# MINDING HER BUSINESS

## WOMEN, ARCHITECTURE, AND DESIGN

Edited by
Alborz Dianat and Kathleen James-Chakraborty

Leuven University Press

This project has received funding from the European Research Council (ERC) under the European Union's Horizon 2020 research and innovation programme (Grant agreement No 101019419).

Funded by the European Union. Views and opinions expressed are however those of the author(s) only and do not necessarily reflect those of the European Union or the European Research Council Executive Agency. Neither the European Union nor the granting authority can be held responsible for them.

The publication of this book was also supported by the KU Leuven Fund for Fair Open Access, and the Open Book Collective (see www.lup.be/obc).

European Research Council
Established by the European Commission

Published in 2026 by Leuven University Press / Presses Universitaires de Louvain / Universitaire Pers Leuven. Minderbroedersstraat 4, B-3000 Leuven (Belgium).



ISBN 978 94 6270 510 4 (Paperback)
ISBN 978 94 6166 738 0 (ePDF)
ISBN 978 94 6166 739 7 (ePub)
https://doi.org/10.11116/9789461667397
D/2026/1869/15
NUR: 648, 656

Layout: Crius Group
Cover design: Daniel Benneworth-Gray
Cover illustration: Maire Gullichsen in 1952. Credit: Villa Mairea Archives.

GPRC
Guaranteed
Peer Reviewed
Content
www.gprc.be

# Table of Contents

# List of figures

# Acknowledgements

This book originated from a conference held in Dublin in June 2024, as part of the ERC-funded project: 'Expanding Agency: Women, Race and the Global Dissemination of Modern Architecture.' Held over three days at the ESB Headquarters and the National Museum of Ireland, the conference examined the overlooked role of women in the global dissemination of modern architecture and design. We thank the speakers, session chairs and attendees for the fruitful dialogue that helped develop the research presented in this book.

We are also grateful for all those who aided in the organisation and delivery of the conference, and particularly: Jenny Devine, Kate Buckley, Nokubekezela Mchunu, Pooja Sastry, George Francis-Kelly, Lynn Scarff, Jade Dillon, Genevieve Whitfield, Pat Boyle, Mia Mercier, and Edel Maloney. The conference was enlivened by a keynote delivered by Nina Stritzler-Levine, for which we are thankful.

We would like to thank Mirjam Truwant at Leuven University Press and the anonymous peer reviewers for their advice and guidance, as well as Isobel Robson for copy editing. We are also extremely grateful for the work of Paula Arning in helping to prepare the manuscript.

This project has received funding from the European Research Council (ERC) under the European Union's Horizon 2020 research and innovation programme (grant agreement No 101019419).

# Introduction

*Alborz Dianat and Kathleen James-Chakraborty*

The recent explosion in the attention paid to women architects and to women as patrons of architecture often overlooks the many other ways women have contributed to the shaping of the built environment. Those identifying as women have been particularly likely to be ignored when they have disrupted the attempts of architects, architecture critics, and architectural historians to insist that architects have been autonomous agents, fully responsible for such matters as the choice of style, interior layout, and construction materials. Instead, as this book will show, architects have often shared agency in ways that neither they nor subsequent historians have consistently acknowledged, with women assuming a wide variety of roles that should not be considered as merely supporting. Although women have also designed and commissioned buildings, much of their impact upon the architecture of the last century – in ways that are easily traceable as far back as the eighteenth century – has instead come from entrepreneurial activities that allowed them to support themselves and their families. This collection shows them manufacturing and marketing construction materials, as well as working as real estate developers and journalists in ways that both extended and challenged their assumed relationship to domesticity. Moreover, as businesswomen they operated the spaces outside the home where key conversations about architecture took place and where innovative designs were marketed. Not all of these activities were frankly capitalist, however. Civil servants, members of religious orders, and philanthropists have been among those who, although not motivated by profit, have also channelled resources to diverse causes influencing the built environment. As this collection considers, women have contributed to developing the infrastructure of newly independent nations in the Global South, improving living conditions for those on society's margins in Ireland, and expanding the facilities of historically Black colleges for women in the United States.

## TOWARDS COLLECTIVE ARCHITECTURAL HISTORIES

Since the 1970s, feminist architects, critics, and historians have drawn attention to the ways in which valorising individual architects, particularly those who pioneered innovative styles, distracts attention from the fact that architecture is always a collaborative act in which everyone from bankers to construction labourers contributes.[1] As early as 1977, Gwendolyn Wright identified a variety of roles through which women have contributed to architectural culture. A handful of exceptional women, she noted, became well-known architects and attained the recognition of their peers, while many more played crucial roles behind the scenes in offices large and small. Others worked as what she termed 'adjuncts', in related fields such as planners and journalists, while yet more were active as reformers.[2] Especially since the 1990s, feminist scholars led by Alice Friedman have paid sustained attention to the role played by extraordinary women, many of them from royal or aristocratic backgrounds, as patrons of innovative architecture and design.[3] The impact of women as consumers, particularly in relation to the home, has not been overlooked either, with the contributions of scholars such as Penny Sparke, joined more recently by Deborah Sugg Ryan.[4] Judith Major, Monica Penick, and Elizabeth Darling are among those who have recounted the importance of women journalists, writing mostly for magazines, while Nina Stritzler-Levine has investigated the shops and design businesses in which women played a leading role.[5] Women's philanthropy, social activism, and social work have also governed the construction, but importantly also the adaptive re-use of the built environment. Marta Gutman has charted the way in which such matronage shaped environments for working-class children in Oakland, California, from the Gold Rush through to just after World War II.[6] More recently yet, Mary Anne Hunting and Kevin D. Murphy, two contributors to this volume, have detailed the ranges of careers assumed by women who studied at the Cambridge School of Architecture and Landscape Architecture (originally the Cambridge School of Architecture and Landscape Architecture for Women) and their contemporaries across the United States.[7]

Despite such revisionist scholarship, many writings on twentieth- and twenty-first-century architecture maintain an emphasis on the heroic contributions of singular architects, with branding assuming such importance that the firm of Zaha Hadid Architects continues to execute new designs years after the death of its titular founder. The authors of the case studies in this book follow an alternative approach. By providing the perspective of entrepreneurs, they underline the collective nature of architectural production, identifying the role of women across the design process. Furthermore, paying more attention to the diverse ways in which female entrepreneurs have had an often unacknowledged impact is part of the contemporary effort by many historians of architecture – and indeed their counterparts from across the humanities – to expose the ways in which architectural culture, as well as in too many cases the study of it, has promoted gendered and racial hierarchies.[8] This must be addressed openly and honestly to provide a foundation for a more inclusive architecture profession, one that is better prepared to meet contemporary challenges because it is less alienated from the publics heretofore largely excluded from entry into it. Uncovering the full impact that a handful of women have already had is at least a step in that direction.

The full range of pursuits through which women impacted architectural culture has yet to be fully acknowledged, much less permeate standard histories of the subject.[9] This book both complements existing publications and expands our understanding of women's contributions to modern architecture and design by delving into the variety of entrepreneurial efforts women have pursued. This entails accepting the degree to which women have had an impact not just when they challenged patriarchal systems, including the capitalist marketplace, but also when they worked effectively within them, deploying them for their own ends.[10] In some cases such women may have been too busy earning a living to have the time or energy to seek to overturn other established norms at a time when relatively few middle and upper class women worked outside the home. In others, their quest for personal independence, although often paired with the desire to find an outlet for creative expression, otherwise consciously supported the status quo. This is scarcely surprising considering that, whatever their national and ethnic background, the women profiled in this collection were all well-educated and at least middle class. Race, religion, and at least moderate wealth, as well as access to education all bestowed authority upon our subjects in ways that were not available to most women, wherever they lived. So too, in some cases, did marriage to well-connected men. These advantages need to be balanced against the recognition as well that many of the women profiled in these pages shied away from drawing attention to themselves in ways that would have been regarded as unseemly, and that their ambition was for the same reasons, if admitted, often discreetly masked.

There were multiple ways in which entrepreneurial women involved in architecture extended rather than rebelled against the association of women with domesticity, hospitality, and fashion. Already in the nineteenth century, women working or undertaking voluntary activities outside the home were most likely to find acceptance when they wrote or otherwise acted in support of such gender stereotypes.[11] It is hardly surprising therefore that many of the figures profiled in the following pages concerned themselves with housing, including the interior decoration of the home, asserting an expertise derived at times as much simply from being female as from any formal training. The ability to be a successful hostess has also long been a prized female attribute in many societies, making the way in which women created commercial spaces in which architectural dialogue flourished far from a revolutionary activity.[12] Many women, especially those of means, have also often been trained to be able to recognise visual nuance, not least through the attention they pay to how they dress and how others do, whether or not they are actively serving as markers of conspicuous consumption.[13] This skill is perhaps the trickiest to integrate into histories of architecture as it threatens to equate attentiveness to architecture and design with 'mere' fashion, in fact one of the principal ways open to many women with sufficient funds to construct identity. Often the first steps in recognising the degree to which women have shaped the built environment include acknowledging not only that contributions have emanated from non-architects, but also accepting the degree to which taste has exerted an influence. Although this is beyond the scope of this collection, this has been true even in socialist societies.[14] Such recognition entails turning away from issues of production to those of consumption, and paying sustained attention to the interplay between consumer demand and what architects, especially those not heralded as stylistic innovators, actually design.

Architects, as well as critics and historians who document and often celebrate their work, have been extremely hesitant to admit the role taste plays in deciding how buildings are designed, and even more importantly, in determining what gets built. The fictive gulf between design and taste has been maintained in spite of accounts outlining the social and economic factors that determine what building types are erected, out of what materials and at what scale. Yet the image of a building, and the impression provided by its façades and interior spaces, stages identity, just as do deciding whether to wear a bathing suit, work clothes or a ball gown. Also key to the impression that both make is the ability of many to discern what price point either a building or an article of clothing likely represents. Whether as designers or, more broadly, as consumers, women have long been condemned for their proximity to fashion. The danger that modern architecture, in particular, might be dismissed as fashion, despite – or indeed perhaps because of – the strong links between dress reform and that of the appearance of the homes in which flapper dresses and cloche hats were worn or the shops in which they had been purchased, has clearly long troubled many advocates of stylistic reform, even as others understood this as a reason to support it.[15] Writing in 1929 in the Boston-based magazine *House Beautiful*, Dorothy Todd, the former editor of the British edition of *Vogue*, for instance, equated the designs of Le Corbusier and Marcel Breuer with the recent revolution that had shortened the hemlines, loosened the waists, and simplified the hair styles of her readers:

> We have an interesting precedent to guide us in the field of women's clothes. In the course of the last ten years, a remarkable sense of style has been developed in that connection. This was not accomplished in a day, but through a process of slow and careful elimination. The results have been so successful as to enable America to boast, to-day, the best-dressed women in the world.[16]

This attention to style, and its detachment from issues of engineering and construction, clearly threatened to brand what became known as the International Style as being governed by an aesthetic, albeit an industrial one, rather than a rational relationship between skeletal steel or reinforced concrete construction and the functional organisation of space.[17] Its early defenders took this stance even as Ludwig Mies van der Rohe partnered with Lilly Reich to design the Silk and Velvet Café for an exhibition of women's fashion held in Berlin in 1927, and Erich Mendelsohn was responsible for the boldly functional architecture of boutiques and department stores erected across Germany between 1924 and 1932.[18] As scholars such as Andreas Huyssen have pointed out since at least the 1980s, such associations were dangerous for those who upheld the new architecture as a dispassionate response to the spirit of the times since mass culture was trivialised, even vilified, for much of the twentieth century in part because of its association with women.[19]

Many male architects and advocates in the twentieth century criticised the influence of female consumers, defining modernism as an opposing 'masculine' movement.[20] Relatedly, those working in architectural partnership with women had portions of their work attributed to the supposedly frivolous tastes of their collaborators. One male critic remarked on Charles Rennie Mackintosh's collaboration with Margaret Macdonald Mackintosh: 'It would appear to have been the florid coarseness of her wholly inferior decorative talent and a firm insistence on "me too" that too often led him into an uxorious ornamental vulgarity.'[21] In 1995, Penny Sparke considered such attempts efforts to bring 'an end to the rule of women's tastes.'[22]

Yet how changes in taste were marketed proved as important to the success of new architectural styles as metaphors for mass production. Women, particularly those who were economically independent and well-educated, applied their agency within capitalist economies by focusing on both innovation and tradition, thereby forging path-breaking careers and shaping consumer choices.

## A COLLECTION OF CASE STUDIES

This book is not definitive. Opportunities abound for scholars to further address the impact women have had upon the built environment, only some of which can be categorised as entrepreneurial. For instance, women in some societies in the Global South and in some indigenous cultures displaced by settler colonialism in the Global North have long been responsible for the construction as well as design of dwellings and other structures.[23] Their contributions remain to be integrated into standard histories of architecture while their perspectives and expertise could inform contemporary practice in ways that might also promote sustainable design. The case studies provided here are nonetheless widely dispersed geographically. While several examples relate to the Anglophone world (Britain, Ireland, the United States, and Australia), others address activities in Turkey, Finland, Chile, Singapore, and Kenya. They are divided into four distinct (though occasionally overlapping) fields, reflective of the breadth of roles women have occupied in the design process through entrepreneurship. These span the construction industry, editorial production, the cultivation of social spaces, and the delivery of humanitarian interventions.

Today, architectural history is finally paying sustained attention to materials, above all because of their importance to mitigating the outsize contribution the construction and maintenance of buildings currently makes to climate change.[24] Yet there are other reasons to highlight their importance. One of the perhaps most surprising ways in which women have contributed to the making of the built environment across the last two centuries and more has been through their participation in the manufacture, sale, and adoption of innovative construction materials and systems. Although in many parts of the world, women were or continue to be actively engaged in construction, in Europe by the middle ages the guild system prioritised the contributions of men.[25] Today the building trades in Europe and elsewhere in the so-called 'west' remain dominated by men, despite two generations of effort by women to make inroads in gaining access to what are often relatively well-paid, unionised jobs.[26] There remains much work to be done on the building site, but historians can at least highlight what women have already achieved. This collection opens with a section entitled 'Materials and Construction' showcasing three inspiring examples.

First, Dana Arnold interrogates the thriving business of the Coade Artificial Stone Manufactory, producers of stoneware and statues utilised by the most prominent architects of Georgian Britain. She convincingly demonstrates Eleanor Coade's success as a businesswoman, not least as Coade's product remains admired today for the way in which it provided architects with a durable and economic alternative to stone. As a ceramic product made in moulds, this material had the additional benefit of allowing easy duplication of motifs. Coade thereby impacted both the construction industry and the highest echelons of architectural culture. At the same time, Arnold is attentive to the ways in which history has been written to privilege male architects, entrepreneurs, and developers, like Robert Adam and Josiah Wedgwood, who have long been central figures in the history of Georgian architecture, design, and taste, while it has at times proved difficult for scholars highlighting Coade's importance even to publish. Arnold's contribution further demonstrates that, although occupying a key position within Georgian architecture and decoration and being anything but unknown in her own day, Coade was widely overlooked for a century and a half following her death in 1821, while Adam and Wedgwood remained central figures in accounts of the taste of their time. How we remember can be as important as what actually happened at a given time; in other words, it is not that women were consistently absent from the architectural culture of their own day, but that their contributions were subsequently more easily overlooked than that of their male contemporaries. It is also, of course, because supplying the means for architects like

Adam or John Soane to express themselves creatively has not counted as much as the actual design of the building, unless, that is, one was named Wedgwood. Moreover, advances in pre-fabrication are presumed to be meaningful when they relate to structure rather than ornament and are developed by male engineers rather than female entrepreneurs.

Many of the same issues also relate to the following chapter, in which Jenna Snow and Andrea Thabet survey the career of Mary Louise Schmidt. Unlike Coade, Schmidt was not responsible for the manufacture of a particular material. Instead of making her name by overseeing technological innovation in the production process, and through a shrewd sense of what designs would sell, as Coade did, Schmidt created a new interface between the construction industry and the architectural profession. Moreover, she did this in interwar and postwar Los Angeles, at the coalface of innovation in the design of domestic architecture in the United States, where new ideas, only some of them emanating from Europe, were popularised before spreading across the country and around the world. Organising the display of building materials from a range of manufacturers, Schmidt supported the architectural industry and bridged the gap between professionals and the public. Even more remarkably, perhaps, she relied on an all-female salesforce to staff her businesses, although this cannot be regarded as being entirely progressive, as she did not retain any who married. That she could be forward thinking in other ways is demonstrated, however, by the degree to which she showcased Paul Revere Williams, the nation's most prominent African American architect of his generation, even at the expense of celebrated white peers such as Richard Neutra.

Women did not simply manufacture and market new materials and construction systems. They also employed them in their work as architects as Gabriela García de Cortázar Galleguillos demonstrates in her survey of the work of Myriam Ratinoff. As an architect in Chile, Ratinoff exploited Multibloc, an innovative construction system of reinforced concrete blocks produced by her husband. Her houses served to promote the Multibloc system and fomented the use of modern technological and material approaches in the country's rapidly industrialised construction sector. But recognition has been lacking, in part due to Ratinoff's lack of engagement with academic circles and because her work was not published in the country's professional press. By drawing attention to Coade, Schmidt, and Ratinoff, the first section of this book stimulates greater attention to the varied contributions of women in the construction of buildings, despite the field's perceived masculine associations.

Less startling are the ways in which women found opportunities for creative expression and economic empowerment through their relationship to the home as outlined in the section 'Domesticity in Journalism and Real Estate'. That women's involvement in architecture can emerge from their gendered association with domesticity is hardly news, as it has formed the basis of much feminist scholarship related to architecture since the 1980s.[27] The second grouping – which focuses on examples from the Ottoman empire, Britain, and the United States – nonetheless expands our awareness of the ways in which women have used this stereotype to their own advantage. Even Schmidt's exhibitions targeted housewives, as well as architects and builders, with her displays in Los Angeles including a 'Homemakers' Exposition'. Acceptance of this gendered division of labour could also serve as the reason to finally admit women to architecture schools. In 1917, the head of London's Architectural Association (AA) Robert Atkinson declared domestic design to be the focus of women at the school: 'The chief reason why we have decided [to accept female students] is that women's help alone can solve the chief problem before us – the planning of the servantless house.'[28] Far more women took charge of the design of the interiors of their homes, or supported themselves as interior decorators, however, than studied at the AA and the handful of other architectural schools that would admit them. Moreover, much of this activity was supported by the many women who forged careers writing for newspapers and magazines, as well as publishing advice literature in book form. Especially in the United States and Britain, but also elsewhere, the explosion of print culture that had occurred already in the nineteenth century, coupled with the rise of advertising that addressed the women who made consumer choices for their households, made this a viable way for educated women like Dorothy Todd to earn a living and have an impact.[29] Presumed to be experts on the home, they not surprisingly often addressed domestic architecture and interior decoration in articles and books that often targeted female readers. By the early twentieth century, as Damia Göre shows in the opening article in this section of the collection, such writing was being both undertaken and read by women far beyond the anglophone world.

The Arts and Crafts movement in Britain and the United States provided many with such a path, one moreover which was also often closely tied to the suffrage movement.[30] Göre demonstrates that already in the early twentieth century Ottoman advice literature charged well-to-do emancipated women with using their craft skills to ensure the beauty of their homes, which were no longer entirely private sanctuaries. From the suffragist mouthpiece *Kadınlar Dünyası* to the more mainstream magazine *Süs*, male and female authors advised a female readership in matters of aesthetics and interior design. Moreover, interior decoration became an acceptable occupation for women already in the late nineteenth century, pioneered in London by Agnes and Rhoda Garrett, and in the United States by Candace Wheeler.[31] In 1913, Elsie de Wolfe, the foremost American interior decorator of her day, famously quipped that 'A man may build and decorate a beautiful house, but it remains for a woman to make a home of it for him', a remark that left considerable room for the activities of amateurs, as well as professionals like herself.[32]

Fashion magazines charged with keeping their readers abreast of changes in dress that would encourage them to buy new wardrobes invariably, and their critics argued frivolously, emphasised the new. Female journalists wrote for women readers, many of whom did not work outside the home. They had to balance a respect for conventions to which they themselves did not necessarily adhere in their own personal and professional lives with the responsibility they often owed advertisers to promote what was new. They also had a commitment to keeping their audience well informed. No one mastered this precarious feat better than Alice Maud Head. Alex Banister profiles her editorship of the British edition of *Good Housekeeping*, established in 1922, highlighting how the magazine informed the period's design tastes and conceptions of modern living. While not endorsing a fundamental restructuring of gender roles, the magazine incorporated a variety of content to support the easing of women's labour in the home at a time when servants were becoming less affordable to the middle classes and when technology was beginning to offer an increasingly affordable alternative to at least some of the work they had performed. Women contributors included Daisy Cottington-Taylor, the director of the Good Housekeeping Institute, and Joyce E. Townsend, who held a degree from the AA and contributed content on housing. Like *House Beautiful* in the United States, *Good Housekeeping* also occasionally published strikingly novel architecture, such as Nimmo House in Buckinghamshire designed by Serge Chermayeff and Erich Mendelsohn and featured in August 1934.[33]

But there were other ways that women could exploit their understanding of home design. During the interwar years and in the immediate postwar period, real estate development offered the potential on both sides of the Atlantic to turn a profit, although many of the women who engaged in it were more concerned with building affordable housing and championing innovative styles. In Britain, as Alexandra Quantrill details, Laura Annie Willson founded a development company in 1925 and oversaw the design and construction of nearly 600 modest houses in Yorkshire and Surrey over the course of the next three years. This was also the period in which she served as president of the Women's Engineering Society, while she was also a founding member of the Electrical Association for Women. Not surprisingly, although the houses were aesthetically conventional, Willson ensured that they were equipped with a range of modern conveniences. The modernism she prioritised emphasised efficiency, and thus aligned with perceptions of electricity's potential to ease domestic drudgery.[34] Thus, although the image of the home Willson and those who chose to inhabit her houses differed, their understanding of the benefits that technology could potentially provide dovetailed with that espoused by the Austrian architect Grete Schütte-Lihotzky in her celebrated Frankfurt kitchens.[35]

In the United States, women quickly found a foothold as real estate agents but here, too, their activities extended into development as well as design and construction.[36] As Mary Anne Hunting and Kevin D. Murphy demonstrate, women played a critical role in the introduction of modern architecture to New England, beginning with the Boston suburbs. The most celebrated example is Helen Osborne Storrow's funding of the house Walter Gropius and Marcel Breuer designed for Gropius and his wife Ise in Lincoln. Hunting and Murphy establish, however, that this was far from a unique case, establishing a context that also included the activities of Amelia Peabody and Olga Monks Pertzoff and continued into the 1960s. In many cases women, including the architects Eleanor Raymond, Sarah Pillsbury Harkness, and Emily Stewart Lansingh Muir, also participated in the design of the housing on land that they and other women developed.

These examples are particularly important because the global dissemination of what became known as the International Style is too often related to the movement of people and images. The term was popularised in *House Beautiful* well before the publication of the book for the 1932 exhibition at the Museum of Modern Art in New York.[37] The essays in this second section demonstrate how the appetite for innovation came to flourish already in the Ottoman Empire before World War I, and continued to do so on both sides of the Atlantic in the interwar period and beyond, in part stimulated by the myriad activities of women excited by the possibility of change.

While claiming special expertise in regard to the domestic, woman also exerted authority far beyond the home, nurturing institutions in which designs could be crafted and sold, as well as public spaces in which architecture and design could be studied, discussed, and advanced. The third set of chapters examines this manner of entrepreneurial activity, detailing women's roles in running businesses across Europe, as well as in Australia and Singapore. Entitled 'Nurturing Spaces for New Ideas', it explores the breadth of forms this could take, including design businesses, coffee shops, and bookstores that functioned for the exchange not merely of products, but also of ideas by a variety of participants in the architecture and design communities.

Maire Gullichsen is best known for her role as one of the four founders of the Finnish furniture manufacturer Artek and as the patron of the Villa Mairea, designed by her Artek partners Alvar and Aino Aalto.[38] Sidelined, as a woman, from a leadership role in her family's timber firm, which her husband claimed in her stead, Gullichsen instead channelled her entrepreneurial skills towards the arts. She organised exhibitions, collected artworks, and cultivated contact with elite figures to stimulate cultural initiatives. Sini Rinne-Kanto adds to this familiar story by focusing upon Gullichsen's engagement with Norrmark Handcraft, which she founded in 1961 in collaboration with the silversmith and designer Bertel Gardberg. The company's operations extended beyond sales in an attempt to revitalise handicraft traditions and foster local job growth in the part of southwest Finland where Gullichsen was born and where the A. Ahlström Corporation, founded by her grandfather, was based. Norrmark Handcraft also provided the template for Gardberg's role as a founder of the Kilkenny Design Workshops in Ireland in 1963.[39] Finally, and equally importantly, Norrmark addressed ecological concerns and engaged with the material economy and logistics chain, with some products featuring knock-down and flat-pack packaging.

While Gullichsen, initially in collaboration with Gardberg, ran a firm that encompassed the manufacture as well as sale of a wide variety of design products, including everything from textiles to furniture, women elsewhere established businesses that mattered because of the physical space they provided for discussion. Andrew Murray shines a spotlight on the contribution made by Barbara Hill, proprietor of the Shiralee, an unassuming coffee shop established in 1956 and frequented by architectural professionals, in furthering modern architecture in Perth. Although its appearance was not remarkable, nor probably was the food and drink it provided well out of the ordinary, the Shiralee fostered discussions around modern architecture and community, providing, as Catherine

Cranston and Charles Rennie and Margaret MacDonald Mackintosh had decades earlier in Glasgow, an inclusive alternative to a pub culture that did not yet welcome women.

Hill was the wife of an architect, as was Lena Lim. Her Select Books, which opened in Singapore in 1976, played a similar role in that city's architecture culture in its heyday as that of the Shiralee in Perth, as Eunice Seng considers. Located in a shopping centre designed by her husband William Lim, it quickly became a hub of the city-state's architectural and literary culture. Dissatisfied with lingering colonialist emphasis on western culture, Lena Lim focused on introducing her clientele to the literary and visual worlds of Southeast Asia, eventually extending her activities to publishing books about architecture. She also co-founded organisations advocating for women's rights and historic preservation.

The position of Hill and Lim as wives of professionals, not to mention Gullichsen's position as perhaps her country's wealthiest heiress, highlights that most of the women featured in this volume were relatively affluent and well-connected, with sufficient financial and social capital to undertake architecture-related pursuits whose economic outcome could seldom be predicted in advance. Hill and her husband could afford to run the Shiralee without making a profit. Others were not only financially secure but frankly ambitious when it came to earning a living. Banister notes that as managing director of *Good Housekeeping*, Head was probably the highest paid woman of her time in Britain. The promulgation of modern design trends in her magazine aligned with the pursuit of personal profit, capitalising on the public appeal of these issues. In many situations, the dissemination of modern architecture and design can be interpreted as the by-product of commercial ambitions, running ambiguously alongside social reform ideals. Rinne-Kanto details the sales tactics but also the strong sense of social responsibility that undergirded Gullichsen's involvement in Norrmark Handcrafts and her community.

Thus, it should not be surprising that the fourth and final section of the book, 'Social Entrepreneurship', addresses the way in which women extended the role of Lady Bountiful in more modern directions. The fourth section addresses female-led international aid efforts, church-based charitable activities, and African American philanthropy in Kenya, Ireland, and the United States, all intended to improve the lot of others, many of them women. While many modern architects aspired to challenge market forces, they remained important in non-socialist states. Yet even within capitalist societies, women who were not architects were active in championing alternatives, and the extent of the charitable activities long considered appropriate for them, now expanded to encompass state funded initiatives and even international development aid.

While many women (and men) engaged in philanthropy in part to cultivate their own reputations, others operated in the shadows, never seeking or attaining individual recognition. Maryia Rusak investigates Joan Tyrrell, an obscure yet highly influential figure working as a civil servant in post-independence Kenya's department of the treasury. She finds evidence of Tyrrell's influence primarily within inconspicuous correspondence, often only signed 'JT'. With a responsibility over financial decisions, Tyrrell, a white descendent of British settlers, liaised with Nordic international aid donors to enable infrastructure projects in Kenya. While it was left to architects to give form to commissioned projects, they would not have been possible without her support and assistance.

In Ireland, Sister Stanislaus Kennedy has been far from invisible in her advocacy for the homeless. A member of the order of the Sisters of Charity, she was a pioneer in studying and addressing the issue in Ireland. She chaired Combat Poverty and set up Focus Point (now Focus Ireland). In their chapter, Ellen Rowley and Haylee Derrickson examine Stanhope Green, the housing scheme she sponsored, which was designed by Gerry Cahill and realised between 1988 and 1991, and the subsequent conversion, also by Cahill, of a second former convent at George's Hill. They use oral history and drawings to document Sister Stan's transition of an ethic of social justice into built form in this renovation and expansion of a neo-gothic former convent. Her role in the architectural process may thus be understood as a form of care, evidenced by both her efforts in the processes that anticipated the intervention of the architect and those that continued after its initial occupation.

In the final chapter of the collection, E. James West explores the role of Camille Cosby in providing financial support for Spelman College, the oldest historically Black women's college in the United States. After providing in 1988 a 20-million-dollar donation with her husband Bill build a new academic centre, Cosby was closely involved in selecting a Black architectural firm to lead the project. The story of the construction and media representation of the Camille Cosby Academic Center, completed eight years later, triangulates the agency of three women. It provided Cosby with the opportunity to step beyond the shadow of her megastar husband and placed her within a long history of Black female philanthropy. But even philanthropic agendas held opportunities for personal gain, if not economically then reputationally. Just as Gullichsen's charitable efforts perpetuated the dynastic authority of the Ahlström family in the Noormarkku region of Finland, Camille Cosby's donation served to propel her prominence in America's public consciousness alongside her husband. Meanwhile for the architect Donna deJongh, the design of the Camille Cosby Academic Center was a chance to cement her position among a small group of prominent Black female architects. Furthermore, the building's construction provided the college's president, Johnnetta Cole, with concrete evidence of her visionary leadership and beloved role as Spelman's 'Sister President', which she would parlay into positions as president of Bennett College and later director of the National Museum of African Art in Washington, D.C.

## DIFFICULTIES AND OPPORTUNITIES

Whether occupying prominent positions within society or operating on the sidelines, many of the women considered in this book remain unseen even in a literal sense. That in at least one case our author has been unable to locate a photograph of her twentieth-century subject is indicative of the degree to which some of their roles were obscured even in their own time.[40] The traces of Tyrrell's impact survive primarily through the recurring evidence of her initials on official documents and the testimonies of her contemporaries. Rusak's survey of Tyrrell is one of several in this collection that confronts – and overcomes – archival silences. Elizabeth Darling has considered the limitations of repositories that focus on the papers of individual architects and the gendered decisions around what type of material has been collected and kept.[41] The historic over-emphasis on designers, drawings and the tangible aspects of construction has at times limited the preservation of material on women working in more varied roles. Such issues can extend even to primary publications, with Banister similarly encountering women's usage of initials – or even their husband's names – in the realm of journalism. Expanding architectural history requires researchers to go against the grain, fighting the biases of their source material.

Authors in this collection supplement their research at times by oral history, to bring to the surface contributions that have too often been obscured not simply by sexism, but by the overly narrow way in which agency in the creation of the built environment has been acknowledged.

For instance, the social spaces cultivated by Hill and Lim now often exist through the recollections of those to experience their intangible influence. Also key, however, have been published texts written more often for female than male readers, which are too often overlooked for exactly that reason.

Intersectional issues are addressed throughout. Hilde Heynen and Lucía Pérez-Moreno have surveyed the usage of intersectionality in writings on women architects, distinguishing experiences through multiple intersecting social categories.[42] Applying such an approach to the figures considered here, this collection recognises how regional conditions, individual identities and cultural contexts helped, hindered, or otherwise affected the contributions of women entrepreneurs. The construction of Spelman College for instance reveals how the intersection of race with gender affected architectural developments, evident in the financial issues faced by Black colleges and architect Donna deJongh's complex navigation of Atlanta's Black community. Gullichsen's case shows how wealth and class-based authority informed influence and patronage in Finland. Tyrrell's actions in post-independence Kenya reveal opportunities within lingering colonial governance networks. Religious identities also feature prominently, from the middle-class Muslim readership of magazines in Turkey, to Ratinoff's membership in Chile's Jewish community, and Sister Stan's Catholic vocation. Consideration of such intersections reinforces the nature of this collection as a series of case studies, rather than a single, universally applicable model.

Across countries and centuries, women have shaped the built environment and the design of interior space through a multitude of entrepreneurial roles. As we hope this collection demonstrates, the writing of histories that acknowledges this agency expands our understanding of who shapes the choice of building materials, how stereotypical domesticity can be manipulated to create substantive opportunities for women to transcend it, how for-profit businesses can create new and more inclusive conversations, and how women-led philanthropic initiatives have created more equitable spaces.

Minding Her Business
Women, Architecture, and Design

## NOTES

1 Susana Torre, ed., *Women in American Architecture: A Historic and Contemporary Perspective* (New York: Whitney Library of Design, 1977) is a key text in this regard. See also Carol Willis, *Form follows Finance: Skyscrapers and Skylines in New York and Chicago* (New York: Princeton Architectural Press, 1995); and Christine Casey, *Making Magnificence: Architects, Stuccatori, and the Eighteenth-Century Interior* (New Haven: Yale University Press, 2017).

2 Gwendolyn Wright, 'On the Fringe of the Profession: Women in American Architecture', in *The Architect: Chapters in the History of the Profession*, ed. Spiro Kostof (New York: Oxford University Press, 1977), 284.

3 Alice T. Friedman, *Women and the Making of the Modern House* (New York: Harry N. Abrams, 1998); Erin Griffey, *On Display: Henrietta Maria and the Materials of Magnificence at the Stuart Court* (New Haven and London: Paul Mellon Centre in association with Yale University Press, 2016).

4 Penny Sparke, *As Long as It's Pink: The Sexual Politics of Taste* (London: Pandora, 1995); Deborah Sugg Ryan, *Ideal Homes: Uncovering the History and Design of the Interwar House* (Manchester: Manchester University Press, 2020).

5 Judith Major, *Mariana Griswold van Rensselaer: A Landscape Critic in the Gilded Age* (Charlottesville: University of Virginia Press, 2013); Monica Penick, *Tastemaker: Elizabeth Gordon, House Beautiful, and the Postwar American Home* (New Haven: Yale University Press, 2017); Elizabeth Darling, 'The Avant-Garde in the Drawing Room: Women, Writing, and Architectural Modernism in Britain', in *Women, Periodicals, and Print Culture in Britain, 1890s–1920s: The Modernist Period*, ed. Faith Binckes and Carey Snyder (Edinburgh: University of Edinburgh Press, 2019); Nina Stritzler-Levine, ed., *Artek and the Aaltos* (New York: Bard Graduate Center, 2016); and Nina Stritzler-Levine, *Svenskt Tenn: Interiors* (London: Phaidon, 2025).

6 Marta Gutman, *A City for Children: Women, Architecture, and the Charitable Landscapes of Oakland, 1850–1950* (Chicago: University of Chicago Press, 2014).

7 Mary Anne Hunting and Kevin D. Murphy, *Women Architects at Work: Making American Modernism* (Princeton: Princeton University Press, 2025).

8 See for instance, Aggregate Architectural History Collective, *Governing by Design: Architecture, Economics, and Politics in the Twentieth Century* (Pittsburgh, University of Pittsburgh Press, 2012); Aggregate Architectural History Collaborative, *Writing Architectural History: Evidence and Narrative in the Twenty-First Century* (Pittsburgh: University of Pittsburgh Press, 2021), as well as Patricia Owens, *Erased: A History of International Thought Without Men* (Princeton: Princeton University Press, 2025).

9 For instance, Colin Davies, *A New History of Modern Architecture* (London: Lawrence King, 2017) lists just thirty-one women in its index.

10 Judy Giles, *The Parlour and the Suburb: Domestic Identities, Class, Femininity and Modernity* (Oxford: Berg, 2004); and Penny Sparke, *Elsie de Wolfe: The Birth of Modern Interior Decoration*, ed. Mitchell Owens, (Wellington: Acanthus Press, 2005).

11 Ann Douglas, *The Feminization of American Culture* (New York: Alfred Knopf, 1977).

12 Note the prominent role that being a hostess plays in Susannah Gibson, *The Bluestockings: A History of the First Women's Movement* (New York: W. W. Norton, 2024), although it is ostensibly a history of women writers.

13 Thorsten Veblen, *The Theory of the Leisure Class: An Economic Study of Institutions* (New York: Macmillan, 1899). See also Carma Gorman, '"An Educated Demand:" The Implications of "Art in Every Day Life" for American Industrial Design, 1925–1950', *Design Issues* 16 (2000): 45–66; and Ruth I. Iskin, *Modern Women and Parisian Consumer Culture in Impressionist Painting* (Cambridge: Cambridge University Press, 2014).

14 Mary Pepchinski and Mariann Simon, eds., *Ideological Equals: Women Architects in Socialist Europe, 1945–1989* (London: Routledge, 2018).

15 Deborah Fausch, Paulette Singley, Rodolphe El Khoury and Zvi Efrat, eds., *Architecture: In Fashion* (New York: Princeton Architectural Press, 1977); and Mark Wigley, *White Walls, Designer Dresses:*

*The Fashioning of Modern Architecture* (Cambridge, MA: MIT Press, 1996) were breakthrough works in examining this connection.

16 Dorothy Todd, 'Some Reflections on Modernism', *House Beautiful*, 66 (1929): 416.

17 William Jordy, 'The Symbolic Essence of Modern European Architecture of the Twenties and Its Continuing Influence', *Journal of the Society of Architectural Historians* 22 (1963): 177–87.

18 Robin Schuldenfrei, *Luxury and Modernism: Architecture and the Object in Germany, 1900–1933* (Princeton: Princeton University Press, 2018). See also Kathleen James, *Erich Mendelsohn and the Architecture of German Modernism* (Cambridge: Cambridge University Press, 1997); and Kathleen James-Chakraborty, 'Ausstellungen erleben. Lilly Reichs Produktdisplays 1927–31', in *Sowohl als auch dazwischen. Erfarhungsräume der Kunst*, ed. Jörn Schafaff and Benjamin Wihstutz (Paderborn: Wilhelm Fink, 2015), 56–76.

19 Andreas Huyssen, *After the Great Divide: Modernism, Mass Culture, Postmodernism* (Bloomington: Indiana University Press, 1986).

20 Jessica Kelly, *No More Giants: J.M. Richards, Modernism and The Architectural Review* (Manchester: Manchester University Press, 2022), 72–24.

21 Alborz Dianat, 'The Re-Making of Charles Rennie Mackintosh: A Study of the 1933 Memorial Exhibition', *Architectural History* 62 (2019): 150.

22 Penny Sparke, *As Long as It's Pink: The Sexual Politics of Taste*, 117.

23 Something pointed out already by Doris Cole in *From Tipi to Skyscraper: A History of Women in Architecture* (Boston: i Press, 1973); and Labelle Prussin in *African Nomadic Architecture: Space, Place, and Gender* (Washington: Smithsonian Institution Press, 1995).

24 Kiel Moe, *Unless: The Seagram Building Construction Ecology* (New York/Barcelona: Actar, 2021); and Peter H. Christensen, *Precious Metal: German Steel, Modernity, and Ecology* (State College: Penn State University Press, 2022).

25 For an analysis of a later period, see Conor Lucey, 'Women and the Construction Industry in Georgian Britain and Ireland', *Architectural History* 66 (2023): 127–54.

26 In Ireland, for instance, in 2023, women made up just 9% of the labour force in this area. See 'Women in the Irish Construction Industry: Statistics and Facts', 13 February 2023, https://www.sig.ie/women-in-the-irish-construction-industry-statistics-and-facts/.

27 For instance, Dolores Hayden, *The Grand Domestic Revolution: A History of Feminist Designs for American Homes, Neighborhoods, and Cities* (Cambridge, MA: MIT Press, 1982); and Gwendolyn Wright, *Building the Dream: A Social History of Housing in America* (New York: Pantheon, 1981).

28 Lynne Walker, 'An Irresistible Movement', in *AA Women in Architecture, 1917–2017*, ed. Elizabeth Darling and Lynne Walker (London: AA Publications, 2017), 13.

29 Margaret Beetham, *A Magazine of Her Own? Domesticity and Desire in the Woman's Magazine, 1800–1914* (London: Routledge, 1996); Catherine Clay, ed., *Women's Periodicals and Print Culture in Britain, 1919–1939: The Interwar Period* (Edinburgh: Edinburgh University Press, 2017).

30 Karen Livingstone, *Women Pioneers of the Arts and Crafts Movement* (London: Thames & Hudson, 2024); Zoë Thomas, *Women art workers and the Arts and Crafts Movement* (Manchester: Manchester University Press, 2022); and Catherine Zipf, *Professional Pursuits: Women and the American Arts and Crafts Movement* (Knoxville: University of Tennessee Press, 2007).

31 Elizabeth Crawford, *Enterprising Women: The Garretts and their Circle* (London: Francis Boutle Publishers, 2002); and Amelia Peck and Carol Irish, *Candace Wheeler: The Art and Enterprise of American Design, 1875–1900* (New York: Metropolitan Museum of Art, 2001).

32 Penny Sparke, 'Elsie de Wolfe and Her Female Clients, 1905–15: Gender, Class and the Professional Interior Decorator', in *Women's Places: Architecture and Design 1860-1960*, ed. Brenda Martin and Penny Sparke (London: Routledge, 2003), 47.

33 J. Fernley Rivington, 'A Home for To-day and To-morrow', *Good Housekeeping*, August 1934, 28–29, 113. On *House Beautiful* see Kathleen James-Chakraborty, 'Expanding Agency: Ethel Power, *House Beautiful*, and the Writing of the History of American Architecture', *Women and Architectural History: The Monstrous Regiment Then and Now*, ed. Dana Arnold (London: Routledge, 2024), 152–68, https://doi.org/10.4324/9781003224662-13.

34 For a similar equation of modernism with domestic infrastructure see Barbara Penner, 'Farm Kitchens and Home Economy: Demonstrating Care', *gta papers* 7 (2021): 38–43, https://doi.org/10.54872/gta-4647-03.

35 Susan R. Henderson, 'A Revolution in the Woman's Sphere: Grete Lihotzky and the Frankfurt Kitchen', in *Housing and Dwelling: Perspectives on Modern Domestic Architecture*, ed. Barbara Miller Lane (Abingdon: Routledge, 2007), 248–58.

36 Jeffrey M. Hortstein, *A National of Realtors: A Cultural History of the Twentieth-Century American Middle Class* (Durham: Duke University Press, 2005). The activities of Alice Washburn in Connecticut are also important in this regard. See Eve M. Kahn, 'Still Mysterious, Architect Gets her Due', *New York Times*, 1 March 1990, 62.

37 For a recent example, see Andrea Bärnreuther, ed., *Taking a Stand? Debating the Bauhaus and Modernism* (Berlin: Bauhaus Archiv, 2021). See also Philip Johnson, 'Two Houses in the International Style', *House Beautiful*, 70 (1931): 307–9, 356.

38 Nina Stritzler-Levine, ed., *Artek and the Aaltos* (New York: Bard Graduate Center, 2016).

39 Nick Marchant, *Kilkenny Design: Twenty-One Years of Design in Ireland* (London: Lund Humphries, 1985).

40 For a notorious case of female invisibility, see Beatriz Colomina, 'Battle Lines: E.1027', in *The Sex of Architecture*, ed. Diana Agrest, Patricia Conway and Leslie Kanes Weisman (New York: Harry N. Abrams, 1996), 167–82.

41 Elizabeth Darling, 'In Plain Sight: Women In and Around the Archive', in *Women and Architectural History*, 99–111.

42 Hilde Heynen and Lucía C. Pérez-Moreno, 'Narrating Women Architects' Histories. Paradigms, Dilemmas, and Challenges', *arq.urb* no. 35 (September-December 2022): 110–22.

PART 1

# MATERIALS AND CONSTRUCTION

## Chapter 1

# Written in Stone

## Eleanor Coade and the Building World of Late Eighteenth- and Early Nineteenth-Century Britain

*Dana Arnold*

If Eleanor Coade (1733–1821) had been a man, there would be no need for this essay. She was a crucial actor in the design and building world of the late eighteenth and early nineteenth centuries in Britain. Her significance and achievements equal the innovation of entrepreneurs and manufacturers such as Josiah Wedgwood through her perfection of the production of the artificial stone Lithodipyra, also known as Coade stone. The designs of the Coade Artificial Stone Manufactory were an essential component in the successful practice of the most famous Georgian architects, including Robert Adam, James Wyatt, Samuel Wyatt, William Chambers, John Nash, and John Soane. The durable weather-resistant stoneware, statues, and decorative features that are vital characteristics of their designs and that still endure today, would not have been possible without Coade stone.

In contrast to many of her contemporary male counterparts, Coade was a highly successful businessperson. Unlike Robert Adam, for example, she was never bankrupted. Indeed, her business was highly lucrative.[1] Like many of her male equivalents Coade was an adept self-publicist. In 1784 she published *A Descriptive Catalogue of Coade's Artificial Stone Manufactory at Kings Arms Stairs, Narrow Wall, Lambeth.*[2] Why do we not hear of this as a comparator to Thomas Chippendale's *The Gentleman and Cabinet-Maker's Director* (1754) or Robert and James Adam's *The Works in Architecture* (1773)? There is no doubt that Coade's entrepreneurial, business, and marketing skills combined with her high-quality manufacturing and artistic talent should have positioned her in the pantheon of British designers and manufacturers. Instead, she remains a somewhat anomalous, feminine footnote to one of the most notable and productive periods in British architecture and design.

Coade's impact on architectural design and practice could stand on its own as an important, if inconvenient, truth that disrupts the canonical masculinist narratives about the building world in this period. But the analysis becomes much richer when entwined with the historiographical treatment of her endeavours – not least the monographic survey by Avery Alison Kelly, *Mrs Coade's Stone* (1990).[3] This chapter recognises the importance of the contribution of pioneers such as Kelly (1913–2016) to the retelling of architectural history. Both the history and historiography of Coade show that women actors are not confined to the modern period. Together these two strands combine (and please forgive the phrase) to break the mould of the canonical, masculinist narratives of late the eighteenth- and early nineteenth-century building world to show that they are not written in stone.

My chapter introduces those not familiar with Coade to her significance as an innovative manufacturer and as a businessperson. Of particular interest is her little-recognised contribution to the knowledge economy in Britain during the late eighteenth and early nineteenth centuries. I then consider the historiography of Coade and addresses her absent presence in many standard canonical works on Georgian architecture. Here, I would also like to think about the broader implications for methods of writing women into masculinist histories and about the language we might use. In this way, we see how Coade challenges canonical norms and how she might point to ways in which we might reconfigure these givens to think differently about the business and practice of architectural design in this period. This re-thinking may well have implications for other epochs.

## MINDING HER BUSINESS

When compared to the heroic master narratives of the period, women's endeavours in the Georgian building world have appeared unimportant, secondary, or even trivial. Women were invisible or at best a bothersome footnote in these masculinist histories. Recent scholarship has begun to address this imbalance showing that in the long eighteenth century women engaged both in the patronage and business of architecture, design, and manufacturing.[4] My aim here is not to present a case study that places a woman in the male pantheon of architects and entrepreneurs of the period. Instead, I would like to explore what might happen if we ask different questions of the archive and focus on different elements or actors.

Figure 1.1: The yard at the Coade Manufactory, London, c. 1804. The London Picture Archive.

There is no doubt that Coade was a shrewd businesswoman and a significant innovator operating at the highest level of architectural production. This was a crowded field in our period with an established terrain mapped out by historians comprising the canonical giants of British architecture and manufacturing. But I want first to think about Coade in her own right before seeing how she might relate (or not) to the male-dominated context.

Coade's early life gives us few clues about the evolution of her technical skills but indicate there may well have been some important lessons about commerce. She was born in Exeter, in the southwest of England where her father worked in the vibrant wool trade. Nevertheless, he went bankrupt in 1760, so the family moved to London. By the mid-1760s, Eleanor Coade was running her own business as a linen draper in the City of London. In 1769 her father died after having been bankrupted for a second time. In the same year, Coade bought an artificial stone factory at Narrow Wall, Lambeth from Daniel Pincot, where she lived on the premises.[5] She developed the business as Coade's Artificial Stone Manufactory (Fig. 1.1) and within two years had sacked Pincot and was directly managing the factory by 1771 at the latest.[6]

The technical details of Coade stone or *Lithodipyra* (meaning stone fired twice) have been ably covered elsewhere and are not the focus here.[7] Suffice to say it was a ceramic-based artificial stone that stood out from its predecessors and contemporary competitors for its high quality and durability. There is no doubt that the innovative technical qualities of Coade stone equalled the much-lauded achievements of Wedgwood's Jasperware.[8] By all accounts, Coade perfected both the formula and the firing process of her stone. How she acquired the necessary knowledge to do this remains enigmatic, especially as her background was in textiles. Perhaps the closest antecedent was Richard Holt's 'liquid metal' which was in fact an artificial stone that was poured into moulds and then fired.[9] It was claimed that Holt's final product was stronger than stone or marble. In 1730 Holt had published *A short treatise of artificial stone, as 'tis now made, and converted into all manner of curious embellishments, and proper ornaments, of architecture*. Probably, as a consequence of competitors, lawsuits, and the slump in the building trade, Holt's business had failed by 1732.

Coade's acquisition of the manufactory in Lambeth coincided with the resurgence of a much-expanded building trade, fuelled by the country house building boom and the growth of London and other major cities in Britain. The desire on the part of both patrons and architects for a broad range of classical stylistic references in their commissions was stimulated by increased contact with the architecture of antiquity through travel and the proliferation of printed studies of the antique. Coade stone met the needs of the more sophisticated taste in design in two ways. First and perhaps of more immediate importance, the product was less expensive than stone or marble thus facilitating the illusion of grandeur or all'antica on the cheap. In addition, some of the more intricate design of architects like Robert Adam would not have been possible were they to be carved in stone. Arguably, the physical possibilities of Coade Stone enabled innovations in design – a point to which I shall return.

The architectural sculpture, decorative features, and free-standing statues and ornaments made from Coade stone were not carved but formed from moulds into which the liquid formula was poured before being fired. The durability of the ceramic moulds ensured the efficiency and quality of the production process. Moreover, as the moulds were reusable, architectural and sculptural elements became reproducible. As we will we see, this became an essential hallmark in Coade's intervention in the building world.

## THE BUSINESS OF STONE

The formula for Coade stone was a closely guarded secret and this may well have been part of the reason behind the success of the business.[10] Secrecy certainly helped avoid the lawsuits and patent disputes that dogged other ventures in the world of artificial stone. We have already seen the problems faced by Richard Holt. There were similar instances in the latter part of the century but here the manufacturing process was different as the artificial stone was cast rather than moulded and fired. Composite, a form of stone paste, often referred to as 'compo', was patented by David Wark in 1765; a similar product was patented by John Johnson in 1777. Although it required a lower level of craftsmanship, composite produced a superior result to plaster ornament while being less expensive and easier to produce than traditional architectural details carved from wood or stone. It seemed to be the ideal material for the residential commissions and speculative developments that proliferated in the building boom of the latter part of the Georgian period. But composite was not a consistently reliable material; consequently, relationships between architect and patron often became fraught, if not litigious.

Perhaps the most notorious example of the failings of composite is the hasty partnership formed in 1774 between William Adam and his sons (James, Robert, and John) and the former Swiss clergyman John Liardet.[11] Only one year earlier, Liardet had entered the competitive world of the inexpensive production of artificial stone. His 'Composition or Cement for all Branches concerning Buildings', known as Liardet stucco, was a kind of cement that could be used either as an external render or for such internal architectural details as cornices, architraves, wall panels, picture rails, and dados. The flexibility of Liardet stucco at first appeared to meet the needs of the Adam family when executing the applied decoration that was a hallmark of their designs. The product was largely untested and only a year after his invention was patented, William Adam and his sons formed a partnership with Liardet. Indeed, Liardet produced his artificial stone in the Adam's premises in the Adelphi. But the relationship soon became unstuck as Liardet's formula was flawed and the frequent failure of the product prompted many lawsuits from disgruntled clients of the Adams.

There is a stark contrast between the business acumen and ability to choose the right employees and partners of Coade and the contemporaneous relationship between the Adam family and Liardet. We can infer that Coade knew who the 'boss' was from the outset as, after purchasing the factory in 1769, she wasted little time in sacking Pincot, 'for representing himself, instead of herself, as the proprietor of the factory'.[12] Soon after, her decision to appoint John Bacon as supervisor and designer (including model maker) ensured the high standard of production. He remained at the firm until his death in 1799. In that same year, Coade made her cousin John Sealy a partner, and the firm became 'Coade and Sealy's Artificial Stone Manufactory'. When Sealy died in 1813, she appointed William Croggon as manager and the firm reverted to being in Coade's name only. Croggon bought the business after Coade's death in 1821. He enjoyed some initial success and around five years later opened a second manufactory on New Road, St. Pancras. Arguably, Croggon lacked Coade's business acumen, and he went bankrupt in 1833.[13] Coade's accomplishments as a businesswoman and the superior design, quality, and durability of her product combined to ensure her success with the architects of her day. Even 'star' manufacturers such as Josiah Wedgwood found little purchase with these important clients, noting to his partner Thomas Bentley that 'we could not prevail upon the architects to be godfathers of our children.'[14]

The range of products made from Coade stone was impressive and met the needs of clients from speculative developers to royalty. The material was used by the London speculative building trade to upgrade the streetscape. This can still be seen today in examples such as 40–54 Bedford Square (Fig. 1.2) and 61 and 63 Cavendish Street, as well as the finely modelled herms supporting the porch at Schomberg House, 80–82 Pall Mall (1791). At the other end of the social scale, George III and the Prince Regent were amongst Coade's more illustrious clients, and the Coade Stone Manufactory was granted the Royal Warrant to King George III.[15] Coade stone was used at Carlton House, the Brighton Pavilion, and Buckingham Palace as well as St George's Chapel, Windsor. The diversity of style demonstrated the versatility of Coade stone and the skill in its manufacture. Of particular note is the commission to replace the organ screen and loft at St George's with a new screen, six feet deep and spanning the width of the nave. This project posed technical challenges as the artificial stone had to match the original gothic stonework of the Chapel and the precision of the moulding on the vaulting succeeds in giving the impression of intricate carving. Moreover, the quality of the items in the Coade standard catalogue was such that a Coade stone font presented to the Chapel by one of the Canons was not specially commissioned but was purchased from stock.[16] Coade also had a significant impact on the urban streetscape and the way in which we continue to experience the

Figure 1.2: 44 Bedford Square, London. Alamy Stock Photo.

city. The embellishments of speculatively built Georgian townhouses in London, for example, lifted the metropolitan aesthetic by punctuating the 'monotony' of the rows of rate houses with refined details, made from a material that continues to endure.[17] If we reorientate the narrative to focus on architecture as a collective endeavour requiring a range of skills and technical prowess Coade would come to the fore as a prime mover.

Although most of Coade's manufactures were intended to imitate fine-grained limestone, some were also painted to resemble bronze or wood. These were usually candelabras, chimneypieces, and other items for interior decoration. There are also examples of outdoor painted Coade stone such as the King George III statue at Weymouth. The variety and technical prowess of Coade stone has been ably covered by Kelly and others.[18] Here I would like to focus on an aspect of Coade's career that has been overlooked – her role in the knowledge economy of the late Georgian period.

## COADE AND THE KNOWLEDGE ECONOMY OF LATE GEORGIAN ERA

The interaction between Coade and the major architects of the day had many dimensions. First, she was a highly competent, reliable manufacturer of the architectural components which they designed. We see this, for example, in the garden front at Heaton Hall which was remodelled using sandstone ashlar with dressings of Coade stone by James Wyatt for Sir Thomas Egerton between 1772–89. The façade is composed of a two-storey centre with five bays and a prominent window bow, flanked by two single-storey seven-bay wings with tall colonnades mounted on steps and linked to slightly higher octagonal single-storey pavilions. The capitals of the giant Ionic semi-columns in the bowed central bay and the panels between the two storeys depicting classical rustic scenes are made in Coade stone from Wyatt's design. It is notable that Wyatt commissioned Coade not long after her manufactory had opened. But perhaps more importantly, the moulds formed for Wyatt's commission for Heaton Hall became part of the Coade catalogue of architectural elements that could be bought off the peg by other architects and builders. We see this in Figures 1.3 and 1.4 showing a design for one of the capitals from the garden

Figure 1.3: Heaton Hall garden front remodelled by James Wyatt, Prestwich, Bury, 1789. Photo by Mike Peel, Wikimedia Commons.

Figure 1.4: Catalogue for Coade's Artificial Stone Manufactory, c. 1784. Yale Center for British Art.

front at Heaton Hall which could be replicated from the mould and was available for purchase and use elsewhere.[19]

Here, I would like to reflect on the Coade catalogue, specifically its sources and users as well as how it produced and spread knowledge and facilitated design and building process. *A Descriptive Catalogue of Coade's Artificial Stone Manufactory at Kings Arms Stairs, Narrow Wall, Lambeth* (1784) was an important interface between Coade and the building world of the period. It comprised a list, dimensions, and illustrations of designs for interior and exterior use including statues, whole panels, friezes, balusters, and chimneypieces.[20] On one level it can be seen as a trade catalogue, comprising 69 etched designs on 36 leaves, depicting over 746 Coade stone works produced by Coade's Artificial Stone Manufactory. There is no doubt of its significance in this regard. I would like to offer a new layer of meaning to our understanding of this publication and its place in the architectural culture of its day.

It is important to think about the sources for the plates in the catalogue. As noted, some of the designs were produced by leading architects who had engaged Coade to manufacture them. In addition, many of the unsigned plates, which are variously dated from 1777 to 1779, were probably the work of Eleanor Coade and John Bacon. Indeed, prior to the publication of the catalogue 'Miss Eleanor Coade, sculptor' had exhibited annually at the Society of Artists from 1773–78, and again in 1780. It is not clear if these works were modelled by herself or produced in her name.[21] But this does not necessarily rule out her role in the designs themselves as there is evidence from Kelly of the sources that must have been familiar to Coade.[22] Kelly demonstrates that Coade owned volumes illustrating well-known collections including the Capitoline museums in Rome. This interest in surveys of antique Roman architecture remained live, as seen for example in Coade's purchase of C.H. Tatham's *Etchings of Ancient Ornamental Architecture* 1799.[23] Indeed, in the same year she produced a design for a pair of monumental thrones, the arms of which are in the form of sphinxes whose wings sweep up to touch the tops of the throne backs; these were exact copies of a Roman throne drawn by Tatham in the Vatican. Examples of this product still survive at Parham Park, Sussex.[24]

Coade also had knowledge of new archaeological discoveries that had an impact on architectural design. These included the excavations at Pompeii and Herculaneum and the striking examples of the baseless Doric order found at Paestum and Agrigento. Furthermore, like many designers of the time, Coade copied items brought back from Italy and housed in British collections, including the Townley collection of marbles and the Warwick Vase. These 'ready-made' architectural or sculptural elements, whether based on work commissioned by architects from their own designs or the designs of Coade or Bacon, played an important part in the architectural production of the day. Moreover, Coade was known internationally. For example, her work was featured in German in a magazine focusing on fashion and luxury, *Journal des Luxus und der Moden*, in 1787.[25] It is notable that this was only the second volume of the journal. The following year the whole Coade catalogue was printed in instalments in the magazine.

The significance and reach of the Coade catalogue lasted well into the early nineteenth century. John Soane's use of ready-made Coade stone in his family mausoleum (Fig. 1.5) gives us a clear indication of the role Coade played in the knowledge economy and how this influenced design. Soane took his death and legacy very seriously as witnessed in the terms

Figure 1.5: J. M. Gandy perspective of Soane Monument, John Soane, London, 1816. © Sir John Soane's Museum, London.

of the bequest of his museum to the nation and in the adaptations to the living space, especially after the death of his beloved wife Eliza in November 1815.[26] Perhaps surprisingly, after her death, Soane also used Coade stone in the design of his family tomb in St. Giles in the Fields burial ground (now St. Pancras Gardens).[27] This was a deeply personal design which Soane exhibited at the Royal Academy in 1816.[28] The monument was raised on a plinth surrounded by an enclosing wall. The materials used were mostly Carrara marble and Portland stone, but off-the-peg Coade stone balusters were considered of appropriate quality in terms of both their material and aesthetic for Soane to include them in the parapet wall as the design neared its final stage (Stage V). Two drawings in Soane's hand dating from 8 and 12 March 1816 show details of ready-made balusters, 34 of which were supplied in March-April 1816 by Mrs Eleanor Coade's 'Ornamental Stone Manufactory'.[29] Given the importance of this design for Soane and his meticulous attention to the details, this use of Coade stone is more than notable.

There are other ways in which Coade became a key player in the knowledge economy of the late Georgian period. Coade's cousin, John Sealy, became her business partner in 1799, and in the same year they opened Coade & Sealy's Gallery (Fig. 1.6), located at the southern end of

Westminster Bridge on the corner where Pedlar's Acre/Narrow Wall met Westminster Bridge Road. It was known as 'Coade's Gallery, or, Exhibition [...] of statues, vases, busts, pedestals, and stoves, medallions and panels in bass-relief, models from the antique, chimney pieces, monuments, fonts, coats of arms', all of which were made at the manufactory, a short distance away. On one level, it was a showroom for the goods produced for the architectural trade and already publicised through the Coade Catalogue. This interpretation presents Coade as secondary or in a supporting role to contemporary architectural and design practices. What has been overlooked here is the role the manufacture and display of these artefacts played in disseminating new artistic ideas and knowledge about the past. As noted, Coade was aware of new discoveries and publications about the architecture and design of the ancient world. The gallery made replica all'antica artefacts and as well as the designs of leading architects available in three dimensions to the viewing public. In this way, the Coade Catalogue and Coade & Sealy's Gallery contributed to the circulation of knowledge of architecture and design.

There is also a broader context for the significance of Coade & Sealy's Gallery. The late Georgian city was a site of display comprising urban entertainments ranging from the edifying to the spectacular. The slippage between reality and fantasy or original and fake was palpable, and the art and architecture of the past was part of this new visual realm. The cult of the past encouraged the production of facsimiles of antique artefacts often made from casts of the original. Initially they were displayed in country house sculpture galleries alongside genuine remnants of antiquity. The house museum, many of which were occupied by well-known architects or designers, was the inheritor of this trend and became a prominent feature of metropolitan society. And here again we find more than a trace of Coade.

For instance, the collector and designer Thomas Hope travelled extensively in Europe and beyond before settling in London around 1796. By 1799 he had bought a house in Duchess Street, London, designed by Robert Adam.[30] Nevertheless, Hope remodelled the interior with a series of themed rooms to display his ever-growing collection of objects purchased during and after his travels, including antique sculpture, vases, and artefacts alongside modern paintings and sculpture. In 1802, Hope hosted a grand opening of his house/museum for the social elite with invitees including the Prince of Wales. The divide between private residence and public gallery blurred further when only two years later Hope decided to issue admission tickets to members of the Royal Academy.

Figure 1.6: An illustration of the grand entrance to Coade & Sealy's Gallery, London, 1799. The London Picture Archive.

Subsequently there were numerous other visitors to the house including leaders of society, artists, scholars, and designers. Visitors to the Duchess Street Mansion experienced a range of styles including Egyptian, Greek, Roman, Indian, and French Empire. The themed rooms included the Vase Room containing his extensive collection of Greek Vases, a Statue Gallery, and The Egyptian Room. Hope's house museum was also known to a broader public including potential clients through his very influential publication, *Household Furniture and Interior Decoration* (1807).[31] Coade was engaged by Hope to produce artefacts to his designs for his Duchess Street Mansion and his country house, The Deepdene. The method of manufacture meant that these items could then become available to others as the moulds could be re-used. Perhaps more notable is Hope's inclusion of Coade ready-mades in his interiors. The illustration of the Picture Gallery in Hope's *Household Furniture*, for example, shows two monumental seats and a tripod table (Fig. 1.7).[32] The seats described by Hope as 'stone seats adorned with sphinxes and lotus flowers' are identical to the Roman throne drawn by C. H. Tatham in the Vatican in 1799 and, as noted above, replicated by Coade with extant examples at Parham Park.[33] The tripod

Figure 1.7: Thomas Hope, *Household Furniture and Interior Decoration* (1807), Plate II. Smithsonian Libraries and Archive.

table design comprising three lion-faced monopodia is copied from a table in the House of the Cervi, Herculaneum. In 1783, Coade had made a copy of this classical piece for Sir John Griffin Griffin at Audley End, Essex, but the moulds would still have existed at Lambeth, and the design was in the Coade catalogue. Coade's copies of ancient artefacts sat alongside the original relics of antiquity collected by Hope. In this way Coade's ready-mades contributed to the dissemination of new knowledge about antiquity through the visual spectacle of the Duchess Street Mansion as well through publications by both Hope and Coade.

The house museum became an increasingly popular urban phenomenon in the early years of the nineteenth century. Between 1808–12 John Soane constructed his drawing office and museum adjacent to two houses he owned and had built between 1792 and 1794 in Lincoln's Inn Fields in London. He used Coade stone as part of both the interior and exterior design. In 1812 Soane added a pair of Coade stone caryatids on the balcony at the top of the projecting 'loggia;' on the front of No. 13 Lincoln's Inn Fields. The figures are modelled on the caryatid figures supporting the roof of the south porch of the Erechtheion on the Acropolis in Athens, one of which was in Lord Elgin's collection. It is possible that Coade had access to use this as a model before it was acquired by the British Museum in 1816.[34] Soane's house contained a significant number of genuine antique artefacts as well as copies some of which were made from Coade stone.

The entire collection was part of a 'visual library' of design that was available to Soane, his pupils, and other members of his office. There were similar displays of originals and replicas at John Nash's house at 14 Regent Street c1820. Nash's drawing office was on the ground floor, and on the first floor was the finest room in the house, the 70-foot-long picture and sculpture gallery.[35] Likewise, Decimus Burton displayed casts of ancient architecture and sculpture throughout his house in Spring Gardens.[36]

Coade's role in the knowledge economy can be contextualised further if we consider the role of women in the staging of urban entertainments. Credit for The Pantheon (1772) on Oxford Street is mostly given to the architect James Wyatt. It was an architectural spectacle combining elements of the Santa Sophia at Constantinople and Roman decoration offering London's elite the experience of opulent all'antica interiors and various entertainments and distractions. But the proprietor Philip Elias Turst was greatly influenced by his wife's wealthy friend Margaretta Maria Ellice, 'a person of fortune' who persuaded him of the need for a 'Dome, Building or Pantheon' for winter evening entertainments.[37] She became Turst's business partner and provided a great deal of capital for the project in return for 'the chief conduct and management of the said intended Pantheon.'[38] Ellice had experience in the staging of urban entertainments as she had a principal role in planning the distractions at another such venue: Mrs. Corneley's in Soho Square, which had 'met with the highest approbation'.[39]

The interplay between Coade, her ready-mades, and the production of architectural style has the potential to reveal much about the business of building in the late Georgian period and the collective practice of the production of design. Her interventions in the display and consumption of architecture and design reveal histories that foreground women. Perhaps if we re-orientate these narratives or, if you will, re-align the actors, Coade (and indeed other women) would come to the fore.

## WRITING COADE

As noted above, Coade's impact on the production of architecture could stand on its own as an important, if inconvenient, truth that disrupts the masculinist, canonical narratives about the building world in this period. But the analysis becomes much richer when entwined with the historiographical treatment of her endeavours. The monographic survey by Avery Alison Kelly, *Mrs Coade's Stone* (1990), is the principal source of our knowledge.[40] Kelly was an authority both on Coade and on Wedgwood, with her study of the latter leading her to the former. Kelly's earlier work on Wedgwood, including *The Story of Wedgwood* (1962) and her *The Book of English Fireplaces* (1968) were taken up by major publishing houses.[41] Perhaps surprisingly, her substantial monograph *Mrs Coade's Stone* was self-published with some support from the Georgian Group, despite Kelly being an established author. Moreover, Kelly had already published widely on Coade including a series of significant articles in such high-profile periodicals as *Country Life* and *Connoisseur*, and several scholarly journals.[42] Would this be the case had either Eleanor Coade or Alison Kelly been a man?

At this point I would like to step back and think more broadly about my motivation for revisiting Coade and Kelly in the context of this volume and think about how we might write women from whatever epoch into architectural history and its historiography without subsuming them into a masculinist canon. First, although the focus of this book is the modern period, women were not invented in the twentieth century and, as we have already noted, recent scholarship shows that Eleanor Coade is not a unique example from earlier times. Second, and perhaps more importantly, I have spent a great deal of time thinking about how we find the feminine presence in architectural history and its historiography as women can be both subjects and objects of architecture.[43] This chapter offers me the opportunity to reflect on these preoccupations as regards both a female actor and a female author who are indexical of what has been the near invisibility of women in the canon of architectural history and historiography. A feminist history or historiography could emancipate women from their anonymity and write them into the histories of architecture. To some extent Kelly's pioneering work does this. But this raises questions in my mind about inserting women in canonical histories. Does this mean we are making women fit into the established masculinist narrative structures. Adding women's involvement with architecture to a history that is predicated on the contribution of individual men would surely be a process of subsumption. Equally, constructing an alternative history of known women practitioners/patrons would risk replacing one hegemony with another. Moreover, I worry that I might project my views back on women in the past. It is not always evident that they saw themselves as oppressed unless we look at that past through the lens of the present. My dilemma is clear – should I as a historian privilege my own interpretation of another's life, itself a hallmark of masculinist ideology or should I compromise my commitment to challenging oppression even if the historical subject does not identify it as such? Here, I have two historical subjects who lived in different centuries and who present different challenges. I will begin with Coade.

We know very little about Coade's own thoughts about her position in the building world of the period. However, actions speak louder than words and the records of her manufactory demonstrate that the business was successful and well regarded. Alongside working with the major architects of the time, she received royal commissions, and the Coade Stone Manufactory was granted the Royal Warrant. Coade also had a significant impact on the urban streetscape and the way in which we continue to experience the British city. The embellishments of speculatively built Georgian townhouses in London, for example, lifted the metropolitan aesthetic punctuating the 'monotony' of the rows of rate houses with refined details, made from a material that continues to endure. Perhaps if we reorientate the narrative to focus on architecture as a collective endeavour requiring a range of skills and technical prowess Coade would come to the fore as a prime mover.

This view may well be supported by Coade's business acumen and achievements which were greatly admired in her obituary notice. It appeared in *The Gentleman's Magazine*, in December 1821.[44]

> November 18th at Camberwell in her 89th year, Mrs. Eleanor Coade, sole inventor and proprietor of an art which deserves considerable notice. In 1769 a burnt artificial stone manufactory was erected by Mrs. Coade at King's Arms Stairs, Narrow Wall, Lambeth. This manufactory has been carried on from that time to the present on a very extensive scale, being a property peculiar to itself of resisting the frost and consequently of retaining that sharpness in which it excels every kind of stone sculpture and even equals marble itself. It extends to every kind of architectural ornaments, in which it comes much below the price of stone, and in many cases cheaper than wood.

Is this really the epitaph of a woman who was invisible to her male peers? But Coade was invisible or at least an inconvenient truth to many architectural historians. Was she in fact the right woman at the right time? Caroline Stanford links Coade's early success to the rising popularity of Robert Adam.

> The other, much grander, opportunity was that the launch of Coade stone coincided with Robert Adam's embellishment of Palladian prototypes with graceful and delicate classical ornamentation, to an extent completely impractical in natural stone.[45]

Alternatively, we could argue that Adam could not have achieved the architectural effects that were his hallmark without Coade. Indeed, the unfortunate relationship with Liardet might add weight to this point of view. John Summerson's summing up of the achievements of Robert Adam is an interesting example of the need in canonical histories for a Roarkist male-author genius:

> The feeling for the externals of architecture changed, after the arrival of Adam, from the grimness of a mask to the delicacy of a feminine 'make-up'. Stucco and Coade stone have a slightly cosmetic character; they suggest, faintly and agreeably, the artificiality of powder and rouge.[46]

Coade stone is merely a product, whereas Eleanor Coade as an important innovator and successful entrepreneur is invisible. The failings of stucco (and by default the disastrous Adam/Liardet business relationship) is forgotten. The feminine presence in architecture is a modification that requires note, and here it is artificial and superficial. Indeed, Summerson's remark makes me think about the language we use to write about women and architecture. The most obvious examples are qualifiers such as 'despite being' or 'even as' a woman/female, which persist. But I remain intrigued by the effect when a feminising adjective is used in conjunction with an abstract or concrete noun. Coade stone is reduced to the merely cosmetic – artifice not genius – something that is added as an aesthetic qualifier. In this way design becomes feminised design. Does it then become inauthentic?

Kelly presents me with a different set of conundrums. As noted above, she had an established reputation as an historian and had already published work on one of the best-known designers, manufacturers, and entrepreneurs of the Georgian period – Josiah Wedgwood.[47] The success of *The Story of Wedgwood* was long-lived and it went into paperback in 1975. Both versions were published by Faber and Faber, a prestigious London publishing house. In the intervening thirteen years Kelly had authored *The Book of English Fireplaces* (1968). Kelly began publishing on Coade in the early 1970s. A short piece for the journal *Furniture History* 'Furnishings from the Coade Factory in Lambeth'.[48] ends with the statement 'Alison Kelly's book on Coade Stone will be published by Faber and Faber'.[49] Further articles on Coade followed until Kelly's extensive monograph *Mrs Coade's Stone* was published in 1990.[50] My interest here is in why there was a sixteen-year gap between the announcement of the Coade monograph and its eventual appearance. The project had the necessary ingredients – Kelly was an established author and Coade was an important subject who had contributed a great deal to the business of design in the late eighteenth and early nineteenth centuries. Moreover, as the number of articles published by Kelly in major academic journals grew, so surely must interest have been piqued in Coade as a key player? Arguably, the only discernible difference between Wedgwood and Coade is that in this instance Kelly's biographical subject was a woman. Recently correspondence has come to light from Kelly to John Summerson written in February 1979 where she outlines the difficulties she is experiencing in getting the book published.[51] My aim here is not to venture into the realms of psycho-biography – that is a topic for others, but there is an undoubtedly rich seam that could be tapped in this regard.[52]

In her letter, Kelly states that Faber and Faber had broken their contract with her even though she had offered to lend them money to publish her book. Consequently, she wanted to apply to the Marc Fitch Fund for a subvention for her monograph on Coade. At this point she did not have a publisher, but the fund agreed to accept her application 'without a proper estimate and without a publisher' She had also named Summerson as sponsor of the publication as he 'so kindly said I could'.[53] The subvention from the Fitch Fund would, in Kelly's view, improve her chances of finding a publisher:

> I am told that a guarantee might be an inducement to a publisher to venture on such a book. I take this with a salt-cellar of salt, as I offered Fabers a loan, but this did not prevent them from breaking their contract. However, perhaps things are getting a little better. Books are now getting published at about 3 times what Fabers said was an uneconomic price. Speriamo![54]

This is an enigmatic glimpse into the evolution of a publishing project which took another eleven years to come to fruition. Kelly's book was finally published in 1990 by the Self Publishing Association with assistance from the Georgian Group. Summerson is not acknowledged nor is the Fitch fund. In the Foreword to the book, Roger White, the Secretary of the Georgian Group recognised the importance of Coade stone as part of the 'new technology' that produced advances in architecture noting that

> [...] its popularity amongst architects and clients was in direct proportion to its subsequent anonymity, since its success in imitating the real things [stone] was the reason for both its widespread use and for the fact modern writers have tended to ignore its existence.

He goes on to acknowledge that Coade stone made it possible for the best-known architects of the day to design ornament that would have been impractical if carved from natural stone. Importantly, Kelly's significance is recognised as the book 'performs a great service in quantifying and illuminating Mrs Coade's achievement'. It is hard to disagree with these remarks.

Finally, I return to my worry that in revisiting Coade and Kelly I might project my views back on women in the past. There is little evidence to suggest that they saw themselves as oppressed no matter how much I might see that when I look at their different pasts through the lens of the present. Nor am I claiming Coade or Kelly as a proto feminist either as a person or as a scholar. Instead, I am interested in trying to understand the disunity of the experience and agency of female subjects and objects of study rather than recreating a teleological notion of reality. Perhaps this approach might work to disrupt the gender binaries in architectural history and its historiography.

This chapter recognises the important contribution of such highly successful but rather unrecognised figures as Eleanor Coade and such historians as Alison Kelly in the retelling of architectural history to show that women actors are not confined to the modern period. As a preamble to the main substance of this book, I would suggest that if we think about knowledge economies and architecture as a collaborative, interactive process rather than the product of the Roarkist genius author and we think carefully about the discourses that are produced as a consequence, we might break the mould of the canonical, masculinist narratives of late eighteenth- and early nineteenth-century building world that are not written in stone.

## NOTES

1 On her death Coade's estate was c £8,000 (approx. £2,000,000 in today's money) probate, PROB 8/214, The National Archives, United Kingdom (TNAUK).

2 *A Descriptive Catalogue of Coade's Artificial Stone Manufactory at Kings Arms Stairs, Narrow Wall, Lambeth* (1784) On one level it can be seen as a trade catalogue, comprising 69 etched designs on 36 leaves, depicting over 746 Coade stone works produced by Coade's Artificial Stone Manufactory. Many of the items depicted are listed, with dimensions and prices. Plates are variously dated from 1777 to 1779. All plates are unsigned.

3 Alison Kelly, *Mrs Coade's Stone* (Upton-upon-Severn: Self Publishing Association, 1990).

4 See inter alia: Amy Boyington, *Hidden Patrons: Women and Architectural Patronage in Georgian Britain* (London: Bloomsbury, 2023) and Conor Lucey, 'Women and the Construction Industry in Georgian Britain and Ireland', *Architectural History* 66 (2023): 127–54.

5 'Coade's Artificial Stone Works', in *Survey of London*, vol. 23, *Lambeth: South Bank and Vauxhall*, ed. Howard Roberts, Walter H Godfrey (London: London County Council, 1951), 58–61.

6 According to Alison Kelly, there is evidence that Coade was directly managing the factory by 1771 at the latest. See Kelly, *Mrs Coade's Stone*, 23.

7 Caroline Stanford, 'Revisiting the Origins of Coade Stone', *Georgian Group Journal* 24 (2016): 95–116.

8 For a discussion of Wedgwood's Jasperware see, for example, Robin Reilly, *Wedgwood Jasper* (London: Thames and Hudson, 1994) and Hilary Young, ed., *The Genius of Wedgwood* (London: V&A Publications, 1997).

9 For a technical discussion of Richard Holt's invention see Stanford, 'Revisiting the Origins of Coade Stone'.

10 For an analysis of the composition of Coade Stone see Ian Freestone, M. Bimson, and Michael Tite, 'The Constitution of Coade Stone', in *Ancient Technology to Modern Science*, vol. 1, *Ceramics and Civilization*, ed. W. David Kingery (Westerville, OH: American Ceramic Society, 1985), 293–304. Ian Freestone, 'Forgotten but not lost: The secret of Coade stone', *Proceedings of the Geological Association* 102 (1991): 135–38.

11 For a discussion of the troubled relationship between the Adam family and Liardet see Frank Kelsall, 'Liardet versus Adam', *Architectural History* 27 (1984): 118–26.

12 'Eleanor Coade' in *Oxford Dictionary of National Biography*, Alison Kelly and Caroline Stanford, 2004, revised 2022, https://doi.org/10.1093/ref:odnb/37296.

13 Kelly, *Mrs Coade's Stone*, 49–50, 301–9.

14 As quoted in Alison Kelly, *Decorative Wedgwood in Architecture and Furniture* (London: Country Life, 1965), 76.

15 Kelly, *Mrs Coade's Stone*, 2.

16 The font has not survived intact, but similar fonts were ordered for Debden Church, Essex, and Milton Abbas, Dorset.

17 The Building Act of 1774 established the system of classifying terrace houses by their size and value, with first-rate houses being the largest and finest, and fourth-rate houses being the most modest. The exteriors of these houses were built using established proportions and were largely identical offering little or no distinctiveness between individual dwellings.

18 Kelly, *Mrs Coade's Stone*, and Stanford, 'Revisiting the Origins of Coade Stone'.

19 I have no evidence of Wyatt's view about his design being replicated and sold by Coade. It is perhaps worth noting that copyright at this time applied solely to the copying of books and was defined in *An Act for the Encouragement of Learning, by vesting the Copies of Printed Books in the Authors or purchasers of such Copies, during the Times therein mentioned* (1710).

20 Many of the items depicted are listed, with dimensions and prices. Plates are variously dated from 1777 to 1779. All plates are unsigned. Kelly suggests a publication date of not before 1784. Kelly, *Mrs Coade's Stone*, 18.

21 Coade's role in the production of these exhibits is not clear. However, Stanford draws the conclusion that the documentary evidence implies that they were produced in her name. See Stanford, 'Revisiting the Origins of Coade Stone', 97

22 Kelly, *Mrs Coade's Stone*, 92–3.

23 Charles Heathcote Tatham, *Etchings, Representing The Best Examples Of Ancient Ornamental Architecture; Drawn From The Originals In Rome, And Other Parts Of Italy, During The Years 1794, 1795, And 1796. By Charles Heathcote Tatham, Architect; Member Of The Academy Of Saint Luke At Rome, And Of The Institute At Bologna* (London: Thomas Gardiner, 1799).

24 Kelly, *Mrs Coade's Stone*, 94

25 According to Alison Kelly, 'Coade Stone in Georgian Architecture', *Architectural History* 28 (1985): 92, note 3, an article in German appeared as 'Über Herrn Coade's Lithopodipira oder Kunst Backerstein-Fabrik zu Lambeth in England', *Journal des Luxus und der Moden* 2 (1787): 171–73. Following the article, Coade's *A Descriptive Catalogue of Coade's Artificial Stone Manufactory at Kings Arms Stairs, Narrow Wall, Lambeth* (1784) was published in instalments in subsequent issues of the magazine. Kelly states this was according to information from Simon Jervis of the Victoria

and Albert Museum. I have not been able to confirm the publication of the article or the catalogue. The journal remained in print until 1826.

26 See John Summerson, 'Sir John Soane and the Furniture of Death', in *The Unromantic Castle and Other Essays*, (London: Thames & Hudson, 1990), 135-37; Michael Hall, 'Mending monuments', *Country Life* June 14, 1990, 302–3; Dorothy Stroud, *Sir John Soane, architect*, (London: De la mare, 1996) 100–2, 114–5; Giles Waterfield and Christopher Woodward, 'Soane's Family Tomb, 1816', in *Soane and Death*, ed. Giles Waterfield (London: Dulwich Picture Gallery, 1996), 106-10.

27 See Sue Palmer, et al., *Death and Memory. Soane and the Architecture of Legacy* (London: Sir John Soane's Museum, 2015), and especially Tom Drysdale's essay '"With trembling hand this tomb he rears": drawing the Soane Family Tomb', 18-27. Drysdale discusses the evolution of the design including drawings by Soane, George Basevi and Gandy whose drawings relate to the various Stages (I–V) of the project. Of particular interest here is Stage IV of the design which includes: entrance gateway to the vault, enclosing walls and balustrade, 28 February 1816, 2 March 1816 by George Basevi, see SM 63/7/20–23 inclusive.

28 Soane exhibited two drawings of the monument at the Royal Academy (R.A. exhibition Nos 799 and 810) and it is assumed that these were drawings SM 14/4/8 and SM F83 (201).

29 SM 63/7/29 and SM 63/7/30. The 34 ready-made balusters were supplied in March–April 1816 by Mrs Eleanor Coade's 'Ornamental Stone Manufactory / Lambeth' at six shillings and sixpence each that, with cartage of four shillings, came to £11.9.0. (See Soane Museum Bills, 16/17/2).

30 For a full discussion of Hope, see David Watkin, *Thomas Hope and the Neoclassical Ideal* (London: John Murray, 1968). The Duchess Street house was demolished in 1851, its contents were taken to Hope's country house, The Deepdene, where they remained accessible to the public.

31 Thomas Hope, *Household Furniture and Interior Decoration* (London: Longman, Hurst, Rees, and Orme, 1807).

32 Hope, *Household Furniture and Interior Decoration*, Plate II. Details of the sides and front of the seats are shown in Plate xix.

33 Kelly, *Mrs Coade's Stone*, 94.

34 SM E6 and SM E7: Soane paid £41 to Coade and Seeley at Lambeth for the caryatids in November 1812. Soane used similar figures in the staircase hall at Buckingham House, Pall Mall (now demolished), at Pitzhanger Manor, Ealing (his country house from 1800-1809) and in the dome of his Rotunda at the Bank of England.

35 John Summerson, (1980). *The Life and Work of John Nash, Architect* (Cambridge, MA: MIT Press, 1980), 132.

36 See Dana Arnold, *Re-Presenting the Metropolis Architecture, Urban Experience and Social Life in London, 1800-1840* (Aldershot: Ashgate, 2000) and (2nd ed. London: Routledge, 2017), 130.

37 The influence Margaretta Maria Ellice had on the design is described in a bill of complaint for dishonest treatment filed by John Sampey, one of the shareholders, against Philip Turst in 1773. The outcome is unknown. PRO C12/408/29, TNAUK.

38 By articles of agreement dated 22 May 1769, Miss Ellice agreed to pay Turst £10,000 at specified dates, and in return she was to receive thirty of the fifty shares issued to fund the project. The total estimated cost of the Pantheon was £15,000. C12/387/19, TNAUK.

39 Ibid.

40 Coade stone was also the subject of an article with a technical focus by Stanford, 'Revisiting the Origins of Coade Stone', and Eleanor Coade was included in a survey by Lucey, 'Women and the Construction Industry'.

41 Alison Kelly, *The Story of Wedgwood* (London: Faber & Faber, 1962); *The Book of English Fireplaces* (Feltham: Country Life, 1968); see also Alison Kelly, *Wedgwood Ware* (London: Ward Lock, 1970).

42 See inter alia Alison Kelly, 'Furnishings from the Coade Factory in Lambeth', *Furniture History* 10 (1974): 68–70; 'Mrs Coade's Gothic', *Country Life*, 2 June 1977, 1514–16; 'Mrs Coade's Stone', *Connoisseur* 197 (January 1978): 14–25; 'Coade Stone in Georgian Architecture', 71–101; and 'Coade Stone in Georgian Gardens', *Journal of Garden History Society* 16, no. 2 (Autumn 1988): 109–33.

43 See, for instance, Dana Arnold, *Reading Architectural History* (London and New York: Routledge, 2002), 199-204; and Dana Arnold, ed., *Women and Architectural History: The Monstrous Regiment Then and Now* (London and New York: Routledge, 2024), especially chapters 1 and 2.

44 *The Gentleman's Magazine* 91, no. 2 (December 1821): 572.

45 Stanford, 'Revisiting the Origins of Coade Stone', 99.

46 John Summerson, *Georgian London* (New Haven and London, Paul Mellon Centre, 2003) 130.

47 Kelly, *The Story of* Wedgwood and *The Book of English Fireplaces.*

48 Kelly, 'Furnishings from the Coade Factory in Lambeth'.

49 Kelly, 'Furnishings from the Coade Factory in Lambeth', 70.

50 Kelly, 'Mrs Coade's Gothic', 'Mrs Coade's Stone', 'Coade Stone in Georgian Architecture', and 'Coade Stone in Georgian Gardens'.

51 My thanks to Professor Elizabeth McKellar for bringing this letter to my attention.

52 Alison Kelly's personal papers are held at the Religious Society of Friends Library (Ref. 2018A14). Like Coade, Kelly was a Quaker.

53 Alison Kelly to John Summerson, 23 Feb 1979, SuJ32/2, RIBA Archives.

54 Ibid.

# Chapter 2
# A Woman on the Margins
## The Trailblazing Career of Mary Louise Schmidt and the Making of Los Angeles in the Twentieth Century

*Andrea Thabet and Jenna Snow*

When Mary Louise Schmidt launched her first building materials business in 1914 to support local architects, no one could have known how essential she would become to the residential architecture industry in Los Angeles. Schmidt began her career as an 'office girl' for architect Arthur Kelly in 1912, doing his bookkeeping and writing specifications. At the time, Los Angeles was merely a rural outpost of a little over 300,000 people. By the time she died in 1974, the Los Angeles area had grown into one of the world's largest metropolises with a population exceeding nine million. As is still true today, governmental officials were grappling with how to house such a rapid influx of residents. From 1914 and through the next six decades, through two world wars and the Depression, Schmidt was at the forefront of the housing conversation. Not as an architect – because of her gender, that profession was not readily available to Schmidt – but rather

Figure 2.1: Mary Louise Schmidt seated at her desk, n.d. Photo by Robert C. Cleveland, Mary Louise Schmidt Archives.

as a proponent for new and modern building materials. Schmidt launched several iterations of a building materials exhibit to showcase the latest in homebuilding materials and architectural plans as a way to highlight the latest trends in home design. As modern architectural design was shaped by new building materials, Schmidt irrevocably influenced the dissemination of modern architecture in Los Angeles and around the world. Her innovative businesses boosted the careers of architects by creating a foundation from which to launch and build their careers, and she created opportunities for architects to connect with clients, manufacturers, and each other. Furthermore, her businesses served to legitimise the architectural profession itself at a time when American architects were still struggling to distinguish themselves as career professionals with formal training, rather than mere tradesmen. Schmidt's entrepreneurial spirit helped shape the careers and businesses of the very same men who would influence residential architecture and design for more than a generation.

In addition to showcasing new materials that would find their way into innovative designs *and* fostering the careers of male architects who would go on to transform modern architecture after the Second World War, Schmidt also created employment opportunities for women. While there were certainly a small handful of women architects, most women interested in design were denied access to the profession, Schmidt included. Schmidt provided an alternative path for young, college-educated women to engage with the architecture and design fields in a meaningful way by employing and training them to inform architects about the latest building materials and assist with building specifications. This helped women to build their own careers, or at the very least earn a living. Schmidt's innovative businesses and trailblazing career influenced the residential construction industry in Los Angeles by creating a centralised hub for the building industry that disseminated information, encouraged community, and connected professionals. In the process, Schmidt left an indelible mark on Los Angeles's built environment.

## SCHMIDT'S EARLY LIFE AND CAREER

Mary Louise Schmidt was born in Denver, Colorado, on 25 July 1890. She spent the first nine years of her life in Denver before her entrepreneur father moved the family to Mexico in 1899, initially as an accountant for American Smelting and Refining Company and later opening an import grocery store for ex-pat Americans. As a young woman, Schmidt did not care much for the authority of anyone but her parents, nor what society expected of women – a sentiment encouraged by a family that valued female independence. In the early 1900s, Schmidt was sent to boarding school in St. Louis, from which she graduated in 1908. After high school, Schmidt attended Smith College in Massachusetts at a time when few women went to college, but her stay only lasted one semester. According to her grandson, when Schmidt discovered Smith was a serious university committed to education, where 'fun was not a priority' and there were no boys, she returned to her family's home in Mexico. By 1911, Mexico's political turmoil necessitated the Schmidt family's move to Los Angeles.[1]

Once settled in Los Angeles, Schmidt began taking classes in architectural drawing and shorthand at Polytechnic High School. As the family still struggled financially, it was necessary that Schmidt become 'employable', according to her grandson. Schmidt was fascinated by architecture, even though this was a profession generally closed to women practitioners. Not only did she pursue drawing classes, she reminisced that she 'often went to watch homes being built, sketching the ones she liked'.[2] When her father purchased land in Alhambra several years later, Schmidt designed a small home for the property. At her first job at Kelly's architectural firm, Schmidt wrote building specifications and revamped office bookkeeping. When business was slow, she picked up extra work from other architects, which she completed during lunch or after hours.

In the 1910s, the architectural profession was still in its infancy in the United States, especially in Los Angeles. The field of architecture as a profession gradually emerged and distinguished itself from master builders and carpenters in the United States throughout the second half of the nineteenth century, not necessarily to further better design but in 'response to [...] economic, social, and ideological issues'.[3] The first architecture school in the country, the Massachusetts Institute of Technology, was established in 1865, soon followed by Cornell University (1871), the University of Illinois (1873), and Columbia University (1881). The architecture school at University of California at Berkeley opened in 1901; it was the first on the west coast. The first institution to offer an architectural degree in Los Angeles, the University of Southern California (USC), admitted the first students to its architecture school in 1919. The American Institute of Architects (AIA) was established in 1857 in New York City while the Western Association of Architects was established in 1884 in Chicago.

Around the same time that the two organisations merged in 1889, the AIA began to push for states to require licensure.

None of these advancements in the architectural profession meant that the field was open to women. Certainly, there were a few women architects. Both MIT and Cornell University, as land grant institutions, were required to admit women.[4] In addition, both the University of California Berkeley and University of Southern California admitted women from their inception. However, it was not sufficient to simply possess an architecture degree to become a licensed architect. In 1901, California was one of the first states to pass a law setting up licensing procedures. Among the requirements was not only a degree from an approved four-year architecture school, but also three years of experience in an architect's office. Women in the United States were often discouraged from even entertaining the idea of a career in architecture, an attitude that lasted for decades. Like Schmidt, they were relegated to supporting roles, if employed at all. In 1948, when the editors of the *Architectural Record* sent out 1,119 questionnaires to women graduates of architectural schools, only 231 replied and, of those, only 108 were practicing architecture.[5] Not surprisingly, the article noted that most of these women focused on residential work. Even in 1972, when UC Berkeley conducted a poll of their women graduates, women architects were often still unable to secure a job in the field following their graduation.[6]

While working in Kelly's office in the early 1910s, Schmidt began to build relationships with both early career architects and notably, other industry professionals. In 1913 she 'assisted' in organising the annual exhibition of the Los Angeles Architectural Club, of which Kelly was the president.[7] Due to her success assembling what seems to be her first exhibit, Schmidt was brought on by the Hollywood Women's Club to organise an 'arts and crafts festival' to raise money for the club's new $20,000 clubhouse.[8] Setting a precedent for her future endeavours, the week-long festival had free admission, as 'the club women will raise the funds for their new quarters by selling floor space to firms manufacturing or selling arts and crafts household equipment'.[9] Held in the newly completed Toberman Building in the centre of Hollywood,[10] the festival offered such 'special entertainment features [...] every afternoon and evening' as 'noted coloratura soprano' Katheryn Leonore.[11] To drum up attendance, Schmidt, along with her 'assistant' Imogene Henry, 'turned out as bally-hoo artists through the streets of Hollywood'.[12]

After spending two years in Kelly's office observing the inner workings of the architectural profession, Schmidt recognised a business opportunity that would allow her to build a career on the margins of the industry while simultaneously legitimising the role of professional architects in Southern California homebuilding. Not quite two months after the Hollywood festival closed, Schmidt launched the building materials exhibit at the Metropolitan Building in downtown Los Angeles. She believed that architects 'wanted an easier way to find and choose materials than rummaging through the enormous *Sweet's* catalogue'.[13] Profiled in *The American Magazine* seven years later, Schmidt remembered thinking 'Why [...] would it not pay building material men to exhibit samples of their materials in one place? And why wouldn't it pay the architect? And why wouldn't it pay someone to bring the architect and the building material men together?'[14]

Despite later mythologising, the idea of a building materials exhibit did not spring fully formed like an Athena from Schmidt's mind. As early as 1886, in connection with the three-day convention in Chicago of the Western Association of Architects, there was a 'building material exhibit, and an architectural drawing display, which brings before each member all the latest materials and appliances used in building and the latest works of the best architects'.[15] By 1890, there were building material exhibits in several cities, such as Chicago, Philadelphia, New York, and Brooklyn. As noted in one article from 1895, 'To architects, whose business it is to be familiar with the best and most economical method of solving any building problem, it is often difficult to find the information desired, as the field is so wide and the inventions and improvements multiply so rapidly'.[16] The first building materials exhibit on the west coast was held in San Francisco. Contemplated in 1897, the exhibit opened in 1908 in the Ferry Building, not long after the earthquake and fire of 1906 had decimated the city and destroyed at least 80% of its buildings.[17] In its contribution to rebuilding the city, the San Francisco building materials exhibit intended 'to make a showing which will demonstrate that nearly all the structural materials and also the industrial ones that are in use are produced in California and that there is no need to send abroad for them'.[18] There were two major differences between Schmidt's building materials exhibit and its precedents. While the earlier ones had a wide variety of building materials and architectural drawings for diverse building types, Schmidt focused on residential design and specifically, single-family homes. Another distinguishing feature was that the earlier building material exhibits were run as an educational service by the local chapter of the AIA while Schmidt, although still educational, ran hers as a money-making business.

Schmidt's exhibit took over the entire sixth floor of the Metropolitan Building, a large open space divided into booths, with a receptionist and demonstrators on site to answer questions.[19] As at the festival she organised for the Hollywood Women's Club, manufacturers paid rent to display materials, while architects paid nothing to visit the site or take advantage of services like finding materials for their projects, or obtaining building specifications. Schmidt also displayed architectural plans and renderings designed by local architects of small, single-family homes that were available for purchase. The rent she received from the manufacturers allowed Schmidt to 'gross six hundred dollars a week', a significant amount for the 1910s.[20] In doing so, she established herself as 'the link between California's architectural profession and the building material industry', a position she would maintain throughout several iterations of her businesses over the years.[21] Between showcasing building materials and highlighting their small home designs, Schmidt's business model was a boon to local architects.

It is perhaps no coincidence that Schmidt took up residency one floor below the Los Angeles Public Library, which occupied the seventh through ninth floors of the Metropolitan Building. Open to all, every day of the year (except the Fourth of July and Christmas), the Los Angeles Public Library was a bastion of education for the public. Association by proximity, Schmidt's building materials exhibit served not only to educate architects on the latest building materials, but, perhaps more notably, to share with the general public, some of whom may have had the public library as their destination, the role an architect could play in design of their future home.[22]

As Schmidt's business grew, so too did her family. Having delayed marriage as long as she could, Schmidt finally married, at the age of thirty-two, local attorney Byron Dick Seaver in 1921. Prior to the marriage, Schmidt made no secret of her disdain for the institution. She believed 'romance ended on the nuptial day [...] and women were always the big losers'. It was one of the reasons she only hired unmarried women in her businesses – she abhorred any kind of 'spousal interference' with her employees or in her offices. Schmidt chose Dick Seaver because he 'challenged her and didn't fawn'.[23] She also may have chosen him for his familial connections. While Schmidt's family were transplants to Los Angeles, the Seavers were well established in Pomona, a town a short train-ride from downtown Los Angeles, where her father-in-law founded the first bank and her mother-in-law was a founding member of the

Figure 2.2: Florence Schmidt, younger sister and collaborator of Mary Louise Schmidt, at the Architect's Building, Los Angeles, seated next to displays of residential architectural drawings and photographs, c. 1930. Mary Louise Schmidt Archives.

women's club. Over the next eight years, Schmidt gave birth to their four children, but she never chose family over career like most women of her time. Instead, she continued to use her maiden name professionally and was listed independently of her husband in the phone book. The Seavers employed Mexican housekeepers, nannies, and cooks, allowing Schmidt to focus on her career ambitions.

Mary Louise Schmidt could not have accomplished all that she had without the help and support of her much younger sister, Florence Schmidt (Fig. 2.2). While Schmidt was the innovator behind their endeavours, Florence was the implementor. Schmidt's grandson remembered, 'Were it not for Tia, now the family's grand matriarch, my grandmother's personal and professional life might have become impossible [...] [they had an] enduring and poignant a partnership as can be forged by the greatest possible love between two sisters.'[24] Florence began working for her sister around 1923, when she was 19 years old, at the building material exhibit at the Metropolitan Building. When Schmidt separated from her

Figure 2.3: Architect's Building at 5th and Figueroa Streets, downtown Los Angeles, 1929. The stripped-down Beaux Arts style echoes that of the newly constructed Central Library, visible on the left. Security Pacific National Bank Collection / Los Angeles Public Library.

husband in 1935, she and her children moved into the house Florence shared with their father. If Florence was clearly intertwined in family relations before the separation, she became even more so after. If Schmidt did not have time to pick her children up from school or drive them somewhere, Florence dropped what she was doing to take care of her nieces and nephew. The sisters' lives were also inseparable professionally. Beginning in 1931 and continuing for several decades, Florence penned the 'Construction Primer', a weekly advice column in the real estate section of the *Los Angeles Times*. According to family lore, Florence secured the job after Schmidt recommended, she 'offer to write it'. Schmidt thought the column was 'uninformed and dull' and could use some flair that Florence could provide. It did not hurt that Schmidt received 'many years of publicity from her younger sister's by-line'.[25]

By 1926, it was clear Schmidt's business had outgrown its single floor in the Metropolitan Building. Needing more space for her building materials exhibit, she convinced a realty firm that she could fill a new building exclusively with architect offices at no charge to them in exchange for the use of three full floors for her building materials exhibit. By the time the building opened in November 1927, Schmidt had the building 90 percent leased.

The Architect's Building was a 12-storey, reinforced concrete edifice located at the southeast corner of 5th and Figueroa Streets in downtown Los Angeles (Fig. 2.3). Stripped almost entirely of architectural ornamentation, the Architect's Building was thoroughly modern. The building contained 460 tons of reinforcing steel. The concrete walls were unfinished with multi-light steel casement windows inset between piers. Like the new Los Angeles Public Library, a block to the west, the Architect's Building harmonised with its neighbour through its smooth, unadorned wall surfaces as well as incorporating carved bas-relief panels, 'depicting the development of architecture, the arts and crafts'.[26]

Just how involved was Schmidt in the construction of the Architect's Building? Numerous *Los Angeles Times* articles prior to, during, and after the building's construction point to Schmidt's influence, ranging from 'chief builder' to designer and project manager.[27] One article from after her death even noted how she supervised construction while 'pregnant and ankle-deep in mud from recent storms'.[28] Although the building permit named three architects, newspaper articles credited a larger group of architects, all of whom Schmidt worked closely with.

It took fifty movers to relocate the materials' exhibit four city blocks from the 6th floor of the Metropolitan Building to the Architect's Building in mid-November 1927. While she only occupied one floor of the Metropolitan Building, in her new space at the Architect's Building, Schmidt took over the ground floor, mezzanine, and basement. This allowed her to expand from fifty exhibitors to more than twice that number. The ground floor was 'divided into streets of attractively designed miniature buildings', while 'a large hall' in the basement was 'devoted to special meetings and to exhibits of architectural drawings'.[29] Although its name was generic, the building materials exhibit, and the architectural plans, focused on single family home design. By the end of 1930, Schmidt was showcasing over 150 building material manufacturers.

After more than ten years of supporting the work of early and mid-career architects, Schmidt had clearly earned their respect and trust as evidenced by Los Angeles architects' willingness to move their offices. Another key motivation for such a move might have been prestige by proximity – that so many professional architects gathered in one place added to the importance of hiring a licensed professional. Noted landscape designer Katherine Bashford moved into the Architect's Building in

1928, sharing an office on the 7th floor with architect Roland Coate. Around the time she moved into the Architect's Building, Bashford noted of the collaboration with architects:

> There has been of necessity a revision in the technique of landscape architecture, influenced first by the crystallization of the modern tendencies in architecture, and fostered by the very general co-operation of the architect and the landscape architect. With the common desire of giving to the client a home possessing all the charms of liveableness both inside and out, the architect realizes fully the necessity of bringing the garden into close relationship with the house, while the landscape architect thinks in terms more architectural and less purely horticultural.[30]

Bashford underscored what would become a tenet of California Modernism – an integration of interior and exterior spaces. These partnerships were possible through close collaborations such as Bashford and Coate, and facilitated by Schmidt at the Architect's Building. In collaboration with the Los Angeles chapter of the AIA and the Architectural Club of Hollywood, Schmidt hosted 'an informal get-together and discussion' the second Tuesday of every month to 'establish closer contact and a feeling of mutual understanding'.[31] Schmidt created a literal foundation on which architects could launch and build their careers which not only benefitted her business, but would also foster connection, collaboration, and community amongst the professional architects, landscape designers, and building materials manufacturers located within the Architect's building.

The exhibit of building materials was clearly essential not just to the architects who had moved into the building, but architects throughout Los Angeles. Writing letters of praise, they complemented Schmidt on the usefulness and value of the exhibit. One architect wrote, 'I moved into this building because of the convenience of having samples of and information as to building materials readily at hand.' Another said, 'The Architects' Building Material Exhibit is daily playing a more important part in the architectural development of Southern California.' Schmidt's former employer, Arthur Kelly, wrote: 'The Exhibit is most comprehensive, and I find it invaluable as a means of getting the different materials before my clients, practically all of whom visit your display rooms.'[32] In this sense, Schmidt's move to the Architect's Building allowed her to expand her previous business model by creating space not only for connection between architects, but also for architects to connect with their clients.

Schmidt also understood women's traditional role as hostesses, and she may have deployed hospitality as a tool for drawing outside women visitors to her exhibit. Given the domestic focus of the exhibit, clearly the target audience was women who were either contemplating, or in the midst of constructing, their own homes. With substantially more builders and contractors than architects, it would have been possible for a woman to visit the exhibit, choose a model home plan, and then specify materials she would like to see. In between special exhibits of photographs and drawings by local architects, European artists, and luncheons for architects, a list of special activities from 1928–30 included multiple meetings of various local women's clubs.[33] For example, in addition to hosting her mother-in-law's women's club, the Ebell of Pomona in July 1929 for a tea, Schmidt also hosted a tea for the Federation of Women's Club presidents.[34]

In April 1930, Schmidt hired her first non-family member employee, Florienne Curry, to be the 'kitchen consultant'. White, middle-class, and college-educated, Curry was described in newspaper articles as 'a junior club girl'.[35] Curry's job description included 'confer[ing] with women who are planning to build homes, and help[ing] them assemble their ideas to present to their architect or builder'. Curry also worked 'with the home economics departments and American home sections of the women's clubs'.[36] That same month, Schmidt announced a 'Perfect Kitchen Competition' inviting both 'housewives' and architects to rethink kitchen design with modern technological advancements.[37] The competition was open to both architectural professionals as well as 'housewives and non-professionals' with substantial cash prizes granted in both categories. First prize in the professional category went to an 18-year-old woman who was working with her architect father after graduating from high school. A mother of three won first prize in the 'housewife' category.[38]

While Schmidt ran a successful, well-respected, well-connected business, journalists regularly portrayed her work in gendered terms that obscured her business acumen. One profile called forty-four-year-old Schmidt a 'young, brainy and engaging [...] woman', while another author would have readers believing she was just 'gentle and sweet' and a 'clever' girl who looked out for architects out of the goodness of her heart. This contradiction in portrayals shows how women in the 1930s were rarely portrayed in terms of work, labour, or the economy. Rather, assigning working women a maternal role served as justification for their labour, as evidenced by *Los Angeles Times* columnist Alma Whitaker's remark that 'Louise and Florence Schmidt run the Architects' Exhibit Building and sort of god-mother the profession'.[39] Yet there was no doubt many of these architects came to see Schmidt's business as essential to their own careers, as did building materials manufacturers who paid to display their products.

Despite its initial success, the building materials exhibit was hard hit by the Depression, and it was forced to close in the spring of 1935, the same year Schmidt separated from her husband Dick Seaver, although they never divorced. Schmidt was not one to wallow in failures. She knew her business was crumbling, and she was ready to launch a bigger and better idea that would take advantage of the 1934 National Housing Act, which marked a critical turning point in the American housing industry. The 1934 Act was designed to address an ongoing housing crisis by creating national housing standards for building materials and construction and overseeing changes in the home finance industry that would make home ownership more affordable for white, middle-class Americans. In 1936, Schmidt constructed a permanent model home exhibit, the California House and Garden Exhibition that served to both educate changes to home finance and promote the construction and modernisation of small homes that would meet the new standards. The 1936 Exhibition (Fig. 2.4) showcased six model homes in six distinct architectural styles by well-known Los Angeles architects using the latest building materials. The Exhibition was constructed on a large parcel of land on Wilshire Boulevard in the newly fashionable Miracle Mile neighbourhood directly across the street from what would become, nearly 30 years in the future, the Los Angeles County Museum of Art. Among the six houses were an all-steel house designed by the first Black man admitted to the AIA, Paul Revere Williams, and a house made of plywood designed by Austrian-born modernist Richard J. Neutra.

Displaying architect-designed model homes in different architectural styles set the California House and Garden Exhibition apart from previous housing exhibits in Los Angeles. Visitors could not only view each of the homes and carefully explore design features, they could also purchase the plans, and, if interested, hire any of the vendors or contractors featured on site. Because Schmidt had established relationships within the architectural community of Los Angeles, and because she had already proven her value to them, she likely had an easy time convincing her chosen architects to contribute to the Exhibition. Schmidt's chosen architects may have viewed the 1936 Exhibition to introduce greater numbers of Angelenos to their work. Nearly every publication covering the Exhibition identified each architect by name, and almost 50,000 people visited during the first week. Further, these architects valued the opportunity to

Figure 2.4: Aerial view of California House & Garden Exhibition on Wilshire Boulevard, Los Angeles, c. 1936. Six full-sized houses were constructed around a central courtyard. Mary Louise Schmidt Archives.

demonstrate the importance of a good architect in constructing elegant small homes. Schmidt secured print coverage aimed at local and national audiences, including a detailed article in the nationally circulated trade journal *Architectural Forum*, which appraised the quality of architecture and design.[40]

Furthermore, the Exhibition was put on by women *for* women. During 1936 and 1937, Schmidt extended the familiar feminine role of hospitality even further by targeting a primarily female audience and creating promotional literature and events aimed at drawing in women. For example, as part of the mission to educate and entertain women, Schmidt planned a two-day Homemakers' Exposition in September 1936, hosted by Marian Manners, Director of the *Los Angeles Times* Home Service Bureau. Along with an afternoon tea, six 'nationally known Home Economists from the Natural Gas Bureau' acted as hostesses at each of the homes with 'table settings and foods typical of the six homes in which they are displayed'. Complimentary recipes were also handed out during this two-day event.[41]

The Exhibition also featured occasional garden parties and weekly women's club events on the tearoom patio. Schmidt often recruited women – actresses, models, and dancers – to act as hostesses inside the model homes, as was common in the era's housing exhibitions, 'to both attract audiences and regale them with explanations of particular display and design ideas'.[42] Actress Mae Clarke presided over a 'housewarming' for the California Cottage with 1200 people reportedly in attendance, while a reception at the New Orleans house celebrated the opening of a Federal Housing Administration (FHA) booth and featured the home's 'co-architect, Edla Muir, playing hostess'.[43] These events appealed to white, lower to upper middle-class women who could imagine themselves as homemakers, wives, and mothers in well-appointed homes, and they illustrate Schmidt's marketing savvy in creating spaces for women to gather and immerse themselves in a fantasy world of model living.[44]

The California House and Garden Exhibition undoubtedly contributed to a surge in new housing construction in Los Angeles after 1936 and served several purposes. The Exhibition made visible all aspects of residential housing – from introducing floor plans and architects to the public, to tangible displays of building materials, through furnishings and décor and gardens, to informing visitors of financing options through FHA representatives. Schmidt's ambitious approach breathed new life into residential housing in Los Angeles, and moreover, the innovative architectural designs and materials on view became models for future residential construction, both for individuals and housing developers. Williams's Better Homes Cottage was a prototype of a prefabricated house made by Lea Steel Homes. In 1937, fifteen houses of the same model were constructed around a large court in Reno, Nevada as a rental property named the El Reno Apartments. Made almost entirely of steel, the Better Homes Cottage was labelled by the architect's biographer 'a modern interpretation of a California ranch house' that 'reflected Williams's ability to reference historical ideas while making use of modern materials'.[45] As *Los Angeles Times* columnist Alma Whitaker argued: 'Architects, contractors and others allied with the project credit [...] Schmidt with having given a hefty boost to the new home-building activity here.'[46] As Schmidt intended, the California House and Garden Exhibition was both aspirational and educational. However, that surge was short-lived as a looming world war stalled new homebuilding. And while the innovative Exhibition was wildly successful in its first year, unforeseen financial challenges forced Schmidt to close the California House and Garden Exhibition in 1938.[47]

## BUILDING NEW BUSINESSES IN THE POSTWAR YEARS

After 1938, Schmidt pivoted once again, launching a new business that drew on her previous ones but ultimately created something new – and this time it was a lasting success. Schmidt was no fool. She knew a housing boom was on the horizon in Los Angeles and across the country. She launched the Architects & Engineers Service soon after the end of the Second World War. The A & E, as it would come to be known, provided valuable services to subscribing architects at no charge, such as assembling data and writing specifications for specific jobs, listing job openings for draftsmen, and securing 'more and better bids from sub-contractors and manufacturers'.[48] Pasadena-based architect Thornton Ladd noted: 'we are saved the trouble of being bothered by a multitude of salesmen showing similar items or talking about products for which we haven't the slightest use.'[49] Schmidt's employees educated architects and engineers on the latest in all aspects of homebuilding materials by answering inquiries, and making office visits with catalogues and material samples in tow. And who better to make those office visits than charming, young, college-educated women? Schmidt's A & E business was unusual because it was woman-driven, woman-staffed, and only relied on men for menial labour.[50] Schmidt ran classified ads in the *Los Angeles Times* that sought '[a] College Girl, Recent Grad. With car for contact work with Architects & Engineers Service. Openings in No. & So. Calif. [Northern and Southern California], Oregon, Washington & New York'.[51] Another classified ad instructed potential employees to 'apply in person'.[52] Yet another classified ad noted 'no experience necessary', on-the-job training, and promised 'rapid advancement'.[53] While Schmidt made no mention of race in the ads, all photographic evidence shows she only hired white women.

Schmidt had always deployed gender as a business practice and consistently created opportunities for young women to build a career on the margins of the architectural industry. A profile on two of Schmidt's employees noted that her 'all-woman organization [...] has been engaged in this masculine-type information service since before enactment of the $19^{th}$ amendment'. Schmidt consistently recruited recently graduated college 'girls' with no prior experience or training needed. The only requirement, 'then as now, was for intelligent and attractive young college graduates'. Her employees 'think their woman's job in a man's world is a pretty interesting way to earn a living.' They described how they made appointments to visit 'an average of two architectural or engineering

Figure 2.5: Building Center employees in front of the Center's entrance, Los Angeles, c. 1957. Mary Louise Schmidt Archives.

firms a day', to discuss products 'in a professional and business-like way'.[54] One former employee remembered Schmidt's mentoring: 'Her advice and encouragement were extremely important to me at a rather crucial time of my life [...] She took great amounts of her valuable time to counsel us, and her advice was greatly valued.'[55]

While her ideas about women and work were somewhat ahead of her time, Schmidt had her limits. Her public relations representative noted that although the job was 'not a job for a flighty type [...] our turn-over is terrific [...] we can't keep our girls from marrying our clients'. While it is unlikely most employees married the clients, it is accurate that there was a decent amount of employee turnover. Schmidt typically terminated any employee who got married, if they did not quit first.[56]

Schmidt's longstanding cultivation of professional relationships with architects, engineers, and building materials manufacturers paid off as she built her new business. By 1952, she had opened five branch offices in San Francisco, Seattle, Phoenix, New York, and Portland, Oregon. At the height of its influence, the A & E reached 'more than twenty-five

Figure 2.6: Lunch meeting at the Building Center, Los Angeles, n.d. Mary Louise Schmidt Archives.

hundred architects across the country'.[57] But Schmidt still had bigger ideas. In December 1957, she opened the Building Center (Fig. 2.5), a centralised permanent exhibit of building, landscaping, and interior design resources that also served as headquarters for the A & E Service. The Building Center was located on the corner of Third Street and Fairfax across from the original Farmer's Market and around the corner from the recently constructed CBS Television City.[58] The property featured 'a series of pavilions [...] grouped around three large garden areas, all different in design and lighting'.[59] Alternating with solid brick walls, pierced concrete block lining the sidewalk provided glimpses of the landscaped courtyards. The pavilions of the Building Center exploited large sliding glass doors to create a flow of indoor and outdoor space, a hallmark of modernist design in Los Angeles. For the first time in Schmidt's career, the Building Center showcased landscape design and interior design. These two professions were far more inclusive and open to women than architecture, thus the new enterprise gave an increasing number of women professionals a platform to promote their work.[60] While architects previously sent their clients to view materials at the Architect's Building, the pavilions and garden setting at the new Building Center provided a more pleasant environment for client meetings. Upon arrival, visitors received a printed checklist where they could 'indicate the materials on which they need[ed] further information'. As in the past, Schmidt served as a gatekeeper for which building materials were on display, 'carefully screened to include only materials of merit from reputable manufacturers'.[61]

Schmidt was not content to rest on her laurels. True to her entrepreneurial spirit, she created numerous opportunities to draw new clients and frequent visitors to the Building Center (Fig. 2.6). A special indoor architectural gallery featured rotating exhibitions of the work of Southern California architects, typically launched with evening receptions for clients and friends. In its first decade, the architectural gallery showcased the work of architects William L. Pereira, Wallace Neff, Lloyd Wright, Paul Williams, and Richard Neutra, among many others.[62] The Building Center also hosted an annual garden party in January, complete with a buffet dinner in the gardens, musical entertainment, and door prizes for attendees. The 1961 garden party, for example, broke 'attendance records' with 'over 1200 members of the building professions and manufacturers' attending. Winners of the very popular door prizes – over 50 in total – included architects Neutra, Neff, Pierre Koenig, and landscape architect Gregory Ain.[63] Many architects, interior designers, and landscape architects also attended the daily Luncheon Club for a casual, low-cost lunch that fostered camaraderie and networking with their colleagues. In the evenings, the Club Room held frequent dinner meetings, social gatherings, and special celebrations.[64] Among the special celebrations, in 1962, Schmidt hosted a reception for Neutra's 70th birthday to honour his contributions to architecture. It was well attended by his family and peers.[65]

The Building Center became essential as the place for information, samples, specification writeups, and professional connections. Visitors could access an architectural reference library. It also quickly became a place for professional training. A Club Room in the Center's Administration wing provided space for industry professionals to hold daytime meetings, seminars, and classes. Professors and teachers from local universities and high schools visited the Building Center for field trips or held class meetings there. An architectural history seminar from the USC School of Architecture met at the Building Center every Wednesday evening in the Spring of 1961 to prepare for the State Board of Architecture examinations.[66] USC's School of Architecture also featured senior student projects in the Architectural

Gallery, giving students an opportunity to showcase their work and connect with alumni and the professional community.[67] In the winter of 1973, the University of California, Los Angeles's Department of Arts and Humanities collaborated with the SoCal AIA's Women's Architectural League to present a lecture series for course credit titled 'Tomorrow Today with Architects of Southern California'. The lecture series was billed as 'an opportunity for contemporary citizens, students, and professionals to communicate with the men who are shaping the environment and changing the quality of our lives'. The list of lecturers was a veritable who's who of Los Angeles architects: John E. Lautner, Robert E. Alexander, Albert C. Martin, William L. Pereira, and several others.[68] The Southern California AIA wrote to Schmidt that the success of their educational seminar program was 'heavily dependent upon the use of the Building Center facilities'.[69] These activities demonstrate the centrality of Schmidt's businesses to the educational training of a generation or more of architects.

The Building Center was the final iteration of a business idea that would drive Schmidt's innovative, decades-long career, and it became 'firmly established as the nucleus of almost all activity in the building industry in Southern California'.[70] Within ten years, the Building Center's reputation as a mecca for residential housing construction, and as a business and educational model for architecture and design support services was drawing visitors from abroad, including Australia and Japan. A schedule of events for March 1961 at the Building Center noted a tour by Japanese Industrialists, and possibly as a consequence Japan's Ministry of Construction established its own Building Center of Japan in 1965. Although Schmidt did not pioneer the idea of showcasing new and innovative building materials, her Los Angeles model provided a prototype that influenced other domestic and international examples. By 1968, an International Union of Building Centers counted forty-four members from all over the world.[71]

## CONCLUSION

Mary Louise Schmidt's entrepreneurial spirit, business savvy, and sheer moxie allowed her to carve a space for herself on the margins of a male-dominated industry. Schmidt trailblazed her own career path by establishing businesses that supported male architects, and she created career opportunities for women at a time when few women were welcomed or encouraged to work in the architectural profession. Schmidt also consistently provided space for women's organisations that encouraged careers in the industry, to gather for meetings, lunches, and social events. Yet, she had a complicated relationship with gender roles and expectations. At the height of the A & E Service's success, Schmidt employed thirty young women and she remained committed to her women-only hiring practices over the course of her career, yet she terminated employees when they married. She never used her husband's name professionally – preferring to be called Miss Schmidt – and she continued to work full time while raising four children. Meanwhile, her businesses allowed her to maintain independence within her own marriage, and then to extricate herself from its constraints when it no longer served her.

There is no doubt Schmidt encouraged the use of modern building materials throughout Los Angeles and the world over her sixty-year career. Through every iteration of her businesses, she influenced a generation of architects who dedicated themselves to the use of innovative building materials and contributed to the amplification of Los Angeles as a bastion of modern architecture – both residential and commercial. Countless architects relied on Schmidt's businesses – the building exhibits at the Metropolitan and Architect's Buildings, the A & E Service, and the Building Center – to save them time, energy, and cost.[72] In the process, they came to see Schmidt's business as essential to their own work and success.

Schmidt's grandson called her 'a fulcrum of California's building industry' and a 'darling of the architects, to whom she was part expert and part flirtation'.[73] Those who knew her – especially the people she cultivated decades-long business relationships with – saw her as a formidable woman who was sharp, direct, trustworthy, and extremely knowledgeable. They recalled her 'immaculately tailored suits and expensive low-heeled shoes [...] her smile and how when she looked at you, her eyes fixed as though there was nothing else worth seeing'.[74] Her legacy may have been forgotten but she left an indelible imprint across the built environment of Los Angeles and beyond.

## NOTES

1 Keith A. McAllister, 'Connections in the Magic Kingdom', BA Thesis, (Amherst College, 1984), 28–40.

2 McAllister, 'Connections in the Magic Kingdom', 43, 47.

3 Mary N. Woods, *From Craft to Profession: The Practice of Architecture in Nineteenth-Century America* (Berkeley and Los Angeles, CA: University of California Press, 1999), 2.

4 Land grant universities were established on land provided by the federal government, authorised by the Morrill Act of 1862.

5 'A Thousand Women in Architecture', *Architectural Record* 103, no. 3 (March 1948): 105.

6 Teresa Grimes, 'A Woman in a Man's Profession: Edla Muir and the Architectural Community of Los Angeles', Master's Thesis, (University of California Los Angeles, 1992), 10.

7 'Architects Will Open Exhibition Wednesday', *Los Angeles Express*, 3 February 1913.

8 'Festival to Aid Club', *Los Angeles Times*, 13 April 1914.

9 'Fountain For Festival', *Los Angeles Times*, 15 April 1914.

10 The Toberman Building now houses Ripley's Believe it or Not!

11 'Festival to Aid Club', *Los Angeles Times*; 'Exhibit to be Held in Hollywood to Raise Funds for Women's Clubhouse', *Los Angeles Express*, 20 April 1914.

12 'Pretty Young Women Bally-Hoo on Streets of Hollywood for Club's Benefit', *Los Angeles Express*, 1 May 1914.

13 The *Sweet's Catalogue*, first published in 1906, was an attempt to systemise and regularise the increasing proliferation of trade catalogues by binding them into one large reference book with an index.

14 Max B. Cook, 'A Girl with a Very Practical Dream', *The American Magazine* 92, no. 3 (September 1921): 62.

15 'Progressive', *The Fort Wayne News and Sentinel*, 18 November 1886.

16 'Building Exhibit', *The Brochure Series of Architectural Illustration* 1, no. 6 (June 1895): 91.

17 'Museum of Architecture', *The San Francisco Call*, 15 August 1897.

18 'To Exhibit Building Materials', *Los Angeles Herald*, 9 February 1908.

19 The Los Angeles Public Library occupied the seventh through tenth floors of the Metropolitan Building, moving to their new, permanent building in 1926.

20 Alma Whitaker, 'Building Hobby of Woman', *Los Angeles Times*, 9 April 1934.

21 McAllister, 'Connections in the Magic Kingdom', 50–54.

22 Likewise, it may not have been a coincidence that when Schmidt moved her business to the Architects Building in 1927, it was located one city block from the new Los Angeles Public Library building.

23 McAllister, 'Connections in the Magic Kingdom', 43–52, 55–70.

24 McAllister, 'Connections in the Magic Kingdom', 95.

25 McAllister, 'Connections in the Magic Kingdom', 83.

26 'Architectural Sculpture in Local Rebirth', *Los Angeles Times*, 11 December 1927. The Architect's Building is now demolished, and the site occupied by a late modern monolith.

27 'Builders' Unit Contract Let', *Los Angeles Times*, 27 February 1927.

28 Cecilia Rasmussen, 'On Architects' Turf, She Built a Tribute', *Los Angeles Times*, 15 September 1997. The author clearly took some liberties with the description. The rainy season in Los Angeles typically lasts from October through March. While rainstorms are not unheard of in April, they are quite rare. Typically, there is no precipitation between March and October. During the 1926–27 rainy season, Los Angeles received 17.76 inches, which is slightly higher than normal. As April 1927 was fairly dry, with less than one inch of rain, it was unlikely Schmidt was ankle-deep in mud. Also, Schmidt was not likely pregnant. Her third child, Barbara, was born in 1925 and her fourth child, Joan, was born in 1929. While it is possible Schmidt had a miscarriage in 1927, there are no primary sources suggesting a fifth pregnancy.

29 'Fifty Builders Move Exhibit', *Los Angeles Times*, 13 November 1927.

30 Steven Keylon, 'The California Landscapes of Katherine Bashford', *Eden: Journal of the California Garden & Landscape History Society* 16, no. 4 (Fall 2013): 7.

31 'Architects of City Fostering Building Unity', *Los Angeles Times*, 22 April 1928.

32 Unpublished pamphlet, SCH004_0035_001_0105 – SCH004_0035_001_0108, Mary Louise Schmidt archives (hereafter MLS archives).

33 Unpublished pamphlet, Untitled, SCH004_0035_001_0003, MLS archives.

34 Unpublished pamphlet, 'Special Activities of the Architects Building Material Exhibit, 1928-1929-1930', SCH004_035_001_0003, MLS archives.

35 Florienne Curry met Schmidt through her sister-in-law, Manilla Seaver. In 1928, Seaver was scheduled to talk to a women's club about the building material exhibit at the Architect's Building, but Curry took her place when Seaver became ill. See 'Society: Juniors Plan for Attractive Social Events', *Foothill Review*, 30 November 1928.

36 'Junior Club Girl Becomes New "Kitchen Consultant",' *Los Angeles Record*, 22 April 1930.

37 'Modern Kitchen Competition Launched', *Los Angeles Times*, 11 May 1930.

38 'Girl Student's Entry Takes First in Kitchen Competition', Los Angeles Times, 29 June 1930; 'Detail of Ideal Kitchen Listed', Los Angeles Times, 6 July 1930.

39 'Successful L.A. Business Women, No. 6: Miss Mary Louise Schmidt', *Los Angeles Times*, 20 May 1934; Alma Whitaker, 'Sugar and Spice', *Los Angeles Times*, 2 May 1936.

40 'Exhibition House Group', *Architectural Forum* 65, no. 1 (July 1936): 37–9.

41 'Homemakers' Exposition', *Los Angeles Times*, 14 September 1936.

42 Ruth Wallach, *Los Angeles Residential Architecture* (Charleston, SC: The History Press, 2015), 11.

43 Alma Whitaker, 'Houses Amid Gardens Show Building Trends', *Los Angeles Times*, 9 August 1936; 'House Warming to Mark Arrival of Federal Booth', *Los Angeles Times*, 19 July 1936.

44 Architectural historian Ruth Wallach notes it was common practice for model home exhibition publicity to use socially and racially coded language to appeal to certain female populations (white, middle-class) but not others. See Wallach, 15–16.

45 Marc Appleton, Stephen Gee, and Bret Parsons, *Paul R. Williams* (Santa Barbara, CA: Tailwater Press; Santa Monica, CA: Angel City Press, 2020), 123.

46 Whitaker, 'Houses Amid Gardens Show Building Trends'.

47 All six houses are extant. For more information on each house and individual architects, see Jenna Snow and Andrea Thabet, 'A Women's Project: Mary Louise Schmidt and the 1936 California House and Garden Exhibition', (Los Angeles: Friends of Residential Treasures: Los Angeles, March 2023), https://www.fortla.org/trails-films-research/trails/.

48 'Architects and Engineers Digest', *Southern California Edition* (April 1952), 16, SCH001_0004_006_0010, MLS archives. The print run lasted from 1952 – 1954 at least, probably longer. See also: 'The Building Center', *Pacific Builders Review* (October 1962): 10.

49 Margaret Stovall, 'Designed for Man's Work: Pasadena Young Women Build Career in Architectural Field', *Pasadena Independent*, n.d., SCH001__0007_022_0001, MLS archives. Details in the article suggest it was published in 1959.

50 McAllister, 'Connections in the Magic Kingdom', 103. Information on Schmidt's employment practices and employees can be found in Box SCH001, Folder 0004, MLS Archives.

51 'Classified Ad', *Los Angeles Times*, 22 August 1951.

52 'Classified Ad', *Los Angeles Times*, 10 February 1952.

53 'Classified Ad', *Los Angeles Times*, 16 June 1953.

54 Stovall, 'Designed for Man's Work'.

55 Christine Shirley to Florence Schmidt, undated, SCH001_0009_009_0001, MLS Archives.

56 Stovall, 'Designed for Man's Work'.

57 McAllister, 'Connections in the Magic Kingdom', 106.

58 Schmidt constructed the Building Center on property leased to her by old friend Earl Gilmore at low cost. CBS Television City directly abuts land owned by the Gilmore family and the family homestead. CBS Television City was one of the first and largest complexes built for television production and broadcasting.

59 Dick Kidson, 'Farmers Market Today', *Los Angeles Times*, 8 April 1958.

60 As noted by Mary N. Woods, 'Many women, white and black, were shunted away from architecture into allied fields like drafting but also interior design and landscape architecture, decoration and gardens being considered appropriately feminine spheres.' See Woods, *From Craft to Profession*, 76.

61 'The Building Center', *Pacific Builders Review* (October 1962): 8.

62 'Party Bulletin', April 1961, SCH001_0006_034_0001, MLS archives. Pereira was featured several times, including in an exhibit about Pereira's university master planning for UC Irvine and Pepperdine University. See Louise Schmidt to Jack R. Weber, January 12, 1971, SCH001_0006_023_0001 – 0002; 'Calendar of Coming Events at the Building Center – 1961', SCH001_0006_036_0001; 'Gallery', March 1966, SCH001_0007_005_0001; SCH_001_005_024_001, MLS archives.

63 'Building Center Annual Garden Party', 10 January 1961, SCH001_0006_039_0001. See also 'Door Prizes for Architects at Building Center Annual Party', 8 January 1960, SCH001_0006_038_0001, MLS archives.

64 These services and activities are documented in several archival sources, including several brochures about the Building Center. For example, 'The Architects and Engineers Service and the Building Exhibition Center of California', c. 1959, SCH001_0007_002_0001 – 0003, MLS archives.

65 Neutra birthday reception invitation, c. April 1962, SCH001_0006_004_0001, MLS archives.

66 *Pacific Builders Review* (March 1961): 3, SCH001_0006_035_0001; 'A Day at the Building Center', 19 April 1961, SCH001_0006_037_0001, MLS archives.

67 'Special Exhibition', SCH001_0006_043_0001, MLS archives.

68 'Architects & Engineers Service Subscriber Bulletin', 15 February 1973, SCH001_0006_028_0001 and SCH001_0006_028_0005, MLS archives. The other named architects were MacDonald G. Becket, nephew of Welton Becket of Welton Becket & Associates, and James Luckman, son of Charles Luckman of Charles Luckman Associates.

69 Arthur F. O'Leary, A.I.A. to Louise Schmidt, 9 February 1966, SCH001_0005_155_0001, MLS archives. As another example, a list of meetings at the Building Center for May 1961 included the Southern California Designer-Craftsmen Association, the SoCal AIA Chapter, American Institute of Landscape Architects, Association of Women in Architecture, Mechanical Engineers Association, and the Women's Architectural League, SoCal Chapter. See 'Calendar of Coming Events at the Building Center – 1961', SCH001_0006_036_0001, MLS archives.

70 'The Building Center', *Pacific Builders Review* (October 1962): 8.

71 Pacific Builders Review, March 1961, 3, SCH001_0006_035_0001; Brochure: 'The Building Centre of Japan', 1-2, SCH001_0007_079_0001 – 0010, MLS Archives.

72 A & E Service, 'About Architects & Engineers Service and the Building Exhibition Center: A Cross Section of Comments by Architects', no date, SCH001_0006_014_0001; additional testimonials in 'Special Bulletin', 20 February 1958, SCH001_0005_030_0001 – 0002, MLS archives.

73 McAllister, 'Connections in the Magic Kingdom', 84.

74 Ibid.

# Chapter 3
# Myriam Ratinoff
## A Concrete Architectural Practice in 1960s Chile

*Gabriela García de Cortázar Galleguillos*

Myriam Ratinoff Brodsky (1926–2019) graduated as an architect from the University of Chile in 1950. She designed and built a large number of houses, many of them in an unprecedented construction system of reinforced concrete blocks. She worked as a designer, undertaking projects for different clients, for her own construction company and for small-scale real-estate developers. Until now, however, Ratinoff had been an unknown figure, and her work had not garnered scholarly attention. The specific construction system had not been studied either, nor the relation of her work to a larger historical-cultural context.[1] Although Ratinoff started her professional practice in an expanding and teeming scene of architectural discussion in mid-century Chile that saw the creation of new journals and the establishment of the first professional association, neither she nor her work have ever featured in the public discussion in Chile, let alone abroad. This chapter presents her work through her own house, the Kohn-Ratinoff house – and through it, her practice. It also situates her *ouevre* in a much broader architectural discussion on technique and design, mainly that of the modernist avant-gardes. Finally, it considers why she has been overlooked by her peers and by history, and proposes a reading that allows the work to go beyond the merely material.

### THE HOUSE

The Kohn-Ratinoff House, designed by Myriam Ratinoff Brodsky in 1962, is located on the corner of Dinamarca Street and El Belloto Street in what is now the Providencia district of Santiago.[2] On a raised front garden, the architect placed two volumes of different heights, perpendicular to each other (Fig. 3.1). The volume facing El Belloto Street has two floors and is more hermetic, while the volume facing Dinamarca street

Figure 3.1: The Kohn-Ratinoff house, Myriam Ratinoff Brodsky, Santiago, 1962, viewed from Dinamarca Street. Photo by Macarena Álvarez.

is one storey high and completely transparent. The complex expresses horizontality through its use of continuous windows and of planes that intersect to generate interior spaces. The site, acquired by Ratinoff and her husband Sergio Kohn in 1958, is shaped like a right triangle, with the two streets corresponding to the short sides of the triangle, and its back, to the hypotenuse.[3] Uniquely in the neighbourhood (and perhaps also in the residential areas in Santiago developed in the second half of the twentieth century), the house has no perimeter fences: the boundaries are established by the two perpendicular volumes, parallel to the two streets, which, through smaller constructions, such as a garage and a second open parking lot, bridge the distance between the house and the party walls. These boundaries also define a triangular-shaped interior patio. The building, commissioned by Ratinoff and Kohn, contains two independent properties, in a variant of the 'double houses' popular in Chile in the 1960s.

The house's modern forms were realised with an innovative construction system employing concrete blocks, which are used not only in walls (as in other masonry systems), but also as a load-bearing structure, including beams and slabs. This can be seen, for instance, in the roof slab of the two-storey volume, which rests on beams made of blocks. The eaves of the house are also made of blocks, this time laid flat, while the walls of the volume on the second floor protrude beyond the plumb line and are effectively cantilevered. In these, the laying of the block does not even attempt to bond them.

Termed Multibloc, this system was developed by Kohn through Inein SA, a company that began operating in 1962. Multibloc consists of machine-made modular concrete pieces, which cover all the needs of a smaller scale construction and was particularly suitable for housing.[4] The system is composed, in effect, of thirty-one pieces: eleven for walls; seven for beams, bond beams and joists; two for slabs; five for very specific purposes (lintels, gutters, ducts); and four for various purposes. Only the last four of these are solid; most are hollow. All employ a module of 39x19x19 cm. This module was designed so that it could accommodate 1 cm of mortar, resulting in closed measurements of 40 cm and 20 cm: the 'block plus mortar' unit produces a module of 40x20x20 cm or 20x20x20 cm. The construction system implies that the hollow modules can be assembled by passing steel rebars through the blocks, which must also be filled with concrete.

The Kohn-Ratinoff house contains two dwellings: 'House A', with access from Dinamarca Street, which has housed the Kohn-Ratinoff family since 1962, and 'House B', with access from El Belloto Street, which was originally intended as an office for Ratinoff and later used as a rental unit. In the project, 'House A' was developed on a large portion of the first floor of the building, and included large common spaces (entrance hall, living room, and dining room), a kitchen with a lunch area, service spaces, two bedrooms and two bathrooms.[5] 'House B' originally occupied two floors, with a large bedroom on the first level (labelled 'Bedroom 3'), and the public spaces on the second floor. These consisted of a living room and dining room, plus a small kitchen. A side hallway led to a bathroom and two bedrooms. This configuration changed over time, as the large bedroom on the first floor eventually became part of 'House A'.

In general, inside 'House A' the concrete block is always used in combination with other materials to define the interiors; in 'House B', or apartment, the concrete block is left bare, only receiving a coat of painting. In the entrance and hallway of 'House A', blocks are used in walls, while the flooring is in a *terrazzo* in reddish tones, the ceiling is plastered, and partitions are made of wood and grooved glass. A planter links the interior with the exterior and adds a vegetal presence to the space. In the living room and dining room, a different block is used. The fireplace wall, a central element in the living room, with a cantilevered base covered in black marble, features blocks of a more horizontal format; this block is also used to cover the dining room wall. In these spaces, the floor is wooden *parquet* and the ceilings are also plastered and painted white. The main bedroom also has plastered and painted walls and ceilings. In 'Bedroom 3' the blocks comprising the walls and ceilings are left exposed as they are throughout 'House B'. The latter reveals the material from which it was built: the entire volume of the second floor is crossed by beams made of exposed blocks, which rest on the walls (the space between beams is closed in with windows); at the same time, the ceiling of the apartment reveals the use of blocks in the ceiling slab; and the walls show the blocks arranged orthogonally, without bonding them.

The Multibloc system is based on the standardisation of measurements and on the modularity of all components. Its industrial manufacture minimises errors on site. In structural terms, the system depends on the hollow core of the modules through which steel rebars pass. The structural design includes standard solutions. There are four types of block-made vertical load-bearing structures, addressing all recurring situations: end-of-wall pillars, T-shaped pillars, 90-degree corner pillars and pillars supporting beams. There are block-made beams in the second floor, and block-made floor and ceiling slabs. There are also *ad-hoc* solutions, made by adjusting existing blocks, such as corner pillars of obtuse shapes, in response to the form of the site, and bond beams to tie down walls, made by adjusting beam blocks. There are also a few elements constructed with traditional methods such as the concrete inverted beams over the public spaces of 'house A' and the steel pillar next to the windows. Most building elements have been made within the finite, closed system of blocks. An X-ray analysis would show a three-dimensional mesh of steel rebars that are tied together, achieving a solidary system, despite its obvious manufacture from discrete pieces. The house, although made of parts, acts structurally as one: the concrete that was cast inside the blocks and within the steel rebars penetrated the pores of the blocks and consolidated the whole system into a unit.[6] From this case, it can be understood that the Multibloc system has the benefits of a simple masonry work, but the structural behaviour of reinforced concrete.

## THE ARCHITECT

Myriam Ratinoff Brodsky began her studies at the University of Chile in 1945 and graduated five years later. Herself the daughter of an architect, Abraham Ratinoff, she worked until at least 2004. Ratinoff studied in a school in transition, at a time when the School of Architecture at the

University of Chile was changing to a Bauhaus-inspired curriculum.[7] According to the records kept in the registrar's office, Ratinoff was part of a first year cohort of 119 students, of whom only 42 students were promoted to the second year; eight were women and 34 were men.[8] Among her first-year classmates, there are several names that would later play a key role in shaping the public debate about architecture in Chile.[9]

Ratinoff's first year at the School of Architecture involved training according to the 1933–1934 curriculum, which had already incorporated some innovations coming at the time from Europe but was still under intense scrutiny for its Beaux-Arts basis.[10] From her second year onwards, however, her studies were shaped by a curriculum that was the fruit of a more radical modernist-oriented reform. This reform, promoted by the students, crystallised into a comprehensive new programme largely due to the work of local professors and students, together with Hungarian *emigré* Tibor Weiner, a former collaborator of Hannes Meyer.[11] These changes sought to promote the training of a 'comprehensive architect': 'a technically efficient but cultured professional – with universal culture, in broad contact with the life and reality of his time and his country –, with an eminently creative conscience.'[12] As stated by the Teaching Commission responsible for the new curriculum, the education of the architect at the University of Chile should generate an architect who is a 'technician with complex knowledge [...], with great flexibility of spirit to accommodate his solutions to increasingly different conditions', which required 'great capacity for analysis and [...] knowledge that is the result of a much more universal and complex education'.[13] The new plan of studies sought to generate modern architects who

> [had] sufficient horizon to judge socially and economically the effective needs of their countries; who plastically [knew] how to find the total expression of the man-nature-society relationship that is being formed in our century; who technically [achieved] mastery of all the problems posed by construction and [completed] the structure of the theories that explain the static work of the new materials.[14]

The 'methodological field' of the 1946 reform was the articulation of three areas: philosophical, technical, and artistic – much along the line of the Bauhaus programme.

The 1946 curriculum had two cycles: an 'Analysis Cycle' (first and second year) and a 'Synthesis Cycle' (third to fifth year), followed by the degree project in the sixth year. The objective of the Analytic Cycle was to provide 'systematically organised knowledge around the artistic, philosophical and technical aspects, as well as certain general concepts that would set in motion the creative work and the basic knowledge that rationally controls this work'[15] Ratinoff only undertook the second year of the Analytic Cycle. However, she was taught the Synthesis Cycle in full, which sought to 'integrally solve problems of Architectural Composition; that is, to design'[16] The most important subject in this cycle was the Central Studio (Architectural Composition), in which 'integrally conceived architectural projects [were carried out]',[17] Ratinoff excelled in this subject, as the registrar's records show.[18]

In 1950, Ratinoff developed her degree project under the guidance of Roberto Dávila Carson, one of the architects who had travelled abroad and had been directly in contact with the European modern masters.[19] She received her degree on the 15 December 1950. Several other notable Chilean architects graduated alongside her. They correspond to a second generation of modern architects, a generation that produced work significant both for its unique character and for developing real estate practices that gave a modern form to the new suburbs.[20] The generation that graduated from the University of Chile in the early 1950s was also the one that would later found *AUCA* magazine, an architecture and arts journal that published both projects and cultural debates.[21] It also supported the establishment of a national debate on architecture through the recently founded first professional association, the *Colegio de Arquitectos* (1942).[22]

Ratinoff did not participate in these cultural and professional debates. She worked as an architect, carrying out one-off projects on commissions, designs for her own construction company and for small-scale real estate companies. She married engineer Sergio Kohn, whom she had known since her schooldays, while she was working on her degree project. Kohn also studied at the same university. They had three children: Roberto, Luis, and Eduardo. She had her office in the centre of Santiago. She also painted, largely in a modern, abstract style. She was affiliated with the *Colegio de Arquitectos* but was also active in the *Cámara Chilena de la Construcción*, as was Kohn, who later served on its board.[23] The couple also participated in the Jewish Community, and had a group of friends who were politically, ethnically, and religiously diverse.[24]

## HER WORK

The Multibloc system was unprecedented in its time: it was Kohn's determined and persistent attempt (through Inein SA) to introduce reinforced block construction to the Chilean environment. Kohn had already been working with concrete block construction since 1952. The first blocks he worked with were hand-made, but after 1955 they were industrially produced. In 1960, he acquired a Besser machine, imported from Alpena, Michigan, USA, which he adjusted from the imperial system to the metric system to produce blocks in the 39x19x19 cm module. The machine produced 7,500 compressed and vibrated blocks per day. Ratinoff demonstrated the potential and scope of the Multibloc system through her built work. Her own home was the first, but several others followed, both commissioned by others and developed by her and her husband.

The Brodsky Rosemblüt house (1962) (Fig. 3.2), also a double house, is one of these, as are the two-storey house for Samuel Drobny (1967), and two houses on Vista Hermosa Street (1967). In the sixties, Ratinoff also developed housing complexes for the middle class using the Multibloc system, through the construction company Hogar Propio Ltda., which she and Kohn co-owned. These complexes share an urban typology of a central or lateral street. Among them, we can find the seven houses on Holanda Street (1963) (Fig. 3.3); nine houses on Roberto López Meneses Street (1970); ten houses on Ortúzar Street (1975); five houses on Pucará Street (1980); and twelve houses on General Gorostiaga Street (1988). She also designed other large-scale works, such as a warehouse with a steel structure and block walls, in the Quilicura industrial neighbourhood, and participated in real-estate developments for third parties, also using Multibloc, such as the Waterloo Street complex (1970), for Jaime Majlis.

Ratinoff not only carried out projects using the Multibloc system, but between 1940 and 1994, she also had a prolific practice designing houses and projects using traditional systems. These include a group of one-storey masonry houses, around Villoslava Street, in the Suárez Mujica neighbourhood, Ñuñoa (1952); and a group of nine one-storey houses in concrete and brick masonry, eight of which have been demolished, built for her mother Berta Brodsky, on El Aguilucho Street (1954–1955). There are also more double houses: for example, the two-storey house at Los Españoles Street (1967–1969), with a concrete structure and brick masonry walls, for Abel Vieira; and another at Los Hidalgos Street (1969–1971), whose interior takes advantage of the sloping terrain to work on interior half-levels. Ratinoff

Figure 3.2: The Brodsky Rosemblüt house, Myriam Ratinoff Brodsky, Santiago, 1962. Photo by Ignacia Villanueva.

Figure 3.3: The Holanda complex, Myriam Ratinoff Brodsky, Santiago, 1963. Photo by Ignacia Villanueva.

also built some multi-family buildings in the boroughs of Providencia, Ñuñoa and, Vitacura, among which sit the two-storey building with four independent apartments on Marchant Pereira Street (1952) and the building, also with two floors and four independent apartments, at Francisco de Aguirre Street (1962).

Ratinoff's work reveals several architectural interests. Perhaps the clearest in the houses of the sixties, at least, is the expression of horizontality. Large roof planes, on different levels, which are often articulated with stand-out walls are possibly a manifestation of her admiration for Frank Lloyd Wright. Among the houses that demonstrate this horizontality are her own house in Dinamarca Street and the double houses in Los Españoles and Los Hidalgos – the latter resembling Asian structures in its articulation of levels and roofs, in addition to its angled eaves and the lush vegetation surrounding it. Also characteristic of Ratinoff's work is the care she puts into the design of the access sequence, in the distribution of hallways, and in the definition of the boundaries between the different spaces of the houses. Doorways are characterised by such details as steps and doors that use translucent and coloured panes, sometimes covered in protective and decorative grilles; surrounding walls are often accentuated using ceramic tile cladding. Interior spatial sequences often present changes in direction, customised flooring (reddish marble *terrazzo*, as opposed to *parquet* flooring), and the use of planters (between interior and exterior). Public spaces are generally characterised by such central elements as fireplaces that simultaneously demarcate a boundary and tie spaces together. Finally, perhaps given the nature of her commissions (especially for single-family houses), Ratinoff could develop the typology of the double house, which in many cases also involved half-levels for the organisation of the interiors. Her objective as an architect was to develop relationships, both between spaces and between materials.

## DESIGN TECHNIQUES

The Kohn-Ratinoff house was built entirely using the Multibloc system. Walls, pillars, bond beams, beams, and slabs were made with blocks from the system, as well as such elements as lintels and cladding. The house also displays a modern formal language, thanks to the horizontality of the first floor, as well as the presence of elements that reveal the structural behaviour of the house – mainly, the beams, slabs and cantilevered walls that crown the second floor. The house unites modern form and structure, exploiting the plastic possibilities of the Multibloc technology, in a calculated effort to commercially introduce it in Chile.

Multibloc was presented as a direct competitor to reinforced concrete construction as it was cheaper and faster. The system that the Kohn-Ratinoff house presented offered the benefits of masonry construction, efficiency in the use of labour (thanks to the size of the pieces, which were designed to be handled by one worker and which required only one crew for the assembly of the entire house) and general economy of construction (by eliminating the expense that formwork entailed). In addition, it offered earthquake-resistant structural behaviour, since the walls are reinforced and concreted to function as a single structural unit, resistant to compression and traction, which was also possible to standardise and normalise, given the industrial origin of the elements.[25] Multibloc's introduction to the market occurred just after the devastating Valdivia earthquake of 1960, a 9.6 magnitude earthquake that impelled the drafting of a more comprehensive seismic regulation in Chile.[26]

The architectural problem associated with the Multibloc system, however, was how to make attractive, for both clients and architects, the industrial and rough material intended to be left exposed. In other words, the problem was how to elevate the mere construction system to architecture. This is where Ratinoff's talent came into play. She adopted the laws of the system with ease: all the dimensions in the plans derive from the blocks and are strictly applied in the building. However, when challenged by needs, she adapted the system: in the Kohn-Ratinoff house, the obtuse corners that respond to the site, and the adaptation of beam-blocks to make bond beams, demonstrate the flexibility with which she used it. The house proves how she was able to foresee, especially through drawing, the problems and accidents inherent to a construction site. In this project, all problems are solved at the design stage, within the system. Ratinoff finds an architectural expression (spatial and formal) that converses with both construction industry and architectural design in equal measure. The house is both a catalogue of the system and a desirable example of modern housing.

The complex synthesis that Ratinoff achieves in her own house is something that she worked on to varying degrees in her subsequent works, but with certain divergences. The Brodsky Rosemblüt house (1962) is more restrained in structural terms, since it does not have block-made beams or cantilevered walls: the house does not present elements that defy gravity. Her quests were not only structural, however. In this house, for example, and the set of seven houses on Holanda Street (1963) she explored strategies to deal with the roughness of the concrete block, which implied adaptations of the block itself, carried out in the factory. The Brodsky Rosemblüt house uses a block with a raised triangle on its façades, which is then arranged in different directions in an alternating manner, while in the complex in Holanda Street the block used has four vertical grooves that divide its length. In both cases, the adaptations of the faces of the block (in the case of the Holanda Street houses, also of the internal face) imply a reduction of the scale of the element, bringing it closer to human proportions.

Ratinoff's work synthesises two forces: an industrialised system for construction, Multibloc, and the modernism imbued into her by the University of Chile's 1946 curriculum reform. For Ratinoff, her greatest professional realisation was in the different housing complexes that she carried out for her company *Hogar Propio Ltda.* As her widower explains, she deeply valued the possibility of offering quality housing for the middle class and those with fewer resources, that is, houses with a low construction cost (given the speed of the works) and with efficient structural behaviour. In terms of design, however, it is probably her higher-standard single-family homes that make a greater contribution.

## BUILDING TECHNOLOGY

Although one of the first architectural explorations of concrete block technology is the concrete masonry Huis ter Heide house in Utrecht, 1915, by the Dutchman Robert van't Hoff, this was for Sigfried Giedion 'a building process with virtually no followers'.[27] Le Corbusier used blocks in the Villa Roche (1923), as a filler in the column and beam system that structures it, but stuccoed it.[28] He also used it at Pessac (1920–1926) and its industrial potential is part of the project's argument, although it is ultimately not visible.[29]

The block-making industry dates back to the late nineteenth century in the United States. Of artisanal origins, mass production only became possible after the invention of a machine with adjustable sides and removable core, and the standardisation of the raw material, Portland cement.[30] By the early twentieth century, concrete block construction had taken off in North America, both because of the relative low cost of concrete block production and construction (usually requiring unskilled labour) and because of the rising costs of wood construction at the time. Concrete block construction occurred almost in parallel with the development of reinforced concrete, although the blocks were not intended to fulfil the monolithic function of concrete, which allowed 'ceilings, beams, and columns to be joined together in a continuous unit.'[31]

It was Frank Lloyd Wright who raised the concrete block to new heights, moving it away from its secondary use as filler or as a material 'condemned to cladding, [...] partition walls, and [...] factories in the slums.'[32] It was not easy. Wright mused: 'The concrete block? The cheapest (and ugliest) thing in the building world. It lived mostly in the architectural gutter as an imitation of "rock face" stone. Why not see what could be done with that gutter-rat?' He proposed that

> Steel wedded to it cast inside the joints and the block itself brought into some broad, practical scheme of general treatment then why would it not be fit for a phase of modern architecture? It might be permanent, noble, beautiful. It would be cheap.[33]

He tested the hypothesis at two points in his career and with different objectives. After using it in part in the Imperial Hotel in Japan (1923),[34] Wright conceived four villas that explored the possibilities of what he called 'textile construction in concrete blocks:' the houses for Alice Millard in Pasadena, California, and for John Storer (both 1923), and those for Samuel Freeman and Charles Ennis (both 1924).[35] These houses experimented with the possibility of taking advantage of the plastic qualities of the material, through the design of patterns on the visible faces of the block. Wright's second approach to concrete blocks occurred twenty-five years later, as part of his search for low-cost housing after the Depression, when he developed the so-called 'Usonian' houses. If the first Usonians were made of wood and brick, around 1950, Wright designed a concrete masonry system that he called 'Usonian Automatic', which was intended to introduce the possibility of self-construction.[36] In total, there are between ten and twenty houses built in the United States using the Usonian Automatic system. Both the 'textile block' and the Usonian Automatic systems use solid blocks, which were arranged in a continuous joint and woven with steel rebars.

Wright's work, while addressing questions about economics and industrialisation, showed an approach in detail: each block was special. The next generation of architects that worked with blocks did so with machine-made industrial blocks, identical to each other, of standard shapes. The shape of the blocks was the same as that which Le Corbusier stuccoed and which Wright had identified as despicable. However, some architects used it without hiding it. In the United States, Louis Kahn used concrete blocks for the Trenton Bath House in New Jersey (1954–57), the Tribune Review in Greensburg, Pennsylvania (1958–61), and the interior of the Unitarian Church in Rochester (1969). In the Netherlands, Gerrit Rietveld used concrete blocks for his pavilion for the Third International Sculpture Exhibition in Sonsbeek Park in Arnhem, in 1954, while Aldo van Eyck also used concrete blocks for his Sonsbeek pavilion in 1966 and his Catholic church in The Hague (1968). Jaap Bakema and Johannes van den Broek also designed the church in Nagele in concrete masonry (1958–1962), as well as several other projects, while Aarno Ruusuvuori, in Finland, also used it in his projects including the church in Tapiola (1965). Herman Hertzberger, as well, used concrete blocks in Centraal Beheer (1968–1972), the Apolo Montessori schools (1980) and in Delft (1960–1966), as well as in the Diagoon housing project (1967–1970) and the Tivoli Vredenburg Theatre (1977). Other architects who explored the possibilities of concrete blocks in the second half of the twentieth century were Soldevila and Llorens in Spain (in houses with simple exterior forms, with half-storeys *à la* Hertzberger, and with piping outside, brutalist style), and the architects of the Swiss Ticino region including Mario Botta and Tita Carloni, among others.

The presence of concrete block masonry in Chile is not limited to Ratinoff's work, although there is possibly no work as consistent and challenging, in terms of both presence in the city and ideas, as hers. A pioneering case from 1935 were David Downey's 'Thermo' blocks, with which Downey designed and built a family home on the Chilean Pacific coast. A non-exhaustive compilation of other works in concrete blocks would include the Hostería Chañaral Honsa, by Bresciani, Valdés, Castillo, Huidobro (1960–1961), plus, the same architects' one- and two-storey houses in Pedro de Valdivia Norte and Los Conquistadores Street, and the Hostería Castro Honsa by Emilio Duhart (1962). Concrete block masonry does not contribute to the architectural qualities of any of these Chilean works. The only project that does use concrete blocks in a way that is central to its design is the Pensioners' Payment Centre of the Banco del Estado de Chile, now demolished, by Christian de Groote (1964–1965).[37]

At the time when Ratinoff began her work using Multibloc, the architectural and construction *milieu* in Chile was exploring questions of prefabrication and industrialisation, especially regarding the production of housing – although not necessarily in concrete.[38] Among the industrialised products in concrete, Depetris' prefabricated warehouses and Inapreco's prefabricated houses stand out, in addition to a series of other manufacturers of discrete industrially produced elements.[39] When Ratinoff was a student, *Arquitectura y Construcción* included articles on both concrete blocks and issues of prefabrication and industrialisation; she may have known these publications.[40]

However, even though the context seemed to be ready for a system such as that developed by Kohn and Ratinoff, their integration of the building system with its design logic and the resulting aesthetics was not mainstream: as Kohn put it 'it never took off'.[41]

## A CONCRETE PRACTICE

Despite her work being such a clear synthesis of design and technology; despite her building several houses using the Multibloc system in different ways and for different budgets; despite the fact that her practice very much aligned with the interests and quests of her generation of Chilean architects, Ratinoff's work has not yet been studied, nor was it published at the time. This is true of her houses and the system out of which they were built. They were not addressed in relation to the existing technology, the challenges she faced or the solutions she developed. Their material aspects were ignored, as were the connections to the work of her peers at home and abroad. How, and why, was such a clear architectural work and consistent practice overlooked?

It cannot be said that the scene was not prepared for a work such as hers, given the discussions on both industrialisation and housing that characterised Chile in the period prior to the *coup d'état* in 1973.[42] Her work, however, did not appear in either of the country's main architectural journals – *AUCA* and *CA* – except in Multibloc ads, which sometimes showcased one of her houses. These featured at least once in every issue published between 1966 to 1970.[43] Multibloc was not just advertised in magazines for architects: it was also heavily advertised in the *Revista de la Construcción* (*Building Journal*, a magazine from the *Cámara Chilena de la Construcción* or Chilean Construction Chamber, published between 1962 and 1972).[44] In all three magazines, the ads focus either on the shape of the block, or on specific qualities through close-up photographs, or they put the focus on construction techniques, or they show results – the latter, the more architectural.[45] In addition to advertising, Inein S. A. had a presence in the *Revista de la Construcción* through letters and articles.[46] *Revista de la Construcción*'s price listings also included concrete blocks starting from issue 8 (1962), with information initially provided by Inein S.A. and from 1963 by two additional sources.

Perhaps Kohn and Ratinoff's dissemination efforts were primarily directed towards the construction industry, rather than onto architects. It is indeed true that both Kohn and Ratinoff had better relations with the Chilean Construction Chamber than with the architects' association. Furthermore, Ratinoff was not close to the architects of her generation who took part in architectural debates, perhaps because she did not teach in the university, as Schapira, Bendersky, the Mardones brothers and others did.[47] It is thus not entirely surprising that she did not establish ties to the *CA* journal or the *AUCA* magazine, beyond advertising Multibloc. Ratinoff operated exclusively in a professional environment, rather than within the discipline, or culture, of architecture. Her field of action was comprised by Inein S. A., which often served as investor for real-estate developments[48], as well as developers such as Jaime Majlis or Max Piper,[49] together with the private commissions she could get.[50] Her work was of a practical, concrete, sensible nature because her architecture was part of a real estate business.

It would thus be inaccurate to say that she was 'left out', or overlooked, since it can be understood that she *chose* to operate in this way. Whatever the origin of this neglect, her Santiago buildings are thankfully still available for scrutiny and assessment. And with this distance in time, the first reading that emerges is a cultural and historic one. Her work appears as not only practical, but deeply imaginative; not only concrete, but resourceful; not only sensible, but sensitive. From our standpoint, it is possible to see that her command of both technology and design allowed her to be both reliable *and* experimental. The buildings are not only responses to the needs of a specific construction system, but also to questions such as how to design in conversation with technology, how to make the most of a closed-system technology, and what is the architecture (the form, the aesthetics, the spaces) of this specific system. At the same time, Ratinoff's houses lend themselves to new inquiries: what are the design techniques that make a rough, or cheap, material desirable to live within? What are the humanising techniques of architecture, and what can they do? These interrogations allow Ratinoff's buildings to engage in a conversation that perhaps she did not have fifty years ago, and whose answers can be both useful and inspiring for contemporary architects. Along the way, the study of Ratinoff's practice also pushes us to wonder about how architecture's business should also be its culture.

## NOTES

1 Myriam Ratinoff as an individual and her work were unknown until the research project behind this article. Except for an appearance on a local TV show 'City Tour', conducted by Federico Sánchez and Marcelo Comparini (available at: https://www.13c.cl/programas/city-tour/capitulos/una-joya-de-la-arquitectura-moderna) and an article on Pablo Altikes' website (https://www.arq-modern.com/2014/02/24/caso-n07/), there was no information about her or her work, nor a critical assessment of it. I am very grateful for the generous collaboration of Sergio Kohn, the architect's widower and of her sons Roberto and Eduardo Kohn in reconstructing Myriam Ratinoff's career.

2 The present article is part of the ongoing research project 'El sistema Multibloc, el diseño y la ciudad. Apogeo y crisis de la modernidad arquitectónica en el Chile de los '60', FONDECYT Iniciación, Folio 11241129 (2023–27). Some of the material used here also comes from a previous research project, 'Myriam Ratinoff, una arquitecta de vanguardia. La casa Kohn Ratinoff (1962)', possible by the U-Inicia seed fund, from the Vice-Rectory for Research and Development (VID) of the Universidad de Chile, project code UI 008-21 (2022–23); the article emanating from the U-Inicia research project is García de Cortázar, Gabriela, 'The Kohn Ratinoff House (1962). A Pioneering Dialogue', *Revista ARQ* 115 (2023): 29-47.

3 The site, now at the intersection of Dinamarca and El Belloto streets, is part of a 1950s urban development of a former farm known as Lo Belloto. Although it is not possible to establish the exact date of the urbanisation, nor who was in charge (whether the owners of the Lo Belloto farm or others), '[i]n Lo Belloto, we observe houses starting from the year 1950, and others from 1960 and even constructions that were only erected in the 1970s before any buildings were erected on the perimeter'; see Renzo Siña Banchero, 'Las Cajas de Previsión y su papel en la urbanización del barrio alto: El caso de la población El Belloto de Ñuñoa 1950–53' (BA dissertation, Universidad de Chile, 2020), 22. For a general history of the Ñuñoa and Providencia districts, see René León Echaíz, *Ñuñohue* (Buenos Aires: Editorial Francisco de Aguirre, 1972); see also Montserrat Palmer, *La comuna de Providencia y la ciudad jardín: un estudio de los inicios del modelo de crecimiento actual de la ciudad de Santiago* (Santiago: Ograma, 1984).

4 'Multiblocs [sic]' catalogue, 1962–63. Courtesy of the Kohn family.

5 According to plans held in Providencia's building authority (Dirección de Obras Municipales, DOM). The municipal folder contains five plans associated with the project, three of the architecture project (for building permit purposes), signed by Myriam Ratinoff, and two of the structural design, signed by engineer Raúl Campusano. The technical specifications of the house have not been kept.

6 In fact, as two separate structures: the two-storey one in separated with the one-storey by an expansion joint.

7 See David Maulén de los Reyes, 'Experiencias docentes. Inclusión/ exclusión del espacio urbano y social 1933/1945/1964', *Revista De Arquitectura* 12, no. 14 (2006) and Daniel Talesnik, 'Tibor Weiner y su rol en la reforma: una re-introducción', *Revista De Arquitectura* 12, no. 14 (2006).

8 The Registrar's Office of the *Facultad de Arquitectura* holds records for Ratinoff's studies for the years 1945, 1946, 1947, 1948 and 1949, missing only the records of her last year. These records contain the year's final grades for every course taken and establish whether the student is promoted to the following year.

9 For example: Osvaldo Cáceres, who worked in Concepción city and co-founded the current School of Architecture at the University of Bío-bío; Pedro Etcheverry Orthous, younger brother of Gastón Etcheverry, who was dean during the Chilean military dictatorship; Carlos Sergio González Espinoza, who later became a Socialist member of parliament and part of the team of architects

who built the UNCTAD III building, a key building not only in architectural but also political terms; for more on the building, see Talesnik, Daniel, 'Monumentality and Resignification. The UNCTAD III Building in Chile', in *Latin American Modern Architecture*, ed. Patricio Del Real, and Helen Gyger (London: Routledge, 2012); and the brothers Julio and Gonzalo Mardones Restat, sons of the engineer and dean Francisco Mardones Otaíza and younger brothers of the National Architecture Prize winner Héctor Mardones Restat. Julio and Gonzalo would found the TAU office in 1954 together with Pedro Iribarne Ríos, Sergio González Espinoza and Jorge Poblete Grez. Records of 1945, Registrar's Office FAU, Universidad de Chile.

10 The 1933 curriculum sought to 'harmonise [...] two European trends': 'one of an artistic nature, which [predominated] in France, and another of a technical nature, which [had] special development in some schools in Germany'. Patricio Basáez, ed., *Ciento cincuenta años de enseñanza de la arquitectura en la Universidad de Chile 1849–1999* (Universidad de Chile, Facultad de Arquitectura y Urbanismo, 1999), 70. Author's translation.

11 After completing his training as architect in Hungary, Weiner enrolled in the Bauhaus in 1929, while Hannes Meyer was directing it. When Meyer was expelled in 1931, Weiner and six other students joined him in Russia, and worked as the *Hannes Meyer Brigade* developing state projects, such as schools and urban plans. In the 1937 Great Purge, Weiner left Russia for Paris, where he married and from which in 1939 he departed to Chile. There he worked as an architect and, through Carlos Sandor (a Hungarian structural engineer), met Abraham Schapira, then a student at the school, and one of the most vocal proponents of reforms. Weiner particularly helped in the 'development of the [new] curriculum and its contents[.] His stay at Meyer's Bauhaus and his later work in the Soviet Union had given him an incomparable experience for the Chilean *milieu* and made him suitable to help the leaders of the reform materialise their objectives. Weiner helped [them] define the academic objectives [of the reform].' Daniel Talesnik, 'Tibor Weiner y su rol en la reforma: una re-introducción', *Revista De Arquitectura*, 12, no. 14 (2006): 66. Author's translation.

12 Patricio Basáez, ed., *Ciento cincuenta años de enseñanza de la arquitectura en la Universidad de Chile 1849–1999* (Santiago: Universidad de Chile, Facultad de Arquitectura y Urbanismo, 1999), 105. Author's translation.

13 Basáez, *Ciento cincuenta años*, 101. Author's translation.

14 Ibid.

15 Basáez, *Ciento cincuenta años*, 107. Author's translation.

16 Ibid.

17 Ibid.

18 See Records of 1947, 1948, and 1949. Registrar's Office FAU, Universidad de Chile.

19 After graduating as an architect from the Universidad de Chile in 1925, and joining the School in 1929, Dávila went to Paris in 1930 on a Chilean government scholarship, where he studied under Theo van Doesburg and George Vantongebo. He attended the XX CIAM in Brussels, and later joined the Vienna Akademie der bildenden Künste, from which he graduated in 1932; in that year, he worked for six months for Le Corbusier in the atelier in Rue de Sevres. He returned to Chile in 1934, where he worked as an architect and taught design at the University of Chile. Basáez, *Ciento cincuenta años*, 121–22.

20 Such as Jaime Bendersky (July 1950), Raquel Eskenazi (June 1950), Abraham Schapira (November 1950) and Myriam Waisberg (September 1950), as well as Gonzalo Mardones Restat (October 1950 – while Julio would graduate in 1954).

21 In 1963 a new crisis engulfed the School of Architecture of the Universidad de Chile: many teachers proposed new reforms to the curriculum to the University's central authorities, regarding a strengthening of the technical and social areas. These reforms were not accepted, and sixty teachers quit. Among them were many of those who led the 1946 reform, including Abraham Schapira and Sergio González, along with A. Rivera, Juan Cárdenas, José Covacevich, Raúl Farrú, and the then dean, Juan Martínez, many of whom decided to found the *AUCA* magazine (AUCA stands for Architecture, Urbanism, Construction, Art), starting in 1965. See Humberto Eliash and Manuel Moreno, *Arquitectura y modernidad en Chile / 1925–1965. Una realidad múltiple* (Ediciones Universidad Católica de Chile, 1989), 166.

22 The *Colegio de Arquitectos* was created in 1942 after a few years of coordinated professional activities that had resulted in the participation of Chilean architects in conferences such as the V Montevideo Pan-american Congress (1940). Eliash and Moreno, *Arquitectura y modernidad en Chile*, 40.

23 The *Cámara Chilena de la Construcción* (Chilean Construction Chamber, CCHC) is a trade union, a private corporation founded in 1951. As stated in their website, it seeks to gather professionals that participate in the building industry, 'regardless of their size': 'building companies, real-estate developers, purveyors, producers, contractors, together with professionals, academics and regular people' (https://cchc.cl/historia-cchc). The CCHC is considered one of the most influential trade unions, and plays a key role in the national economy as well as in the political arena. Its political allegiances lie with the right-wing parties and the Christian Democracy. (https://www.elmostrador.cl/mercados/destacados-mercado/2012/03/30/cchc/).

24 As stated by Sergio Kohn in a conversation in August 2021.

25 In 1970, Sergio Kohn was part of the Modular Coordination Committee, in charge of the formulation of the Norma Chilena de Arquitectura y Construcción NCh742.EOf.70 [Act of 1970] 'Coordinación modular en bloques huecos de hormigón – dimensiones' [Modular Coordination for Hollow Concrete Blocks – Dimensions], which established the dimensions for hollow concrete blocks.

26 Chile, a seismic country, had from 1931 a general and succinct Act regulating building and urbanisations, the 'Ley General de Urbanismo y Construcciones', which also included a longer and more detailed 'ordinance', the 'Ordenanza General de Urbanismo y Construcciones'. These two Acts first established the need for building permits for new constructions, designed by architects. After the 1962 earthquake, a new and more specific regulation on seismic design was drafted and finally passed in 1972. This Act, revised and modernised several times since 1972, still regulates the building industry, incorporating all the knowledge that the continuous earthquakes have brought on. See José Miguel Sáez, 'Normativa nacional antisísmica en materia de construcción. Bases y proyecciones' (BA dissertation, Universidad de Chile, 2011).

27 Sigfried Giedion, *Building in France, Building in Iron, Building in Ferroconcrete* (Santa Monica: The Getty Center for the History of Art and the Humanities, 1995), 167.

28 Giedion, *Building in France*, 178.

29 Tim Benton, 'Pessac and Lège revisited: standards, dimensions and failures', *Massilia, 2004. Annuaire d'etudes corbuseennes* (Barcelona: Associació d'Idees, 2004), 81–82.

30 The first experiments in the manufacture of concrete blocks occurred around 1870 in the United States, prompting the registration of a large number of patents. Not all of them succeeded. Pamela H. Simpson, 'Cheap, Quick and Easy: The Early History of Rockfaced Concrete Block Building', *Perspectives in Vernacular Architecture* 3 (1989): 108–9.

31 Giedion, *Building in France*, 150–51.

32 Raúl Castellanos Gómez and Débora Domingo Cañabuig, 'Bloques normales', *Revista EN BLANCO*, no. 6 (2011): 6.

33 Wright goes on: 'All that imagination needed to make such a scheme feasible was a plastic medium where steel would enter inert mass as a tensile strength. Concrete was the inert mass and would take compression. Concrete is a plastic material – susceptible to the impress of imagination. We would take that despised outcast of the building industry – the concrete block – out from underfoot or from the gutter – find a hitherto unsuspected soul in it – make it live as a thing of beauty – textured like the trees. Yes, the building would be made of the "blocks" as a kind of tree itself standing at home among the other trees in its own native land'. He wrote these words to present the house for Alice Millard in Pasadena, in his Autobiography, as recollected in Bruce Brooks Pfeiffer, 'Frank Lloyd Wright and the "textile block" construction system', *Domus* 737 (1992), 110-16.

34 According to records: built primarily of concrete, concrete blocks and carved *oya* stone.

35 Pfeiffer, 'Frank Lloyd Wright and the "textile block" construction system'.

36 M.K. Hurd, 'Usonian Automatic: Wright's concrete masonry', *Concrete Construction* (1988): 1028-1030.

37 Christián de Groote, 'Banco del Estado de Chile, local pago de pensionados Santiago', *Auca: Arquitectura Urbanismo Construcción Arte* 6-7 (2020): 73-74.

38 Mainly wood. See *Auca: Arquitectura Urbanismo Construcción Arte,* 4 [Prefabricación en Chile] (1966).

39 Such as Palomer, Depal, Pretesa S.A., Cemento Melón, Pizarreño.

40 For a history of the *Arquitectura y Construcción* journal, see Andrés Téllez and Hugo Mondragón, *Arquitectura y construcción Chile 1945–50: una revista de arquitectura moderna* (Santiago: LOM, 2006).

41 Sergio Kohn, in a conversation on April 2023. Sergio Kohn abandoned INEIN S.A. around 1986. The company continues to fabricate concrete blocks, especially for walls, but the integral, coordinated, system declined in the eighties.

42 As reconstructed by Eliash and Moreno, a new era began in 1952. The 1952–65 period is characterised for these authors as a period of economic growth and of the establishment of institutions whose focus was urban and social progress: the CORVI (Corporation for housing) and the planning authority within the Ministry for Public Works. These institutions, in part, fostered access to housing for both the working class and the middle class, thanks to such Acts as the DFL2 in 1959 (tax exemption for houses under $140m^2$, still in use), and the creation of private-public corporations to fund housing, like the EMPART. Eliash and Moreno, *Arquitectura y modernidad en Chile / 1925–65*, 154–58.

43 Advertising in *AUCA* magazine is found in issues 3 to 9, corresponding to the period between 1966–67 (the magazine was published from 1965 to 1975). There is also advertising in *CA* magazine in issues 1 to 7, which corresponds to the period between 1968 and 1970 (the magazine began publication in 1968). The magazines were examined for the period between 1960 and 1975.

44 In this journal, there is advertising from issues 2 to 10 (1962–63) and then from issues 54 to 98 (1966–70).

45 The research has yielded detailed results of Multibloc's advertising, which, however, would be too long to name here. A longer version of this chapter could include cases that illustrate each type of advertising in a specific way, whose inventory and classification is already done.

46 Such as, for example, letters regarding the stability of block construction in the wake of the 1962 earthquake in *Revista de la Construcción* 37 (1962), or the articles referring to block construction by Inein S. A., in *Revista de la Construcción* 66 (1967) and *Revista de la Construcción* 82 (1969).

47 Ratinoff also shared cultural proximities with many of them (the presence of architects from 'the colony' – of Jewish descent – was strong). Ratinoff, however, did not share their political views – all the above were of leftist sentiments, while she was not, as stated by Sergio Kohn in a conversation in August 2021.

48 'She had investors, as they are called today, [and] that was the firm I was working in; it gave the money to build the [housing] ensembles'. As stated by Sergio Kohn in a conversation in August 2021.

49 Jaime Majlis and Max Piper were both builders and developers, for whom Ratinoff 'drew many plans', for projects both in Santiago and on the coast (for Majlis, Kohn remembers a house in El Quisco, a coastal town; Sergio Kohn, in a conversation in January 2022). Of Max Piper, Kohn says: 'he was one of Mimí's recurrent clients' (Sergio Kohn, in a conversation in September 2022).

50 Many of her clients were family and friends: among those listed as clients in the plans held in the DOMs, we can find María Ortiz de Kohn, Berta Brodsky (her mother), Clara Ratinoff (her sister), Abel Vieira (a doctor friend), and others.

PART 2

# DOMESTICITY IN JOURNALISM AND REAL ESTATE DEVELOPMENT

Chapter 4

# Beauty in Revolution

## Late Ottoman Feminists and the Everyday Aesthetics of Home Crafts in 1920s Women's Magazines

*Damla Göre*

The first wave of Ottoman feminism gained momentum after the restoration of the constitution and the removal of restrictions on the press in 1908. This phase of heightened press activity reverberated for more than a decade and gave birth to several periodicals about or oriented towards women, all of which nuanced aspects of feminist struggle.[1] These periodicals, along with political and economic emancipation, aimed to revolutionise middle-class Muslim-Turkish women and transform them into educated, intellectual, and creative equals to men, and more specifically, into productive forces in a society that had previously denied them self-determination. The authors stressed the aesthetic aspect of women's emerging social position as simultaneously domestic and public figures, designating a new gender identity as a stay-at-home-artist who would use and exhibit her house as her canvas. The visual explosion in the media, involving coloured prints, fashion plates, graphic illustrations, advertisements, and do-it-yourself manuals carried this project even further. Taken together, these texts and images supplied step-by-step and multi-media guidelines on how to develop an aesthetic sensibility via home crafts and small-scale home renovation projects and assigned women the role of a 'beautifier' and domestic 'beauty' as the natural expression of the female self.[2]

This mediatisation of artistic expression served as a harbinger of a female-driven aesthetic discourse on interior architecture that preceded women's acceptance into formal architectural education in Turkey in 1928.[3] Two particularly prominent examples, *Kadınlar Dünyası* (Women's World) and *Süs* (Ornament) (Fig. 4.1 and 4.2), represent a spectrum of feminist perspectives regarding how to define and practice beauty, but there were several others that also specifically targeted female readers.

قادينلر دنياسی

عرض تشكر

حقوق نسوان

قادينلقده سويه

عرفان

Figure 4.1: The article entitled 'Women's Legal Rights', on the very first page of the first issue of *Kadınlar Dünyası*, shows the centrality of feminist concerns in the magazine's editorial policy. *Kadınlar Dünyası*, no. 1 (17 April 1913), 1. IBB Kütüphane ve Müzeler Müdürlüğü Collection, Atatürk Library.

The magazine *Kadınlar Dünyası* was privately founded in 1913 by Ulviye Mevlan (1893–1964), a Turkish suffragist and journalist and was published by Serbesti Press (Serbestî Matbaası) in Istanbul. The magazine, which subsequently became the official organ of the Association for the Defense of Ottoman Women's Rights (Osmanlı Müdafaa-i Hukuk-ı Nisvan Cemiyeti), acted as the think tank for the women's movement by creating an interactive environment for activists, authors, and readers. What marked *Kadınlar Dünyası* as a magazine, and made it almost synonymous with Ottoman feminism, was its radical feminist activism.[4] Beyond this ideological pursuit, though, the magazine hosted quite sophisticated debates on the aesthetics of beauty.

The lifestyle magazine *Süs* (Ornament) was printed initially at the Tanin Press (Tanin Matbaası), and later by Amedi Press (Amedî Matbaası), both

Figure 4.2: The lifestyle magazine *Süs* described itself in its inaugural issue as a 'weekly literary women's magazine whose aim is to adorn the manners and dress, but above all the heart and mind of women'. *Süs*, no. 1 (16 June 1923), 1. IBB Kütüphane ve Müzeler Müdürlüğü Collection, Atatürk Library.

of which were located in Istanbul. Mehmed Rauf (1875-1831), the renowned Ottoman novelist, poet, and publisher, founded the magazine in 1923 and served as its editor-in-chief, until passing it over to Muazzez Yusuf for its last fourteen issues published in 1924. *Süs* was an image-intense magazine of arts, literature, and fashion.[5] It became a lively crossroad for female and male authors, and appealed to a broad female readership. It organised an intriguing and highly visual home decor campaign urging its readers to undertake interior design projects to beautify their homes. Although this campaign may appear to be a hobby column at first glance, it in fact contained a politically charged effort to find beauty in decorative art.

Historians have seldom compared the histories of the two magazines, as the presumption is that politics and aesthetics should be treated as mutually exclusive. Both *Kadınlar Dünyası* and *Süs* contributed to establishing a feminist epistemology of aesthetics by serving, first and foremost, as platforms for women writers to express themselves and expand their audiences. The intertwined political and commercial pursuit of 'beauty' became a key element of the assistance to feminists provided by media targeting Ottoman women. Both the editorial content and the graphic design of *Kadınlar Dünyası* contributed to the creation of a new aesthetic, while *Süs* offered theoretical and practical instructions for home renovations and craft projects that guided its readers in implementing these ideas.

## BEAUTY IN WOMEN'S MEDIA

In the early 20th century, Ottoman magazines and newspapers began addressing new topics, including the philosophy of art and literature.[6] Women's magazines quickly followed suit. Ottoman women's magazines, which had emerged in the 1870s, moved in a totally new direction during the print boom that followed from the revocation in 1908 of press restrictions imposed by Sultan Abdülhamid II.[7] The rise of privately-owned publications also had a profoundly impact.[8] As they sought to sustain themselves, these magazines embraced emerging trends in graphic design as well as editorial content, becoming more engaging than ever before.[9] In this new era, beauty emerged in women's magazines as both an independent subject of philosophical inquiry and a key marketing tool. Moreover, the entangled relationship between beauty and these magazines had a political as well as a cultural and commercial dimensions.

During the Second Constitutional Era (1908–1922), *Kadınlar Dünyası* and *Süs* adopted beauty as a field of study and transformed the discussion of it from an academic to a popular pursuit. Whether motivated by political or economic concerns, this shift contributed to the democratisation of art education and offered writers and readers a platform for changing architectural taste. Ottoman women were not accepted to vocational art schools until the establishment of Women's Fine Arts Academy (İnas Sanayi-i Nefise Mektebi) in Istanbul in 1914, which constituted a smaller and less-ambitious version of the Fine Arts Academy. However, this date hardly marks a milestone in women's engagement with architecture because, even after the school's establishment, it remained accessible only to a select few. Moreover, while the programme included modules on technical drawing, it excluded architecture per se, thereby separating the

Figure 4.3: The magazines conveyed the importance of manual labour for domestic economy both through images of women doing handicrafts such as embroidery and through how-to manuals for such projects. *Kadınlar Dünyası*, no. 104 (23 August 1913), 1. Periodicals Collection, The Women's Library and Information Center Foundation.

curriculum of female students from that of their male peers until 1923.[10] In reality, the Women's Academy did not even start out as a legitimate art school. It was a teacher's training school with a focus on pedagogy; in other words, its purpose was to educate female students to become art teachers, rather than artists.[11] Broaching the discourse on beauty in women's magazines thus had an ideological value, directed against the patriarchal institutions that disadvantaged female students during their education and even after they were admitted to higher studies.

Additionally, beauty implied creativity and had economic significance at a time when middle-class Muslim housewives were being gradually integrated into the workforce, after being isolated from working life longer than their Armenian and Greek and working class counterparts, who had already been earning wages by 1914.[12] The periodicals' primary aim in promoting design skills for female readers was to reduce their reliance on the market for decorative arts and to enable them to contribute to both their household and the national economy through domestic labour.[13] Their broader understanding of this included creative hand labour, such as embroidery, tailoring, and weaving, in addition to more routine domestic tasks like cleaning, cooking, and childcare.[14] Undoubtedly, these manual jobs were already practised among working-class women at home or in small workshops to earn a living, a practice that transcended ethno-religious boundaries. However, for the first time, magazines incentivised handicrafts as a means through which their middle- and upper-class readers could alleviate their economic worries, which were exacerbated in times of war (Fig. 4.3).

These two women's magazines therefore increasingly devoted themselves to this source of creative but unpaid labour, providing their readers with both essays on theoretical debates and practical instructions on craft activities that defined and changed the concept of 'beauty'. In doing so, they adopted a variety of editorial strategies as well as experimented with the latest printing techniques to inspire and equip readers to craft. Moreover, their enactment of beauty on the printed page exploited the materiality of their medium. The attention that has been given to their educational and ideological content has ignored this aspect of their utility in daily life. However, magazines also constituted commodities that sought higher sales numbers, and a stable revenue through advertisements. For these reasons they were also nimble at self-promotion. Recent scholarship on print culture has argued that such magazines embodied an immense vitality that was inextricable from the techniques and economies of publishing technology.[15] Such dynamism characterised Ottoman print culture especially after the print boom, which marked the transition to what became the penny press. Between 1912 and 1914, the number of newspapers and magazines not only expanded but also underwent a veritable visual revolution, introducing new approaches to graphic design, including experiments with headlines, multi-column layouts, typography, and images.[16] In this paradigm shift, publishers recognised the benefits of being able to appeal to a wider audience especially through enhancing the visual appeal of their periodicals.

In parallel with the growing academic interest in the concept of beauty, women's magazines of the post-print boom era adopted beauty as an explicit editorial goal as well as a strategy to increase sales. They aspired to translate beauty onto paper, through their flashy and richly illustrated graphic design, which also encompassed colourful covers plus full-page fashion plates. They justified these trends as the desire to visually replicate the beauty of the female form on their printed pages, referring to women as the ultimate source of elegance and grace.[17] The print media, thus, equated the aesthetics of the femininity with the refined qualities of the paper plane. While the female body, with its modern habitus, was seen as a source of visual desire, the printed page, if designed properly, was seen as a medium where the gaze could find similar pleasure. This forced relationality was epitomised in the numerous images that juxtaposed female figures with their periodicals, consequently rendering them both as desirable objects.

Perhaps the strongest evidence of this ambition lies in the magazines' collaboration with painters, who contributed fashion plates as well as other illustrations depicting female figures. For instance, *Mehasin* (The Beauties), established in 1908 as the first Ottoman fashion magazine published in colour, worked with Ali Sami Bey (who later took the surname Boyar; 1880–1967), in its two supplemental holiday issues.[18] In addition to direct collaboration with painters, the magazine regularly featured lithographs of famous art works, mostly with European female names and even offered the option of ordering larger prints of their selections from European printshops.[19] Similarly, *İnci* (The Pearl), published between 1919 and 1921, commissioned several renowned painters to design its covers.[20] These highly realistic portraits, which straddled the line between lust and fashion, certainly improved the magazine's marketability. Their forebear, *Süs* followed the trend. The magazine enthusiastically announced its partnership, again with the painter Ali Sami Bey, in its seventh issue:

> From now on, Süs will be adorned with the works of the most renowned painters professionally associated with the country's art scene. And there will be a noticeable improvement in printing, which unfortunately has not yet reached the level we would like to see.[21]

It comes as no surprise that Ali Sami was already affiliated with the girls' academy and that he served as the inaugural director of the Women's Fine Arts Academy until 1915. While running the all-girls vocational school, he simultaneously was involved in women's magazines, supplying readers with an alternative form of art education.

The beauty-focused magazines of the era thus reshaped not only how published works were received but also their utility in daily life. Being richly illustrated in this manner gave them an allure that extended beyond the printed word, transforming them into coveted lifestyle accessories.[22] They became 'must-have' items for anyone wishing to adopt the aesthetics of modern life. Though books had long been cherished by Ottoman intellectuals as collectors' items, early twentieth-century women's magazines took this to a higher level, reimagining their issues as decorative objects. They frequently featured pictures and projects of chic libraries, bookshelves, and reading corners, actively promoting reading as a practice to be emulated and books as valuable commodities.[23] This aestheticisation reached new heights in advice columns, where readers were encouraged to match books with flower pots, bibelots, and picture frames, creating colour-coordinated interiors.[24]

Magazines, in contrast, diverged slightly from books in terms of their utility. They offered a more playful and dynamic interaction with the reader and the medium. These image-filled and mostly colourful paper sheets invited readers to engage with them in tactile ways. Compared to books, periodicals were often more vibrant, more ornate, and, most importantly, more interactive. Readers didn't just read; they cut out prints of paintings, tore out embroidery samples, glued favourite photos together, and, as some illustrations suggest, possibly even pieced together their own scrapbooks. Thus, the paper medium itself became a means for creative expression.

Women's media evince the importance of the concept of beauty outside the domains of high art and academia. This reshaped the scope and use of periodicals while simultaneously mediating aspirations of gender equality. These mediations took place in *Kadınlar Dünyası* and *Süs*, both of which regarded achieving beauty in everyday life as a feminist project. In particular, they conveyed and addressed political radicalism with the strategies of commercial journalism.

## 'DIDN'T KANT EVER LOVE?'

In late Ottoman studies of art historical terminology, beauty was known as *hüsn*, and the discipline of aesthetics was referred to as *ilm-i hüsn* or *ilm-i bedâyi*, equivalent to 'the knowledge of beauty'.[25] These intertwined concepts became a burgeoning field of study in intellectual circles, and several journals devoted sections to the scholarly study of the subject, while monographs continued to be published well into the 1920s.[26] Most of this writing, aimed at a general (male) readership, drew on Western thinkers who treated beauty as an abstract concept, and explained it through a linear narrative that stretched from ancient Greece to the works of white, male, Western philosophers. While the women's magazines included these sources, which formed a parallel canon to that of their European counterparts, they developed a different approach. For them, the concept of 'beauty' was largely a social phenomenon that could be used by women as a soft form of power.

One of the most powerful expressions of this idea was formulated in *Kadınlar Dünyası*, in the series of essays entitled 'Women at home and in society' by Mes'adet Bedirhan.[27] Mes'adet Bedirhan, who was an Albanian author married to Süreyya Bedirhan, the heir of the notable Ottoman-Kurdish family, was both a member of the editorial board and a regular contributor. Between 1913–14, she authored fourteen articles until her output suddenly ceased, probably due to the political turmoil surrounding her husband's activism.[28] The point of her articles was to show all Ottoman women that they had the power to change their own destiny and ultimately the course of history through their own resources.[29] 'The duty of beauty', which she formulated in her advice column, symbolised this broad societal transformation originating from the core unit of the home where women held positions of power and influence. She wrote that 'A woman fulfils a duty of beauty first to her family, then to her nation, and finally to all of humanity'.[30] According to Bedirhan, enhancing beauty would make women's productive and managerial skills, whether in the form of caring, housekeeping, or decorating, an integral part of their modern and national identity and thus constitute a crucial step in social progress. Perfecting these everyday and domestic acts would empower all Ottoman women at home and in the public sphere and would thus eventually grant them the respect they had long sought.[31]

Bedirhan's columns were not illustrated. They appeared in seven consecutive issues more as opinion pieces, aligned with the journal's mostly textual content. However, the magazine fulfilled its own 'duty of beauty', so to say, by publishing image-intense covers and full-page posters of women in its final pages, both of which indirectly visualised Mes'adet Bedirhan's plea for beauty as an embodiment of empowered women. Covers displayed women engaged in artistic pursuits, such as reading, writing, creating handicrafts, performing music, or posing artistically for the camera in staged interiors. Full-page portraits of mythical female figures, including Joan of Arc and Amazons, contemporary personalities such as the actress Miss Algins, and unnamed fashionable models, completed each issue. Compared to the few and much smaller images often sprinkled within the rest of each issue, these fashion-plate supplements were obviously tailored to be consumed independently from the rest of the magazine, as they were mostly uncaptioned. That the magazine decided to publish all of this visual content as a bimonthly album in its second year further confirms the high demand for these illustrations and that they were valued as much as its radical content.[32] Additionally, it suggests that the earliest women's magazine to publish an unveiled Ottoman woman not only drastically defied cultural norms but also generated revenue from this act of disobedience.[33]

After a five-year hiatus due to war, the magazine resumed publishing in 1918 with a new editorial policy. Given the changing times and the challenges of publishing from within an occupied city, *Kadınlar Dünyası* adapted both its textual and visual strategies. The owner and founder, Ulviye Mevlan, divided the magazine into theoretical and practical sections. The first supplemented the earlier focus on essays with content that addressed literary, philosophical, historical, educational, and sociological topics, featuring reviews, translated novels, poems, and biographies.[34] The aesthetic status of women was treated here, remaining a central feminist theme for envisioning gender equality in social life. As the magazine's format evolved, the discourse on beauty grew more nuanced and in-depth, drawing on a broader range of references. The contributors' feminist definition of beauty expanded, as they engaged with canonical philosophers and recent publications, while employing a more rigorous citation system.

Seniye Baha's book review on Immanuel Kant exemplifies the magazine's expanded format. Published on 21 January 1921, the article 'What does philosopher Kant say about women and womanhood?'[35] was not a review of his oeuvre, but rather a biographical account, drawn from Alfons Hoffmann's 1902 book *Immanuel Kant. Ein Lebensbild nach Darstellungen der Zeitgenossen Borowski, Jachmann, Wasianski*.[36] This marked the first direct engagement in *Kadınlar Dünyası* with a canonical philosopher writing on aesthetics. What was intriguing, however, was the author's unique approach to Kant. Delving deeply into his biography, the reviewer focused on Kant's views on women, examined through the lens of his romantic life. The author, seemingly perplexed by encountering a prudish bachelor, posed a provocative question: 'Did he never love in his life? Did he avoid love from women?' Despite Kant's known avoidance of marriage, the author forced a 'no' in response, stressing that the philosopher actually had two brief affairs and was known to be a successful matchmaker

Figure 4.4: The covers reflect the stylistic changes in the magazine's self-image between 1913 and 1921. The shift towards more ornate and floral elements from top to bottom reflects the Art Nouveau aesthetic that prevailed in the print media. *Kadınlar Dünyası*, no. 1 (17 April 1913), no. 163 (2 March 1918), 194-2 (8 January 1921), no. 194-5 (29 January 1921). IBB Kütüphane ve Müzeler Müdürlüğü Collection, Atatürk Library and Periodicals Collection, The Women's Library and Information Center Foundation.

among his friends. Based on these insights, the writer further insisted, 'He was not a misogynist', and he made an effort to captivate the reader's interest in Kant's personal life – most probably with the pragmatic goal of sparking conversation at the readers' next salon gatherings. By humanising Kant and other big names, the magazine made them relevant to its readership only to the extent that they touched a woman's life and that they could be considered allies.

In a similar vein, another author, Nezihe Hamdi, developed her own conception of beauty in her essay series advocating for a politically charged and everyday aesthetic understanding. Although not much is known about her early life, Nezihe Hamdi was an erudite intellectual, who published nine articles in the magazine in 1918. Much like Mes'adet Bedirhan, she conceived aesthetics on a social level and as a potent catalyst for societal transformation. The most extensive expression of her thoughts on beauty came to light in her four-part piece 'How should a woman join the social life?' in which she drew on the works of numerous prominent contemporary thinkers, including the aesthetic theories of the German sociologist Georg Simmel (1858–1908) and his French counterpart Gabriel Tarde (1843–1904).[37] Her essays comprised a guide for how the feminist movement could gain wider acceptance, essentially explaining to her readers how they could oppose the regressive currents in their daily lives by identifying strategies on the public, individual, and performative levels. Employing this course of action, she argued, women should not only seek economic and legal parity but also carve out an aesthetic presence within society.[38] It is true that her description of women as aesthetic components of the environment represented a concept characteristic of proto-modernist ideas.[39] Seemingly aware of this fact, she repeatedly underlined the agency associated with this role, writing: 'On the contrary, assigning an aesthetic identity to women would provide an even stronger incentive for them to engage in social life.' Thus, she strongly defended that a women's aesthetic identity (*bedîi hüviyyet*) did not diminish her role as a catalyst in effecting social changes, but rather strengthened it.

The second pillar of the magazine's editorial policy was its refreshed corporate identity, reflecting a broader trend toward diversifying formats and employing an overtly aesthetic language. From 1918, *Kadınlar Dünyası* expanded its visual register, moving beyond full-page spreads to include a variety of graphic designs. The magazine's layout became more cohesive, featuring stylised headlines, end marks, and illustrations, thus creating a more balanced interplay between text and imagery. These changes not only enhanced the magazine's visual appeal, making it distinctly different from its pre-war editions, but also improved its readability. Additionally, the magazine's visual style adopted more deliberate artistic influences, with its graphic designs referencing art historical movements systematically for the first time. Art Nouveau stock illustrations, characterised by floral motifs, abstract natural forms, sinuous lines, and stylised depictions of female figures, adorned the pages (Fig. 4.4). This focus on branding was most evident in the evolving logo, which changed three times in just three years. While retaining the sülüs-style calligraphy for the title, the frames increasingly incorporated floral elements, often paired with seductive feminine portraits, again evoking the Art Nouveau aesthetics.

Finally, advertisements took up more space in the magazine, sometimes appearing as advertorials on the cover, alongside female protagonists, or occasionally dominating the front matter. They could also occupy up to four pages in the back. Likely due to financial constraints, the magazine now depended more on the advertising revenues.[40] Ultimately, this market-oriented approach offered a stable source of income for an otherwise ideological publication. It also opened the doors to more contemporary methods of content creation and presentations of beauty.

## ARTISTS AND THEIR EVERYDAY CRAFTS

*Süs* took a more practical and visual path, departing from the theoretical rigor of *Kadınlar Dünyası*. Its authors broadened the concept of 'beauty' as a total artistic ambition tailored for housewives by transforming it into a do-it-yourself (DIY) art project. This maker movement, emerging during the early years of the republic, proclaimed in 1923, reworked the traditional craftwork associated with the women into a more expansive practice with greater spatial impact. It recalibrated the decorative arts to encompass everyday domestic practices through a deliberate campaign delivered via essays, posters, perspective drawings, and detailed assembly instructions. The magazine turned aesthetic discourse on its head, moving it from the most abstract to the most mundane, and thus made it accessible beyond the realm of professional formation.

The blurring of boundaries between fine arts and applied arts most clearly expressed in the work of Necibe Süreyya. Although we have no biographical information about her, at *Süs* she became a popular writer who would publish on a fairly wide range of topics, including beauty, home decor, pets, womanhood, literature, and hair models.[41] Despite this diversity of subjects, Süreyya's work can best be described as an ode to housewives, particularly to the often-overlooked labour they put into creating beautiful, warm, and welcoming domestic spaces. Her articles especially expanded on the day to day nature of this aesthetic effort. For instance, in one of her articles, she argued that housewives were inspired by 'a desire to create tiny masterpieces' (küçük bir şaheser meydana getirmek arzusu) by creating tasteful living spaces and making them truly worthy of being called home, day after day, hour after hour.[42] She doubled down her praise for everyday decorative practices, as she termed the organisation of the salon with the trinkets and paintings a work of 'art' (san'at) executed with exceptional instincts.[43] Süreyya established an inclusive and democratic concept of beauty by elevating these ephemeral instances of interior design to the same status as the fine arts. This reframing of traditional areas of activity in the domestic sphere aligned with the magazine's commercial strategy to appeal to a broad female readership. On a larger scale, her contributions can also be seen as a subtle response to a male-dominated discourse.

It is worth noting that the designation of the home as the locus of art also defined women as artists. This identity recognised the housewife's manual skill converting her into a productive and creative citizen. First and foremost, the artist-housewife role emphasised women's active participation in domestic economics, which could contribute to national recovery following the financial hardships engendered by a long period.[44] In line with its radical predecessor *Kadınlar Dünyası*, *Süs* called for women to engage in arts and crafts, which it claimed could liberate them from the domination of the furniture industry and their tasteless products. Multiple articles linked a house owner's beauty to the expressiveness of the rooms its mistress designed, likening interior decoration to another layer of clothing.[45] Moreover, this aesthetic identity served as a rebuttal to the orientalist stereotype that portrayed Ottoman-Turkish women as idle figures, merely passing time amidst traditional decor – a common trope associated with the *ancien régime* during the early years of the Republic. As Ece Zerman argued, this discourse reflected what the sociologist and founder of Turkish nationalism, Ziya Gökalp, called 'aesthetic Turkism', which was not only a reaction to external referents, but also a search for a national essence that sought.[46] Thus, the artist-housewife identity provided locus where aesthetics and nationalism intertwined. Throughout, *Süs* championed the revitalisation of the national economy, which aligned with Gökalp'.[47] It condemned any ready-made or foreign goods, underscoring women's vital role as creators capable of shaping the nation's future.

With the aim of crafting 'artist housewives', *Süs* carried out an unprecedented campaign and capitalised on this goal using various commercial methods. The magazine began by outlining potential avenues for artistic expression through a series of illustrated how-to manuals, covering everyday items from cushions to entire armchairs and practices such as sewing, building, and furnishing, all of which framed domestic design practices as real artistic endeavours. This campaign gained momentum after Muazzez Yusuf took over as editor-in-chief from Mehmed Rauf in the

Figure 4.5: The inscription on the poster emphasises the DIY character of the elements. It reads, 'Embroidery or appliqué designs for pillows, curtains, and ceiling chandeliers will feature summer flower motifs, with flowers embroidered on satin and the lampshade made of silk. Alternatively, the flowers can also be painted onto the fabric using a brush and dye. The motif can similarly be applied to tablecloths, umbrellas, and dresses.' *Süs*, no.42 (29 March 1924), np. IBB Kütüphane ve Müzeler Müdürlüğü Collection, Atatürk Library.

last fourteen issues. Under her leadership, the initiative transitioned into a promotional scheme, aimed at attracting regular readership and securing subscribers. The cover of the April 1924 issue excitedly announced the new home decoration campaign and the increasing prominence of illustrations, proclaiming that from now on 'every week we will provide samples of easy-to-build and simple furniture designs for our ladies'.[48] In this new chapter of its history, *Süs* developed a double-edged approach. On the one hand, its back matter catered to its readers' visual pleasure with poster pages, including fashion plates, and full-page colour illustrations featuring architectural details. On the other hand, most of its coverage embraced practical domesticity, offering close-up images of furniture, assembly instructions, and decorative advice, making the otherwise far-fetched ambiances of the poster pages accessible for everyone (Fig. 4.5).

Hadiye Şükrü's one-off contribution delivered those layers of instruction all at once, ushering in the campaign. Although Şükrü is another female author we do not know much about, her prodigiously energetic pen and her technically sound manual deserves a closer inspection. Şükrü began her piece titled 'In order to embellish our homes' with a complaint about the insufficiency of wet spaces in Istanbul's existing housing stock. Instead of simply reporting on this matter, though, she took initiative and urged her readers to transform their own living conditions themselves. She explained the process of converting a yüklük, a built-in wardrobe typical of traditional Ottoman houses, into an elegant vanity. She delved into the intricate details of this ambitious renovation project, step by step:

1. Cover the existing wardrobe surfaces with linoleum
2. Sand the interior surfaces of wooden boards
3. Paint the shelves
4. Take measurements to avoid mistakes
5. Mark the application areas
6. Implant the prepared shelves
7. Add three mirrors to the back and the wardrobe wings[49]

Her endeavour also took on a visual dimension, with two images of potential final results seamlessly blending into the pages with wrapped texts. This balance of text and imagery steered the development of how-to manuals. A multitude of illustrations and furniture sketches detailed the instructions, the most notable example being the series 'How to furnish our houses?' which spanned four issues from numbers 46 to 49.[50] The anonymous author claimed that anyone with 'a bit of good taste and manual skills could own beautiful furniture', critiquing the standard models in trade catalogues and the exorbitant prices of furniture stores.[51] Beauty, they argued, would arise from these do-it-yourself projects and their careful arrangement within the home. To picture this goal, the editorial showered readers with interior designs of multiple scales, ranging from standalone libraries and corner reading sofas to full-fledged living, dining, and bedroom projects. The repository of this carefully curated series was also enriched by other simpler projects, including portable bookshelves, knick-knacks for drawing rooms, and cushions made from ribbons (Fig. 4.6).[52] Readers had countless models at their disposal for their personal designs, described down to the most minute technical details, such as the dimensions of materials and their assembly instructions. Readers could also enhance their sense of taste, as the very same manuals were simultaneously infused with theoretical discussions on principles of interior design.

Figure 4.6: The advice column titled 'How to Decorate Our Homes?' is an example of how the magazine encouraged complex craft projects using both hard and soft materials and different skills. Unsigned, 'Evlerimizi Nasıl Tefriş Edelim?' *Süs*, no. 47 (3 May 1924), 8. IBB Kütüphane ve Müzeler Müdürlüğü Collection, Atatürk Library.

*Süs* achieved multiple accomplishments through this home decor section. These architectural enterprises all demanded the expertise of both an interior decorator and a carpenter, thus combining artistic vision with hands-on labour. Each guide featured a different type of craftsmanship, from carpentry involving screwing, sanding, and brush-painting, to the delicate art of sewing. The diverse range of skills required nullified the traditional divisions between the decorative arts associated with 'feminine' and 'masculine' craftsmanship.[53] Most importantly, however, the home decor section of *Süs* elevated the traditionally marginalised art forms that adorn people, homes, or utensils. It redefined beauty, presenting it as an intimate, domestic, and daily expression of fine art, challenging the conventional boundaries between fine arts (sınaat-ı nefise) and decorative arts (sınaat-ı tezyiniye) in Ottoman scholarship.[54] In doing so, it dissolved rigid hierarchies between definitions upheld by institutions that had excluded women, offering a fresh and feminist perspective on aesthetics.

## TRANSFORMATIVE CAPACITY OF AESTHETICS

The traditional understanding of aesthetics, often portrayed as an intellectual abstraction exclusively tied to academia, was far removed from the feminist perspective found in women's magazines. Authors like Mes'adet Bedirhan, Seniye Baha and Nezihe Hamdi in *Kadınlar Dünyası*; Hadiye Şükrü and Necibe Süreyya in *Süs*; and their colleagues challenged these accepted definitions, which they clearly saw as a patriarchal construct disconnected from their lived experiences. For these women, beauty constituted a powerful instrument for critiquing the state of life during the last decade of the Ottoman Empire. Therefore, reading their efforts reveals an aesthetic model serving feminist ambitions, which aimed to validate, elevate, and solidify the status of middle-class Ottoman women, starting with their immediate environment: the home. In a broader sense, this contributes to the perception of aesthetics as a soft form of power, regardless of the authors' vocal advocacy for their political agenda. As Yuriko Saito has argued in her inspiring work on everyday aesthetics, we are unfamiliar with how such daily judgements affect societal change when they do not result from a specific programme by the government, society, or commercial enterprise.[55]

Late Ottoman magazines for women demonstrate that the medium propagated a feminist take on aesthetics on multiple levels. First, they were artifacts to which publishers, editors, and painters, as much as authors, contributed their own visions. As seen in both *Kadınlar Dünyası* and *Süs*, they were shaped by both journalistic and financial concerns, such as sales. In other words, the paper didn't just transcribe ideas about beauty; it transformed them into multiple visual (cover pages, album supplements, and graphic designs) and experiential formats (craftworks, DIY guidelines, and home renovation projects). Second, these mediations between women's magazines and beauty provide new insights into the relationship between modern design culture and print media. In particular, the manuals for home crafts challenge the often-told top-down narratives that position visionary architects above anonymous makers.[56] None of these authors received formal architectural training. Nonetheless, they produced accessible, trendy, and self-aware designs. Therefore, these seemingly trivial examples show the diversity of protagonists in the Istanbul's design scene in the first quarter of the twentieth century, when the earlier orthodoxy defining good design was set aside.

## NOTES

1 During this era, feminist issues focused additionally on the dynamics of private life, such as couples' social, familial, and sexual lives. For a discussion on Ottoman press from the aspect of gender, see Irvin Cemil Schick, 'Print Capitalism and Women's Sexual Agency in the Late Ottoman Empire', *Comparative Studies of South Asia, Africa and the Middle East* 31, no. 1 (1 May 2011): 196–216, https://doi.org/10.1215/1089201X-2010-067.

2 For more on the beautifier role in the Victorian context, see Penny Sparke, *As Long as It's Pink: The Sexual Politics of Taste* (Halifax: Press of the Nova Scotia College of Art and Design, 2010), 16.

3 Özlem Erdoğdu Erkarslan, 'Turkish Women Architects in the Late Ottoman and Early Republican Era, 1908–1950', *Women's History Review* 16, no. 4 (1 September 2007): 560, https://doi.org/10.1080/09612020701445966.

4 Serpil Çakır, *Osmanlı Kadın Hareketi* (Istanbul: Metis Yayınları, 2016), 164–200.

5 Esra Çon, 'A Decollete Journal for the Ottoman Turkish Women: "Süs" (16 June 1339 (1923) – 26 July 1340 (1924)).' (PhD diss., Boğaziçi University, 2007), 7.

6 One of the first examples of this new paradigm was Hüseyin Cahit Yalçın's (1875-1957) 16-part essay in the journal Servet-i Fünun entitled 'On Aesthetics' (Hikmet-i Bediiye Dair), published in 1898. The fact that this journal represented the 'art for art's sake' movement and became a platform for a group of writers and poets who formed the 'New Literature' (Edebiyat-ı Cedide) circle was no coincidence.

7 Çakır, *Osmanlı Kadın Hareketi*, 60. For an overview of the 1908 press boom, see Erol A. F. Baykal, *The Ottoman Press, 1908-1923* (Leiden: Brill, 2019), 43–71.

8 Baykal, *The Ottoman Press*, 165-184; Schick, 'Print Capitalism and Women's Sexual Agency', 197.

9 Baykal, *The Ottoman Press*, 190–97.

10 What is unsurprising, but worth mentioning, is that the infrastructure of the women's academy was also significantly less well equipped than that of the men's school. Fatma Ürekli, 'Güzel Sanatlar Eğitiminde Osmanlı Hanımlarına Açılan Bir Pencere: İnas Sanayi-i Nefise Mektebi', *Tarih ve Toplum* 231, no. 39 (March 2003): 50–60.

11 Uğurgül Tunç, 'Osmanlı Modernleşmesinde Eğitim, Sanat ve Kadın: İnas Sanayi-i Nefise Mektebi Âlisi Örneği' (MA Thesis, Istanbul Technical University, 2018), 33.

12 Donald Quataert, 'Ottoman Women, Households, and Textile Manufacturing, 1800-1914', in *Women in Middle Eastern History: Shifting Boundaries in Sex and Gender*, ed. Nikki R. Keddie and Bath Baron (New Haven: Yale University Press, 2008), 161–76; Yaşar Tolga Cora, 'Female Labor, Merchant Capital, and Resilient Manufacturing: Rethinking Ottoman Armenian Communities through Labor and Business', *Journal of the Economic and Social History of the Orient* 61, no. 3 (2018): 361–95, https://doi.org/10.1163/15685209-12341453.

13 Mes'adet Bedirhan, for example, likened the economy of family units to smaller versions of state finances writing in *Kadınlar Dünyası*. She emphasised the housewives' essential role as 'providing maximum well-being for her family with minimal expenses' stressing the managerial role of the materfamilias. Mes'adet Bedirhan, 'Evde ve Cemiyette Kadın: Aile Bütçesi', *Kadınlar Dünyası*, no. 104 (20 September 1913): 4–5.

14 For instance: 'Resim albümü için işleme kap', *Hanımlara Mahsus Gazete* (The Ladies' Own Gazette), no. 5 (17 September 1895): 4; 'Biçki ve Dikiş', *Hanımlara Mahsus Gazete*, no. 15 (12 October 1895): 349; 'Yeni Yastıklar', *Mehasin* (The Beauty), no. 9 (14 August 1909): 650–55.

15 Margaret Beetham, *A Magazine of Her Own?: Domesticity and Desire in the Woman's Magazine, 1800-1914* (London: Routledge, 1996), 142-154; Mary Ellen Zuckerman, *A History of Popular Women's Magazines in the United States, 1792-1995* (Westport: Greenwood Press, 1998), 59–77.

16 Baykal, *The Ottoman Press*, 192.

17 Süs expressed 'beauty' as a guiding principle for the design of their new publications with these words: 'This lofty ambition, especially under the name Süs ("Ornament"), the magazine itself acknowledges, is almost "an insolence", considering the unattainable ideal of female beauty.' 'İki Üç Satır', *Süs*, no. 1 (16 June 1923): 2.

18 'Bayram Nüshamız', *Mehasin*, no. 10 (14 September 1909): 1-2; 'Bayram Nüshamız', *Mehasin*, no. 11 (14 October 1909): 1–2.

19 The magazine announced that it would sell enlarged lithographs of paintings by the Italian painter Élisa Koch (1833-1914) and the French painter Francine Charderon (1861-1928) in the third issue for an additional charge of 80 kuruş. To entice readers, the publishers even offered vouchers for photo enlargements and promised a refund if the reader did not like the result. 'Küçük Hemşire ve Hab-ı Masum Levhası', *Mehasin*, no. 3 (November 1908): 1–2.

20 Among these names were such painters and caricaturists as İzzet Ziya Turnagil (1883-1936) and Sedat Simavi (1896-1953).

21 Çon, 'A Decollete Journal', 30.

22 Benjamin C. Fortna, *Learning to Read in the Late Ottoman Empire and the Early Turkish Republic* (Basingstone: Palgrave Macmillan, 2011), 41–43.

23 For instance, *İnci* featured the photographs of the famous poet, writer, and intellectual Tevfik Fikret's library for its readers. *Süs*, in contrast, provided several interior illustrations that were filled with books and models of bookshelves. 'Merhum Fikret İçin', *Mehasin*, no. 8 (8 March 1923): 13; 'Evlerimizi Nasıl Döşemeliyiz?', *Süs*, no. 47 (3 May 1924): 8; 'Seyyar Kitap rafı', *Süs*, no. 46 (26 April 1924): 8.

24 'Evlerimizi Nasıl Tefriş Edelim?', *Süs*, no. 49 (17 May 1924): 8.

25 Kahraman Bostancı, *Mehmet Vahit Bey ve Güzel Sanatlar Üzerine Bir Terminoloji Risalesi* (Istanbul: Arkeoloji ve Sanat Yayınları, 2003), 39.

26 The prime example of the study of aesthetics was the Ottoman philosophy journals. *Yeni Felsefe Mecmuası* (New Journal of Philosophy), published in Thessaloniki in 1911, and *Felsefe Mecmuası* (Journal of Philosophy), published in Istanbul in 1913, are considered the first journals devoted exclusively to philosophical research in the Ottoman Empire. Some later works include: Cemil Sena, 'Bedîiyat: Güzele dair', *Milli Mecmua*, no. 109. (1 May 1928): 1756–1758; Rıza Tevfik Bölükbaşı, *Mufassal Kamûs-ı Felsefe* (Istanbul: Matbaa-i Amire, 1914); Mehmet Emin Erişirgil, *Kant ve Felsefesi* (Istanbul: Büyük Millet Meclisi Hükumeti Maarif Vekaleti, 1923); İbrahim Alâettin Gövsa, *Bedi-i Terbiye* (Istanbul: Tanin Matbaası, 1925); Ziyaeddin Fahri, *Bediiyat* (Istanbul: Devlet Matbaası, 1927).

27 The first of the eight-piece essay series: Mes'adet Bedirhan, 'Evde ve Cemiyette Kadın', *Kadınlar Dünyası*, no. 101 (3 August 1913): 8.

28 Ayşe Kadıoğlu, 'Writing to Exist: Mes'adet Bedirhan's Pleas for Ottoman Women', *Women's History Review* 34, no. 1 (2025):165-69, https://doi.org/10.1080/09612025.2024.2332857.

29 Kadıoğlu, 'Writing to Exist', 8–9.

30 Mes'adet Bedirhan, 'Evde ve Cemiyette Kadın', *Kadınlar Dünyası*, no. 104 (23 August 1913): 4.

31 Mes'adet Bedirhan, 'Evde ve Cemiyette Kadın', *Kadınlar Dünyası*, no. 101 (3 August 1913): 8.

32 In issue 162, the magazine announced that it would publish albums every two months. The price of 5 kuruş for the album corresponded to one fifth of the magazine price in 1914.

33 Certainly, the private consumption of photography among women predates the advent of women's magazines. But the attempt by a popular magazine to do this was still a revolutionary undertaking. For more on private consumption of photography among Muslim women and female photographers, see: Alev Berberoğlu, 'A Portrait of the Artist as a Young Woman: Müfide Kadri's Photograph', *Keshif: E-Journal for Ottoman-Turkish Micro Editions*, no. 2 (2024): 10–19, https://doi.org/10.25365/kshf-24-02-02.

34 Çakır, *Osmanlı Kadın Hareketi*, 158.

35 Seinye Baha, 'Kadınlara ve kadınlığa dair filozof Kant ne diyor?' *Kadınlar Dünyası*, no. 194-4 (22 January 1921): 4.

36 Alfons Hoffmann, *Immanuel Kant. Ein Lebensbild nach Darstellungen der Zeitgenossen Borowski, Jachmann, Wasianski* (Halle: Hugo Peter, 1902).

37 Her article also mentions the liberal Turkish politician Celal Nuri İleri (1882-1936), the German philosopher Friedrich Nietzsche (1844-1900) and a thinker called 'Bogla' [sic], whose name I could not identify while transliterating.

38 Nezihe Hamdi, 'Kadın cemiyet hayatına nasıl girmelidir?' *Kadınlar Dünyası*, no. 187 (17 August 1918): 4.

39 Penny Sparke, *As Long as It's Pink*, 16; Beverly Gordon, 'Woman's Domestic Body: The Conceptual Conflation of Women and Interiors in the Industrial Age', *Winterthur Portfolio* 31, no. 4 (1996): 281–301, https://doi.org/10.1086/496697.

40 Several scholars have examined the function of advertisements in women's magazines. For the Ottoman context, see: Elizabeth Frierson, 'Cheap and Easy: The Creation of Consumer Culture in Late Ottoman Society', in *Consumption Studies and the History of the Ottoman Empire, 1550-1922: An Introduction* (Albany: SUNY Press, 2000), 243–60.

41 Çon, 'A Decollete Journal', 50.

42 Necibe Süreyya, 'Ev Kadını', *Süs*, no. 53 (14 June 1924): 10.

43 Ibid.

44 The male workforce declined dramatically throughout the long era of wars, marked by the Balkan Wars, WWI, and the War of Independence until the 1920s. As an outcome, women's labour emerged as an active force in society.

45 This metaphorical bridge between women's bodies and interiors was iterated over multiple issues. 'Bir Hanım Yazı Odası', *Süs*, no. 14 (15 September 1923): 4; 'Evlerimizi Nasıl Tefriş Edelim?' *Süs*, no. 47 (3 May 1924): 8; 'Evlerimizi Nasıl Tefriş Edelim?' *Süs*, no. 48 (10 May 1924): 3. For an insightful analysis of the juxtaposition of modern house and modern Turkish women as a representation of nationhood, see: Gülsüm Baydar, 'Tenuous Boundaries: Women, Domesticity and Nationhood in 1930s Turkey', *The Journal of Architecture* 7 (Autumn 2002): 17, https://doi.org/10.1080/13602360210155429.

46 Ece Zerman, 'Reappropriating the Orientalist Gaze in the Material Culture of Kemalist Turkey: The Formation of an "Aesthetic Nationalism",' in *Kemalism: Transnational Politics in the Post-Ottoman World*, ed. Fabio Giomi, Emmanuel Szurek and Nathalie Clayer, (London: I.B. Tauris, 2019), 220.

47 Gökalp's ideas, which he expounded in his famous book *Türkçülüğün Esasları* (The Principles of Turkism) in 1923, echoed throughout the magazine published in the same year. Ziya Gökalp, *Türkçülüğün Esasları* (Eskişehir: Anadolu Üniversitesi Basımevi, 2019).

48 'Evlerimizi Nasıl Döşemeliyiz?' *Süs*, no. 44 (12 April 1924): 8.

49 Hadiye Şükrü, 'Evlerimizi Süslemek İçin', *Süs*, no. 39 (8 March 1924): 4–5.

50 Evlerimizi Nasıl Tefriş Edelim?" *Süs*, no. 46 (April 26, 1924): 5; 'Evlerimizi Nasıl Tefriş Edelim?' *Süs*, no. 47 (3 May 1924): 8; 'Evlerimizi Nasıl Tefriş Edelim?' *Süs*, no. 48 (10 May 1924): 4; 'Evlerimizi Nasıl Tefriş Edelim?' *Süs*, no. 49 (17 May 1924): 8.

51 'Evlerimizi Nasıl Tefriş Edelim?' *Süs*, no. 46 (26 April 1924): 5.

52 'Seyyar Kitap rafı', *Süs*, no. 46 (26 April 1924): 8; 'Genç Kız Odaları için Biblolar', *Süs*, no. 50 (24 May 1924): 9; 'Kurdeleden Yastıklar', *Süs*, no. 52 (7 June 1924): 8.

53 Clive Edwards, '"Home Is Where the Art Is": Women, Handicrafts and Home Improvements 1750–1900', *Journal of Design History* 19, no. 1 (2006): 13, https://doi.org/10.1093/jdh/epk002.

54 Bostancı, *Mehmet Vahit Bey*, 36.

55 Yuriko Saito, *Everyday Aesthetics* (Oxford: Oxford University Press, 2007), 57.

56 Judy Attfield, *Wild Things: The Material Culture of Everyday Life* (New York: Fairchild Books, 2020), 58.

# Chapter 5
# Editors and Entrepreneurs
## Women's Writing on Architecture and Design in Britain, 1918–39

*Alex Banister*

Women's magazines have long been overlooked as source material in the history of architecture and design. However, these sources reveal intimate insights into the lives of millions of women. Although often dismissed as inconsequential and trivial, fleeting and short-lived, something that is read and then thrown away, magazines can be re-evaluated as source material that offers a new view of women's experiences of modernity.

It is widely recognised that magazines have the ability to create collective cultural meaning and construct reader identities within the confines of patriarchal capitalist society.[1] However, more work remains to be done connecting this with women's writing on architecture and how modern design could better their lives, both in and out of the home. Whilst women's writing on architecture rarely appeared in architectural journals of the interwar period, women's views were transmitted to wide audiences in magazines targeted at female readerships. Here, writers and editors created important spaces for the presentation and discussion of modern design; reinforcing the idea that architectural modernism was 'dependent on the written word (and the illustration) for its material existence'.[2]

Focusing primarily on the British edition of *Good Housekeeping* magazine during the interwar years (1918–1939), this chapter highlights the ways in which women's print culture shaped the careers, spending habits, and tastes of a new architecture and design audience, and interrogates magazines as a means for change during this period.

### 'FEARLESS, FRANK, AND OUTSPOKEN'

The British version of *Good Housekeeping* magazine was launched by William Randolph Hearst's National Magazine Company and first appeared on shelves in March 1922, following in the footsteps of the highly popular American version. Its opening editorial promised readers articles about 'what concerns them and interests them most', answering 'the burning questions of the day [...] by women who are fearless, frank, and outspoken'.[3] Priced at one shilling and published every month, it was aimed at middle-class women with an annual household income of at least £1000. It provided extensive advice, expert opinions, recipes, and a consumer testing service through the Good Housekeeping Institute, as well as problem pages, letters from readers, fiction serials, and articles on current affairs, from the costs of sending your child to school to women in politics.[4] It quickly became one of the most successful titles of its kind, selling around 150,000 copies annually.

The diverse content reflected the new status of women as modern citizens, but as well as being on the pages of the magazine, these women were also present in the sites of production. The growth in women's publications during the period offered new professional opportunities for women, in fields such as advertising, public relations, and journalism. *Good Housekeeping* employed many women in these entrepreneurial roles, centring women's voices in conversations surrounding modern life and public discourse. Women with professional journalism training or domestic science qualifications had the power to inform opinion in new ways. The rise in expert literature on domestic efficiency and kitchen design, for example, attracted both readers and advertisers. In this way, women shaped design history in ways historians have not previously acknowledged, through words rather than through building.

At the helm was Alice Maud Head (Fig. 5.1), who was appointed Managing Director of *Good Housekeeping* in 1924 and led the magazine until the outbreak of the Second World War. Head was also the managing director of the National Magazines Corporation, and was reportedly the highest paid woman in Britain during the interwar period. When quizzed for the BBC's *Woman's Hour* about the generosity of Hearst's paycheques, she coyly confirmed 'it was very generous indeed'.[5] Through her business strategy and networking skills, Head built up a strong network of contributors to the magazine, including respected fiction writers. She also built solid relationships with advertising agencies, solidifying the magazine's commercial success and therefore its future, whilst also influencing the nation's spending habits. A recent issue of *Good Housekeeping* magazine reflected on Head's influence, describing her as doing 'everything we ask of a business leader today a century ago, in a world far less supportive of women at work'.[6]

Figure 5.1: Alice Maud Head by unknown photographer, 1930s. © National Portrait Gallery, London.

Editor as networker, taste-maker, and design-influencer was a role filled by women at other magazines. British *Vogue*, another Hearst publication with a successful sister in the United States, employed Dorothy Todd as editor. Todd, alongside her work and life partner Madge Garland, the magazine's Fashion Director, revolutionised the magazine, printing articles on interiors by the Bloomsbury Group and architecture by Le Corbusier.[7] Todd's network stretched beyond the borders of Britain to the United States, where she contributed an article to *House Beautiful*, a magazine under the stewardship of another editor-taste-maker Ethel Power.[8] Todd's successor at *Vogue*, Alison Settle, continued to promote modern architecture and design, and later worked for the Council of Art and Industry and the Council of Industrial Design.

At *Good Housekeeping*, Alice Head collaborated closely with her colleague Dorothy Daisy Cottington-Taylor, the Director of the Good Housekeeping Institute. Trained at the National School of Cookery and a recipient of a Certificate in Household and Social Science from King's College for Women, Cottington-Taylor wrote a regular column for the magazine and led the Institute. The monthly feature, 'Household Engineering

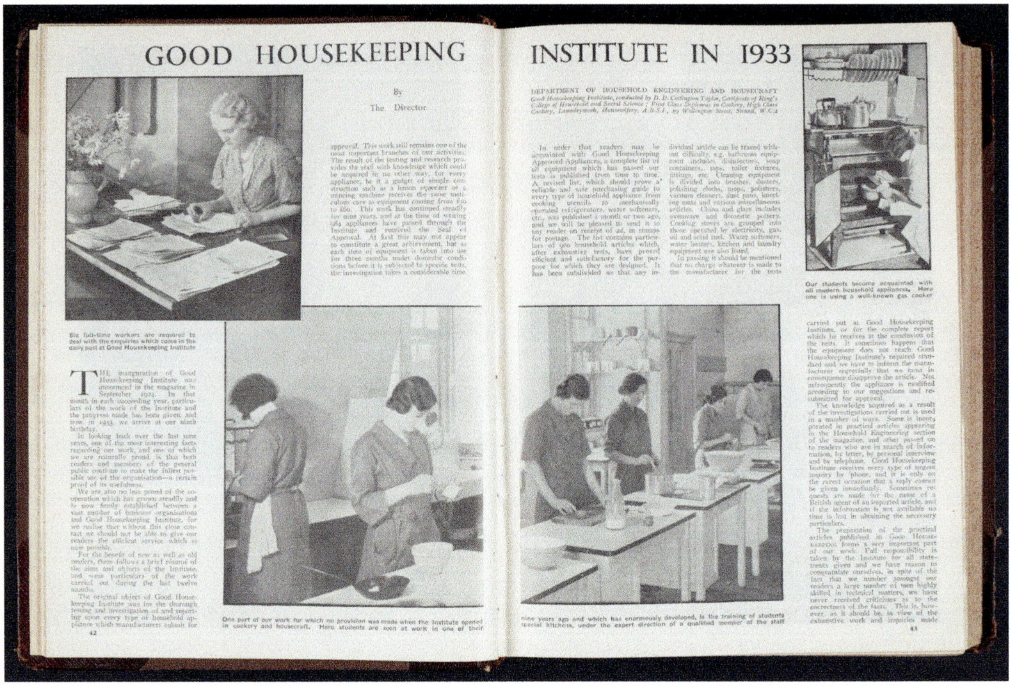
GOOD HOUSEKEEPING INSTITUTE IN 1933

By The Director

Figure 5.2: Dorothy Daisy Cottington Taylor, 'Good Housekeeping Institute in 1933', *Good Housekeeping*, September 1933, 42-43. British Library Collection. 0 P.P.1524.dac.

and Housecraft', provided step-by-step photographs and instructions to guide readers in such tasks as home decoration, laundry, and cleaning. Through the Institute, Cottington-Taylor and her team tested appliances, ran events and lessons for women, and advised on everything from cookery to budgeting. The Institute was run by women, for women, and provided a physical space for these networks to meet, exchange, and socialise (Fig. 5.2). Like Head, Cottington-Taylor was well-connected and influential. She was also very astute in her use of language, styling both the Institute and her writing as forms of 'engineering' and experimental 'laboratories'. The language of technology, scientific management, and industrial rationalisation created an image of the home as a domestic factory and promoted the housewife's role as a profession.

Every issue of *Good Housekeeping* ran one or two architectural features detailing specific homes. These were usually written by male 'experts' affiliated with the Royal Institute of British Architects (RIBA) under the leadership of the magazine's Director of Housing: the first was Herbert Welch FRIBA, one of the architects of the Hampstead Garden Suburb, followed by

Robert Springett AIAA. However, in February 1935, the magazine appointed Joyce E. Townsend as the new Director of Housing. Townsend was one of the second cohort of women who entered the Architectural Association (AA) in 1918. She was elected an Associate of the RIBA in March 1925, and worked on slum re-housing schemes, factory and hospital buildings, alongside almshouses for women. She was also a founding member of the RIBA Women Architect's Committee. In an article introducing her new role at *Good Housekeeping*, the magazine described her as 'broad-minded, tactful, a speaker of no mean talent', highlighting her academic and professional achievements, as well as her love of solo travel.[9] Under her editorship, the architectural pages of the magazine featured homes and designs which would appeal to the needs and wants of women.

Head and Cottington-Taylor's networks ensured a diverse and opinionated group of women contributed to *Good Housekeeping*. Helena Normanton, the first female barrister in the United Kingdom, wrote regular articles on politics and the women's right to vote.[10] Key members of the women's suffrage movement, such as Lady Violet Bonham Carter and Dame Millicent Fawcett, also wrote for the publication.[11] The importance of networks can be seen behind the scenes of such other women's publications as British *Vogue* who employed an impressive roster of authors. Some were architects and designers themselves, such as Doris Lewis, another alumna of the AA and Associate of the RIBA, who wrote under her married name of Mrs Howard Robertson.[12] Nora Shackleton Heald, the editor of British society magazine *The Queen*, was also a keen commentator on architectural modernism with a penchant, like her peer Dorothy Todd, for Le Corbusier.[13] Her magazine also employed Constance Peel, writing under the name of Mrs C. S. Peel, as editor of the household department during the 1910s and 1920s. Peel also worked for the magazines *Hearth and Home* and *The Lady*. She wrote books on household management, including *Marriage on Small Means* (1914) and *The Labour-Saving House* (1917), and, following the First World War, worked for the Ministry of Reconstruction and the British Women Housewives' Association.

Mrs C. S. Peel's use of initials and Doris Lewis's use of her husband's name was not an uncommon feature of female authorship in interwar British journalism. However, the anonymity these forms of ownership present can be challenging when tracing contributors to women's magazines. Without evidence of first names or with the issues of attribution surrounding shared archives of architect-partners like the Robertsons, much work is still to be done to correctly credit the pioneering work of interwar women journalists.[14]

Through their words, editorial decisions, and abilities to network and work collaboratively, women became key agents in discussions surrounding modern politics, social issues, and culture. Far from the dismissive view of women's interwar magazines as frivolous flapper fodder, these 'fearless, frank, and outspoken' women represented a much more opinionated and complex figure of the interwar woman and the ways in which architecture and design could serve her modern way of living.

## 'MILLIONS OF HUMAN BEINGS, OF BOTH SEXES, OF ALL AGES, HAVE NOW BEEN ADMITTED TO THE WHOLE OF LITERATURE'

As well as contributing to magazines, women influenced the sphere of business in architecture and design through their new economic powers and roles as consumers of an increasingly commercialised modern culture. Magazines, particularly those aimed at women, were a key site of debates surrounding the mass consumption of culture.

In July 1927, the writer Virginia Woolf and her husband Leonard Woolf took part in a scripted conversation on a BBC radio programme entitled 'Are Too Many Books Written and Published?' Whilst Leonard argued yes, Virginia praised the possibilities of wider publishing. In riposte to her husband, she debated: 'You must remember that the majority of readers today are reading for the first time [...] Millions of human beings, of both sexes, of all ages, have now been admitted to the whole of literature.'[15] Woolf's belief in the broadcasting of literature can be seen in her regular articles for *Vogue* and in her 'London Scene' essays written for *Good Housekeeping* in the 1930s, which have been described as a means to 'engage the female readers of this publication in a feminist analysis of patriarchal Britain.'[16]

This rise of commercialised publishing and a wider readership of educated women following the First World War met with criticism, often of a gendered nature. In his book *Literature, Money and the Market*, Paul Delaney describes how the 'purchasing power of the female reader' challenged the 'artist's phallic autonomy in the early twentieth century and became a constant target for modernist misogyny'.[17] Andreas Huyssen, in his essay 'Mass Culture as Woman: Modernism's Other', noted that at the turn of the twentieth century the prevailing discourse gendered mass culture as feminine versus authentically high culture as the 'prerogative [...]

[and] privileged realm of male activities.'[18] The 'democratisation of publishing' through the large scale production of books and the publication of new women's magazines which occurred during this time was perceived as a threat to this masculinised realm of the highbrow and the boom in choice of women's magazines and their vast circulation figures gave a new power to women as readers and consumers. This criticism perhaps explains why women's magazines have historically been overlooked as a legitimate source material worthy of academic study.

Women's magazines presented multifaceted texts featuring a mix of cultural subjects, which added to the contemporary anxieties of the threat posed by mass culture to 'authentic' high culture. By situating modernism within the magazine, women's publications contravened these previously gendered cultural boundaries and represented an important site of resistance against gendered discourses. It is, therefore, important to lean into this high / low mix and embrace how, through their wide ranging if sometimes contradictory, content and their consumerist outlook, women's magazines presented opportunities for interwar women.

As customers of culture, women could participate in, and influence debates about, the built environment and the development of new design languages. The cultural identification of shopping with femininity can explain why architectural histories have in the past overlooked this development, preferring instead the image of the designer as separate from the purchaser.[19] British *Vogue*, for example, published features on homes – guided tours which revealed glimpses into the lives of celebrities and socialites and their modern tastes – alongside articles on cocktail making and fashion, book and exhibition reviews. It assumed its readership had some existing knowledge of modern culture and blurred the lines between highbrow and lowbrow in a way not seen before in Britain.

*Good Housekeeping* similarly traversed this high / low dichotomy. The May 1927 issue, for instance, featured an article on 'The New Feminism' by the leader of the National Union of Women's Suffrage Societies, Dame Millicent Fawcett; guidance on travelling in France, Belgium and Italy for solo female travellers; and an article on women graduates, next to articles on food storage and which broom to buy, advice on how to keep youthful skin, and serialised romantic fiction. Content was frequently inconsistent, both within the pages of one issue and across the years. In September 1930, the writer Alice Booth wrote a short story that claimed 'A House needs a Husband', whilst in April 1938, an anonymous barrister informed the readers of their rights under 'The New Divorce Law'.[20]

Perhaps it is tempting to dismiss the mismatched and incongruous content of the magazine as bad editorship. However, this view assumes a readership incapable of critically engaging with diverse definitions of modern womanhood. In these publications, the high and low, the intellectual and the popular, the progressive and the traditional, were not positioned as opposites, and its readership were not forced into being one or the other, but rather they became multifaceted participants capable of navigating different contexts, opinions, and iterations of modern life. Women's magazines promoted a new kind of citizenship for women, in which they were free to be interested in politics and culture, whilst also enjoying shopping, fashion, sport, or film, whether they were housewives, mothers, workers, or all of the above.

These negotiations took place through content, but also through visual and formal constructs, something which makes magazines unique as a historical source of study. In their hybrid use of the visual and textual they provided an experimental site for interwar graphic design. Technological advances in colour printing, photography, and photomontage provided new and exciting ways through which meaning could be communicated. Unlike books, magazines, both in their fast-paced frequency and in their use of text and image, presented a site for reading but also for looking and creating connections. Similarities can be drawn between the pages of magazines and the rapidly increasing popularity of cinema during this period; a pastime with which many women of the 1920s and 1930s would engage. Much as film, magazines provided a space for fantasy and dream.

Fiona Hackney and Julia Bigham have described women's magazines as both a 'window' and a 'mirror'.[21] This metaphor has particular resonance within the architectural pages of *Good Housekeeping*, where fantasies of modern living through tours of other people's homes (magazine-as-window) were featured alongside an acknowledgment of how one could recreate it in their own home (magazine-as-mirror). This scrapbook-like culmination of content provided a site in which women were provided the space to question, negotiate, and explore; to try-on different iterations and identities of the modern woman before making their consumer choices.

The expansion in the consumers of architecture following the First World War created what Jessica Kelly has termed 'the architectural public': a market of consumers who had an interest, but not necessarily an expertise, in design, and who sought specialist opinions as to what to buy.[22] This new commercial side of architecture and design presented questions about how to deal with public taste and how to persuade

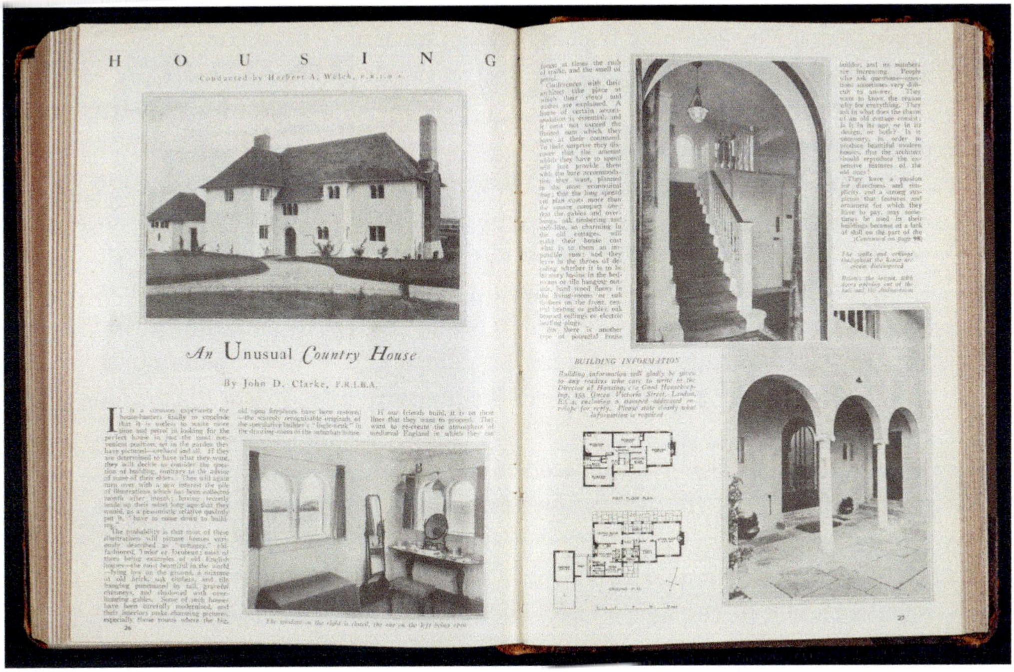
HOUSING

Conducted by Herbert A. Welch, F.R.I.B.A.

An Unusual Country House

By John D. Clarke, F.R.I.B.A.

BUILDING INFORMATION

Figure 5.3: John D. Clarke, 'An Unusual Country House', *Good Housekeeping*, February 1927, 26-27. British Library Collection. 0 P.P.1524.dac.

assumed and intended readerships what constituted 'good taste'. Kelly's term can be expanded from the architectural press to include women's magazines. *Good Housekeeping*'s recommendations were far-reaching, and its architectural features advocated for high quality design which fulfilled everyday needs.

Following the First World War, the state of the housing stock was a matter of concern across the social spectrum. Existing housing was considered unfit for purpose or outdated because of changes in ways of living, such as the decline in live-in servants as well as smaller family sizes. At the same time, the expansion in speculative private suburban house building paired with cheap mortgages meant that homeownership was opened to middle- and working-class households on an unprecedented scale. With these seismic changes in everyday life, women as architectural purchasers were a key demographic targeted by women's magazines of the interwar period, capitalising on the growing home-making and home-owning market and redefining women's new roles. The conversation about what housing should offer involved women, and although the typical *Good Housekeeping* reader may not have necessarily been able to afford to commission a bespoke, architect-designed home, the architectural features in its pages promoted a need for, and right to, a modern domestic environment of her own.

These critical negotiations played out in the magazine's Housing column, which featured a wide-ranging selection of housing types, for varying budgets, in both the city and the countryside. Women's magazines' publication of suburban housing in the cottage or Tudorbethan style, and those evoking English architectural heritage has been dismissed as a backward-looking nostalgia for the solidity and security of times past. However, what canonical histories of modern architecture of the period have overlooked is the focus *Good Housekeeping* had on the ways in which these buildings actually embraced modern design, even if not looking 'textbook modern'. The architecture critic Sarah Williams Goldhagen has contended that viewing modernism as a singular style-based paradigm 'glosses over its complexity and multifarious richness'.[23] Instead, modernism should be considered not through the lens of a formal style, but through one of a less restrictive discourse and set of practices, opening the field up to re-evaluate architecture which has previously been overlooked for not being 'modern' enough in canonical histories.

Photographs from the article 'An Unusual Country House' from February 1927 seem at first glance to offer an unremarkable reinterpretation of the past: a house with a pitched roof, large chimney stacks, and arched windows and doors (Fig. 5.3). However, the article promotes simplicity in ornamentation and an inquisitiveness in house building, encouraging readers to question

> the reason why for everything [...] in what does the charm of an old cottage consist; is it in its age, or in its design, or both? Is it necessary, in order to produce beautiful modern houses, that the architect should reproduce the expensive features of the old ones?[24]

The article concludes that this house may appeal to readers who believe that good design is something that can be expressed in many ways.

Beyond ornament, architectural discussions in *Good Housekeeping* highlighted the way in which the modern home should and could serve the modern woman. For example, the January 1934 issue featured an article written by the architect Geoffrey Bryant Hobbs on 'Buying an Estate

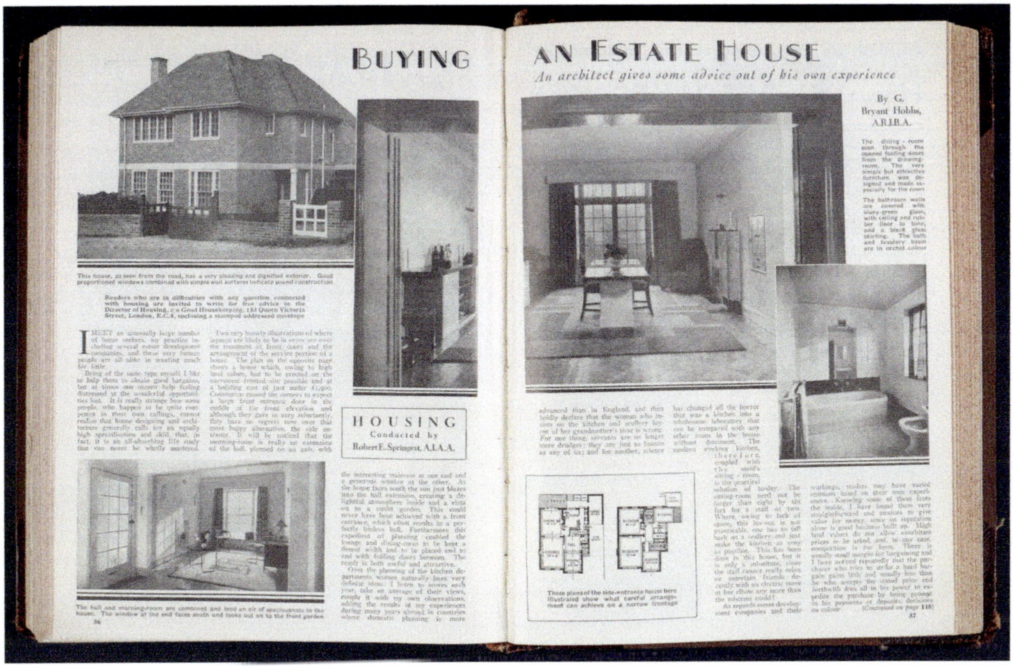


Figure 5.4: G. Bryant Hobbs, 'Buying an Estate House', *Good Housekeeping*, January 1934, 36-37. British Library Collection. 0 P.P.1524.dac.

House' (Fig. 5.4). Speaking to the reader as an astute consumer, the article described the purchase of a house as 'possibly the one big financial investment of their lives', and a decision which involved women. Through text, exterior and interior photographs, and detailed floorplans, Bryant Hobbs promoted to the *Good Housekeeping* reader the merits of consulting an architect, while remaining attentive to costs. He suggested, for instance, moving the front door to the side rather than the central-front as making economic sense due to high land values, whilst remaining 'useful and attractive'. And although the house in question lacks the style readily associated with canonical modern architecture, its kitchen is still undeniably modern, which, according to Cottington-Taylor's Institute, Bryant Hobbs defines as a laboratory for food preparation:

> The woman who insists on the kitchen and scullery layout of her grandmother's time is wrong [...] science has changed all the horror that was a kitchen into

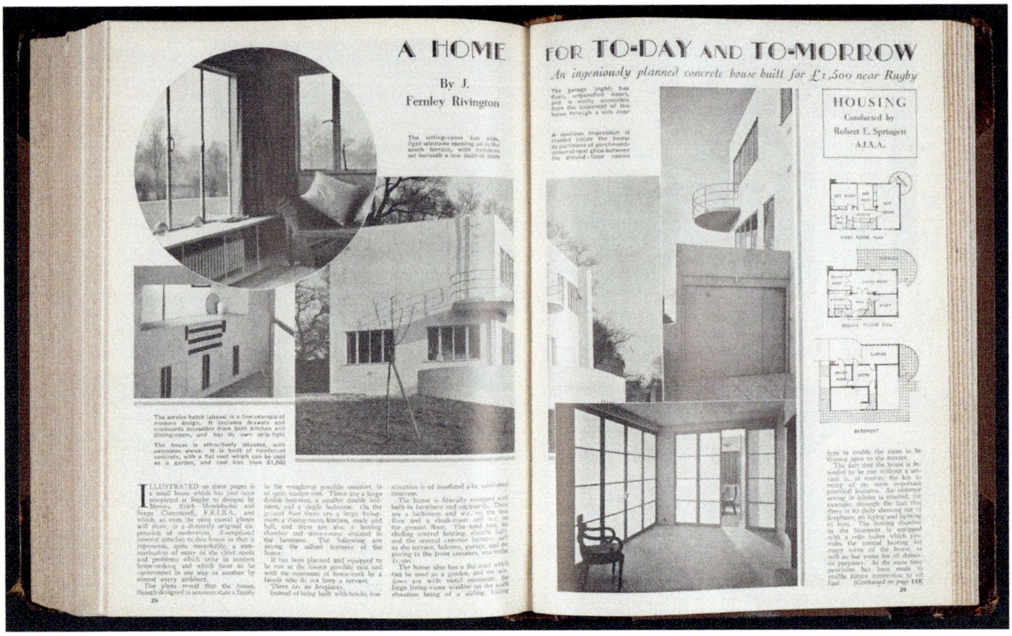
A HOME FOR TO-DAY AND TO-MORROW

*An ingeniously planned concrete house built for £1,500 near Rugby*

By J. Fernley Rivington

HOUSING
Conducted by
Robert E. Springett
A.I.A.A.

Figure 5.5: J. Fernley Rivington, 'A Home for To-day and To-morrow', *Good Housekeeping*, August 1934, 28-29. British Library Collection. 0 P.P.1524.dac.

a wholesome laboratory [...] The modern working kitchen, coupled with the maid's sitting room, is the practical solution of today.[25]

*Good Housekeeping* also published, like Todd and Shackleton Heald's magazines, the work of prominent architects associated with the modern movement. In August 1934, *Good Housekeeping* published an article entitled 'A Home for To-day and To-morrow', detailing an 'ingeniously planned concrete house built for £1,500 near Rugby' (Fig. 5.5).[26] Completed to designs by Erich Mendelsohn and Serge Chermayeff, the house was praised by the magazine for 'remarkably summarising many of the chief needs and problems which arise in modern home-making', and for providing a modest yet comfortable home specifically for a family without a servant. Appealing to the reader of *Good Housekeeping*, the article highlights the labour-saving considerations of this home, such as not having to clean the fireplaces, as well as the money-saving attributes, such as the 'insulated 4-in. reinforced concrete' walls and coke boiler central heating, which was future-proofed for conversion to oil heating.

## 'WE ARE TRYING TO BLEND OUR OLD WORLD WITH OUR NEW. TRYING TO BE CITIZENS AND WOMEN AT THE SAME TIME'

What were the motivations of the 'fearless, frank, and outspoken' women writing for the 'millions of human beings' now able to be informed consumers of design culture? It is difficult to fully separate their motives from the capitalist agendas of the publishing companies for which they worked and their advertisers upon whom they were reliant for the future success of their magazines. Is it possible to determine whether magazines were capitalising on the desire for societal change, or whether they could be agents of meaningful change for women?

The magazines' framing of shopping as a fundamental part of modern womanhood is inextricably linked to their dependency on advertising revenue. *Good Housekeeping* went as far as to 'guarantee' its adverts, featuring the slogan 'Advertised Goods are Good Goods' in the corners of its commercial pages, reassuringly blurring the lines between editorial and commercial content. This structuring and mediating of content extended to architecture. An article from the January 1934 issue discussing the minimum home asserted that 'the bachelor flat, the single-apartment dwelling, the minimum house, call it what you will, is one of the social developments of our age'.[27] The article praised the minimum home's prioritisation of light and air, and its modern use of tiles in the kitchen and bathroom. These features are echoed in the later pages of the same issue in an advertisement for the new Sloane Square Avenue Mansions (Fig. 5.6), an 11-storey apartment block in Chelsea designed by George Kay Green, which had opened the year before. The advertisement reads:

> Small, Convenient, Inexpensive! You are invited to inspect the most modern, best appointed, labour-saving small flats in central London. Ideal homes for the business man or woman; an ideal pied-a-terre for the country resident. Electric lights; telephone for each flat; garages for residents' cars; central heating; constant hot water; private balconies [...] dainty kitchenette and tiled bathroom included.

Such threads actively linked products with Cottington-Taylor's construct of the modern woman as domestic manager, linking social liberation with freedom from drudgery. Modernism offered women convenience; something which, as Kathleen James-Chakraborty notes, was not 'the modernism on which the Museum of Modern Art focused', but one

Figure 5.6: 'London's Latest Luxury Flats', advertisement in *Good Housekeeping*, January 1934, 127. British Library Collection. O P.P.1524.dac.

that was still significant and transformative.[28] These links may have garnered results for advertising companies, but did the convenience of the labour-saving devices promoted by magazines contribute to women's liberation in more radical and tangible terms? Once freed of domestic drudgery through the informed consumer choices and recommendations from the Good Housekeeping Institute, what would women do? In the case of *Good Housekeeping*, its editors and journalists encouraged readers to focus as much on life outside of the home as within it, through a new outlook on citizenship and new-found career opportunities. The ability to run an efficient household equated to the ability to run an efficient woman's organisation, or even to run the country. The journalist Sidney Dark argued that women's practical skills as housewives made them highly suitable to the governmental jobs which men 'still monopolise'.[29]

*Good Housekeeping* also made its readers aware of politics beyond the borders of Britain. The magazine had a decidedly international outlook, exploring other cultures and encouraging women to travel.[30] Helena

Normanton's long-standing column 'The World as it Passes' updated readers on women's rights and achievements from around the world. Following the introduction of universal suffrage in 1928, and informed by the internationalist movements of the period, the magazine tapped into the activism of the interwar pacifism, such as the politics of organisations including the Women's International League for Peace and Freedom. The article 'Women and Peace' commented that the 'women's vote in England is undoubtedly a peace vote', and that the political influence of women had already strengthened adherence to and support of the League of Nations.[31]

New opportunities for women in the world of work were a key consideration in *Good Housekeeping* throughout the interwar period. As well as the professionalisation of the role of the housewife, encompassing rationalisation, budgeting, and efficiency, the magazine took women out of the home. The concept of home changed from being a place of retreat from society to a site from which one could, and should, engage with the wider community. Articles regularly encouraged paid work and discussed women's employment rights. 'This is a generation which realises that worth-while happiness can be found in work' asserted Beatrice Kean; Ellen Dorothy Abb detailed 'Careers from Abroad' for women who 'have initiative and dislike stereotyped occupations'; while Vera Brittain explained 'Why I think Mothers can have Careers'.[32] A dedicated section of the magazine advertised courses and professional development, there was also a regular column on wide-ranging career paths for women, from pharmacy and dispensing (October 1936) and the medical profession (August 1936) to veterinary surgery (June 1937) and dairying (July 1937).

This progressive and positive promotion and recognition of women as capable and active participants in life outside of the home was not matched by the domestic sphere opening up to men: *Good Housekeeping* never challenged the concept of housework as women's work. Despite arguing for the professionalisation of the housewife when Violet Bonham Carter pondered 'Should Wives have Wages' in December 1924 or Helena Normanton demanded 'Wages for Wives' in November 1928, her domestic labour remained unpaid, a conversation that still resonates today.[33] Despite enhanced choices, expectations for women in reality became heightened, creating in effect more work. Again, we see *Good Housekeeping* as a site of contradictions: of progress but also conservativism, of empowerment through choices but disempowerment through expectations, of feminism but within a still patriarchal system. These conflicting gender politics were also class-based. Whilst the middle-class readers of *Good Housekeeping* may have seen work as emancipatory, working-class women may have understood full-time housewife duties as freedom from paid labour, which had often been domestic service for others or factory work.[34]

Magazines therefore presented a site for negotiation and compromise, and whilst criticism can be levelled against their reliance on advertising and their commercialised linking the housewife and labour-saving appliances with social liberation, they did offer a plurality of choice. They presented the figure of the housewife as an emblem of modern life, as much as the 'female politician, the film star, or the sportswoman' of the time.[35] In her introductory editorial for *Woman* magazine, the journalist Margaret Lane argued: 'We are trying to blend our old world with our new. Trying to be citizens and women at the same time. Wage-earners and sweethearts. Less aggressively feminist than independently feminine. It is a difficult balance to strike.'[36] The old with the new is a key mediation in *Good Housekeeping* during a time when women (and men) were adjusting to the aftermath of the First World War, to women's increasing employment rights, to universal suffrage, to a fast-paced shopping culture, and to new ideas about marriage, family, and how to live.

## 'WHAT IS THE FUTURE OF WOMEN?'

Women's periodicals of the interwar period in Britain advocated for a multiplicity in modern femininity, reflecting the complex and diverse nature of being a woman during a time of social, political, and cultural change. The *Good Housekeeping* reader was not a homogenous creature, standard and singularly dimensional in her identity as housewife, but rather varied and sometimes contradictory, reflecting the plurality of opportunities available to her. The diverse pages of these magazines, with their mixture of high and low culture, editorial and commercial content, suggest readers were expected to negotiate the juxtapositions and complexities of feminine modernities.

'What is the future of women?' asked the Labour MP Joseph Kenworthy in 1930, predicting that 'future historians, writing of the first part of this twentieth century, will put the sudden advancement of women to a status almost of complete equality with men in the very forefront of the great events of our times'.[37] Writing this in the pages of *Good Housekeeping*, Kenworthy's comment reflects the opening up of professions in journalism, where figures such as Alice Head, Dorothy Todd, Ethel Power, and Nora Shackleton

Heald commanded authority and contributed to complex debates about modern ways of living. Their networks of writers and editors exemplify how architecture and design are collaborative practices; ones which are shaped outside circles controlled by professional architects and studied beyond the built. In highlighting these previously unheard voices, and considering architecture through journalism by and for women, the study of women's magazines can expand agency, reveal an energetic and engaged discourse which informed architectural consumerism, and reveal different accounts of modern architectural culture in Britain during this time.

The new economic powers of the female consumer made these magazines sites for experimentation with modern living. Through the composite relationship of text and image, editorial and advertising, magazines created a fantasy space, through which women could engage with different forms of womanhood, at different stages of their professional and personal lives. These forms of womanhood embraced new opportunities, promoting the modern woman as having responsibilities and choices, such as the right to work and earn money, to spend it in an informed way, and to use her political freedoms to seek change in Britain and beyond. Although on the surface progressive, magazines were also a site of problematic negotiations of modern womanhood. Nonetheless operating within the confines of a patriarchal society, its presentation of the housewife as manager of her own home sought to encourage active citizenship and change. Despite fast-paced advances, both during Kenworthy's lifetime and beyond, 'future historians', nearly a century later, still see much work to be done, both in the pages of magazines and beyond.

## NOTES

1 For example Judy Giles, *The Parlour and the Suburb: Domestic Identities, Class, Femininity and Modernity* (Oxford: Berg, 2004); and Margaret Beetham, *A Magazine of Her Own? Domesticity and Desire in the Woman's Magazine, 1800–1914* (London: Routledge, 1996).

2 Elizabeth Darling, 'The Avant-Garde in the Drawing Room: Women, Writing, and Architectural Modernism in Britain', in *Women, Periodicals and Print Culture in Britain, 1890s–1920s: The Modernist Period*, ed. Faith Binckes and Carey Snyder (Edinburgh: Edinburgh University Press, 2019): 134.

3 'The Reason for Good Housekeeping', *Good Housekeeping*, March 1922, 11.

4 For example Marjory Royce, 'The Problem of School Bills', *Good Housekeeping*, October 1929, 218; and Dame Millicent Fawcett G.B.E., 'The New Feminism: What Has the Women's Vote Accomplished for the Country?', *Good Housekeeping*, May 1927, 23, 112.

5 Sue MacGregor, 'Alice Head', *Woman's Hour*, aired 3 May 1976 (London: BBC Radio 4, 1976), radio broadcast.

6 Lizzie Broadbent, 'Meet the woman who created Good Housekeeping', *Good Housekeeping*, January 2022, 48.

7 Although most existing research on British *Vogue* in the interwar years has focused on literary modernism and the Bloomsbury Group under the editorship of Dorothy Todd, the pages of the magazine remain a key source for discussions on architecture. For example Anne Pender, 'Modernist Madonnas: Dorothy Todd, Madge Garland and Virginia Woolf', *Women's History Review* 16, no. 4 (2007): 519-533; Christopher Reed, 'A Vogue That Dare Not Speak its Name: Sexual Subculture During the Editorship of Dorothy Todd, 1922-26'; *Fashion Theory* 10, no. 1-2 (2006): 39-72; Aurelea Mahood, 'Fashioning Readers: The Avant Garde and British Vogue, 1920-9'; *Women: A Cultural Review* 13, no. 1 (2002): 37-47; Jane Garrity, 'Selling Culture to the "Civilised": Bloomsbury, British Vogue, and the Marketing of National Identity', *Modernism/Modernity*, 6, 2 (1999): 29-58; Nicola Luckhurst, *Bloomsbury in Vogue* (London: Cecil Woolf, 1998).

8 Dorothy Todd, 'Some Reflections on Modernism', *House Beautiful* 66 (1929): 416-17, 470-76. For more on women writing on architecture *in House Beautiful*, and journalism as a viable career path for women, see Kathleen James-Chakraborty, 'Expanding Agency: Ethel Power, House Beautiful, and the Writing of the History of American Architecture', in *Women and Architectural History: The Monstrous Regiment Then and Now*, ed. Dana Arnold (Abingdon: Routledge, 2025) 152-68.

9 C. Romanne-James, 'Introducing Joyce Townsend A.R.I.B.A.', *Good Housekeeping*, February 1935, 66.

10 For example Helena Normanton, 'Representative Women of Great Britain: An Appreciation of those who are in Parliament and of those who Ought to be', *Good Housekeeping*, February 1929, 48–49, 130; Helena Normanton, 'The New Women M.P.'s' *Good Housekeeping*, August 1929, 16–17, 134; Helena Normanton, 'The Members we Elect: Would they be better legislators if we were better voters?', *Good Housekeeping*, March 1931, 42–43, 153.

11 For example Millicent Fawcett, 'What Eight Million Women Will Do With Their Votes', *Good Housekeeping*, April 1922, 10–11; Violet Bonham-Carter, 'The Political Future of Women', *Good Housekeeping*, October 1922, 11–12.

12 For more on Doris Lewis and other women who studied at the Architectural Association, see Elizabeth Darling and Lynne Walker, *AA Women in Architecture: 1917–2017* (London: AA Publications, 2017).

13 For example Nora Shackleton Heald, 'Towards a New Architecture: When Engineer and Architect Work Together', *The Queen*, November 1927, 17–20.

14 Of particular note in the case of Doris Lewis: upon her marriage to Howard Robertson in 1927 – he was at that time the principal of the AA where she studied and had his own practice (Easton and Robertson) – she reportedly decided 'unilaterally that one architect in the family was enough', ending her architectural career in favour of journalism. See Elizabeth Darling. 'Robertson [née Lewis], Doris Adeney, Lady Robertson (1899–1981), architect, interior designer, and writer', *Oxford Dictionary of National Biography*, 11 July 2019, accessed 16 September 2024. https://www.oxforddnb.com/view/10.1093/odnb/9780198614128.001.0001/odnb-9780198614128-e-369119

15 Virginia Woolf and Leonard Woolf, 'Are Too Many Books Written and Published?', 15 February 1927, BBC Written Archives Centre Caversham, in Melba Cuddy-Keane, 'Are Too Many Books Written and Published?' *PMLA* 121, no. 1 (2006): 242.

16 Alice Wood, 'Made to Measure: Virginia Woolf in *Good Housekeeping* Magazine', *Prose Studies* 32, no. 1 (2010): 22.

17 Paul Delaney, *Literature, Money and the Market: From Trollope to Amis* (Basingstoke: Palgrave, 2002), 150.

18 Andreas Huyssen, *After the Great Divide: Modernism, Mass Culture and Postmodernism* (Bloomington: Indiana University Press, 1986), 47.

19 For more about the relationship between designer and consumer see Katie Lloyd Thomas, 'This Strange Interloper: Building products and the emergence of the architect-shopper in 1930s Britain', in *Suffragette City: Women, Politics, and the Built Environment*, ed. Elizabeth Darling and Nathaniel Robert Walker (Abingdon: Routledge, 2020) 110-35.

20 Alice Booth, 'A House needs a Husband: A Short Story', *Good Housekeeping*, September 1930, 26; A Barrister, 'The New Divorce Law', *Good Housekeeping*, April 1938, 58.

21 Fiona Hackney and Julia Bigham, 'A Cottage of One's Own: Making Modern Women Through Word and Image in Interwar Women's Homemaking Magazines', *The Journal of Modern Periodical Studies* 13, no. 1 (2022): 134.

22 Jessica Kelly, *No More Giants: J. M. Richards, Modernism and The Architectural Review* (Manchester: Manchester University Press, 2022): 14.

23 Sarah Williams Goldhagen, 'Something to Talk about: Modernism, Discourse, Style', *Journal of the Society of Architectural Historians* 64, no. 2 (2005): 144.

24 John D. Clarke, 'An Unusual Country House', *Good Housekeeping*, February 1927, 27.

25 G. Bryant Hobbs, 'Buying an Estate House', *Good Housekeeping*, January 1934, 36–37, 115.

26 J. Fernley Rivington, 'A Home for To-day and To-morrow', *Good Housekeeping*, August 1934, 28–29, 113.

27 W. F. Crittal, 'Experimenting with the Minimum Home', *Good Housekeeping*, January 1934, 40–41, 116.

28 James-Chakraborty, 'Expanding Agency', 162.

29 Sidney Dark, 'Why Women Should do the Dull Work', *Good Housekeeping*, March 1928, 10.

30 For example Katharine Tynan, 'Family Life in Germany To-Day', *Good Housekeeping*, January 1923, 17; Lilian T. Mowrer, 'Housekeeping through Europe', *Good Housekeeping*, November 1938, 11, 84; Marion Cran, 'Let's Fly to Kenya!', *Good Housekeeping*, June 1937, 18–19, 119; Constance Malleson, 'Through Lapland by Electric Train', *Good Housekeeping*, July 1937, 28–29, 108.

31 Lt Commander the Hon J. M. Kenworthy MP, 'Women and Peace', *Good Housekeeping*, April 1929, 13.

32 Beatrice Kean Seymour, 'Modern Girls WANT to Work', *Good Housekeeping*, September 1933, 10–11, 100; Ellen Dorothy Abb, 'Careers from Abroad', *Good Housekeeping*, April 1936, 218; Vera Brittain, 'Why I think Mothers can have Careers', *Good Housekeeping*, April 1930, 55.

33 For example: Oliver Burkeman, 'Dirty secret: why is there still a housework gender gap?', *The Guardian*, 17 February 2018, accessed 19 September 2024, https://www.theguardian.com/inequality/2018/feb/17/dirty-secret-why-housework-gender-gap, Mark Easton, 'Women still do more housework, survey suggests', *BBC*, 21 September 2023, accessed 19 September 2024, https://www.bbc.co.uk/news/uk-66866879.

34 For analysis on the middle-class readership of *Good Housekeeping* in contrast to the working-class readership of *Modern Home* magazine and their national versus international outlooks, *see* Alice Wood, 'Housekeeping, Citizenship, and Nationhood in Good Housekeeping and Modern Home', in *Women's Periodicals and Print Culture in Britain, 1918–1939: The Interwar Period*, ed. Catherine Clay, Maria DiCenzo, Barbara Green and Fiona Hackney (Edinburgh: Edinburgh University Press, 2018), 210–224.

35 Fiona Hackney, 'Women are News: British Women's Magazines 1919–1939', in *Transatlantic Print Culture, 1880–1940: Emerging Media, Emerging Modernism*, ed. Ann Ardis and Patrick Collier (Basingstoke: Palgrave Macmillan, 2008), 116.

36 Margaret Lane, 'Woman: Where She Stands Today, What She Has Paid, Was It Worth It?', *Woman*, June 1927, 7.

37 Lt Commander the Hon J. M. Kenworthy MP, 'What is the Future of Women?', *Good Housekeeping*, April 1930, 16–17, 112.

# Chapter 6
# 'A Live Career for Women'
## Building Homes for the Working Class in Interwar Britain

*Alexandra Quantrill*

In a 1931 talk on 'Professions for Women', Virginia Woolf famously described how she first had to kill 'the Angel in the House' – the embodiment of feminine grace and compliance – in order to develop an autonomous creative voice.[1] Exhorting women to vanquish the phantom angels impeding their professional growth, Woolf conjured a metaphorical house to be reimagined and reclaimed:

> You have won rooms of your own in the house hitherto exclusively owned by men [...] the room is your own, but it is still bare. It has to be furnished; it has to be decorated; it has to be shared. With whom are you going to share it, and upon what terms?[2]

According to Woolf women would only break free of docile domesticity by first owning the house – or winning financial freedom – and then shaping it into a liberatory space in order to dictate the terms for their professional lives.

At the time, Mrs. Laura Annie Willson, frequently described as Britain's first woman home builder, had been performing a similar act of conflating, and then inverting, women's domestic and professional roles (Fig. 6.1). A non-expert who learned the craft of construction and the business of development on the job, Willson showed how building and housing offered fruitful career paths for women at a time when their aptitude for commercial and technical work was largely dismissed.

Acutely aware of financial obstacles facing women, Willson had begun work at age ten as a half-timer in a textile mill, becoming a full-timer at thirteen, and continuing until she married the owner of a lathe workshop outside Halifax. She was a suffragist, even going to prison for the cause, and fought to establish labour rights for female textile workers. During the First World War, Willson oversaw seventy women employed on

THE VOTE.
JAN. 1, 1926.

# EQUAL FRANCHISE THIS YEAR!

# THE VOTE

## THE ORGAN OF THE WOMEN'S FREEDOM LEAGUE.

NON-PARTY.

VOL. XXVII. No. 845. (Registered at the G.P.O.) ONE PENNY. FRIDAY, JANUARY 1, 1926.

**OBJECT:** To secure for Women the Parliamentary vote as it is or may be granted to men; to use the powers already obtained to elect women in Parliament, and upon other public bodies, for the purpose of establishing equality of rights and opportunities between the sexes, and to promote the social and industrial well-being of the community.

PRINCIPAL CONTENTS.

A WOMAN HOUSING ENGINEER. Mrs. G. H. Willson, M.B.E.
WOMEN AT HOME AND ABROAD.
QUEEN ALEXANDRA'S MEMORIAL.
NATIONAL UNION OF WOMEN TEACHERS.
EQUAL FRANCHISE THIS YEAR!
CRIMES AGAINST CHILDREN.
ANOTHER RAILWAY OUTRAGE!
BOOK REVIEWS. D. M. N.

## A WOMAN HOUSING ENGINEER.

MRS. G. H. WILLSON, M.B.E.

Mrs. Willson is the new President of that extraordinarily active concern the Women's Engineering Society. Her career began at the early age of ten, when she entered a textile factory as a "half-timer." She soon became interested in the Trade Union Movement, and its efforts to obtain better conditions for women in industry, and later she identified herself very completely with the most active phases of the struggle for woman's suffrage.

Her marriage with the head of a well-known firm of lathe makers provided her with still wider scope for her energies, for during the war she took over the entire charge of the women's work in her husband's factory. For this work Mrs. Willson was awarded the M.B.E., and she is justly proud of the fact that her name appeared in the very first list of the Order of the British Empire, containing the names of women recommended by the Ministry of Munitions. At the close of the war, in 1918, she became one of the earliest members of the newly founded Women's Engineering Society.

Since the war Mrs. Willson has devoted her abundant energy to housebuilding, with special reference to the labour-saving aspects of the homes she is putting up. Some of these houses, in fact, are more or less demonstration houses for electrical apparatus, and it is possible that others will be devoted to the latest developments in gas appliances.

MRS. G. H. WILLSON, M.B.E.

The housing scheme with which she is principally occupied at the moment is in Yorkshire, on the outskirts of Halifax. Though the scheme was not discussed with her contractors until July 22nd of last year, some of the houses were nevertheless ready for occupation by the end of November, and many more will soon be ready for occupation. Mrs. Willson's plan is for 64 houses, built 600 feet above sea level on a crescent, with communal greens for bowling, tennis, etc. Each house has a living-room, scullery, pantry, coals, and bathroom on the ground floor, and three bedrooms upstairs, and can be bought for the astonishingly small price of £400. Mrs. Willson is no great believer in the various modern building substitutes. She prefers to deal with Accrington brick materials that have already stood the test of time, with slate tiles, and good stout timber. She has also devised the most attractive hearths in her houses, because she knows how dear these are to the heart of every Yorkshire woman.



Figure 6.1: 'A Woman Housing Engineer, Mrs. G. H. Willson, M.B.E.', *The Vote: The Organ of the Women's Freedom League* 27, no. 845 (January 1, 1926): cover. Courtesy of Carnegie Library.

munitions production in her husband's factory.[3] Around 1922, however, she left industry to become a speculative builder of houses.

While she lacked professional qualifications, Willson actively participated in debates over housing and industry, shrewdly combining the objectives of commerce with the needs of working housewives. Like many women of that era, she never seriously challenged the domestic role they had been assigned. In *Women's Work in Modern England* (1928), feminist Vera Brittain cited Willson for her advances in engineering and housing, adding that her parallel roles as businesswoman, wife, and mother only strengthened arguments for women's professional capacity, since a married housewife posed no threat to the social order.[4] Despite encouraging women to engage in a range of jobs, from ship captains to engineers, Willson was equivocal in her assertion, 'We do not want to be feminists and talk too much about what we have done, but I ask you the question, "Are our women duds?" and I am not afraid of the answer'.[5]

Unlike Woolf, who had an independent income, women like Willson could not operate in 'a room of one's own'. She required investors, planning agreement, and willing consumers to establish her company, and lamented she 'would build houses in every county in England', if only she had the resources.[6] What might the scarce evidence on Willson's work tell us about modernisation, housing, and women's role in the political economy of interwar Britain?

## HOUSING, C. 1920S

The creation of affordable housing was vital to Britain's reconstruction in the aftermath of the Great War. In recognition of women's increasing political power as well as their domestic knowledge, a Women's Housing Sub-Committee (WHSC) was formed in 1917 to advise the Ministry of Reconstruction and the Local Government Board (LGC) in charge of administering housing guidelines.[7] The sub-committee included several Women's Labour League members, including Chief Woman Officer of the Labour Party Dr Marion Phillips, and architect Averil D. Sanderson Furniss, who had begun an inquiry into working-class homes.[8] Their findings, compiled in a 1918 Women's Labour League pamphlet, *The Working Woman's House*, described a typical home with only one room for cooking, dining, and bathing, and no hot water. The pamphlet included detailed architectural plans for comfortable cottages with 'good working conditions' to ease working-class women's domestic burden and household expenses. Following Women's Labour League guidelines, the WHSC recommended houses with three bedrooms, a bathroom with hot and cold running water, scullery for food preparation, living room, and a separate parlour for recreation.[9] The 1919 Housing Act proposed newly built communities of single-family houses that adhered to the garden city principles laid out by Raymond Unwin, chief architect to the Ministry of Health, and incorporated all of the WHSC's suggestions except for the parlour, which the all-male Housing Committee dismissed as a middle-class pretension.[10]

Like their Women's Labour League pamphlet, Phillips and Sanderson Furniss's 1919 book, *The Working Woman's House*, foregrounded the perspectives of working-class women, attempting to redress the fact that architects employed by 'well-to-do' families incorporated the suggestions of both husbands and wives, whereas the 'the working woman, to whom it is so infinitely important to secure a comfortable and convenient home, has never been consulted at all'.[11] Along these lines, *The Woman in the Little House*, a 1922 book by journalist Leonora Eyles, imagined how women would solve the housing problem. Describing the daily life of a typical working-class woman living in cramped accommodations, Eyles wrote: 'There are many things Mrs. Britain would ask for if a clever woman architect came to her with plans and plots [...]' She laid out a list of demands including efficient planning to avoid women having to carry bedroom slops through the living room, ample cupboards to keep spaces clear, and central heating to reduce coal consumption, which produced smoky, dust-filled interiors. Defying the notion that the poor were unwashed and slovenly, Eyles's Mrs Britain also requested a separate bathroom, as 'cleanliness is an acquired taste following on civilization – if it were more accessible it would be more general'. Not simply aimed at efficiency, these architectural interventions were to improve the quality of life, creating 'room to live'. In her contribution to the housing debate, Eyles foregrounded the emotional lives and desires of the working class: 'If people are herded on top of each other, soul and body alike will grow stunted.'[12]

As women continued to weigh in on housing design, the discourse grew beyond spatial requirements to encompass questions of energy economy. Several WHSC members spoke at a conference on 'Labour Saving in the Home' held as part of the 1920 Daily Mail Ideal Home Exhibition. Discussions focused on design features like smooth surfaces and rounded corners to ease cleaning, and new technologies[13] A Miss Peel from the WHSC proposed kitchens scientifically planned along the lines of a 'modern, well-managed factory', to reduce the distance travelled in preparing a meal from 350 to 30 feet. The presenters, many of whom had helped to craft the 1919 Housing Act guidelines, framed housewives as overworked labourers lacking legal protection, and suggested that efficient layouts and scientific management principles would help them achieve the 8-hour workday limit already won by unions. Despite these demands, the conference itself positioned women's input on housing as good business for the builders and companies whose model homes and appliances filled the exhibition grounds where it was held.

This push and pull between public and private interests pervaded Britain's efforts to expand housing in the interwar years. While housing realised under the 1919 Act fell short of demand, additional government subsidies were granted to local authorities in 1924. These state funds facilitated the completion of one and a half million new homes in Britain during the 1920s and 30s, but another two and a half million were built with private money.[14] As much as public discourse shaped the design of interwar housing, therefore, its construction was largely the work of private developers.

## 'A HOMELY WOMAN'

The first woman elected to the National Federation of House Builders, Willson spotted a business opportunity in the need for working-class housing. As the new president of the Women's Engineering Society in 1926 she touted her savvy in construction, declaring there was 'no such thing as a housing problem, but a great boom in housing'.[15] By that time she had over 200 houses completed or underway in and around Halifax.[16] A year before she had hired an architect to design 64 houses 'of the working-class type' on a site across from her husband's factory, portraying this development as 'a small garden city', with houses arranged in a semicircular plan, and communal tennis courts, a bowling green, and croquet lawn positioned at its centre (Fig. 6.2).[17]

Willson described housing as 'very much a woman's question, [...] engineering of the domestic kind'. At the same time, she underscored her working-class background, and was described in the press as a 'homely woman'[18] who made sure the living room in each of her houses had an open hearth, 'dear to the heart of every Yorkshire woman'.[19] Interior layouts were configured to accommodate young couples of limited means,

Figure 6.2: Advertisement for 'Workmen's Houses' in Halifax by Laura Willson, *The Woman Engineer* 2, no. 5 (December 1925): cover, overleaf. IET Archives and WES.

with a front hall, living room, kitchen, larder, three bedrooms, and bathroom. Like many private builders, Willson excluded the coveted front parlour to save costs; a strict economy that disregarded the desires of working women, but enabled her to price the houses at £400, comparable to the cost of a new council house subsidised by the state.[20] Affordable construction, maintaining a strict bottom line, was also a selling point.

Amidst material and labour shortages in the years following the First World War, the British government imposed market restrictions on commonly used building components, and underwrote building experiments with new materials, such as the prefabricated timber and steel Weir houses.[21] Although she claimed to be 'keenly interested' in such explorations, Willson critiqued imposed restrictions slowing construction and 'keep[ing] stocks at the brickyard'.[22] Her homes used traditional materials like robust Lancashire Accrington 'engineering brick', and slate for the roofs.[23] Rebuffing complaints about intransigent tradesmen, she professed to be 'rather proud of [...] English bricklayer[s]', who had been 'mismanaged [...] or greatly slandered' in the past,[24] and claimed she had 'no ca'canny' in any of her workmen.[25]

While Willson resisted the homogenising tendencies of modernisation, and dismissed 'faddists' who created what she saw as 'monstrosities

[...] under the name of town planning',[26] she embraced new forms of energy that could reduce domestic labour.[27] Her Laurel Crescent scheme included 'demonstration houses for electrical apparatus' and 'the latest [...] gas appliances'. Willson fully furnished two houses to show how they could be outfitted for a frugal £100. In contrast to labour-saving fittings like tiled fireplaces for easy cleaning, she selected traditional fumed oak sideboards, mantelpieces with bevelled mirrors, and carpet and curtains to match the velvet sofas, for 'an air of comfortable elegance'.[28] These furnishings were more in line with typical working-class interiors, far from the austere forms of Margarete Schütte-Lihotzky's 1926 Frankfurt Kitchen, a visual language of efficiency that had yet to take hold in Britain.

Whereas Schütte-Lihotzky disparaged women for being 'remarkably uninterested in the new ideas', preferring 'old knick-knacks' and 'a snug and cozy home' to modern rationalised design, Willson catered to these predilections, marketing her houses as preserving traditional English forms. Schütte-Lihotzky presented her labour-saving kitchen as representing both functionalism and modern 'clarity and beauty' in its standardised construction, muted colours, and simple materials. Although she suggested that 'the not-too-distant future belongs to the electrical kitchen', she hesitated to incorporate electricity within her Frankfurt Kitchen design, suggesting it remained impractical for lower income families.[29] By comparison, Willson showed herself to be relatively progressive when it came to energy, if not modern aesthetics, when she developed a model electrical working-class home.

The principles of labour-saving evoked by both women derived from American home economist Christine Frederick. Schütte-Lihotzky attributed the spatial organisation of her Frankfurt Kitchen to the concepts set forth in Frederick's 1919 book, *Household Engineering: Scientific Management in the Home*. By early 1927, Frederick was well-known in England, although apparently more for her promotion of electricity than for her work on efficiency through spatial design. Vera Brittain described a London lecture in which Frederick stated that 'the first step in the application of science to the home has been the installation of good electric lighting and heating systems'.[30] In 1927 Frederick addressed the Electrical Association for Women (EAW), dedicated to liberating housewives from domestic drudgery through electrification, and published an article in their journal in which she described the design of compact homes with efficient heating, water, and lighting systems, along with the installation of copious electrical appliances.[31] As president of the Women's Engineering Society

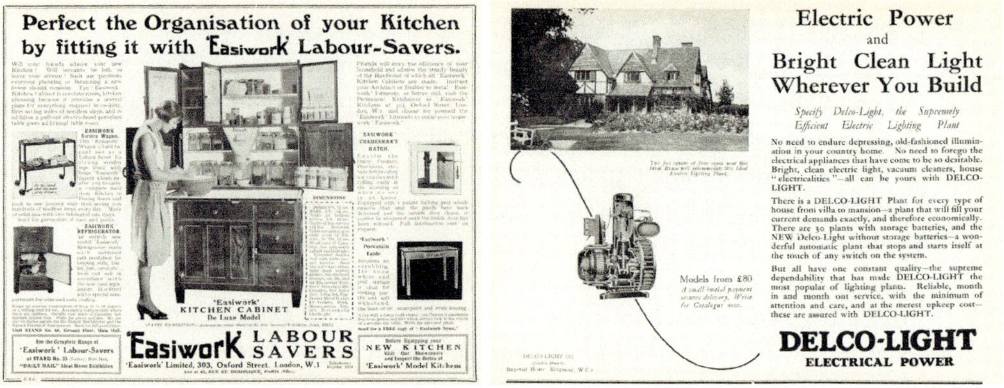


Figure 6.3: Advertisements for 'Easiwork Labour Savers' and 'Delco-Light Electrical Power'. *The Daily Mail Ideal Houses Book: Reproductions of the Best Designs Entered in the 'Daily Mail' Ideal Houses Competition for Architects, 1927.* (London: Associated Newspapers, 1927), xxx, xxxiii. Avery Classics, Avery Architectural & Fine Arts Library, Columbia University.

and a founding member of the EAW, Willson was undoubtedly aware of Frederick when she planned her own houses 'along labour-saving lines', although she focused more on the inclusion of appliances that would speed domestic tasks rather than on novel spatial layouts or materials. Drawing directly from the cottage plans outlined in the Housing Acts of 1919 and 1924, Willson deliberately chose materials typical of traditional Yorkshire cottages.[32]

Perhaps due to a uniquely British conservative mindset, the influence of scientific management on housing design was slow to take hold, leading to a strange aesthetic dichotomy in the late 1920s. This was evident in a 1927 Architects' Competition sponsored by the *Daily Mail*, which solicited designs for houses demonstrating principles of beauty, utility, and value for money, which could become models for builders and housing authorities. While the winning entries were all cottage revival or neo-Georgian style houses, the competition catalogue also included an article on 'Planning a Work-Saving Kitchen' by Canadian entrepreneur G.E.W. Crowe, who evoked principles of scientific management as she called for compact space planning incorporating her company's Easiwork storage units. This juxtaposition of modern systems and techniques with conventional forms is echoed in the catalogue's advertisement for a Delco-Light personal power plant next to the Tudor revival cottage it would serve (Fig. 6.3).[33]

## FINANCING DEVELOPMENT

Although she espoused traditional materials and aesthetics, Willson developed progressive financing models. Disparaging the state as 'a kind of wet nurse' for subsidising council-built rental homes, she urged private developers to compete by obtaining council subsidies, and posited that home ownership would improve the lives of working people: 'I do not think any apology is needed from those who build houses to sell [...], [t]here are people who have talked about the workman being a wage slave [...] yet they now want to make him into a permanent rent slave.'[34] For her 1926 estate in Luddenden Foot, Halifax, she secured a subsidy of £20 per house from the local council, allowing her to set a price of £380. With her husband's financial backing, she offered a second mortgage of £55 to buyers who put £25 down, enabling them to obtain a building society loan and repay her in weekly instalments over 21 years. Addressing the council, she denied any 'philanthropic motives' behind the payment scheme, confident that it would generate profit.[35]

In 1927 Willson moved her business to Englefield Green, in Surrey, embarking on a scheme of 210 brick houses of four types laid out with wide roads and green verges as an 'up-to-date garden village' (Fig. 6.4). She commissioned an architect to design homes for a typical lower-middle-class 'clerk who wants a charming house for his wife, who can run it in the least expensive manner'.[36] Photographs of a demonstration house (Fig. 6.5) show labour-saving gas heaters and appliances, with electric lighting. Houses were priced between £450 and £550, and Willson took £30 deposits from prospective buyers, the remainder to be paid in weekly rent.[37]

While she was 'constantly in and out of the houses' during construction, 'issu[ing] orders through the foreman [...]', Willson refused to go up on the roofs, blustering that '[h]igh finance, but not high building is my motto'.[38] In her view, women would be judged for their capacity to '[deal] with finance on a large scale'.[39] As they generated increasing revenue, society would begin to accept that, instead of robbing men of jobs, women could create new work. Vaunting the quarter of a million pounds her housing business earned in its first three years, she stated: 'I am proud to have played some little part in helping to make business a live career for women instead of a fad.'[40]

Figure 6.4: Willson Road, Englefield Green, Surrey, c. 1930. Credit: Chris Phillips.

Figure 6.5: Kitchen of Englefield Green demonstration home, Surrey. Promotional booklet, c. 1928. Private collection.

## ELECTRICITY AND MODERNISATION

When feminist author Winifred Holtby asked in 1934, 'Is There a Woman Problem?', she queried a widespread suspicion of women's 'right to earn', writing: 'The old dread of woman's magic power is added to the new dread of her industrial competition at lower wages.'[41] After the Pre-War Practices Act of 1919 pushed women out of industrial jobs they held during the First World War, many saw greater opportunity in newly developing industries like electricity, where there was less competition with men. In 1927 Willson joined Caroline Haslett and Margaret Partridge to establish Electrical Enterprises, a power company operated entirely by women. Spurred by the establishment of a national grid to expand distribution, they opened a generating plant in Suffolk, postulating that women were best equipped to convey electricity's 'domestic and hygienic' advantages to rural households.[42]

Haslett was director of the Electrical Association for Women and Partridge, an electrical engineer, was a founding member, along with Willson. The first major EAW campaign was to write a 'Women's Specification' for home builders, enumerating outlet provision to maximise the use of electrical appliances without cumbersome wiring. Unlike Haslett and Partridge, who remained unmarried, Willson stressed that her first-hand experience as a housewife and mother as well as a builder informed her work in shaping the specification.[43] At the time, Willson saw new market opportunities in electrified housing, and at a 1929 conference for builders and architects she presented her recent projects to illustrate how to put the Women's Specification into practice.[44] She had already embarked on a second Surrey estate in Walton-on-Thames, which included houses and bungalows, as well as the conversion of an existing mansion into six larger flats for families, and seventeen two-room flats for single occupants, presumably unmarried women.

Increasing numbers of so-called 'surplus women' in the aftermath of the Great War challenged a patriarchal property system centred on the nuclear family, prompting new forms of accommodation.[45] By the early 1930s, the EAW's magazine was advertising 'Bachelor Girl' flats with cheap electricity and amenities to ease single women's working lives. A 1930 article in the same journal featured Willson's Walton-on-Thames flats, for which she employed an electrical engineer and wiring contractor to help realise what was described as a 'practically [...] all-Electric' building.[46] She paid to electrically heat water for the building, contracting with the local

Figure 6.6: Magnet 'Minor' Cooker in a two-roomed flat for a single woman. 'A Woman Builder and Electricity', *Electrical Age for Women* 1, no. 16 (April 1930): 629. IET Archives.

electricity department to pay a fixed charge for all shared current. Each flat was given an electric cooker, and heating outlets in every room. Tenants paid for personal use through slot meters. Electricity was expensive, having not yet reached an economy of scale, so women were encouraged to control household energy budgets by tallying units of consumption, a managerial logic applied to energy use. Notwithstanding the cost, Willson extolled this new form of domestic energy; she professed to be 'charmed by the use of Electricity, and [...] using it freely' in a flat of her own.[47]

Looking closely at the tightly cropped photograph of an interior corner (Fig. 6.6), we see it centres on a small Magnet Minor cooker, on top of which sits a copper electric kettle, indicating this is a two-roomed flat for a single occupant. Mounted above the cooker is its control unit and socket, and a utilitarian fuse box issuing forth current through exposed wires. On the walls, papered in a leafy pattern, are two small framed pictures, hung awkwardly high. We see the edge of a simple wooden spindle chair atop a practical smooth, speckled floor covering. While this décor is clearly not modern in its sensibility, the article's emphasis on the novelty and efficiency of the electric fittings makes clear this interior was seen to represent *modernisation* in women's domestic lives. This fragmentary image of housing for single women by a female developer presents the compact utility of the electric cooker, with its clean white enamel door and prominent controls, as a stark contrast to coal-powered cast iron kitchen ranges: hot, heavy, and perpetually dusty. Connected to an electrical infrastructure just beginning to fan out across Britain, this single apparatus is rendered as both catalyst and symbol of extensive social and technological modernising processes.

Compare Willson's flat to one designed contemporaneously by architect Edna Mosley for the EAW (Fig. 6.7), as part of an exhibition dedicated to the lifestyle of the 'Bachelor Girl'. Intended to minimise domestic toil, freeing

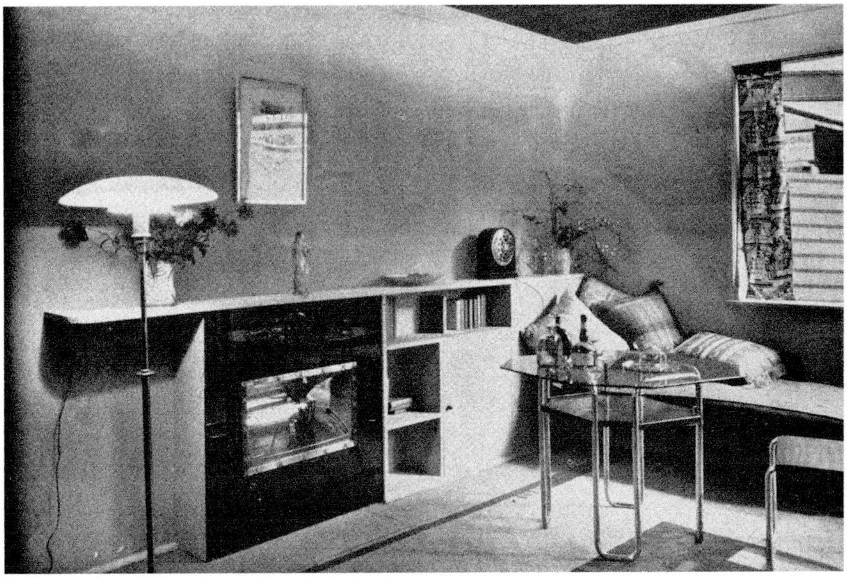

Figure 6.7: Bachelor Girl's Flat, Edna Mosley for the Electrical Association for Women, 1930. *The Decorative Art Journal* (1933): 55. RIBA Collections.

women to focus on professional pursuits, the flat incorporated copious electrical equipment: from a shiny chrome and glass fireplace, to thermostatically controlled heating, fridge, bed warmer, and radio. Mosely's spare design language of smooth planes and built-in furniture reinforced the depiction of electricity as propelling new forms of existence. Much like the efficient organisation of the Frankfurt Kitchen, Mosely's Bachelor Girl flat manifests a shift towards representing domestic electricity as integral to modern aesthetic ideals.

## A WOMAN WHO MEANT BUSINESS

By the early 1930s, just as modern design began to permeate British domestic interiors, Willson retired from building houses. For 'women who meant business', however, the question of how to reconcile their roles as domestic and economic producers remained. In Virginia Woolf's critique of patriarchal capitalism, *Three Guineas*, she bemoaned how women remained stuck between the hypocritical world of the private house and a professional sphere that paid them so little they stayed trapped under the dominion of husbands and fathers. 'The one shuts us up like slaves in a harem', she wrote, and 'the other forces us to circle, like caterpillars head to tail, round and round the mulberry tree, the sacred tree, of property'.[48] For Woolf, it was the British property system – as both dwelling place and economic structure – that continued to deny women independence.

By making property her business, fusing feminine domesticity with commercial development, Willson betrayed the ambiguity of these circular confines. While housing created professional opportunities for women, it limited them to domestic concerns, one of many paradoxes Willson negotiated. Even as she disavowed feminism, her career modelled economic autonomy – a critical focus for interwar progressive feminists like Brittain, Holtby, and Woolf. She created financing plans to enable working-class home ownership, although she only selectively adopted Labour women's demands. While she showed no interest in modern design, her embrace of electricity implied a radical transformation of the domestic interior. Piecing together evidentiary fragments, a picture emerges of a woman pushing against boundaries between masculine professional expertise and feminine domestic knowledge, technological development and cultural modernism, thereby exemplifying the complexities of women's role in modernising labour and housing in interwar Britain.

## ACKNOWLEDGMENT

The author would like to thank Anne Kirker, Nick Barber, the Surrey History Centre, and the Englefield Green Association for their invaluable assistance in her research.

## NOTES

1 Virginia Woolf, 'Professions for Women', in *The Death of the Moth and Other Essays* (New York: Harcourt Brace & Co., 1942), 237-38.

2 Ibid., 242.

3 'The Woman House Planner', *The Sphere*, 1 October 1927, 28.

4 Vera Brittain, *Women's Work in Modern England.* (London: Noel Douglas, 1928), 37-54.

5 'Woman Engineer Now Heads Firm, Not Afraid of Answer to Question "Are Women Duds"', *Montreal Daily Star*, 24 October 1928; 'Threat of Invasion into Mens Jobs', *Manchester Evening News*, 16 September 1927, 6.

6 'Woman Builder', *Daily News* [London], 15 February 1926, 5 noted that 'She considered it a great honour for a woman, who was born in humble circumstances, to have had the privilege of building homes for the people.' See also 'Woman Builder's Confession', *Leeds Mercury* (25 February 1927): 2.

7 Committee members were appointed by Christopher Addison, Minister of Health under the Ministry of Reconstruction, who saw the tides were turning when it came to women's political

involvement. After years of protests, some during the First World War, the Women's Suffrage clause of Representation of the People Bill received overwhelming support when it came before the House of Commons in June 1917, and, despite opposition in the House of Lords, was finally passed into law in February 1918. The WHSC advised the Local Government Board (LGC) in charge of administering housing guidelines.

8 Also on the WHSC was Maud Pember Reeves, who in 1913 published *Round about a Pound a Week*, documenting the life of working-class families sharing a 2-storey townhouse in South London. Each family had one living room and one bedroom. They shared a scullery and 'copper' to heat water on the ground floor, there was no running hot water in the house and no running water at all upstairs, so women had to carry water up and down stairs. The only source of heat for warmth and cooking was an open grate in the living room kept black with lead, and the WC was outside. See Matrix, *Making Space: Women and the Man-Made Environment* (Verso, 2022 [London: Pluto, 1984]), 29.

9 Marion Phillips, 'The Working Woman's House', *The Labour Woman* 6, no. 23 (March 1918): 7-8. *See also* Matrix, *Making Space*, 32, Deirdre Beddoe, *Back to Home and Duty: Women between the Wars*, 1918-1939 (London: Pandora, 1989), 89-91; and 'The Kind of House a Working Woman Wants', *The Labour Woman* 4, no. 20 (December 1917), 2. To complement their proposed layout, the women appealed for technologies to minimise toil, such as a gas stove and electric cooking appliances, which could quickly warm the parlour without the hassle of keeping a fire going. Cleaner electric light was preferable to gas in all spaces, and additional stipulations included wide windows facing south and south east to maximise light, set low to minimise curtain costs. Walls were to be painted with light colours and given rounded corners to ease cleaning. The report sought to minimise dangerous physical labour like carrying large tubs of hot water for bathing, cooking, or laundry, aiming to create opportunities for women's recreation.

10 Mark Swenarton, *Homes Fit for Heroes: The Politics and Architecture of Early State Housing in Britain* (London: Routledge, 2018), 92-109. Calling for the construction of 500,000 new houses and demonstrating how to materialize them, the Tudor Walters report became a guiding reference for the crafting of state housing policy, beginning with the Addison Act, passed in 1919 under the banner of 'Homes fit for Heroes'.

11 Marion Phillips and Sanderson Furniss, *The Working Women's Home* (London: Swarthmore Press, 1919), 10.

12 Margaret Leonora Eyles, *The Woman in the Little* House (London: G. Richards, 1922), 46-53.

13 *Women and Housing: Labour Saving in the Home; Report of a Conference of Women's Organisations Held at the 'Daily Mail' Ideal Home Exhibition, Olympia, London, on February 10th, 1920.* (The Garden Cities & Town Planning Association, 1920), 9-12. The exhibition displayed the winning entry of a design competition for the best labour-saving home, as well as concepts for various labour-saving devices. Alarm over 'the servant problem' was also used to bolster arguments for an electrified domestic sphere, which was presented as saving middle-class housewives from having to perform the labour of servants they could no longer afford.

14 Beddoe, *Back to Home and Duty*, 95-96. 213,000 houses were built under the Addison Act – a number far short of the projected need for a million new homes. A 1924 Wheatley Act funnelled state funds to subsidise local authorities, who were encouraged to build along the garden city principles proposed by Unwin and the WHSC. By 1932 the government abolished all building subsidies except for slum clearance. See also *The Housing Problem: A Statement of the Present Position* (Housing Sub-Committee of the Consultative Committee of Women's Organisations, July 1924).

15 'Women's Engineering Society Conference', *Common Cause* (17 September 1926): 298.

16 Len Chaloner, 'The New President of the Women's Engineering Society: A Glimpse of Mrs. Willson's Remarkable Career', *The Woman Engineer* 2, no. 5 (December 1925): 109. 'The first houses were built, between July and November 1925, with several more planned to be roofed before the cold of winter, usually a time of tribulations and setbacks to the prospective builder.' The first houses built in the Laurel Crescent development were already occupied by autumn 1926.

17 'Woman Builder', *Daily News* [London], 15 February 1926, 5. 'Bowling Green Open for Play', *Halifax Evening Courier*, 13 May 1929.

18 'Houses at £400 Apiece – A Woman Shows How to Do It – Director of Firm of Engineers – Ovendon Experiment to Help Newly-Weds', *Leeds Mercury*, 6 January 1926.

19 Len Chaloner, 'The New President of the Women's Engineering Society', 109. See also 'A Versatile Halifax Woman', *Yorkshire Evening Post*, 18 December 1925, 5, 'A Versatile Halifax Woman', *Yorkshire Evening Post* (18 December 1925): 5, and 'The Ideal Home', *Perthshire Advertiser* (20 January 1926): 17.

20 'Presidential Address by Mrs. L. A. Willson, M.B.E. (Delivered at Leeds University, September 3, 1926)', *The Woman Engineer* 2, no. 8 (September 1926): 153. 'Woman Builder', *Daily News* (London), 15 February 1926, 5.

21 A government Committee for Standardising New Methods of Construction was formed in 1920 to study alternative building materials and economies of labour. Chaired by Sir Ernest Moir, its research on alternative building materials and low-tech construction techniques to utilise unskilled labour became the basis for the formation of a Building Research Board with a demonstration site at Acton. The Ministry of Health declared alternative materials and construction methods would be 'interesting and instructive to those Councils whose schemes are being delayed through lack of bricklayers'. Quoted in Harry Harrison, Stephen Mullin, Barry Reaves and Alan Stevens, *Non-Traditional Houses: Identifying Non-Traditional Houses in the UK 1918-75* (Garston: Building Research Establishment, 2004), xiv. The Labour movement weighed in on these questions of materials and labour in party publications such as *The Labour Woman*, whose articles covered the lack of available builders and related issues.

22 'A Woman's Housing Scheme', *The Woman Engineer* 2, no. 4 [Special Number on the First International Conference of Women in Science, Industry, and Commerce] (September 1925): 100. Willson complained that 'a lot of time was being wasted talking about substitutes in the building trades'. Quoted in Len Chaloner, 'The New President of the Women's Engineering Society', 109.

23 'The Ideal Home', *Perthshire Advertiser*, 20 January 1926, 17. Accrington brick was produced in Lancashire.

24 'Presidential Address by Mrs. L. A. Willson, M.B.E. (Delivered at Leeds University, 3 September 1926)', *The Woman Engineer* 2, no. 8 (Sept 1926): 153.

25 'The Ideal Home', *Perthshire Advertiser*, 20 January 1926, 17.

26 'Presidential Address, Delivered at the Bristol University, September 21, 1928', *The Woman Engineer* 2, no. 16 (September-October 1928): 311.

27 Willson stated: 'The use of electrical appliances, the much more general use of electrical or gas ovens, as against coal ovens, makes for ease and comfort inside the home and leaves the town much less smoke laden'. 'Presidential Address by Mrs. L. A. Willson, M.B.E. (Delivered at Leeds University, September 3, 1926)', 152.

28 Len Chaloner, 'The New President of the Women's Engineering Society', 109. In the end, only one of Willson's Laurel Crescent houses was supplied with electric appliances, and one with gas.

29 Margarete Schütte-Lihotzky, 'Rationalization in the Household', trans. Don Reneau, in *The Weimar Republic Sourcebook*, ed. Anton Kaes, Martin Jay, Edward Dimendberg (University of California Press, 1994), 462-465. Schütte-Lihotzky's essay was first published as 'Rationalisierung im Haushalt', *Das neue Frankfurt*, no. 5 (1926-1927): 120-123.

30 Brittain, *Women's Work in Modern England*, 44-45.

31 Mrs. Christine Frederick, 'How The American Housewife Achieves Leisure Through Electricity', *Electrical Age for Women* 1, no. 3 (January 1927): 98-100.

32 'The Ideal Home', *Perthshire Advertiser*, 20 January 1926, 17.

33 *The Daily Mail ideal houses book: reproductions of the best designs entered in the 'Daily Mail' Ideal Houses Competition for Architects, 1927, together with designs of houses and a bungalow exhibited at the Ideal Home Exhibition at Olympia, 1927* (Associated Newspapers, 1927). See also Deborah S. Ryan, *The Ideal Home through the 20th Century* (London: Hazar, 2007).

34 'Presidential Address by Mrs. L.A. Willson, M.B.E. (Delivered at Leeds University, September 3, 1926)', *The Woman Engineer* 2, no. 8 (September 1926): 153-154; 'Presidential Address, Delivered at the Bristol University, September 21, 1928,' *The Woman Engineer* 2, no. 16 (September-October, 1928): 311.

35 'Warley Wood Housing, Mrs. Laura Willson Explains Her Scheme, Luddenden Foot In for a Good Thing', *Halifax Daily Courier and Guardian*, 15 April 1926, 7.

36 'The Woman House Planner', *The Sphere*, 1 October 1927, 28. Willson commissioned an architect to design the houses.

37 'The President's New Housing Scheme', *The Woman Engineer* 2, no. 10, (March 1927): 193.

38 'New Careers for Women', *Halifax Evening Courier*, 16 September 1927: 8. Her husband provided financial support and acted as masonry and plastering contractor.

39 'Presidential Address', *The Woman Engineer* 2, no. 12 (September 1927): 232.

40 'Presidential Address, Delivered at the Bristol University, September 21, 1928', *The Woman Engineer* 2, no. 16 (September-October, 1928): 312.

41 Winifred Holtby, *Women* (London: John Lane the Bodley Head, 1934), 7, 188-189.

42 'Electrifying the Country Areas', *Halifax Evening Courier*, 8 September 1927; 'Women Deal with Electrical Distribution', *North Mail and Newcastle Chronicle*, September 8, 1927, 3; and 'Electrical Enterprise, Ltd.', *The Woman Engineer* 2, no. 12 (September 1927): 248.

43 Haslett appears to have been dedicated to her career above marriage, while Partridge lived for years with engineer Margaret Rowbotham, who had worked with her in Electrical Enterprises.

44 Peggy Scott, *An Electrical Adventure* (London: Jas. Truscott & Sons, Ltd., 1934): 45. See also *Electrical Age for Women* 1, no. 12 (April 1929): 481.

45 Holtby wrote that one condition of women's equality would be what she termed 'greater elasticity in domestic organization', encompassing co-operative arrangements of housing and work to allow single women, married women, and men, to share the burden of household labour. Holtby, *Women*, 191.

46 'A Woman Builder and Electricity', *Electrical Age for Women* 1, No. 16 (April 1930): 629.

47 Ibid.

48 Virginia Woolf, *Three Guineas* (New York: Harcourt, Brace and Company, 1938): 90.

## Chapter 7

# Not Her Mother's Suburb

## Women in American Real Estate and Their Promotion of Modern Architecture in the Mid-Twentieth Century

*Mary Anne Hunting and Kevin D. Murphy*

Since the nineteenth century, the American home has been widely recognised as the domain of women. Paradoxically, this fundamental association also enabled women to emancipate themselves from their homes for careers in a variety of fields, including real estate and development. Though historian Jeffrey M. Hornstein examined how American women came to dominate real estate sales in *A Nation of Realtors: A Cultural History of the Twentieth-Century American Middle Class* (2005), less is known about their role in residential suburban development.[1] Women did, in fact, take a variety of roles in the process, ranging from architect and landowner to activist and developer or a combination of these. In some instances, women also provided the crucial funding to create 'radical suburbs', as historian Amanda Kolson Hurley calls them since suburbanisation is grounded on progressive social and environmental principles.[2] In this chapter, we examine the stories of several women who – alone or with partners – contributed to a modernist approach to real estate development in the United States. We argue that male participants in the planning of progressive residential neighbourhoods have overshadowed the crucial roles carried out by women in real estate who participated by means of money, social clout, organisational skill, and an historic affiliation with the concept of home.

Several women were active professionally in the city of Boston and its surroundings, a centre of the Progressive Movement in the early twentieth century. Women architects trained at the all-women's Cambridge School of Architecture and Landscape Architecture between 1916–42, as well as at the Massachusetts Institute of Technology and elsewhere, formed strong networks through which they influenced the shape of contemporary building. Though not professionally trained, Amelia Peabody (1890–1984),

Figure 7.1: Helen Osborne Storrow at Pine Tree Camp, Plymouth, Massachusetts, 1934. Records of the Massachusetts Girl Scouts, Schlesinger Library, Radcliffe Institute.

Olga Monks Pertzoff (1911–80), and Helen Osborne Storrow (1864–1944), all of whom lived in the fashionable Back Bay neighbourhood, made an impact as they applied portions of their family fortunes to construct modern dwellings. Amelia Peabody used the inheritance from her family of financiers to commission the Cambridge School-trained architect Eleanor Agnes Raymond (1887–1989) to design residential and farm buildings on her estate in Dover, Massachusetts; Olga Monks Pertzoff funded the purchase of property in Lincoln, Massachusetts, for her husband, Constantin Alexander Pertzoff to subdivide for modern house construction; and Osborne Storrow (Fig. 7.1) underwrote the construction of five residences, three of them designed by émigré modernist architects Walter Gropius and Marcel Lajos Breuer, on the subdivision she laid out on her Lincoln farm (Fig. 7.2).

While these projects feature significant examples of modern architecture, they also demonstrate the varied ways or degree to which women

Figure 7.2: Site plan of the Woods End Road Historic District in Lincoln, Massachusetts, showing the location of the houses built on the property of Helen Osborne Storrow.

could be involved in residential development. Peabody, for example, did not subdivide her property for modern house development but nonetheless provided a model for women developers. Given Raymond's potent network of Cambridge School graduates and students, the multiple structures she designed for Peabody in Dover from the 1930s through the 1970s may well have exerted an important influence on others that followed, in which women of Peabody's class similarly provided the means for a modern suburban idiom to emerge. Her peers would have noted how bold Peabody was as a patron who provided the land and capital for an ambitious modern architect to introduce New England to a largely unfamiliar idiom.

Women in real estate development drew upon the late nineteenth-century effort to make residential architecture more plentiful and efficient, something historian Dolores Hayden famously dubbed 'material feminism'.[3] Subsequent generations benefitted from a heightened consciousness of domestic design and functionality brought about by the Better Homes of America campaign, begun in 1922 to promote home ownership, modernisation, and beautification. Marie Mattingly Meloney (1876–1943), editor of the women's magazine *The Delineator*, initiated the concept, even though not long afterwards the secretary of commerce, Herbert Hoover formalised the program as an educational foundation in Washington, DC and gave the executive director position to James Ford, an

Figure 7.3: Watercolour drawing of a proposed development in Belmont, Massachusetts, completed in 1942 at the Cambridge School of Architecture and Landscape Architecture (1916–42) by Suzanne Marjorie Stockard (1917–2001), Marjorie Elizabeth Robbers (1919–2008), and Jeannie Patrie Allinson (1918–2006). Private collection.

associate professor of sociology at Harvard University. Mattingly Meloney was marginalised by the professionalisation of housing reform, if not sexism, when she simultaneously transitioned into an advisory role, but she remained a leader in resolving what was becoming one of the most critical issues of the day.

From at least the 1930s through the immediate postwar period, new business facilities and residential neighbourhoods on the East Coast began to occupy former farmland due to government investments in regional highway and public transportation systems that made it more feasible to commute between a city and a suburb. For many of the women who contributed to suburban real estate development, Modernism in residential architecture was viewed as more than a style that could be used to distinguish one development from another. Rather, it provided a progressive approach to planning by taking into consideration domestic living arrangements, social engagements, community amenities, building preservation, land conservation, and more.

Many women were introduced to housing design as students when between the two world wars architecture schools gradually introduced it into their curricula. As the work of the Cambridge School students

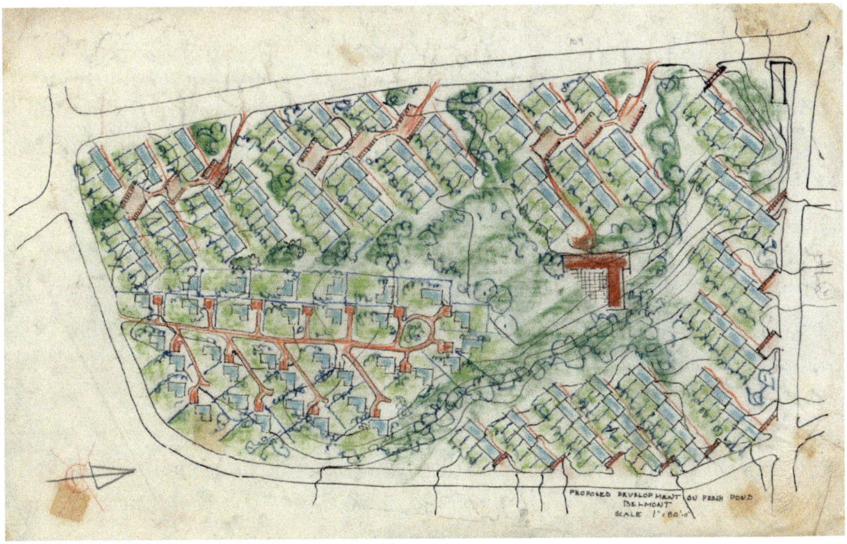


Figure 7.4: Watercolour drawing of a proposed development in Belmont, Massachusetts. Private collection.

demonstrates, women were especially trained to design modern suburban developments.[4] The proposed plan for a development on Fresh Pond in Belmont, Massachusetts (Fig. 7.3 and 7.4), a collaborative project of three of its students dating to 1942, illustrates their tactic by treating the housing and landscape as a single design problem, as they were taught to do by their instructors, some of whom were also Harvard faculty. Their drawings show popular contemporary features such as small lot sizes, each with private green space; detached and semi-detached houses (presumably with labour- and time-saving equipment); and cul-de-sacs for privacy and safety. Many of these planning concepts became central features of the suburban developments distinguished by their modern architecture from the Boston area's many other contemporary bedroom communities where traditional New England architecture predominated.

## THE SUBURB AS A LIVING ORGANISM

Following their graduation, some continued to be engaged in modern suburban development. Frances Baxter Quarton (1918–2017), who attended both the Cambridge School and Harvard's Graduate School of Design (GSD), partnered with the Columbia and Harvard-trained architect Constantin

Pertzoff to create two neighbourhoods on, respectively, Woodcock Road and on Twin Pond Lane, in Lincoln, a fifteen-square-mile town with a notable colonial history. Interestingly, the developments were funded not by a man, as was customary, but by Olga Monks Pertzoff, a descendant of the well-heeled Gardner family in Boston and, more specifically, a niece of the famed art collector and patron Isabella Stewart Gardner (1840–1924). Cultural philanthropy was a socially acceptable arena through which affluent women could have an impact on their communities. Although the breadth of Gardner's art patronage was exceptional, she undoubtedly served as an important model for other women who sought to use their wealth to enrich the Boston area. Accordingly, Monks Pertzoff chose to patronise the arts by staging concerts and theatrical performances at the couple's Lincoln home. Yet she had an entrepreneurial spirit as well, evidenced by her financial role in the developments for which her husband and Baxter Quarton designed modern suburban homes.

In planning their two small developments, Baxter Quarton and Pertzoff relied on the traditional New England town as a touchstone. An article that appeared in *Architectural Forum* in 1944, of which Pertzoff is a co-author, argues that an '*urban community is a living organism*'. Unlike the historic seaports of Portsmouth, New Hampshire, and Marblehead, Massachusetts, for instance, where narrow streets and densely positioned houses facilitated social interaction, large contemporary cities, the authors maintained, were overwhelmed by automobile traffic and were 'discouragingly impersonal'. They suggested that cities be broken down into small social units so that each could be more manageable and have a recognisable identity.[5] The plan of the Twin Pond Lane subdivision reflects these ideas in that fourteen modest plots, as well as the nearby pond and recreation area, are accessed from this primary artery while the automobile traffic flow is isolated on the perimeter (Fig. 7.5). Correspondingly, the house designs by Baxter Quarton and Pertzoff are relatively small so that they fit neatly into and coalesce with the natural landscape. The one they designed in 1963 for Lowell and Florence Scott Hollingsworth is situated at the top of a steep site so that the rear façade could be three-stories high (instead of two) to accommodate a 400-square-foot studio for silversmith Scott Hollingsworth in a daylit basement as well as a spacious screened porch on the top floor overlooking the preserved wooded property and pond (Fig. 7.6).[6]

Such projects expanded on earlier developments for which women had principal responsibilities. An important example is the Mariemont (1920–26) development, 'a demonstration of far-sighted town planning

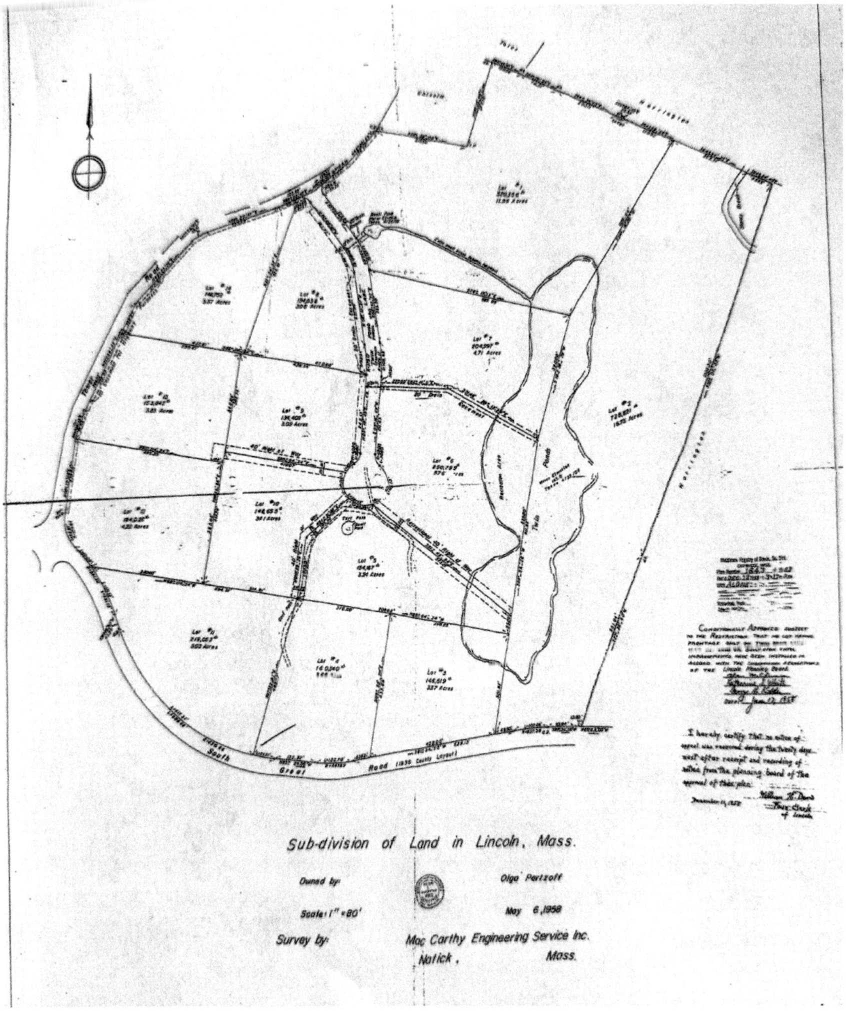


Figure 7.5: Plot plan of the Twin Pond Lane development in Lincoln, Massachusetts, funded by Olga Monks Pertzoff (1911–80) and planned by Constantin Alexander Pertzoff (1899–1970) and Frances Baxter Quarton (1918–2017), 6 May 1958. Photograph courtesy of the Town of Lincoln Building Department.

and good housing', according to its master planner, John Nolen. Located on 365 acres about ten miles outside of Cincinnati, Ohio, Mariemont was conceived by Mary Hopkins Emery (1844–1927) and financed with her inheritance from her husband, an industrialist and real estate developer.[7] The *Women's Journal* insisted that this ambitious 'woman's project' represents the responsibility that women "*must*' take in town

Figure 7.6: House for Lowell M. and Florence Scott Hollingsworth, 18 Twin Pond Lane, Frances Baxter Quarton and Constantin Pertzoff, Lincoln, Massachusetts, 1963. Photograph courtesy of the Town of Lincoln Building Department.

planning. Even so, of the twenty-six firms invited to provide architecture designs, only one was composed of women – the Boston firm of Eleanor Manning (O'Connor; 1884–1973) and Lois Howe (1864–1964). Nonetheless, the Mariemont project provided a unique opportunity to give coherence to suburban developments in contrast to communities that looked as if there was no planning at all, a criticism made by James Ford a decade later: Still in 1933 he contends

> that suburbs had developed in an unguided and unintelligent manner to the point where the vacant land in the outskirts of our large cities is already laid out according to fixed and, unfortunately, usually inappropriate plans. For the protection of our future suburban dwellers from ugly and inconvenient land-planning, the trend for the future in the field of land subdivision should be in the direction of increased social control and should involve legally authorised and scientific re-planning of residential areas already plotted.[8]

## A DEVELOPMENT OF MODERN ICONS

The 'social control' to which Ford refers was built into the subdivisions spearheaded, at least in part, by women amenable to modern architecture. Although there is no evidence that Olga Monks Pertzoff was acquainted with Helen Osborne Storrow, they came from the same social milieu and their families had Boston townhouses near one another. Their respective subdevelopments in Lincoln benefitted from both their connections and also the progressive ideas to which the two women had been exposed. Osborne Storrow's project, today known as the Woods End Road Historic District, resulted from a convergence of her interests in social reform, craftsmanship, and building spaces. Raised in the Victorian era in Auburn, New York, Osborne Storrow was apparently not offered an opportunity for higher education. She was, however, reared by a family with extensive reformist interests: her great-grand parents on her mother's side were abolitionists and their home was a stop on the Underground Railroad; her grandmother, Martha Coffin Wright (1806–75) and great aunt, Lucretia Coffin Mott (1793–1880), as well as her mother, Eliza Wright Osborne (1829–1911) were avid and influential suffragists.[9]

Osborne Storrow had no experience in modern design but used her inheritance from her industrialist father as well as from her husband, James Jackson Storrow, a financier who died in 1926, to support progressive causes. Influenced by the national settlement house movement, she joined the board of the North Bennett Street Industrial School (NBSIS) in 1898, which supported the Italian and Eastern European immigrant community in Boston's North End.[10] Her personal involvement increased as its reading room programme transitioned to local library clubs, many for the education and empowerment of women, including the Saturday Evening Girls Club (SEG) for which Osborne Storrow 'led folk-dancing classes, taught genteel behavior, and got to know the girls'.[11] When, in about 1908, the SEG started the Paul Revere Pottery, Osborne Storrow procured equipment and then funded two production facilities.[12]

Correspondingly, Osborne Storrow partook in the movement for domestic reform as president of the American Homemakers in Boston, which likely led to her chairmanship of the Massachusetts committee of Better Homes in America and a position on its board of directors. She also took a leading role in the Boston Home Information Center, founded in 1930 to provide expert advice, information, and instruction to homemakers.[13] These projects were complemented by her chairmanship role for the Home Department at the Eastern States Exposition in Springfield, Massachusetts. With the guidance of the Society for the Preservation of New England Antiquities (now Historic New England), between 1927 and 1938 she purchased and moved historic buildings to the exposition grounds to create a New England village with the assistance of preservation architect Joseph Everett Chandler.

Storrowton, as it later became known, was just one of many philanthropic projects Osborne Storrow undertook with a particular focus on providing spaces or buildings to charitable organisations. For instance, she acquired a townhouse at 18 Hull Street in Boston's North End for the Paul Revere Pottery. She also built camps and acquired buildings, both in New England and in Europe for the Girl Scouts, an organisation that became a central focus of her charitable giving and indeed of her life.[14] Osborne Storrow's interest in architecture had been kindled decades earlier, in 1883, when she spent the summer in France and Switzerland with her older brother Thomas Mott Osborne who had studied Gothic architecture at Harvard College, likely under Charles Eliot Norton. As Osborne Storrow recalled in the 1930s, 'At that time appreciation of Gothic architecture was not as common as it is now, but Tom had made a special study of it and had us about among the great cathedrals of the Isle [sic] de France with a sure feeling for all parts of their beauty as well as a detailed knowledge of their history'. She remembered, 'We climbed every tower'.[15]

Norton was close to artist and theorist John Ruskin, one of the principal proponents of the Arts and Crafts Movement whose writings enjoyed a large readership in the Unites States. Thomas Osborne likely served as the conduit from Ruskin and the British Arts and Crafts to Osborne Storrow whose house in Lincoln, completed in 1905 by Walter Thacher Winslow and Henry Forbes Bigelow, was inspired by contemporary domestic architecture in England.[16] The house was considered at the time as 'modern' and as 'simpler' than contemporary suburban houses in historic styles; nonetheless, it was traditional in its brick masses topped by steeply pitched roofs and in the symmetrical compositions of its front and rear elevations.[17] Craftsmanship was emphasised in its construction, for instance, in the use of ceramic tiles from the Moravian Pottery and Tile Works as well as in the green ceramic tile vaults made by the Guastavino Fireproof Construction Company.[18] Osborne Storrow continued to stay abreast of domestic reform movements, writing in 1931, 'There is reason to hope that within the next decade there will be a revolution in house building, home furnishing, and home life in America'.[19] Osborne Storrow expressed this sentiment in the context of an article in which she advocates for improved housing for African Americans through Better Homes of America, published in *Opportunity: A Journal of Negro Life*.[20] The article demonstrates that her commitment to progressive causes, especially through the lens of architecture and, more specifically, domestic architecture, continued into the Depression years.

As deep as her interest was, however, Osborne Storrow was unprepared for Modernism – at least in the form to which she was introduced to it by Gropius, who had recently arrived from Germany via London to teach at Harvard. In a letter to Gropius thanking him for the loan of a book on the subject – probably his own *The New Architecture and the Bauhaus*, published in English in 1935 – Osborne Storrow explained that his 'type of architecture' was 'startling' to her but that she nonetheless looked forward with great interest to having him build a house on her property – if he decided to do so.[21] Even though she was then a widow in her mid-seventies, Osborne Storrow did not waver from her commitment to advancing new design ideas and concepts despite there being few examples in New England. The so-called colony of houses for which Osborne Storrow provided the land and the capital was cohesive – both socially and artistically – even though the town of Lincoln was still a bastion of traditional architecture (see Fig. 7.2).[22]

To some extent, Osborne Storrow's project paralleled that of Amelia Peabody twenty miles away in Dover – another largely rural town dotted with historic houses. While Peabody made it possible for Raymond to design and build multiple buildings that remained in her ownership, Storrow extended the concept further by facilitating the work of multiple architects who could eventually purchase the homes.

The first house in Osborne Storrow's iconic project was designed by Gropius and Breuer for Gropius and his family at 68 Baker Bridge Road. Following its completion in 1938, Gropius and Breuer built two other modern houses on parcels adjacent to the Gropius house: a bachelor's 'studio-house' for Breuer at 5 Woods End Road and a house for James Ford and his second wife, Katherine Marrow Ford (1905–59), on the largest piece of property at 10 Woods End Road. A fourth house at 9 Woods End Road was designed by the architect Walter Francis Bogner, whose descendants still inhabit it.[23] A fifth house for John F. and Mary Loud, the latter a friend of Storrow's through their shared interest in English folk dancing, designed by the Cambridge School-trained architect Constance Mumford Warren (1903–87) at One Woods End Road, was Colonial Revival.

The Harvard professors – Gropius, Breuer, and Bogner – had already shown their familiarity with Modernism through their teaching: As chairman of the Department of Architecture at Harvard's GSD, which had been established in 1936, Gropius was leading a design studio for master's students in architecture. Both Breuer, who had studied under Gropius at the Bauhaus, and Bogner were associate professors in architecture there, while Bogner was also teaching at the Cambridge School, where he familiarised alumna and students alike (including Frances Baxter Quarton) with his own building process on Woods End Road. As an associate professor in sociology, Ford taught such topical courses as Community Organization and Urban Sociology, both relevant to regional planning. With his wife as the co-author, he had already published *Slums and Housing: History, Conditions, Policy* (1936). As the Ford house was being constructed, they were likely compiling their two other publications, both with multiple printings: *The Modern House in America* (1940) and *Design of Modern Interiors* (1942). Though Osborne Storrow had previously not known Gropius or Breuer, she did have a close working relationship with Ford through their affiliation with Better Homes in America.[24]

Despite Osborne Storrow's associations with leaders in the field of modern housing, her Woods End Road project has never been adequately acknowledged for what it truly is: an early, influential subdivision of modern architecture in the United States created by a highly capitalised developer. Osborne Storrow had agreed to subdivide about seven percent of her more than two-hundred-acre farm; finance the house construction; and lease it to the inhabitants at six percent of the construction costs (which continued until after her death in 1944 when the renters were given the option to buy their houses). She was recognised by a peer at the time for her interest 'in everything that is progressive and creative'; according to Gropius's second wife, Ilse Frank Gropius (1897–1983) she also believed that the newly arrived immigrants should be given a chance to demonstrate their talent.[25] In her monograph on Breuer, Isabelle Hyman states that the development was like a 'miniature *Siedlung*' perhaps conceived as 'an unconscious re-creation of European housing exhibitions wherein a tract of land was developed with modern houses.'[26]

While Hyman's analogy seems fitting, Osborne Storrow's project represents much more. First, it stemmed from a strong collaboration between the developer, architects, and inhabitants; second, it shows how social networks can play such a key role in development (allegedly, Henry Richardson Shepley, the Boston architect of another project Osborne Storrow had funded, introduced her to Gropius); and third, it promoted Modernism in the region as well as the architects themselves.[27] By associating the subdevelopment with contemporary German housing estates, Hyman de-emphasises the extent to which it grew out of earlier efforts made in the United States to lend spatial and architectural coherence to suburbanisation. Moreover, by calling it a 'miniature *Siedlung*', a German term closely associated with housing for the working and lower middle class, she implies that Gropius and Breuer were the sole inspiration and that Osborne Storrow with her combined experiences in social welfare, architecture patronage, and domestic modernity had not made an equal, if not more, meaningful contribution.

## POSTWAR MODERN DEVELOPMENTS

The group of modern houses in Lincoln attracted considerable critical attention and the concept of a stylistically coherent subdivision in which Modernism was the norm rather than an aberration gained a certain number of followers, although it never displaced the primacy of traditionally designed tract houses. Gropius and Breuer had tremendous influence on the next generation of modern architects, especially on their Harvard students, some of whom participated in the small movement of suburban developments that followed. The best known is Six Moon Hill in Lexington, Massachusetts, developed between 1947 and 1953 by Gropius's seven equal architect partners in the firm The Architects Collaborative (1945–95; TAC). The group intended to raise their own families on the twenty-acre, steeply sloped site chosen for its proximity to such local amenities as shops and schools as well as to both Cambridge and Boston. Their ideas for Six Moon Hill were emblematic in conception, design, operation, and proprietorship of the firm's organising precept of collaboration. Each property owner was entitled to two voting shares – so that spouses could vote separately but equally – in the nonprofit corporation that oversaw the property and infrastructure. Although the design of the houses was the responsibility of the owners, all of them had to pass a community planning board review.

Since Six Moon Hill was initially developed for personal use instead of speculation or on commission, the usual pattern of postwar residential development that prioritised profitability over respect for the land and for the composition of the community was averted. Thus, the prevailing model of development in most suburbs, whereby male developers employed architects to design houses was upended here. Although there

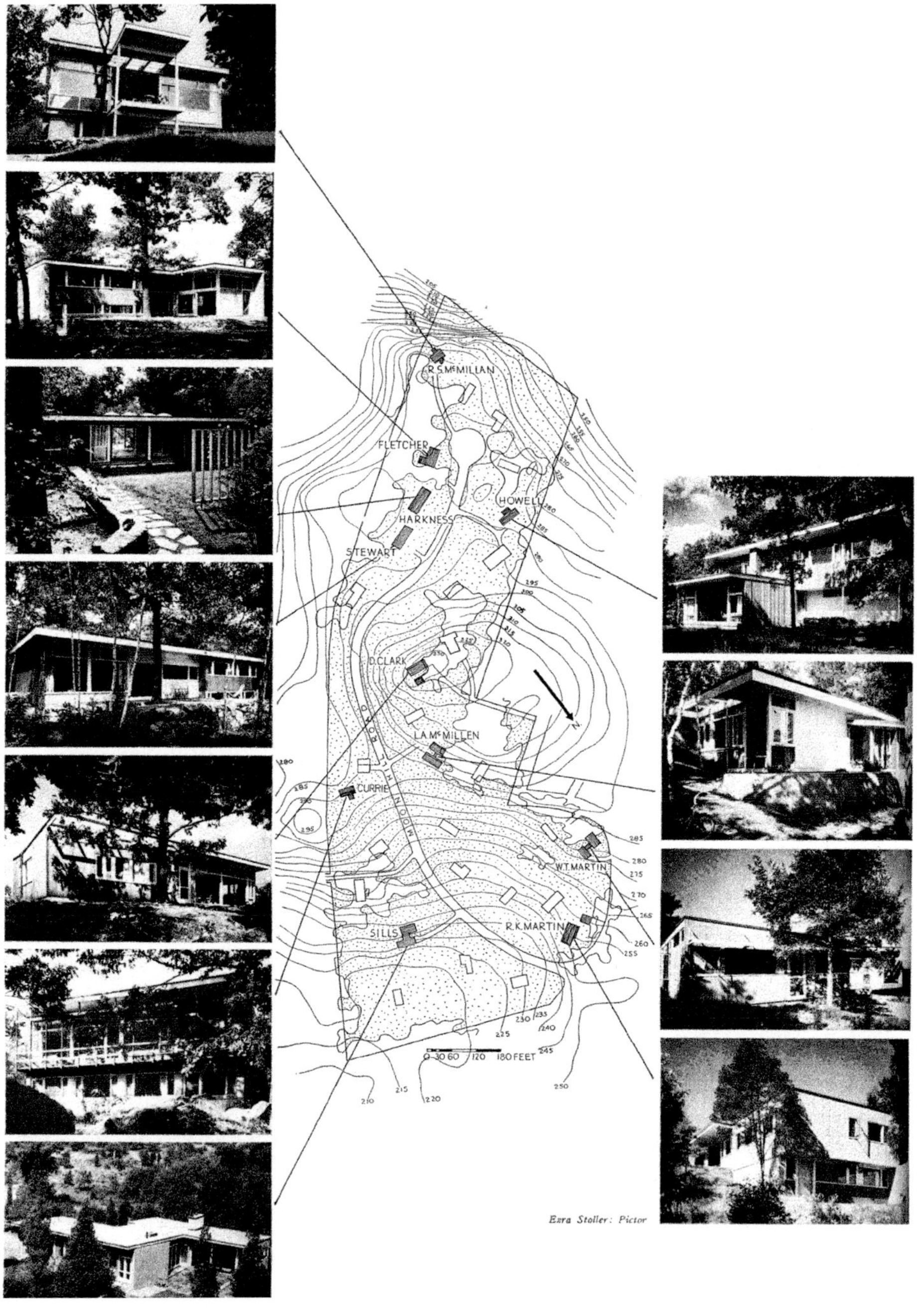


Figure 7.7: Site plan and houses in the Six Moon Hill development in Lexington, Massachusetts, designed by seven architect partners of The Architects Collaborative (1945–95), in 'Six Moon Hill', *Architectural Forum* 92, no. 6 (June 1950): 112.

was not a single progressive individual to provide the capital, as was the case in the Lincoln developments, Six Moon Hill was similar in that conventional suburban planning and architecture were avoided.

The relationship of the houses to their respective landscapes as well as to other homes was of vital importance (Fig. 7.7). The initial plan called for twenty-nine half-acre lots for individual houses as well as four acres of common land for recreation, including a swimming pool and tennis court, for shared use.[28] While every house was based on the distinctive needs of its occupants, all of them adhered to modern design principles. Much as in the development of Twin Pond Lane by Baxter Quarton and Pertzoff, the founding architect developers reluctantly integrated automobiles into the plan. 'We thought cars were the enemy', recalled Sarah Pillsbury Harkness (1914–2013), one of the two TAC architect wives who lived there.[29] As an unfortunate necessity, a single street runs through the centre of the property to provide access to each lot but ends in a cul-de-sac to reduce traffic through the neighbourhood. As a safe space for neighbourhood children, who at one point numbered nearly one hundred, the street was a place where adults could socialise spontaneously as well.

By 1950, nineteen houses had been erected at Six Moon Hill at a cost of between $10,000 and $22,000, in a period when according to the Census Bureau the average house in the United States cost about $7,000. The success of the development inspired the TAC architects to produce a larger group of sixty-eight houses in Lexington, Massachusetts, called Five Fields. They began planning the project in 1951 and within five years all the lots were sold.[30] The houses in Five Fields were not as distinctive as those at Six Moon Hill, in part because the architects were not designing for themselves, but for profit.

In contrast, the suburban development called Pepper Ridge, located in Pepper Pike just four miles outside Cleveland, Ohio, featured completely individualised houses. It was specifically planned in 1940 to attract young, educated, and cultured buyers with families who sought solutions to the environmental degradation and social isolation that suburbs often brought about. It grew out of collaborations with Robert and Ann Halle Little (1914–2012), who had studied architecture, respectively, at Harvard and at the Cambridge School.[31] Robert Little's association at Harvard with Gropius and Breuer led to an introduction to the Cleveland architect J. Byers Hays. Recognising their challenge in obtaining approval to build modern houses in a region where the chief developer, the Van Sweringen family, insisted on predictable revival styles, Hays in turn led the Littles to Frances Prindle Taft (1921–2017), an art historian, and husband Seth, a lawyer, politician, and grandson of President William Howard Taft. The Littles and the Tafts shared an interest in Modernism and together were determined to provide 'the things that seem desirable for a small community just beyond the noise and smell and traffic of a big city'.[32]

According to the original family members, Pepper Ridge became more than anyone initially envisioned. As Little recalled, they succeeded in composing a tight-knit community of 'some unstuffy people and their twenty-seven kids' living in a 'suburban Shangri-la'. No one was judged by race or religion but rather by their enthusiasm for living in a community based on planning principles outside the postwar norm.[33] The initial three families, including the Littles, who were related to the family that owned Cleveland's legendary Halle Brothers department store (1891–1982), purchased sixty-five-acres of farmland on a strip overlooking a deep river valley. The group was free to determine the landscape plan, the siting of the houses, and even the signage. They subdivided the property into twelve lots, varying in size from one to seven acres, depending on topographical and environmental dispositions with particular attention given to seasonal sunlight, breezes, and commanding views. They set back the lots from a primary road installed only after the individual parcels of land had been determined, they created small lakes to slow runoff, and they laid out meandering smaller roads to enhance the intimacy of family life (Fig. 7.8).[34] Likely with the input of his wife, Little designed eight of the eleven original houses, between 1941 and 1957, including their own, which helped promote the development as well as Little himself. As at Six Moon Hill, the houses designed by others were required to be reviewed for stylistic continuity by an architecture committee formed by the residents. Low-lying common land provided for neighbourhood recreation, including a swimming pool and tennis court.[35]

The Harvard-educated architects Edgar Hunter and his wife, Margaret King Hunter (1919–97) envisaged a smaller, though no less inspirational community in New Hampshire's White Mountains. Unlike the Littles, the Hunters formally established a professional partnership, in 1945, in Hanover, where, as an undergraduate Edgar Hunter had attended Dartmouth College. Though in 1948 they found a 'lovely' thirty-three-acre site with a panoramic view, neither could afford to develop it and so they convinced his older brother to purchase it.[36] As at Six Moon Hill, in Hanover the site was close to amenities but steeply sloped and potentially difficult to build on, which may have explained why it was available. The

Figure 7.8: Topographic map by Robert Andrews Little (1919–2005) of the Pepper Ridge subdivision he created with his wife, Ann Murphy Halle Little (1914–2012) and others in Pepper Pike, Ohio, c. 1950. Cleveland Architecture Foundation.

architect couple divided the property into five parcels, making site plans, laying out roads, and looking for congenial neighbours – all of whom, in the end, would be associated with Dartmouth.[37] The community design shared principles with the subdevelopments of the Harknesses and the Littles – whom they would have known at Harvard – including private, wooded home sites with views and a communal area for socialisation. According to the deed restrictions – a customary way at the time to ensure coherent, middle- or upper-middle-class enclaves – on each piece of property there could be only one domestic structure that cost no less than $5,000 (about $1,000 below the median price of a New Hampshire home in 1950).[38] The restrictions in the Hanover community did not stipulate that the houses be modern or that the Hunters design them, although the architect couple did design the first four.[39] An article in *Architectural Record* in November 1953 on the earliest houses and their plans illustrates how the Hunters took into consideration the siting as well as climatic conditions and how each home was modern in its flexible open plan and mostly vernacular materials.[40]

## A WOMAN AS DEVELOPER AND ARCHITECT

This blend of modern and traditional elements is commonly found in New England, including at the Gropius house where contemporary concepts and regional features and materials – such as a screened porch and wood siding – are combined. Such amalgams appealed to buyers in resort developments elsewhere, typically situated in rural communities with prevalent vernacular construction. Indeed. some developments adopted a hybrid modern and traditional aesthetic as their signature style, for instance at Eastman, a four-season White Mountains resort in Grantham, New Hampshire, where in the late 1960s developer Emil Hanslin insisted upon an architecture based on the traditional New England barn. He adapted the characteristic materials and open spatial experiences of the pre-modern barn to the production of contemporary vacation homes, all sited to conserve the wooded landscape. Hanslin had pioneered his planning concepts earlier in Massachusetts, at New Seabury on Cape Cod, where eleven villages were laid out on three thousand acres with the assistance of Pietro Belluschi, dean of architecture at MIT. There however, a variety of architectural styles were accepted – from Corbusian by Robert Damora to Colonial Revival by Royal Barry Wills.[41]

A woman rarely – if ever – designed, alone, all the houses in a particular development. An exception to this generalisation was possible when a woman acted as both developer and architect – another rarity. One example is that of Emily Stewart Lansingh Muir (1904–2003) who created a development and designed the houses for it in Downeast Maine, while Hanslin was working in New Hampshire. With postwar highway construction, second homes became increasingly common along the seacoast, even in such remote locations as Deer Isle, Maine, where the village of Stonington had once prospered through fishing and granite quarrying. After a bridge was constructed from the mainland in 1939, Deer Isle attracted more visitors, especially visual artists like Lansingh Muir, a painter.[42] Though lacking formal architecture training, she embarked on a small-scale practice that included a house and studio for her sculptor husband, William and her own painting practice.[43] Eventually, Lansingh Muir designed some forty-six houses on Deer Isle, thirteen of which were part of a development she laid out around Crockett Cove on a wooded parcel she purchased in 1959.[44] Explaining her intention, Lansingh Muir said that the houses 'turned out contemporary, but they're not copies of anything I ever saw. They're meant to fit the needs of the landscape'. Because they were frequently situated in wooded settings – as opposed to open fields, where original farmhouses still existed – she adopted a specific tactic of putting 'the drama' on the Penobscot Bay side.[45] Thus, soaring walls of glass face the water while wood siding and other 'friendly' materials flank the less prominent sides, complementing the modest vernacular dwellings she admired (Fig. 7.9).

Figure 7.9: House for Robert J. and Dorothy H. Ralston, 129 Barbour Farm Road, Emily Stewart Lansingh Muir (1904–2003), Stonington, Maine, 1968. Photograph by Maura McEvoy.

More than just acting as an architect, however, Lansingh Muir functioned, too, as a developer. Her capital, like that used by other women developers, undoubtedly came from her family since both parents had died a few years before she purchased the Crockett Cover property. Her father, Van Rensselaer Lansingh, an engineer who wrote and spoke widely on the use of lighting in commercial and residential spaces, was successful enough to purchase a cooperative apartment on Park Avenue in Manhattan in 1943; at about the same time, he acquired extensive property in Stonington.[46] His daughter is remembered for using her inheritance to introduce ideas about environmentally sensitive real estate development into coastal Maine, where highly prized oceanfront and ocean-view homes were more typically squeezed onto tiny lots. Furthermore, Lansingh Muir set aside a substantial portion of her Crockett Cove property as preserved open space with hiking trails. Even though she diminished the potential economic benefit for herself, she demonstrated that her goals as a developer were fundamentally different from those of her mostly male contemporaries.

Lansingh Muir was part of a cohort of women who received little credit for its influential role in real estate developments. The lack of attention paid to women entrepreneurs is evident, for example, in Hyman's monograph on Breuer, in which she opines that the Lincoln development 'was perhaps realizable in the United States at that time only in the climate created by [Joseph] Hudnut, Gropius, and Breuer at Harvard'.[47] The important contributions of the Harvard instructors are undeniable, but the role of Osborne Storrow in developing the property and financing the path-breaking work of her modernist tenants also deserves recognition, especially because it influenced a subsequent generations of architects and developers.

The receptive 'climate' for Modernism, particularly in the generally conservative field of homebuilding, was produced not only by men with positions in prominent cultural and educational institutions: Women who had the means to fund and manage the creation of residential enclaves featuring modern architecture also played a crucial role although they generally lacked institutional affiliations that could have made their efforts better known. Their work unfolded at a variety of scales: from the group of domestic buildings Amelia Peabody asked Eleanor Raymond to design to the larger neighbourhood of Six Moon Hill that the TAC architects laid out. While the female real estate broker gained ready acceptance, in part because the project was related to the home, her role of developer threatened to impinge on the male-dominated fields of real estate development as well as architecture, regional planning, engineering, and finance. Nevertheless, some wealthy and far-seeing women provided fundamental support for innovative community design as they used their talents and resources to facilitate the creation of modern places that were not their mother's suburbs.

## NOTES

1 Jeffrey M. Hornstein, *A Nation of Realtors: A Cultural History of the Twentieth-Century American Middle Class* (Durham: Duke University Press, 2005).

2 Amanda Kolson Hurley, *Radical Suburbs: Experimental Living on the Fringes of the American City* (Cleveland: Belt Publishing, 2019).

3 Dolores Hayden, *The Grand Domestic Revolution: A History of Feminist Designs for American Homes, Neighborhoods, and Cities* (Cambridge, MA: MIT Press, 1982).

4 Mary Anne Hunting and Kevin D. Murphy, *Women Architects at Work: Making American Modernism* (Princeton: Princeton University Press, 2025).

5 Hermann Herrey, Constantin Pertzoff and Erna M. J. Herrey, 'An Organic Theory of City Planning', *Architectural Forum* 80, no. 4 (April 1944): 133–40, quote at 133 (emphasis in the original).

6 Kay Sieverding, 'Lincoln Sells Historic Hollingsworth House', *Concord* [MA] *Journal*, 20 September 2012.

7 John Noland, 'Mariemont, Ohio – A New Town Built to Produce Local Happiness', in *Better Homes Manual*, ed. Blanch Halpert (Chicago: University of Chicago, 1931), 738.

8 James Ford, 'Trends in Housing', *Social Forces* 11, no. 4 (May 1933): 518.

9 Leonard Ware, *Helen Osborne Storrow, 1864–1944: A Memoir* (Northampton, MA: s.n.,: 1970), 6.

10 Timothy T. Orwig, 'Joseph Everett Chandler, Colonial Revival Architecture, and the Origins of the Historic Preservation Movement in America', PhD Diss. (Boston University, 2010), 420–35.

11 Nonie Gadsden, *Arts & Reform: Sara Galner, the Saturday Evening Girls, and the Paul Revere Pottery* (Boston, Museum of Fine Arts, Boston, 2006), 29.

12 Ibid., 35, 77.

13 Osborne Storrow to Rosa Marie Levis, 17 March 1930, box 7, MC207, Papers of Rosa Marie Levis, Schlesinger Library, Radcliffe Institute.

14 The houses or spaces, including camps, that Osborne Storrow also funded include: a building for the Paul Revere Pottery on Notting Hill, Brighton (1915); Pine Tree Camp Long Pond, Plymouth, for Girl Scouts (GS) (1917+); camp, Saturday Evening Girls Club, Wingaersheek Beach, Gloucester (1917); camp (GS), Winsor School, Boston (1917, 1918); Cedar Hill (GS), Waltham; Levi and Peletiah Gilbert house (1794), West Brookfield, the first of eleven buildings moved to the Eastern States Exposition, Springfield (1927+); Memorial City Hall, Auburn (1929); 1 Walnut Street, for the Judge Baker Foundation, Boston (1931); 'Our Chalet' (GS), Adelboden, Switzerland (1932); 87 Beacon Street (GS), Boston (1934); Old Manse, Concord (1938); Alexander house (1811), Springfield (1939); John Brown House, New York City; Women's Educational and Industrial Union building, Auburn; interior of a cottage at Foxlease for Girl Guides, Lyndhurst, Hampshire, England; and a farm for the Youth Hostel Movement, Meredith, NH. All were in Massachusetts unless otherwise noted.

15 Osborne Storrow, notes for a biography about Thomas Mott Osborne (1859–1926), box 344, MSS 64, Osborne Family Papers, Manuscript Collections, Syracuse University Library. Her notes were for the biography Rudolph Chamberlain, *There Is No Truce: A Life of Thomas Mott Osborne* (New York: Macmillan Company, 1935).

16 The Storrow house and grounds in Lincoln are now owned and occupied by the Carroll School.

17 'Boston Suburban Architecture', *Architectural Record* 21, no. 4 (April 1907): 265. Also see 'A Fireproof Country House', *Indoors and Out* 1, no. 4 (January 1906): 155–64, Vacuum Cleaner Company advertisement; Ralph de Martin, 'The House of J. J. Storrow, Esq.' *American Homes and Gardens* 4, no. 9 (September 1907): 353–57.

18 Osborne Storrow was likely aware of Isabella Stewart Gardner's earlier Moravian Tileworks installation since they were friends. See Maggie Goldstein, 'Henry Mercer's Moravian Pottery and Tile Works at Fenway Court', Isabella Stewart Gardner Museum, 23 January 2024; https://www.gardnermuseum.org/blog/henry-mercers-moravian-pottery-and-tile-works-fenway-court. She would have also known the Guastavino tile installation in McKim, Mead and White's Boston Public Library (1895).

19 Osborne Storrow, 'Better Homes for Negroes in America', *Opportunity: Journal of Negro Life* 9, no. 6 (June 1931), 174–77, quote at 177.

20 Ibid.

21 Walter Gropius, *The New Architecture and the Bauhaus*, trans. by P. Morton Shand (New York: Faber and Faber, 1935). Osborne Storrow to Gropius, 27 October, box: 34, MS Ger 208, (1582), Walter Gropius Papers, Houghton Library, Harvard University.

22 John C. MacLean, *A Rich Harvest: The History, Buildings, and People of Lincoln, Massachusetts* (Lincoln, MA: Lincoln Historical Society, 1987); W. Clifford Harvey, 'Members of faculty of School of Architecture Think Early American Trend is Overdone', *Christian Science Monitor*, 7 July 1939; Harvey, 'Old Homes and New Merge in Lincoln', *Christian Science Monitor*, 9 February 1940.

23 A letter from Mrs. James (Helen) Storrow to Marcel Breuer, 9 November [1938] in the Marcel Breuer Digital Archive references the interest of Marc Peter Jr., a Harvard-trained architect and instructor of interior architecture at the Cambridge School of Architecture and Landscape Architecture, and his wife, Frances Gardiner Peter (1912–92), an alumna of the school, in a parcel of the Lincoln property that Osborne Storrow eventually relinquished to Breuer, https://breuer.syr.edu/Documents/Detail/letter/190764?item=190765, accessed 17 November 2025. According to a summary of fees in the Shepley Bulfinch Archives, in 1940, a John A. Griswold was also considering building there.

24 On 18 January 1932, James Ford wrote to Osborne Storrow, 'I miss very much the opportunity to talk our problems and plans over with you'. The letter is in box 5, folder 16, Better Homes in America records, Hoover Institution Library and Archives, Stanford University.

25 Frieda Napier to Marcel Breuer, quoted in Isabelle Hyman, *Marcel Breuer, Architect: The Career and the Buildings* (New York: Harry N. Abrams, 2001), 105; Ise Gropius, *History of the Gropius House* (Cambridge: SPNEA, 1977), 2, quoted in 'Gropius House', National Historic Landmark Nomination, 14, accessed 24 December 2024, https://npgallery.nps.gov/NRHP/GetAsset/8d4b74a7-3fdf-4532-8c78-a1590a596fcb.

26 Hyman, *Breuer*, 105.

27 Henry Richardson Shepley designed the Memorial City Hall in Auburn (1929), which Osborne Storrow and her sister funded in memory of their father.

28 Hyman, *Breuer*, 105.

29 Sarah Pillsbury Harkness, quoted in Robert Campbell, 'Utopia Revisited: Built by architects seeking a model for community life, Six Moon Hill has thrived for 45 years', *Boston Globe*, 1 April 1994.

30 Keith N. Morgan, 'Six Moon Hill', in *Buildings of Massachusetts: Metropolitan Boston*, ed. Keith N. Morgan, Richard M. Candee, Naomi Miller, Roger G. Reed, et al., (Charlottesville: University of Virginia Press, 2009), 438; Walter Gropius and Sarah P[illsbury] Harkness, eds., *The Architects Collaborative, 1945–1965* (Teufen AR, Switzerland: Arthur Niggli, 1966), 48.

31 A letter from Pillsbury to John Harkness, January 10, [c. 1945], private collection, confirms the closeness of their relationship, 'I got a letter from Ann Halle Little. I must say it was damn nice of her'.

32 'Report to people who may be interested in buying part of the land which Jim Hughes is considering selling', Spring 1950, manuscript, private collection.

33 *Harvard College Class of 1937 Twentieth Anniversary Report*, s.v. 'Robert Andrews Little' (Cambridge: privately printed for the Class of 1937, 1957), 233; Frances P. Taft, 'Folk Tales of Pepper Ridge Road: I, 1950–1970', 7, private collection.

34 Dennis Dooley, 'Robert A. Little, FAIA, Architect, 1919-2005: 1965 Cleveland Arts Prize for Architecture', http://clevelandartsprize.org/awardees/robert_little.html.

35 Michael O' Mallet, 'Pepper Pike's one-of-a-kind community', *Plain Dealer* [Cleveland], 8 November 2006.

36 Registry of Deeds, *Grafton County, New Hampshire*, no. 763, 28 February 1948, 435-37.

37 Margaret King Hunter, 'A Design for Living – or Building', *Wheaton Alumnae Quarterly* 36, no. 3 (July 1957): 14–15.

38 Registry of Deeds, *Grafton County*, no. 788, 6 July 1949, 47–49.

39 Ibid.

40 'Four Small Houses in E. H. and M. K. Hunter, Hemlock Hill, Hanover, N. H.', *Architectural Record* 114, no. 5 (November 1953): 154–65.

41 'Better Living', *Life* 52, no. 16 (20 April 1962): 122–27. Drawings for New Seabury projects are in the Royal Barry Wills Associates Archive, Historic New England.

42 Historic American Engineering Record, 'Deer Isle-Sedgwick Bridge, Spanning Eggemoggin Reach between Sedgwick & Deer Isle at Route 15, Sedgwick, Hancock County', ME, HAER-ME 66, Library of Congress, accessed 22 April 2024, https://www.loc.gov/resource/hhh.me0314.photos?st=gallery.

43 Philip Conkling, 'A Practical Visionary, Remembering Emily Muir', *Maine Magazine* (May 2017).

44 Ibid.

45 'Emily Muir: Mistress of Conscience', interview, *Island Journal* 4 (1987): 52.

46 'Buys an Apartment in Cooperative House', *New York Times*, December 30, 1949; Richard LeVere, 'There From the Start'. *Lighting Design + Application*, 35, no. 2 (2005): 59–60.

47 Hyman, *Breuer*, 105.

# PART 3

# NURTURING SPACES FOR NEW IDEAS

## Chapter 8

# Maire Gullichsen and Norrmark Handicraft

## Matron of Finnish Design and Champion of Postwar Craftsmanship

*Sini Rinne-Kanto*

Norrmark Handicraft was a cottage industry founded in 1961 in Noormarkku in southwestern Finland by Finnish art patron and collector Maire Gullichsen and silversmith Bertel Gardberg. Its initial mission was to produce locally made handcrafted objects, complementing the Finnish furniture brand, Artek. Norrmark Handicraft's founding philosophy also revolved around the idea of social responsibility, with a plan to revitalise the Noormarkku region, keep the traditional craftsmanship skills alive in the countryside, and provide employment for local artisans.

Norrmark Handicraft is a unique experiment that stands out in Gullichsen's career. It was a socially committed project that sought to combine the notions of local and global industry and craft in postwar Finland, which was witnessing the consequences of unequal patterns of industrialisation and rapid urbanisation. Its importance has been largely ignored, probably due to the company's short life span. The ideological foundations on which Norrmark Handicraft was built formed a clear continuum with Gullichsen's other projects – notably Artek – which aimed to create a better everyday environment while at the same time responding to the needs of the time. This cottage industry, founded almost thirty years after Artek, followed a paternalistic logic that Gullichsen, a member of an elite industrial class, had been taught in her childhood home: to foster the local community while providing jobs and a better living environment. But the story of Norrmark Handicraft also represents a break from her earlier projects. While the project sought to respond to the everyday design needs of postwar consumers, it was also firmly rooted in the local and vernacular. As such, it responded to the design thinking of the time: moving away from the cult designer objects Artek had come to symbolise and further towards notions of locality and ecology, the democratisation of art and culture.

The life and work of Gullichsen, a devoted modernist, has been the subject of several biographical publications.[1] Although these shed light on her life's story and work, Gullichsen's accomplishments and profile are often framed in connection to the Aaltos – either her role as one of the co-founders of Artek alongside Alvar and Aino Aalto or as one of the clients for one of the key examples of the Aaltos' modernism, the Villa Mairea. This text seeks to provide a more nuanced look at her career and show how she actively shaped Finland's cultural, artistic and intellectual landscapes and debates from the 1930s to the 1970s. She is an example of the less often discussed complex relationships and roles that women have played in the field of design as patrons, initiators of movements and radical thinkers who have paved the way for the cultural avant-garde.

## INDUSTRIAL ARISTOCRACY: NOORMARKKU AND THE AHLSTRÖMS

To fully comprehend the origins and raison d'être of Norrmark Handicraft, it is essential to consider the historical ties that Gullichsen's family – the Ahlströms – had in Noormarkku, and the role they played in the region's development and modernisation. The industrialist and businessman Antti Ahlström (1827–96), Maire Gullichsen's grandfather, acquired the Noormarkku Works in 1870, making the family fortune in forestry. At the time of his death in 1896, he was one of the wealthiest and most prominent businessmen in Finland. After his passing, Antti Ahlström's second wife, Eva Ahlström, Gullichsen's grandmother (1848–1920), took over the family business and ran it until 1907, becoming one of Finland's first female industrial leaders. She is celebrated in the company's history as the matriarch, and she is 'known in the Ahlström family as the unifying force that held the family together and [who enabled] the businesses to be passed on to the next generation'.[2] Later, Gullichsen's father, Walter Ahlström, the eldest son of Antti and Eva Ahlström, expanded the business into one of the largest industries in Finland, pivoting from the sawmill industry to paper and giving birth to the A. Ahlström Corporation.[3] Although the company had several active industrial plants and sites across western and southern Finland, the headquarters was established in the municipality of Noormarkku, creating a solid bond between the local community and the Ahlström family company for decades to come.[4] The development and growth of the company followed the general pattern of industrialisation in Finland at the turn of the century. It significantly accelerated the shift from an agricultural to an industrial community in the Noormarkku region.[5] The company's activities followed a deeply paternalistic organisational model; the company was omnipresent in the Ahlström factory towns. It provided jobs and housing, built kindergartens, schools and museums, and even introduced electricity to Noormarkku and the neighbouring villages in 1896.[6] When expanding the industrial base for the company's activities, Walter Ahlström understood the urgent need to hire professional architects and interior designers for both A. Ahlström Corporation's numerous building projects and for the architecture plans of his own home. This laid the foundation for the Ahlström family's concern for the creation of better living environments while providing for the whole community in the Ahlström factory.[7]

Antti and Eva Ahlström were known for their philanthropy and charity work, and the latter supported various women's movements in Finland.[8] The company also expanded its activities to other fields, such as glass manufacturing. It acquired the glassworks in Karhula (1915), Iittala (1917), and Riihimäki (1985), thus contributing to the history of the Finnish glass industry.[9] The Ahlström family and company names soon became synonymous with each other: private was public, and the grand narrative and the branches of the Ahlström family tree were entangled with the local memory in Noormarkku.[10] Noormarkku became a symbolic place in both company and family histories and, in Maurice Halbwachs's terms, contributed to the framework of collective memory.[11]

The Ahlström company, still active in the Noormarkku area, has strategically used culture and education throughout its history to extend its reach and influence. It has built its brand not only through its business operations but also through the promotion of culture and education. Museums, exhibitions, and publications have been key in highlighting its unique and lasting relationship with the region. As Halbwachs notes, memories are not just recollections but also models, examples, and elements of teaching.[12] The Ahlström company has been effective in using this concept to strengthen its image and reputation in the region. According to Maarit Grahn, who has extensively researched the Noormarkku area and the Ahlström family history, the Ahlström company's case is a typical example of how companies highlight the ideas of continuity, credibility, and innovation.[13] The crucial role that locality plays in the company's image and brand creates and maintains a horizontal responsibility towards the region, passed from generation to generation and aligned with the idea of *richesse oblige*, a pattern we also witness in the foundation of Norrmark Handicraft.

## FROM PARIS TO HELSINKI: 'THE ERRAND GIRL OF THE ARTS' BRINGS CONTINENTAL VISTAS TO FINLAND[14]

Growing up within her elite industrial family, the early life of Maire Gullichsen (born Ahlström; 1907–90) was 'carefree and lavish, without any particular goals', according to her biographer. She decided to quit school at 17 and was more interested in dancing the Charleston and spending time in restaurants and cafés than in her studies. Her parents decided to send her abroad to learn languages, and young Gullichsen got her way when she was allowed to choose Paris as her destination. The socialite's encounter with the interwar capital of arts during its golden age bore fruit, and she decided to devote herself to the world of arts.[15] During her time in Paris, she became convinced that she wanted to be an artist and studied at Fernand Léger's private *académie*. Its progressive way of teaching and thinking greatly influenced her.

Gullichsen transformed in Paris; she became a cosmopolitan and sophisticated 'garçonne' who decided to continue her art studies in Finland (Fig. 8.1).[16] She became a prominent member of Helsinki's high society, often spending her time in cafés and restaurants in the company of fellow modernists, such as the painters Birger Carlstedt and Yngve Bäck and the art critic and future co-founder of Artek, Nils-Gustav Hahl. But upon returning to her native Finland, she was also eager to put into practice what she had learned and eagerly observed abroad. Gullichsen, together with three other women, Ethel Thesleff, Irja Noponen, and Saara Castrén, founded the Free Art School as a 'counter academy' following the Parisian models. The new institution opened in 1935 and became an alternative to the conservative Ateneum Academy of Fine Arts, free from the constraints of the old world when it came to teaching and praxis. There were no entry requirements, except that students from the Ateneum Academy were not admitted. Gullichsen later explained that the school's aim was not to create opposition to anything, but simply to offer an alternative to the academy teaching, adding that she was not fighting for 'revolution', but for 'progress'.[17] Gullichsen took on a great deal of responsibility in the day-to-day running of the school and was involved in its activities until the 1970s.[18]

In 1931, Maire Gullichsen's father, Walter Ahlström died, which resulted in major changes in the company direction but also in Gullichsen's personal life. Three years earlier, Maire Ahlström had married Harry Gullichsen (1902–54), a Norwegian businessman. In 1932, after the death of Walter Ahlström, Harry Gullichsen became General Director of the Ahlström

Figure 8.1: Maire Gullichsen, 1930. Villa Mairea Archives.

Corporation. Although this meant new restrictions and responsibilities for Maire Gullichsen, it also meant that she was financially freer to do what she wanted. She was convinced that her father would have wanted his daughter to continue his life's work alongside her husband and lead an active role. As her new life was full of social obligations and traveling, she turned the situation around in favour of her art hobby. On trips abroad, she spent all her free time in museums and art galleries, which she believed was the only way to get to know art, and bought the latest exhibition catalogues and art books.[19] Maire Gullichsen took the active lead in many of her initiatives and brought her expertise and wealth to the projects. When Artek was founded, it was the Gullichsens who provided the financial backing, and when financial problems later arose, they helped to keep the company afloat for more than three decades.[20] Given their background, status and wealth, the couple were considered 'uncharacteristically progressive'.[21]

Maire Gullichsen founded Artek together with Aino and Alvar Aalto, and Nils-Gustav Hahl in 1935. The main motivations included the exportation of Aalto furniture and creating something in Finland akin to Wohnbedarf, established in Zürich in 1931, with model interiors within the shop area. Gullichsen was appointed as Artek's first chair and played a very active role in the company, as revealed in the Artek meeting minutes and letters sent to her by Hahl.[22] Her dream, however, was to start an art gallery in Helsinki that would be devoted to modern art. She proactively used Artek, a showcase of modernity, to fulfil her personal ambitions of showing international modern masters in Finland. In 1937, she organised a dual exhibition of works by Fernand Léger and Alexander Calder in its premises.[23]

Artek's exhibition programme allowed Gullichsen to combine her continuing interest in art and design through exhibition-making. Her art world contacts from her Paris years enabled her to introduce pioneering artists and continental perspectives to her homeland, which had only gained independence from the Russian Empire in 1917.[24] She pursued the exhibition programme – which she kept firmly in her own hands – for thirteen years in the Artek store facilities until she decided it was time to establish a separate venue, Galerie Artek, to host art exhibitions and to free up more room for the Artek store.[25] Soon, Galerie Artek held an unparalleled position as the Finnish representative of French galleries, such as Carré, Maeght, and Louise Leiris.[26]

The third project initiated by Gullichsen during the interwar period was the Contemporary Art Association (Nutidskonst – Nykytaide r.f.), which, though founded in 1939, did not begin its work until 1944 because of the delays caused by the war. It sought to organise more prominent, institutional exhibitions of modern art in Finland, something that Artek was too small to arrange, partly because it could not receive public funding to support its endeavours.[27] The association strove to build and accumulate a veritable collection of modern art in Finland, and Gullichsen became the prime mover behind it. She used her extensive personal connections with Finland's industrial elite to encourage people to buy and collect art as well as make donations to major institutions.[28]

In conjunction with these various cultural initiatives and institutions – created within a timeframe of less than ten years – Gullichsen also actively built up her own collection of modern art. More than almost anyone else in Finland, she was, because of her wealth and network, in a position to acquire works of art of the highest quality from both Finnish and international masters.[29] Her collection included works by Pablo Picasso, Jean Arp, and Pierre Bonnard as well as Finnish painters such as Tyko Sallinen, Helene Schjerfbeck, and Ellen Thesleff. For her, buying art was not necessarily just about owning; it was more of a moral obligation and a means to support artists, make goodwill gestures, and cultivate personal relationships.[30]

Gullichsen, along with a circle of Finnish modernists – painters, architects, designers and cultural critics – became arbiters of taste as they sought ways to bring internationalism and functionalism to Finland. Active participants in the Roaring Twenties – a decade of emancipation – they opposed conservative, nationalist and introverted values and were part of a cultural revolution.[31] Gullichsen sought to raise the level of artistic presentation to meet international standards and to create a modern art collection housed in official art institutions.[32] She did this thanks to her extensive network of industrialists, gallerists, and artists in Finland and abroad. The initiatives that Gullichsen undertook or co-founded with her contemporaries were usually interrelated. The Contemporary Art Association, Artek (and later, the Galerie Artek) and the Free Art School were natural continuations of one another, supporting her larger dream of introducing continental perspectives and international modernism to Finland. The 1920s and 1930s saw a major breakthrough in modernism; art education, exhibition practices, art criticism and collecting all advanced in Finland during these crucial decades.[33] Gullichsen played a decisive role in making the Finnish art and cultural scene what it is today.[34]

## DEVOTED REFORMER: DEMOCRATISATION OF THE HABITAT AND *VACKRARE VARDAGSVARA*

Gullichsen had a broad and radical outlook from the start. By her own account, however, it was not until the early 1930s that she became interested in industrial design, mainly through Artek. She took a firmer position in the field during the 1940s, becoming an active voice in Finnish society, discussing the state of the domestic environment and everyday life, for example, in magazine articles. In a 1947 article, she expressed her dismay at the state of the quality of everyday objects:

> Beautiful everyday products are today the privilege of the well-to-do elements of society, and 'more beautiful everyday goods' are now only to be had by private order and at a luxury price. To improve taste, we need constructive and useful criticism, a debate in the press.[35]

The context of the publication was, of course, the nation's post-war reconstruction efforts and rapid urbanisation. While trying to encourage a wider discussion about the situation of Finnish industry and post-war production, she also discussed the notion of the democratisation of everyday products:

> Our times demand the democratisation of everyday products: we need cheap and good wares, but democratisation in this case does not mean that we must be satisfied with the goods that are available today.[36]

Figure 8.2: Maire Gullichsen, 1952. Villa Mairea Archives.

The popular Swedish slogan *vackrage vardagsvara* (more beautiful everyday goods) was also Gullichsen's motto when she lamented the deplorable situation and called for efforts to get rid of junk and trivial bric-a-brac.[37]

Gullichsen's determination to improve the nation's standard of living was not just empty rhetoric; she put it into practice. Throughout the 1940s, while she was busy with Artek and other cultural institutions and curatorial work, she also pursued several projects in the Noormarkku region. From 1945 until his death in 1954, she worked on social responsibility issues at the A. Ahlström Corporation while her husband was the company's managing director (Fig. 8.2).[38] When she asked the board for an official position to work on social responsibility issues, she did not request financial compensation. Instead, she emphasised the need for a woman's perspective on the development of social conditions for workers, especially as regards hygiene issues in the childcare and social welfare facilities that the Ahlström company provided for its employees according to its paternalistic purview.[39] In doing so, she seems to have deliberately claimed expertise in domestic matters. The concern for the creation of accessible, modern living space for employees and their families became important to her, and in this, she followed the example set up before by the Ahlström company.

## HANDMADE MODERNISM FROM NOORMARKKU

While Gullichsen started to claim more agency in public debates related to the nation's domestic well-being, she also became more attached to her home region. Her biographer Helena Woirhaye notes how, despite her frequent travels and holiday houses abroad, her favourite destination remained the Villa Mairea in Noormarkku, and that she was one of the rare Ahlström family members who had registered her permanent address in the area.[40]

On 20 October 1961, Gullichsen delivered a speech at the inauguration of the new Noormarkku Town Hall. On this occasion, she donated to the municipality a tapestry by a Finnish painter and professor at the Free Art School, Unto Pusa (1913–73). 'Tools from a Workshop' (1960–61) presents an abstract, streamlined, modernist composition of wheel equipment from the Makkarakoski ironworks in Noormarkku. Despite the work's connection to the region and its industrial history and its apparent reference to the history of Finnish craftsmanship and the tradition of 'ryijy' production, the tapestry was hand-woven in Aubusson, France. The example of the tapestry, like Gullichsen's speech, creates a link between the past and the present, rural Finland and France, and modern machinery and handicrafts. She concluded her speech by paving the way for Norrmark Handicraft:

> For my part, I am emboldened to hope that this tradition of crafts will be revived in Noormarkku and that the craftsmen who still live in the locality will help me in creating a new vocational tradition in the town, as well as that the newly started Noormarkku Crafts Workshops would include smithery in its programme in addition to woodcarving. In the future, products from Noormarkku may be a match for quality with the best in the world.[41]

Later that year, Gullichsen and silversmith-designer Bertel Gardberg (1916–2007) founded Norrmark Handicraft, which was listed in the trade register as a joint company under the name 'Noormarkun Käsityöt – Norrmark Slöjd, Gullichsen & Gardberg'.[42] Gardberg was known for his designs for everyday objects and his material combinations such as silver and wood. He was one of the well-known figures of the 1950s 'Golden Age' of Finnish design, especially after his success in the Milan Triennale where he won awards in 1954, 1957, and 1960.

Three main motivations for the establishment of Norrmark Handicraft are usually highlighted: to fulfil the desire to revitalise the region, to keep

Figure 8.3: A nut tray designed by Nanny Still. Wooden utensils were among the first products designed at Norrmark Handicraft. Over the years, more than eighty different products were incorporated into the selection. The utensils were designed by Bertel Gardner, Nanny Still, and Birgitta Bergh. Satakunta Museum Collection, Norrmark Handicrafts Archive.

the handicraft traditions and skills alive in the face of rapid industrialisation, and to complement and fill gaps in Artek's product range. In other words, despite its formal connection with Noormarkku, the company was closely linked to Artek's activities since its beginning. Like Artek, also Norrmark Handicraft was financed from the outset by the A. Ahlström company.[43] The finished products 'were to represent the highest standards of craftsmanship', handcrafted in small batches. The objects ranged from small everyday items – such as wooden utensils and wrought-iron utensils – eventually also to encompass furniture (Fig. 8.3).

In its early days, Norrmark Handicraft produced wooden goods mainly from imported woods such as teak and olive, but when it expanded into furniture production, the company opted to use cheaper, such locally available woods as birch and pine.[44] The creative design process or outcome were not entirely based on folk aesthetics or ideals, but can be defined as handmade modernism; such established designers such as Bertel Gardberg and other leading figures in Finnish design provided the design models and sketches that the skilled craftsmen then followed, carrying out the production phase locally in Noormarkku.[45] The artisanal and locally produced products were then marketed mainly to the fashionable urban elite in Artek's Helsinki boutique and at international furniture fairs and exhibitions, but also at the local Noormarkku Crafts handicraft shop.[46]

Gullichsen's interest in crafts was not new. It had followed her through her years at Artek and her many travels abroad before and after the war. She collected North African and Provençal handicrafts to combine with Artek's retail range in the shop.[47] Daniele Burlando discusses how vernacular elements played a role in the Artek philosophy from the beginning. Looking back to the Finnish folk tradition had been part of the romantic nation-building process since the turn of the century, and Artek drew on this tradition. Gullichsen and Aino Aalto not only introduced folk crafts from abroad into Artek's product range – a mixture of boutique and exhibition elements – but the latter also designed carpets and fabrics produced locally in Finnish weaving mills. She also relied on small-scale hand-woven production in 1936 through Gullichsen's contacts in Noormarkku, Aino Aalto pursued the fabrication of rya rugs, a type of Finnish tapestry, to be made by home weavers in the Noormarkku village.[48] Twenty-five years after Aino Aalto employed home weavers in Noormarkku, Gullichsen decided to establish a more formal cottage industry model in her hometown.

## MAIRE GULLICHSEN AT THE HELM OF NORRMARK HANDICRAFT: ON THE VERGE OF AN INTERNATIONAL BREAKTHROUGH

In 1965, four years after the foundation of Norrmark Handicraft, Gardberg, a key figure in the company's early years, moved to Ireland to help establish the Kilkenny Design Workshops. This marked a change in the company's ownership, with Gullichsen taking the helm. The registered name was changed to 'Noormarkun Käsityöt – Norrmark Slöjd, Maire Gullichsen' to reflect the new ownership, under which the company's production range soon expanded, particularly into furniture making. The furniture range

Figure 8.4: Traditional Vanikka bread. Photo by Matti Perävainio, Hinnerjoki Local History Museum.

included designs by architect Kristian Gullichsen, Gullichsen's son, and Ben af Schultén, who had been appointed interior architect at Artek in 1964.[49]

One of Norrmark Handicraft's best-known and most sought-after furniture designs was Vanikka; a name referring to a Finnish word for a type of crispbread that was made during the Second World War (Fig. 8.4). While the traditional shape of the bread was round, Vanikkas were square to reduce the amount of space used during transport to the frontlines and to make it more cost-effective. This version of the wartime crispbread gave its name and shape to the eponymous range of furniture that Kristian Gullichsen designed for the company in 1968.[50]

The functional aspects of Vanikka responded to the non-conformist atmosphere of the time and the needs of the baby boomer generation: it was intended to be affordable, compactly packaged and assembled by the customer on-site while adhering to the principles of material economy. Vanikka made its international debut at the Bella Centre exhibition in Copenhagen in 1968, which resulted in a large order for the small craftsman's workshop (Fig. 8.5).[51] This was the first real test for the young company, and furniture production quickly proved to be more challenging than initially thought. Local craftsmen could not meet the production demands and keep up the required pace, especially to fulfil orders for the

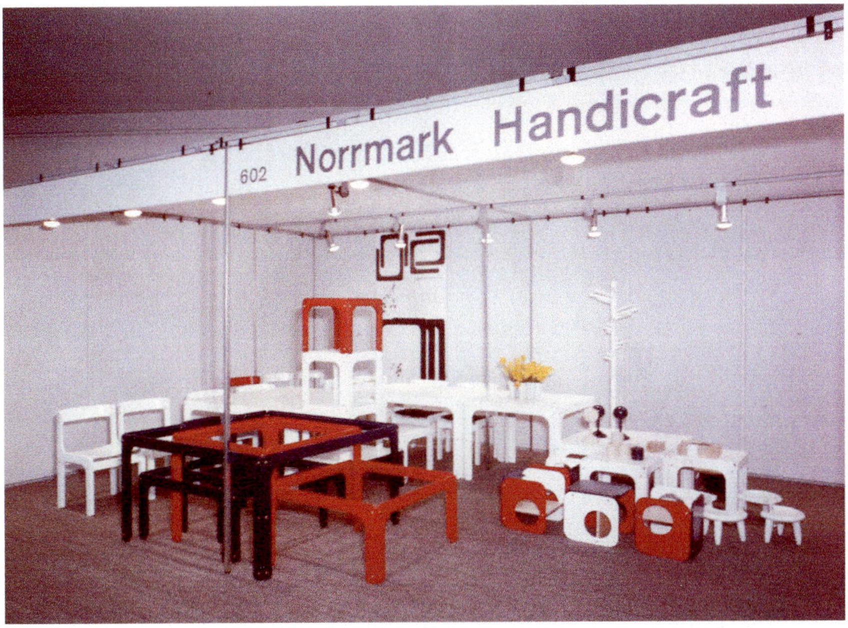


Figure 8.5: The *Vanikka* furniture series shown at the Copenhagen Furniture Fair, 16-19 May 1968. Satakunta Museum Collection, Norrmark Handicrafts Archive.

most popular products. When technical and production challenges arose, the company could not resolve them quickly enough.[52]

A brief comparison between Norrmark Handicraft and Artek's production realities may be useful here. The cornerstone of Artek's furniture production in the early 1960s was the series of models designed and patented by Alvar and Aino Aalto, based mainly on wood carving and plywood moulding. The manufacture of these products required special processing methods developed at the Finnish furniture factory Korhonen and bespoke production conditions for which the factory was specially adapted.[53] In the Noormarkku workshop, an old facility provided by the Ahlström Company, the main tools were a lathe, which was used to make chair parts and small objects, and a band saw and milling machine, which were used to make plywood models (Fig. 8.6).[54] In contrast to Artek's more modern production methods and framework, the Norrmark Handicraft furniture line was created to allow more experimentation and flexibility through trial and error, a kind of experimental laboratory helpful when developing new models yet unsuited for mass production.

Figure 8.6: Maire Gullichsen and Kalle Rajamäki at the Noormarkku workshop in the 1960s. Villa Mairea Archives.

While furniture was being introduced, the range of products was expanded to textiles, with the two becoming the most popular product lines. The weaving workshop had a separate building in the village, and Maire Gullichsen appointed textile artist Elisabeth Gripenberg to run it.[55] Also, local Noormarkku women produced hand-woven rugs for sale at home through the Noormarkku Crafts shop. Despite the popularity of the textiles and furniture, especially the Vanikka series, the company remained unprofitable.[56]

At the beginning of the 1970s, the company's management took various measures to deal with economic challenges. They sought improvements through managerial revisions: Maire Gullichsen became a silent partner, while her son, Kristian Gullichsen, became a general partner. The company evolved into a limited partnership. The economic challenges were coupled with the persisting production issues: the carpentry workshop was deemed too small and outdated, with frequent humidity problems and high temperatures. The poor conditions affected the quality of the products, and several customers complained.[57] As a result, the company tried to find subcontractors, like the Asko furniture company, to ensure the continued production of its popular products. The search was unsuccessful. The company continued to suffer from financial, technical, and production problems.[58]

## CLOSURE AND HERITAGE OF NORRMARK HANDICRAFT

Faced with several challenges, including economic and production issues, the carpentry workshop ceased the production of small items and most of the furniture at the beginning of 1974, reducing its product range and scope of work.[59] At the same time, the company was brought under the Artek umbrella, and its name was changed to Artek Oy Ab Norrcraft. Artek continued to manufacture some of Norrmark Handicraft's most popular products, such as Kristian Gullichsen's 'Vanikka' series, Bertel Gardberg's 'Footstole C.' Anna-Maija Jaatinen's coat rack and Ben af Schultén's furniture in Noormarkku.[60]

Despite the difficulties and the partial merger with Artek, Maire Gullichsen continued to develop new directions within Norrmark Handicrafts. In 1976, she hired the textile artist Estelle Rosenlew as a consultant. Both Rosenlew and Gullichsen were interested in strengthening local identity, and together, they brainstormed about a 'living museum' that would combine local craft traditions with newly produced versions inspired by traditional models. Estelle Rosenlew was supposed to be the consultant and creator of new models, but her ideas for models and the joint idea of a 'living museum' never saw the light of day.[61] Shortly after her appointment, Norrmark Handicraft ceased to exist, and the weaving continued under another association, the regional Satakunta Association of Cottage Industries. Noormarkku Crafts was dissolved on 31 December 1976 after fifteen years of activity.[62]

Norrmark Handicraft had many advantages; from the outset, it had an extensive national and international network, which proved helpful in many ways, as the handicraft objects were exhibited locally and worldwide from the beginning. Its proximity to Artek gave the project an immediate outlet, circulation and visibility, while the continued financial support of the Ahlström company guaranteed its very existence. Gullichsen and Gardberg used their extensive networks to attract and recruit many talented designers to the company's creative roster. The design vocabulary sought to respond to the general mood of the baby boom era through its democratic values, with a strong focus on the design

Figure 8.7: The *Vanikka* series exemplifies the modern flatpack thinking that prevailed at Norrmark Handicraft. Satakunta Museum Collection, Norrmark Handicrafts Archive.

of children's furniture and self-assembled flatpack furniture, following the idea of flatpack customer assembly introduced in Sweden by IKEA in the 1950s (Fig. 8.7). The company's more apparent shortcomings were a lack of organisation and inadequate infrastructure.[63] Although the company faced difficulties, especially in terms of production, it is worth noting that Gullichsen pushed the project forward with new ideas, constantly renewing its direction and products. Despite the attempts to revive the company, the efforts were in vain.

A relatively uncommercial idea that defined the foundation of Norrmark Handicraft had also defined the early days of Artek; in both cases, the company foundations had ideological motivations, and continuing operations were usually more important than making a profit.[64] It is interesting to consider the similarities between these two projects and how, at the moment of founding Norrmark Handicraft, Artek had, in a way, accomplished its original mission; it had created a set of 'elastic standards' that could be serially produced as a set of components from local materials to form an ever larger repertoire of types adaptable to the individual requirements of any number of specially made interiors.[65] While this resolution was fulfilled, Artek simultaneously moved away from its initial manifesto; in the early 1960s, at the moment of Norrmark Handicraft's founding, Artek furniture was, in a sense, already a generation in the past.

Moreover, the creation of Norrmark Handicraft was preceded by somewhat turbulent years at Artek, with clashes over the direction of the company between Alvar Aalto and Maire Gullichsen, the only co-founders still alive in the 1950s. Kristian Gullichsen observed: '[Artek] wasn't a successful business, it became a sort of interior decoration company. He [Alvar Aalto] found that distasteful. He used to say there were too many pot warmers here.' Indeed, the Aalto architecture firm slowly drifted away from Artek during the 1950s, when Alvar Aalto came to see it as bric-a-brac. The drift of the Aalto architecture firm away from Artek was accompanied by an affirming bond between Harry Gullichsen and Alvar Aalto, who worked closely together on many of the larger architectural projects commissioned by the Ahlström Company. When it came to characterising the couple, Harry Gullichsen was defined as 'a man with few inhibitions, in contrast to Maire Gullichsen', and he seemed to be embarrassed by 'her excessively bourgeois background'. 'He was more like Alvar [...] he was really unconventional and of course, he got on famously with Alvar.'[66] The creation of Norrmark Handicraft allowed Maire Gullichsen to make a fresh start in her career, leaving behind a network of complicated and strained relationships in which personal and professional ties were often intertwined.

## FROM THE LIVING MUSEUM TO THE PORI ART MUSEUM

Gullichsen's original ideas for a 'living museum' remained unrealised, but these ideas were instrumental in the creation of another museum in the region, the Pori Art Museum. The idea was fulfilled in the mid-1960s, with Gullichsen bringing in the well-known and influential museum director, Pontus Hultén, for a visit to consult on project plans.[67] In a continuation of Gullichsen's previous projects, the role of the new local art museum was also evaluated through the prism of modernism: its role and functions were to follow the idea of an operational centre that was open to the outside world and actively participating in it. Located in the old customs warehouse in Pori, the museum was designed by Gullichsen's son, Kristian.[68] Gullichsen donated more than three hundred mostly Finnish works to the foundation she established in 1971, which in turn became the core of the new museum.[69] The collection of foreign art remained mainly in Villa Mairea, and its maintenance was entrusted to the Ahlström Company and a namesake foundation she established to look after Gullichsen's legacy.[70]

## VISIONARY NORRMARK HANDICRAFT AS PART OF THE 1960S DESIGN LANDSCAPE

Although Norrmark Handicraft was a unique experiment, it was by no means an anomaly in the Finnish postwar design landscape. The notion of 'return to craft' and the experimentation with the cottage industry model was part of a neo-craft revival in post-war Finland. As Pekka Korvenmaa discusses in the book *Scandinavian Design – Alternative Histories*, some of the leading designers, such as Tapio Wirkkala and Ilmari Tapiovaara, were also concerned about the disappearance of craftsmanship in the rural context and organised courses and workshops to keep the tradition of local craftsmanship alive.[71] Designer, journalist, and teacher Harry Moilanen travelled across Finland and arranged workshops with his students from the Institute of Industrial Arts, and his goal was to support local cultures by recording and revitalising traditional craft techniques.[72]

There were many reasons for this. In general, industrialisation, urbanisation, and welfare improvements in the 1960s influenced and changed attitudes towards handicrafts and industrial arts in Finland. As Gullichsen had reflected upon in her writings, the post-war baby-boom generation and new groups within the population placed increasing demands on the design of everyday objects. At the same time, awareness and understanding of shared environmental problems on a planetary scale were growing.[73] As elsewhere in the world, a new generation expressed their dissatisfaction with the status quo, and the design field was accused of simply being capitalist.[74] As a result, the design debate of the 1960s led to the declining status of the so-called hero designers and the cult objects they had designed earlier.[75]

In the context of the highly politicised decade and debate, Korvenmaa calls this return to craft a 'non-political' alternative to the status quo represented by Artek and others and considers it in a way saying 'no' to modernism. Korvenmaa writes:

> The pastoral past was seen as apolitical and loaded with positive connotations of true Finnishness. Neo-folklore became a trend that also led to collection of

> the remnants of the agrarian past, which now adorned especially upper-middle-class homes in the form of simple wooden vessels and other utensils.[76]

But these calls for equality, freedom, and a return to pre-capitalist modes of production were in fact highly politicised, reflecting the mood of the decade in which these developments took place.

According to Minna Sarantola-Weiss the return to craft also made sense business-wise; as nostalgia had evolved into an important part of consumer culture. People began to decorate their homes with pine furniture, rag rugs, and folk handicrafts. While the return to craft can be considered as part of a broader conversation about ecology and the idealised rural community – the utopian notion of culture from scratch – it must be remembered that the often poor and even backward reality of the countryside was still very much in people's minds, at least of those who did not find themselves in the bigger cities.[77]

The 1960s witnessed rapid industrialisation and a growing need to respond to manufacturing needs, yet it was a moment when a more radical approach to material culture re-emerged. Looking at the history of Norrmark Handicraft and the reasons behind its founding, it seems that the project tapped into the duality that defined this moment, and Gullichsen's newly created patronage project was certainly not outdated. Her interest in the vernacular – fundamental since the early days of Artek – took on a new format, and the result, Norrmark Handicraft, stands out as an unprecedented example of the emergence of a locally organised production model and social patronage combined with the latest trends of the international avant-garde. Norrmark Handicraft managed to create a strategic and delicate balance in its marketed image. While the company's design continued to be signed by the well-known designers, its image was more rooted in the local and the vernacular, thus moving away from the star-cult designer emphasis that was then heavily criticised among the younger generations.

## CONCLUSION

Maire Gullichsen is often associated, both in Finland and internationally, with the Aaltos and with the founding of the furniture company Artek. Her role and achievements are mainly discussed in relation to her projects in the pre- and inter-war period, in both the art and the design worlds. Active and entrepreneurial, her lasting contribution to art, design and architecture in Finland and internationally continued into the 1970s, spanning more than four decades. The significance of Norrmark Handicraft, a unique experiment and socially committed project that stands out in her career, has been largely ignored, probably because of its short lifespan and the fact that she created it at a later stage in her career.

Gullichsen was no ordinary patron of the arts. She was a flag-bearer of modernism, always on the lookout for new forms and ideas, creating projects that reflected the changing society and values around her. She founded major institutions, some of which still exist today: Artek, Galerie Artek, the Free Art School, the Contemporary Art Association, and laid the foundations for the Pori Art Museum. She used her privileged position to broaden Finland's horizons and to introduce Finnish art and design to an international audience. She did not content herself with handing out money or thinking how to make rational investments, but rather gave her labour and expertise, funding projects for which she herself was responsible.

It is easy to ascribe several definitions or roles to Gullichsen. Within the modernist canon, she has always been discussed as the ideal and independent modern woman, matriarch, philanthropist, and protagonist of the artistic avant-garde and modernism. Looking at her practice through a feminist lens, we can see that she did not confine herself to the representative role of the wife of an important industrialist. Although her gendered identity as a patron was perhaps less important to her than her political mission, it should be noted that as she was not given an official position in the Ahlström company after her father's death, she made up for this through her many activities within the company or through projects closely linked to it. Most importantly, she used the Ahlström Company to finance her projects, ensuring their continuation and sometimes even their very existence. These projects, sometimes regarded as a lady's hobby, have left a lasting mark on Finnish art and design history and the history of modernism in the 20th century.

In founding Norrmark Handicraft, Gullichsen sought to create handmade modernism innovatively to reflect the noble idea of social responsibility while balancing vertical and horizontal family legacies and relationships. It was certainly radical for the grande dame of the arts – co-founder of Artek and a notable industrial heiress – to support a cottage industry model and put her money into a social, almost utopian experiment. In seeking to address the complex issues of industrialisation and hoping to keep vernacular traditions alive, Norrmark Handicraft and its founder, Gullichsen, were ahead of their time.

## NOTES

1 For Maire Gullichsen's biography see Helena Woirhaye, *Maire Gullichsen – Konstens springflicka* (Helsinki: Konstindustrimuseet, 2002) and *Maire Gullichsen*, ed. Esko Nummelin and Emilia Siltavuori (Kukkila: Pori Art Museum, 2000).

2 Ahlström – 'A Family Tradition of Progress', Ahlström Company, accessed 13 April 2024, https://www.perilliset.fi/.

3 Woirhaye, *Maire Gullichsen*, 182, and Maarit Grahn, *Perheyhtiö ja paikallisuus – A. Ahlström Osakeyhtiön historian perintö Noormarkussa* (Turku: Painosalama Oy, 2014), 11.

4 Maarit Grahn, 'The Noormarkku Ironworks: Places of Memory and Capital', in *Locality, Memory, Reconstruction: The Cultural Challenges and Possibilities of Former Single-Industry Communities*, ed. Simo Häyrynen, Jopi Nyman and Risto Turunen (Cambridge: Cambridge Scholars Publishing, 2012), 125.

5 Ibid.

6 Maarit Grahn, *Perheyhtiö ja paikallisuus – A. Ahlström Osakeyhtiön historian perintö Noormarkussa* (Turku: Painosalama Oy, 2014), 243.

7 Woirhaye, *Maire Gullichsen*, 14–15.

8 'Ahlström – A Family Tradition of Progress', Ahlström Company, accessed 13 April 2024, https://www.perilliset.fi/.

9 Ibid., 63.

10 Grahn, 'The Noormarkku Ironworks', 125.

11 See: Maurice Halbwachs, *On Collective Memory* (Chicago: University of Chicago Press, 1992).

12 Halbwachs, *On Collective Memory*, 59.

13 Grahn, *Perheyhtiö ja paikallisuus*, 5.

14 See: Woirhaye, *Maire Gullichsen*. Gullichsen's biographer, Woirhaye, notes how Maire Gullichsen used the term 'errand girl of the arts' to describe herself when discussing her activities in the field of art.

15 Woirhaye, *Maire Gullichsen*, 19.

16 Ibid., 43.

17 Ibid.

18 Ibid., 45.

19 Ibid., 41.

20 Ibid., 47.

21 Nina Stritzler-Levine, 'Artek and the Aaltos', in *Artek and the Aaltos: Creating a Modern World*, ed. Nina Stritzler-Levine and Timo Riekko (New York: Bard Graduate Center, 2022), 47.

22 Ibid., 49.

23 Pekka Suhonen, 'Maire Gullichsen, modernism and elegance', in *Maire Gullichsen*, ed. Esko Nummelin and Emilia Siltavuori (Kukkila: Pori Art Museum, 2000), 31.

24 Stritzler-Levine, 'Artek and the Aaltos', 47.

25 Susanna Pettersson, 'Artek – a Bridge to the International Art World', *FNG Research*, no. 3 (2017): 13. https://research.fng.fi/wp-content/uploads/2017/05/fngr_2017-3_pettersson_susanna_article1_2.pdf

26 Ibid., 14.

27 Erik Kruskopf, 'Clear colour, pure form', in *Maire Gullichsen*, ed. Esko Nummelin and Emilia Siltavuori (Kukkila: Pori Art Museum, 2000), 59. The co-founders included: Alvar Aalto, Maire Gullichsen, Nils-Gustav Hahl, Bertel Hintze and Antero Rinne.

28 Elina Melgin, 'The Contemporary Art Association Nykytaide ry', in *Maire Gullichsen*, ed. Esko Nummelin and Emilia Siltavuori (Kukkila: Pori Art Museum, 2000), 158-159.

29 Kruskopf, 'Clear colour, pure form', 59.

30 Ibid., 60–61.

31 Melgin, 'The Contemporary Art Association Nykytaide ry', 158–59.

32 Kruskopf, 'Clear colour, pure form', 59.

33 Pettersson, 'Artek', 3.

34 Kruskopf, 'Clear colour, pure form', 68.

35 Maire Gullichsen, 'Our industry and household objects', in *Maire Gullichsen*, ed. Esko Nummelin and Emilia Siltavuori (Kukkila: Pori Art Museum, 2000), 82. Written originally in 1947.
36 Ibid., 83.
37 Suhonen, 'Maire Gullichsen, modernism and elegance', 33.
38 Stritzler-Levine, 'Artek and the Aaltos', 49.
39 Grahn, *Perheyhtiö ja paikallisuus*, 196.
40 Woirhaye, *Maire Gullichsen*, 182, and Grahn, *Perheyhtiö ja paikallisuus*, 110.
41 Emilia Siltavuori, 'Noormarkku Crafts', in *Maire Gullichsen*, ed. Esko Nummelin and Emilia Siltavuori (Kukkila: Pori Art Museum, 2000), 127.
42 The name of the region is Norrmark in Swedish and Noormarkku in Finnish. The two founding members of Norrmark Handicraft were Swedish-speaking Finns, so the name of the company and the region are often written in both languages.
43 Kirsi Gullichsen, 'Noormarkun Käsitöiden huonekalutuotannosta', in *Noormarkun Käsityöt*, ed. Anni Saisto (Pori: Pori Art Museum, 2021), 48.
44 Sanna Oikarinen, 'Yritystoiminnan keskeiset vaiheet', in *Noormarkun Käsityöt*, ed. Anni Saisto (Pori: Pori Art Museum, 2021), 13.
45 Handmade modernism is a concept borrowed from the scholar Gökhan Karakus, whose particular research focus is design in Turkey. There, cosmopolitan-minded architects and sculptors forged partnerships with artisans, juxtaposing contemporary furnishings with vernacular source material. Through Norrmark Handicraft, Maire Gullichsen sought to apply the same design thinking that many designers had done before her, such as Charlotte Perriand, Lina Bo Bardi, Clara Porset. See Glenn Adamson, 'Perriand's handmade modernism', in *Charlotte Perriand: The Modern Life*, ed. J. McGuirk (London: Design Museum Publishing, 2021), 156–65.
46 Siltavuori, 'Noormarkku Crafts', 127.
47 Suhonen, 'Maire Gullichsen, modernism and elegance', 32.
48 Daniele, Burlando, '"Moroccan" Artek – Colonized Textiles within 1930s Modernist Interiors', *Journal of Design History*, no. 35 (2023): 5–6, https://doi.org/10.1093/jdh/epac035.
49 No written documents mentioning the Ben af Schultén appointment survive, but it is known that Maire Gullichsen was the primus motor in the appointment. See: Ulla Kinnunen: *Ben af Schultén and the Artek Tradition* (Lönnberg Print, Finland: Alvar Aalto Foundation, 2008), 23–25 Later in 1976, Ben af Schultén became artistic director of Artek.
50 Gullichsen, 'Noormarkun Käsitöiden huonekalutuotannosta', 59–65.
51 Ibid., 59.
52 Ibid., 48.
53 Gullichsen, 'Noormarkun Käsitöiden huonekalutuotannosta', 48.
54 Ibid.
55 Oikarinen, 'Yritystoiminnan keskeiset vaiheet', 15–18.
56 Ibid.
57 Ibid.
58 Ibid., 18–22.
59 Ibid.
60 Esko Nummelin and Emilia Siltavuori, eds., *Maire Gullichsen* (Kukkila: Pori Art Museum, 2000), 128.
61 Ibid., 22–25.
62 Siltavuori, 'Noormarkku Crafts', 128.
63 Gullichsen, 'Noormarkun Käsitöiden huonekalutuotannosta', 48–49.
64 Ulla Kinnunen: *Ben af Schultén and the Artek Tradition* (Helsinki: Lönnberg Print, 2008), 13.
65 Harry Charrington, 'Artek and the Aalto Atelier in Postwar Finland', in *Artek and the Aaltos: Creating a Modern World*, ed. Nina Stritzler-Levine and Timo Riekko (New York: Bard Graduate Center, 2022), 589.
66 Ibid., 579.
67 Pontus Hultén was the director of Stockholm's Moderna Museet in 1959–73, and, later, he became the founding director of the Centre Pompidou, which opened in 1977.

68 Esko Nummelin, 'Pori Art Museum', in *Maire Gullichsen*, ed. Esko Nummelin and Emilia Siltavuori (Kukkila: Pori Art Museum, 2000), 206.

69 Martti Sinisalmi, 'Foreword', in *Maire Gullichsen*, ed. Esko Nummelin and Emilia Siltavuori (Kukkila: Pori Art Museum, 2000), 13.

70 Susanna Pettersson, 'From private to public, collector, and the identity of a collection', in *Maire Gullichsen*, ed. Esko Nummelin and Emilia Siltavuori (Kukkila: Pori Art Museum, 2000), 249.

71 Pekka Korvenmaa, 'From Policies to Politics: Finnish Design on the Ideological Battlefield in the 1960s and 1970s', in *Scandinavian Design – Alternative Histories*, ed. Kjetil Fallan (Oxford: Berg, 2012), 233.

72 Kaisu Savola, *Disrespectful thoughts about design: Social, political and environmental values in Finnish design, 1960–80*, (Joensuu: Aalto ARTS Books, 2023), 143.

73 Ulf Hård af Segerstad: *Modern Finnish Design* (Westport, CT: Frederick A. Praeger, Publishers, 1969), 45.

74 Ibid.

75 Ibid.

76 Korvenmaa, 'From Policies to Politics', 233.

77 Minna Sarantola-Weiss, 'Creature Comforts: Soft Sofas and the Demise of Modernist Morality in the 1970s Finland', in *Scandinavian Design – Alternative Histories*, ed. Kjetil Fallan (Oxford: Berg, 2012), 146–47.

# Chapter 9
# Barbara Hill and the Most Intimate Coffee House in Perth, Western Australia, 1956–1960

*Andrew Murray*

## INTRODUCTION

Throughout the twentieth-century coffee shops have been identified as key urban sites of intellectual and social ferment. They are places where ideas can be tested, networks can be formed, and debates may unfold. Historian Nick Beech equates them to 'social condensers' which he defines as 'critical spatial practice[s] immanent to social transformation [...] represent[ing] experiences "in solution" rather than in "precipitate", not "means" towards specific "ends" but lived moments'.[1] Beyond the archetypal bohemian cafes of continental Europe like the nearly mythical *Les Deux Magots* in Paris which are now popular tourist destinations, a host of ordinary coffee shops have provided a comfortable and lively atmosphere in which people meet and discuss ideas 'in solution' over a hot drink and nourishing meal. Some, like the short-lived Partisan Coffee House in London, were established with the specific aim of encouraging intellectual discussion.[2] Others were simply convenient locations that provided neutral grounds and cheap refreshments for meetings.[3] Not just coffee shops of course, but all manner of everyday restaurants and bars have also contributed to important discursive formations, and remain littered throughout historical accounts as physical anchors to otherwise ephemeral conversations and chance encounters outside of the office or the classroom which gave rise to more tangible movements and outcomes.[4]

Excavating these sites from the margins of history can provide illuminating details regarding the mechanics of how particular ideas or projects are crystalised, and the social spaces and networks upon which these formations relied. They provide the ability to chart previously unseen or unexplored networks which lie behind well-established narratives, and to new characters and events that can augment and enrich existing accounts.

Figure 9.1: 17 Howard Street, Perth. The Shiralee's entry was through the door on the far left. Collections of the State Library of Western Australia, Library Board of Western Australia.

Taking these spaces, and the people who were involved in making them, seriously allows for a multitude of voices and experiences to be included within history. A 2018 special issue of *Architecture and Culture* edited by Jessica Kelly and organised around the theme of 'Anonymity and Hidden Mechanisms in Design and Architecture' articulated the benefit and the potential consequences for contemporary scholarship in looking precisely at the kind of spaces such as coffee shops, which have typically not been the focus of discussion. Kelly's intention was:

> To explore the places, practices and people that were hidden in most conventional discussions of architecture and design [...] The sites of production like the office, the conference room, the bar and the objects that furnish them. The overlooked, anonymous designers, the ordinary and everyday people rather than the 'great' or extraordinary [...] The overlaps between professional and personal interactions, such as when an editorial meeting turns into an evening in the pub, or when the studio overlaps with the sitting room and when colleagues are friends or lovers.[5]

In excavating these places hitherto on the margins of history, previously hidden networks are revealed, and a wider cast of actors is introduced into the discourse. This is part of a broader effort to push for the writing of more diverse, inclusive, and robust histories, which Janina Gosseye has described as starting to produce 'a suite of microhistories and stories of everyday spaces as well as unknown and marginal figures [...] in an attempt to dismantle modern architecture's master narrative'.[6]

This chapter looks closely at one of these 'hidden' and 'everyday spaces' that became central to the development of a new, youthful architectural discourse in Western Australia, alongside the 'marginal' figure of one of its owners. The Shiralee, with its tag line of 'Perth's most intimate Coffee House', opened on Howard Street (Fig. 9.1) in the city centre in 1956. It was an initiative of recent arts graduate Barbara Hill and her husband, architect Alfred Alexander (Lex) Hill, along with Lex's parents, Alfred and Kathleen Hill. From its inception until a change of ownership four years later, the space was co-opted by the local architectural community, and it became the social hub for a group of young architects and architectural students. It became so closely connected with the profession that it was known informally among architects and architecture students as 'the architects coffee shop'.[7]

The architects and students who gathered at the Hill's Shiralee ushered in a new and progressive architectural culture that unfolded in Western Australia in the early 1960s and would shape the local profession for decades to come. The 1960s was a decade of profound cultural change in Perth particularly within the arts and the built environment. It was a period of unprecedented building activity spurred on by an enormous economic boom driven by new mineral wealth.[8] This cultural shift was due to a number of factors set largely in motion during the late 1950s. These included but were not limited to: a significant influx of young architects returning from their working holidays in the UK; the maturing of the first group of graduate architects from the Perth Technical College (PTC) course, many now leading their own practices; and the emergence of a robust architectural media landscape with new student magazines and a refreshed Institute journal.[9] The flurry of construction activity and economic prosperity meant there were abundant opportunities for young architects to test out their new ideas in practice. The Shiralee did not directly shape this cultural shift, but it opened precisely as these factors and new ideas were beginning to coalesce. It offered a space outside the office and the classroom where ideas could be tested, networks established, and plans formulated and debated over a hot coffee.

This account of the Shiralee particularly focuses on Barbara Hill (1932–), who, through her entrepreneurial spirit and gregarious nature, was an active participant in the development of this new architectural culture in Western Australia. Barbara was closely involved with the architectural profession of Perth for many decades, both socially and through the running of the Shiralee, but she is someone who traditionally sits outside of architectural history. She is not an architect, a client, a developer nor does she appear in the media. An account of the Shiralee could easily overlook her contribution and focus instead on the role of Lex and on his architectural connections. But the Shiralee was an enterprise that was a product of both Barbara and Lex, and of Lex's parents, and its success and cultural cachet was entirely dependent on and tied to the social atmosphere that Barbara and Lex cultivated. Acknowledging it as an extension of their hospitality, and understanding it as an explicit social enterprise, is crucial to identifying how and why it became such a key meeting place for an emerging young group of the profession. Further, acknowledging both Lex and Barbara in the story of the Shiralee enables us to see that this new architectural culture unfolded within a much wider cosmopolitan shift, one which was grounded in a newly discovered enthusiasm for the city. It was a place that saw various groups of young, culturally attuned people gather to engage in a particular modernity brought together through the openness and generosity of the owners. Ushering in cultural change was not their explicit aim; they just wanted a nice coffee shop where they and their friends could socialise. But in the purposeful act of providing this space, they allowed this shift to unfold.

## A NOTE ON SOURCES

The Shiralee has never been the subject of scholarly attention, and it has never been discussed in depth in any architectural or social history of Perth. I was first made aware of its existence when, during the course of my doctoral research, I conducted a number of oral histories with Perth architects who had studied at Perth Technical College in the late 1950s and early 1960s. It was frequently brought up in passing, but rarely remarked upon. It was just part of the lived experience for these architects. As I went on and the references kept piling up, I was soon put in contact with Barbara Hill, who was now living in Albany, a five-hour drive south of Perth.

Over a number of phone calls, formal interviews, letters and other exchanges, including a drive down to Albany to meet her in 2021, the story of the Shiralee unfolded. Lee's retelling revealed her motivations in opening it and the diffuse social and professional networks that converged there, with the architectural profession just one, albeit central, aspect of it. This account reflects not only her participation in running the shop and the broader context in which it was conceived, but also her perspective on the architectural scene as it developed in Perth during this time. This alternative perspective, one from outside the profession but firmly inside its social networks, provides an invaluable new and alternate understanding of the architectural culture in the state.

The Shiralee was an amateur run affair that lasted for four years under the Hill's stewardship, after which it was sold and became the influential and popular folk music venue for which it is now best remembered.[10] The café deliberately flew under the radar. It never advertised, appeared in the phone book, featured in the news, or became a backdrop to the glamorous social pages of the local paper. There are no photographs or ephemera from the café that have survived and very few primary sources to document it. Instead, the story of the Shiralee presented here has been constructed primarily through extensive exchanges with Barbara Hill, together with the recollection of various patrons.

## BARBARA AND LEX HILL

The story of the Shiralee is largely the story of its owners, Barbara and Lex Hill. It begins in 1954 when the pair, who had recently started dating, set off independently on the well-beaten path to England to live, work and explore. They were following in the tradition of the working holiday, an almost universal rite of passage for young professional Australians and New Zealanders that began in the 1920s and continues today. It is a journey in which groups of young people travel to the United Kingdom after completing their studies to live and work for a period of two or three years before returning home. Barbara Hill, (née Miller) was from a wheat and sheep farming family in rural Western Australia and had graduated with an Arts degree from the University of Western Australia (UWA) in 1953. Lex Hill had recently immigrated with his parents from Belfast to Western Australia and received his Associateship in Architecture diploma from Perth Technical College (PTC), also in 1953. Barbara left first, travelling with her sister Pamela, a kindergarten teacher, aboard the SS Orontes which sailed directly to London.[11] Lex soon followed, travelling aboard a

Figure 9.2: Barbara and Lex Hill outside Barbara's flat in London, with the scooter they drove home to Australia. Photographer: David Moore. Copyright: Lisa, Michael, Matthew and Joshua Moore.

cargo ship and disembarking in Athens before winding his way via train across to London via Italy.[12]

In London the pair lived separately. Barbara moved into a flat in Earls Court (Fig. 9.2) with a group of friends and worked a series of part time jobs including as a typist and a nanny, largely to support her extensive travels throughout the UK and the continent. Lex moved into a flat in Earls Court with a group of other architects from Perth and worked full time for an architectural practice. They married shortly before they returned home. In London they both took full advantage of the excitement that postwar city offered, enjoying the urbanity, food, music, and art of the vibrant scene. In contrast to the conservative, small town and suburban environment of Perth, London was a revelation, one shared by a large group of their friends all living together in close proximity.[13] In particular, the social freedom and late-night culture stood out. The group went to restaurants and the theatre, and gathered at pubs, which were not segregated by gender as they were in Perth, but rather had a warm and inclusive atmosphere with cosy nooks and warm mulled wine in the winter.[14]

But it was the experience of visiting the late-night coffee shops that was most memorable. This was a new type of coffee shop that had developed in London in the early 1950s, and it offered a vibrant new centrally located social space. In a note to me, Barbara described the straightforward motivation, despite the fact they had no experience in hospitality: 'Back in Perth after August 1955, remembering and missing the many coffee shops we'd enjoyed visiting in London and elsewhere, Lex and I, with his parents, were keen to start a coffee shop.'[15] Perth at that time had no coffee shops like it, and Barbara and Lex simply wanted 'a good coffee shop' of their own, while Lex's parents wanted a retirement project.[16] The London coffee shops that Barbara identified were a unique phenomenon and developed a specific and reproducible typology that would spread across the world, largely in major Commonwealth cities like Melbourne, Brisbane, and Auckland.[17] An exploration of the typology and its history provides important context for the Shiralee, and for the Hill's seemingly impulsive decision.

## THE LONDON COFFEE SHOP TYPOLOGY

The London coffee shop was a distinct and identifiable type which emerged in the early 1950s amidst a postwar youth revolution which was unfolding across the city. It was a type that was spatially, aesthetically, and operationally different from the coffee houses of the 17$^{th}$ and 18$^{th}$ century, yet clearly 'redolent of [their] sociability'.[18] The new London coffee shop emerged in the wake of the invention of the modern espresso machine in Italy, which was patented by Gaggia in 1947, and used pressure rather than steam to extract the coffee. The invention of this machine led to what coffee historian Markman Ellis described as a global 'espresso revolution' which would occur across the globe in several different guises and models, among them a specific type known as the London coffee shop.[19]

The London coffee shop came to typify the youth-led cultural shift that occurred in immediate postwar Britain. Markman Ellis describes their impact:

> The espresso-bar revolution had 'exploded like a bomb' in the mid 1950s. Importing an idea and some technology from Italy, it was transformed by London's particular forms of urban sociability, by jazz and skiffle, by teenage fashions and migrant expectations [...] the espresso bars were auguries of the new politics of later decades.[20]

With outrageous interiors, late opening hours, and juke boxes, they became the social hubs for a generation of newly emancipated British youth, who, having seen off the end of wartime rationing, were emboldened with a new sense of free time, money, and a growing appetite for socialising, culture and fun, as well as desperate for a social space they could identify as their own. By 1956, just three years after the first of the new wave espresso cafés was opened by Pino Riservato in his Soho basement, there was an estimated 475 coffee shops in London.[21] Ellis articulates their appeal:

> There was little of the formality, ritual and expense of dining in restaurants; and unlike public houses and taverns, there were no licensing laws regulating the age of customers and hours of business [...] Their clientele was young, fashionable and, most notably, comprised both sexes, men and women.[22]

The coffee houses of London were thus entirely new spaces, free from the historical associations and cultural baggage of other late night or traditional youth-oriented venues. This made them an entirely 'new social space' which allowed for the meeting of 'a hitherto proscribed mixture of people' integral to their success.[23] Shops like the Mocamba Coffee Bar, which the Hills likely visited given it was just around the corner from their Earl's Court flats and that at least one of their close friends, also from PTC, Ross Chisholm patronised it, were exciting social hubs and summed up much of what was so attractive about the experience of living even temporarily in London.[24] These shops quickly spread across the UK and Ireland, and Barbara recalled that, during a particularly memorable visit to a coffee house in Dublin on a holiday in 1954, the idea that she and Lex should open their own coffee shop in Perth crystalised.[25] So when the couple returned in 1955 they drew directly on their experiences in this new coffee shop typology.

## COFFEE SHOP AMATEURS

The freedom and social atmosphere that these night time venues offered in London were a revelation to Barbara, Lex, and their broader social circle that they lived and travelled with in London. In Barbara's words: they were 'refreshing'.[26] In stark contrast, the nightlife and social scene of 1950s Perth was limited. Restaurants were rare and formal, and coffee was largely only available in old fashioned, formal pre-war tea rooms.[27]

The pub, always connected to a large hotel, remained the dominant social space for young people with alcohol as its focus. Public bars in central Perth were still male-only affairs, and those that did allow women had separate 'ladies lounges' that were hidden away, cut off from the main bar area, and drinks were charged an added premium. Indeed, it was not until well into the 1960s and 1970s that it became acceptable for women to drink in the main public bars in Australia.[28] Barbara keenly felt this discrimination. Shortly before she sailed for London, she recalled a time when she was denied entry to the Palace Hotel Bar, located on St George's Terrace, which was then the city architects' main after-work drinking spot. She had gone there to meet Lex but was refused entry and instead directed to the ladies' lounge upstairs with the other 'wives' about which she strongly protested to the owners.[29] Barbara was clear in her discussions with me that this episode was not a direct motivation for wanting to open the Shiralee, but it was an issue that has clearly stayed with her. It provides an insight into the social setting and conservative atmosphere of Perth at the time of which she was acutely aware and which she was actively resisting. It is also an episode which serves to demonstrate her progressive attitude and burgeoning modernity which would only be further stoked within the late-night vibrancy of London.

Invigorated by their experience abroad, the pair decided to open their own coffee shop. It was to be a space where their friends and associates, many of them also recently returned from London, could gather and replicate a cosmopolitanism that was missing in Perth. Lex's mother Kathleen named the Shiralee after a recent eponymous novel by D'Arcy Niland. None had any experience in hospitality or running a café. They were simply interested in the idea and buoyed by the enthusiasm of youth and the optimism of the postwar period. Their seemingly impulsive decision to reproduce the liberating social spaces they had encountered in London speaks particularly to Barbara and Lex's gregarious nature, and of their generous hospitality and inclination for hosting. The pair were well connected socially within Perth's emerging cultural scene, and they sought to extend this to a physical venue that they could share with friends.

The apparently impulsive decision to open the café further aligns the Shiralee with the London coffee shop scene of the 1950s which was dominated by 'amateurs'.[30] Matthew Partington, an authority on the London coffee house scene of the 1950s, notes that this was the result of a number of factors but predominantly the low inflation rates, and the still moribund economy, which meant that rental prices for commercial properties were low enough 'to allow someone with very little capital to rent or lease business premises – it was a chance worth taking'.[31] Another commentator of the day, Martha Gellhorn, noted the charm and benefits of these enterprises as they existed in London: 'No previous experience or training is necessary, and little capital [...] The interior decoration can just as well be home-made as not, if funds are low [...] Amateurism in fact pays, perhaps by setting the desirable tone of intimate harum-scarumry.'[32] A similar economic situation faced the Hills in Perth, and so they were able to take the risk.

## BUILDING THE SHIRALEE

The four set to work transforming a square basement office with no street frontage into 'Perth's most intimate coffee house' as it would be described on their menus. Many of their friends were able to drop by and lend a hand where they could but much of it was built by Lex and Barbara. They constructed all the tables out of plywood tops and hairpin bent steel legs. Barbara made curtains and sewed red and white checked tablecloths. A small kitchen was installed with a sink, electric frypan, soup pot, and vertical sandwich toaster along with a coffee percolator. A bench was built along one side with small stools, and scattered potted plants as well as paintings by their friends enlivened the space. They printed bright yellow menus, which were placed on the tables and hanging on the walls, adding a touch of colour. The hero was the espresso machine, which Barbara bought from a local department store for 25 pounds. A shiny chrome, single group, lever machine sat atop the counter space – the gleaming symbol of the new wave coffee house.

The Shiralee opened on Valentine's Day 1956 to a small crowd of friends and family. Open from 9am until midnight every day, except Sunday when it was closed for private functions and parties, the Shiralee offered a space to meet during the day and socialise at night. It was a cosmopolitan enclave where young culturally attuned people could freely socialise away from male dominated and uncomfortable bars and pubs. The main attraction of the Shiralee was of course coffee, but the modest kitchen also offered a small menu of toasted sandwiches, soup – always with cream – pikelets and Peters' ice cream. It wasn't licensed, but customers were allowed to bring in alcohol at night, which they rarely did. The only time alcohol was really consumed was on Sundays when they held occasional private parties. Lex was busy with his day job at the architectural practice Hawkins and Sands, so Barbara oversaw much of the running of the café in the early days, with Lex dropping in after work to lend a hand. Shortly after opening it was the senior Hills who ran the café as Barbara was busy with a young child, but she would still prepare the coffee and run over ingredients during the lunch break. Kathleen played a particularly important role in the life of the coffee shop and became the social heart of the enterprise. On Saturdays, the busiest night of the week, both Barbara and Lex would run it, essentially hosting an open party, attracting a cosmopolitan in-crowd.

As the first dedicated espresso bar in Perth's central business district, the Shiralee attracted a diverse crowd, but it predominantly catered to those young people involved with the city's emerging cultural scene and was closely aligned to the Hill's wide ranging social circle. Many were looking to extend the enthusiasm and excitement for urban life that they had experienced in London. Some were artists, dancers, actors, and authors who were active participants in Perth's cultural scene. But all were drawn together by a renewed enthusiasm for the city and emboldened by the new cosmopolitanism that postwar prosperity enabled. This engagement with the city centre and nightlife was a far cry from the suburban Perth of their youth. Many, including the Hills, moved into apartments in the middle of the city, and a series of cultural hubs opened up, including art galleries, theatres, and late-night restaurants which provided a vibrant social scene previously unknown in Perth.[33] The Shiralee was a central node in this new urban landscape.

During the Hills' tenure, the Shiralee was best known, however, for its close connection to the city's architectural community. Driven by the fact that Lex was a highly visible and well-known member of the profession, the Shiralee became one of the main places for young architects to meet and discuss.[34] The shop was near the architectural school at the Perth Technical College, which meant it quickly became a student favourite and it was used by its students as both a social space and a meeting place. It became the default place to retire after events like the cricket matches organised by the students and staff and was treated almost like a clubhouse by young architects. Duncan Richards, a prominent architectural historian who studied at PTC in the 1950s recalled 'I went to The Shiralee frequently. It was a good place to meet architectural students, friends [...] [but] the main reason I went to the Shiralee was to be left alone and to read'.[35] Those that gathered at the Shiralee would go on to be key contributors to the local Institute journal, and students who regularly met there would shortly put together a radical student magazine *Aedicule*. The student notes section of *The Architect*, the journal of the Royal Australian Institute of Architects Western Australian chapter, of this period reveals this close relationship, and mentions of the Shiralee are dotted throughout its issues. For instance:

> It is most gratifying to find that a discussion group has developed among the First Year Students. Symposia are held regularly at the Shiralee, and here questions of religion, art, philosophy, etc., are discussed.[36]

Or in another instance:

> The meeting ended at 2255 hours with a mad scramble in the direction of the 'Shiralee' coffee lounge [...] The masses, having settled down within intimate surroundings, were served with tasty sandwiches, cakes, ice cream and hot coffee.[37]

Mentions like this abound. A recent monograph on the work of architect Ralph Drexel recalls that he met his wife Heather Courthope at the Shiralee, and in an oral history leading international architect Kerry Hill recalled that the Shiralee was a large part of what made studying architecture in the city so exciting.[38] There was also a series of infamous pantomimes staged at the Shiralee each Christmas by the local architectural community that have contributed to the folklore of the place.[39] In this way, the Shiralee became central to the production of the progressive architectural culture which emerged in Perth in the late 1950s, offering a space where one could meet, talk, and linger over a coffee, outside of the office or classroom, and apart from the older architectural establishment.

## BARBARA'S CONTRIBUTION

The Shiralee was not just an architect's café, however. Through Barbara's recollection of the venture a more nuanced and complex story of the Shiralee began to emerge, one which clearly identifies a number of adjacent, and loosely connected social and cultural networks that converged there. Examining these various paths allows for a fuller understanding of the intellectual and social ferment that produced a new and progressive architectural culture in the late 1950s. It also situates the development of this culture within broader social and artistic developments and illuminates a whole series of figures connected to an emerging modernity in Perth.

Barbara's recollection naturally focuses upon her social circle, which included architects, journalists, artists, and teachers. Many of these were relationships that had been nurtured during her time at university, where she was involved in the Undergraduate's Guild. An example of these overlapping social groups can be seen in her involvement with the 1952 University of Western Australia Revue, staged by the Guild. This production included a performance by the Architectural Students' Association alongside Barbara, and her friends Anne West, June Eggleston and Joanna Ainslie, with whom she would travel to the UK.[40] These were overlaps that would be replicated at the Shiralee.

Barbara recalled the wait staff, who were just close friends roped in to work, and included influential and high profile members of the new cultural scene such as Paddy Parry, wife of architect Mervyn Parry, Penelope Hanrahan, a professional ballerina, and Jacquie Sprogoe, now a jewellery designer, who was then the secretary for the architectural firm of Hobbs, Winning and Leighton. Sprogoe worked in the coffee shop during her lunchbreaks in order to earn extra money to save up for her own London trip.[41] Barbara noted that the artists Guy and Helen Grey-Smith exhibited their paintings at the coffee shop and that at Christmas Helen would sell fabric and small items like Christmas cards. She recalled other artists like Robert Juniper helped in decorating the shop. Juniper was a regular, alongside cartoonist Paul Rigby, whose wife Marlene Cockburn was a journalist and close friend of the Hills. A regular stream of actors and musicians also came in through the back door from the Capitol Theatre, one of the city's grandest. This meant that musicians performing at the Capitol would regularly duck in after performances, sometimes playing a small show to the coffee shop crowd.

The Shiralee provided the space in which such cosmopolitanism could be enacted. Beth Duncan (née Blair), a close friend of the Hills and wife of architect John Duncan, who had been in London at the same time, recalled: 'The Shiralee was a meeting place. For us it was quite exciting to have a coffee shop in Perth. Up until then there had been virtually nothing like that.'[42]

The Shiralee had a welcoming, intimate atmosphere. It did not make any money, but it did encourage people to linger over a coffee, to talk and to socialise. Barbara described it as 'friendly and inefficient', operating mostly by word of mouth to serve their wider network of friends.[43] It was small, quiet and familiar, a kind of refuge within the city, that transcended Perth's pervasive conservatism. The Shiralee operated more like a social enterprise than a going business concern and it functioned as a direct extension of the Hills' hospitality. Alongside art galleries, theatres, and pool halls, it provided a crucial piece in the transformation of central Perth.

This wider view of the clientele and patronage of the Shiralee begins to sketch out a picture of an emerging cosmopolitanism in Perth, that involved multiple convergent groups and. It demonstrates that the progressive architectural discourse of the time did not emerge in isolation, but rather was a product of an attitude shared amongst a wide range of people, formed in part through their shared experiences overseas and consolidated at a coffee lounge, generously enabled by the hospitable spirit of Barbara and Lex Hill.

## CONCLUSION

In 1959, the Hill family moved to Sarawak, Indonesia where Lex joined the British Colonial Service. His parents continued to run the Shiralee for another year in Barbara and Lex's absence but sold it in 1960 after which it was transformed into a well-known folk music venue. The couple returned to Perth in 1961. Lex went back to Hawkins and Sands, and Barbara looked after the young family. She did not return to the hospitality industry after the Shiralee, but she did continue her close connection with the city's burgeoning cultural community.

In a small city like Perth, with an even smaller and more concentrated cultural scene, a small space or a single moment can galvanise a group. A coffee shop like the Shiralee, supported by the generosity and gregarious nature of its two young hosts, was able to act as a catalyst for an emerging cultural shift that occurred in Perth in the late 1950s. It became a key point at which a number of scenes converged in a highly charged, small, social space.[44] For the four years that the Hill's ran it, it became a key hub in the developing postwar modernity of Perth.

Barbara and Lex Hill had an enthusiasm for city life, awakened in London, that they sought to bring back to Perth. The Shiralee captured the excitement and sophistication of urban life in London, transported and recreated on the edges of the Commonwealth for a willing and eager crowd, and added considerably to Perth's vitality. Through their generous actions they provided a space that both advanced its cultural outlook, and one that was adopted by the local architectural community as a place to meet outside institutional walls and typical drinking spots. Here students could learn outside the curriculum and engage their teachers and other architects in a social setting. This to commissions and relationships that would extend far beyond the small space of the coffee shop.

The Shiralee was a joint venture, shared between Barbara and Lex Hill, and Lex's parents. All played a role in its existence, but specifically highlighting the contribution that Barbara made allows for a richer and more developed understanding of a nascent cosmopolitanism and social group in Perth. This was a group in which architecture was firmly embedded, and in which Barbara played a featured role. Her interest in running the coffee shop was spurred by her frustration at being unable to access social spaces within Perth available to her husband, but also a desire to see a more equitable social space for herself and her friends. In this sense Barbara made a significant contribution to the modernity of Perth, and its architectural culture.

Barbara is not an architect, nor in architectural media, nor is she a client or contractor. But through her vision, in her desire for change, and through her ambition, she played a key role in the development of a new architectural scene of Perth and was a witness to its unfolding. By agitating for change in a pragmatic and practical fashion, she and Lex encouraged a new discourse to develop, one which would ultimately shape much of the future of the built environment of Perth. They brought together people with otherwise disparate ideas who were nonetheless united by their desire for modernity and urbanity. Acknowledging her entrepreneurial contribution allows for a broader and more nuanced understanding of the networks, connections, and social links which underpinned the architectural profession and cultural scene of a small, geographically isolated city.

# NOTES

1 Nick Beech, 'Social Condensation in the Metropole: Locating the First New Left', *The Journal of Architecture* 22, no. 3 (2017): 506.

2 The Partisan Coffee House in Carlisle Street Soho was established in 1959 by Raphael Samuel ostensibly as a club room for the emerging British New Left. See: Beech, 'Social Condensation in the Metropole', 506.

3 An example is the Old Vienna Coffee Inn, Brisbane, which became the informal meeting room for the Queensland Association of Landscape Architects. See Andrew Saniga and Andrew Wilson, 'A League of His Own: Karl Langer's Landscape Australia', in *Karl Langer: Modern Architect and Migrant in the Australian Tropics*, ed. Deborah van der Plaat and John Macarthur (London: Bloomsbury, 2022), 251.

4 See for example: Kirsten Day and Peter Raisbeck, 'The Last Laugh and its Afterlife: Emerging narratives in 1970s Melbourne Architecture', *Fabrications* 31, no. 3 (2021): 336–356.

5 Jessica Kelly, 'Anonymity and Hidden Mechanisms in Design and Architecture', *Architecture and Culture* 6, no. 1 (2018): 7.

6 Janina Gosseye, 'A short history of Silence: The Epistemological Politics of Architectural Historiography', in *Speaking of Buildings: Oral History in Architectural Research*, ed. Naomi Stead, Deborah van der Plaat and Janina Gosseye (New York: Princeton Architectural Press, 2019), 12.

7 Robert Gare, phone conversation with Andrew Murray, 23 September 2021.

8 Pat Duffy, ed., *The David-Foulkes Taylor Years: Invitation Exhibition, WAIT 1982* (Perth: WAIT, 1982), 11.

9 For further information on this shift see: Andrew Murray, 'Tee Square Journal, Phi, Aspect, and Aedicule: The Publications of the Architectural Students Association of Western Australia', *Fabrications* 33, no. 1 (2023): 142–170.

10 For details on the Shiralee when it was a folk venue see: David Hough, 'Eating Places', in *The Historical Encyclopedia of Western Australia*, ed. Jenny Gregory and Jan Gothard (Crawley: UWA Press, 2009), 297–299; Jon Stratton, 'Youth Culture', in *The Historical Encyclopedia of Western Australia*, ed. Jenny Gregory and Jan Gothard (Crawley: UWA Press, 2009), 963–65; Malcolm J. Turnbull, 'The Folk Boom in Perth', *Town Crier: Newsletter of the Western Australian Folk Federation* 32, no. 5 (2004).

11 'W.A. Girls in London Get Car and Jobs', *The West Australian*, 17 May 1954, 14.

12 Kirwan Ward, 'Peepshow', *The Daily News*, 18 September 1954, 16.

13 For further details on this group of West Australians living together in London see: Andrew Murray, 'What To Do with "Thirty Blow-Ins" at a Housewarming Party: Peripheral Figures and Architectural History', in *Proceedings of the Society of Architectural Historians Australia and New Zealand* 37, *what If? What Next? Speculations of History's Futures*, ed. Kate Hislop and Hanna Lewi (Perth: SAHANZ, 2021): 584–89.

14 Mulled wine was a particularly fond memory of this time in London that Barbara shared with me. Barbara Hill, Telephone Communication with Andrew Murray, 22 March 2022.

15 Barbara Hill, letter to Andrew Murray, 13 January 2020.

16 Barbara Hill, telephone communication with Andrew Murray, 22 March 2022.

17 Examples include Il Capuccino (Melbourne 1954); El Cubana (Melbourne 1955); The Arab (Lorne 1956); The Primitif (Brisbane, 1957); and The Attic (Christchurch, 1957).

18 Markman Ellis, *The Coffee-House: A Cultural History* (London: Weidenfeld & Nicolson, 2004), 234.

19 Ellis, *The Coffee-House*, 244.

20 Ibid.

21 Ibid., 228.

22 Ibid., 233

23 Ibid., 245.

24 Ross Chisholm, personal diary, 1954, private collection of Katrina Chisholm.

25 Barbara Hill, telephone communication with Andrew Murray, 24 May 2024.

26 Barbara Hill, telephone communication with Andrew Murray, 8 March 2021.

27 A notable exception was the Van Gogh Coffee Lounge, a student-run bohemian café that opened in 1952.

28 There were different rules for each state, for further details see: Clare Wright, '"Doing the Beans": Women, Drinking and Community in the Ladies' Lounge', *Journal of Australian Studies* 27, no. 76 (2003): 5–16.

29 Barbara Hill, telephone communication with Andrew Murray, 22 March 2022.

30 Matthew Partington, 'The London Coffee Bar of the 1950s – Teenage Occupation of an Amateur Space?' Paper presented at *Occupation: Negotiations with Constructed Space (Interior Architecture Conference)* 2-3 July 2009, University of Brighton, 4.

31 Partington, 'The London Coffee Bar of the 1950s', 4.

32 Martha Gellhorn, 'So Awful to Be Young, or, Morning to Midnight in Espresso Bars', *Encounter* 6, no. 5 (1956): 43, quoted in: Partington, 'The London Coffee Bar of the 1950s', 4.

33 Key establishments included the Skinner Gallery, Latin Quarter restaurant, and Playhouse Theatre.

34 At the time of opening, Lex was joint editor of *The Architect WA*, the local Institute's official journal, and was working in the practice Hawkins and Sands, which was known as the most progressive and ambitious practice in the city.

35 Duncan Richards, email correspondence with Andrew Murray, 25 November 2019.

36 'Students' Notes: From the School of Architecture', *The Architect* (September 1957): 41.

37 'Architectural Students' Association' *The Architect* (March 1956): 31.

38 Kerry Hill, Oral History conducted by the UWA Historical Society, 21 November 2013, accessed 15 May 2024, https://oralhistories.arts.uwa.edu.au/items/show/85.

39 Ian Kelly, curator, *Peter Parkinson: Theatre Architecture* (Perth: York Theatre Festival, 1987).

40 The Guild of Undergraduates of the U.W.A. – *The University Revue*, 1952, booklet, PR8065/THE/475, University of Western Australia Theatres: Collection of Ephemera Material, State Library of Western Australia.

41 Jacquie Sprogoe, telephone communication with Andrew Murray, 13 March 2020.

42 Beth Duncan, interview with Andrew Murray, 10 March 2021, Swanbourne, W.A.

43 Barbara Hill, telephone communication with Andrew Murray, 14 June 2021.

44 It is important to note that there were other key cultural institutions where people gathered, like art openings, theatre, and bars, but the Shiralee offered a dedicated social setting.

Chapter 10

# Lena's Bookshop

## Uncomfortable Knowledge, Modern Architecture, and the Building of a Southeast Asian Space, 1976–2004

*Eunice Seng*

On 1 September 2004, the *Straits Times* newspaper announced the closing of a 'little bookstore' in Singapore's commercial district. The closure was followed by letter tributes and articles featuring the owner, Lena U Wen Cheng, and her twenty-eight-year-old bookshop, Select Books. A journalist described it as a 'near-institution' – a label with which no author, artist, architect, or booklover would disagree.[1] Cheng, known publicly as Mrs Lena Lim after her marriage to the architect-urbanist William Siew Wai Lim ('Willy' or 'Willie') and simply 'Lena' to close friends, founded Select Books with two partners in 1976. Dr Lai Ah Eng, a senior research fellow at the Institute of Policy Studies, described the bookstore as a 'must-visit' for all academics passing through. With a reputation as an 'alternative' bookshop, because it carried books written by opposition politicians, Select Books was as Nancy Chng recalled, the place in Singapore for making friends who shared a common thirst for knowledge.

This chapter situates the founding of Select Books in the 1970s, a transitional period in Singapore of economic growth and heroic nationalism. Channel News Asia (CNA) described the decade as the time when the 'nation [came] of age'.[2] This chapter examines her 'knowledge reversal' project by attending to the entanglements between the cultural 'institutionalization' of the bookshop, the shopping centre, and the intellectual and creative discourses they enabled. In so doing, it considers how the Lims' literary and architectural practices reimagined place-identity and re-centred creative production, and particularly how Lena, as an entrepreneur, cultural figure, and women's rights advocate, built forms of solidarity with individuals and groups on the frontlines of postcolonial knowledge production to envision an intercultural Asia.

## TRANSREGIONAL BEGINNINGS

Lena Cheng was born in Manila in 1937 to Cheng Sing Kwang, a diplomat in the Chinese Republican government's department of foreign affairs, and Kong Fung Shing. Her two eldest brothers and a sister were born in China. She and two other brothers were born in Manila after their father was re-assigned to the Philippines. He was posted to Singapore just before the war but sent back to China months before Singapore fell to the Japanese in 1942. After a year in China, he moved his family to Calcutta – an important posting because overseas American aid went through Calcutta over the Himalayas into Chongqing after the coasts of China were taken by the Japanese. The family stayed in India during the war after which Cheng left government service and moved back to Singapore in 1947. The boys were sent to Chinese schools while the two girls received an English education. Lena described her homemaker mother as a 'liberal person' who believed in equal access to education for boys and girls.[3] In 1956 she joined the Singapore division of the University of Malaya, which in 1962 was renamed the University of Singapore, where she majored in history and geography, with a minor in art history, and graduated in 1960 with an honours degree in history.

The years between 1955 and 1960 were significant for the rising consciousness in Southeast Asia of the region as an interconnected political, economic, and cultural entity. Indian Prime Minister Jawaharlal Nehru described this as the 'new dynamism of Asia'.[4] Singapore's first general election coincided with the first Afro-Asian conference in Bandung, West Java, in April 1955, at which twenty-nine nations were represented. Two delegates of the Labour Front, the newly-elected government, attended as observers and shared updates with other Asian delegates on Malaya's 'fight for independence'.[5] In October of that year, academics from The University of Malaya attended the first conference on South East Asian Studies at the University of Rangoon. It was sponsored by Johns Hopkins University's Centre of South East Asian Studies.[6] The Centre also sponsored a subsequent meeting at Chulalongkorn University in Bangkok attended by academics from Burma, Hong Kong, Indonesia, the Philippines, Singapore, Sri Lanka (then Ceylon), and Vietnam.[7] In 1957, among its efforts to become a main South East Asia centre for the study of oriental languages and culture, the University of Malaya sent several hundred copies of its first volume of a classified catalogue of the collection of Chinese books to universities, libraries and centres of Chinese studies throughout the world including universities and cultural organisations in Beijing and Taipei.[8] It also hosted many inaugural international conferences including the Malay Language and Literary Congress in September 1956, an all-Malayan student conference in April 1959, and a conference on educational policy in Southeast Asia in September 1959.[9]

The foregrounding of women's representation and rights in society were integral to the politics of independence. Between 1955 and 1959, the Singapore Council of Women (SCW) lobbied various political parties to address the injustices faced by women, arguing that 'the attainment of independence will remain an idle dream if the men in this country do not rise to generous heights to grant that independence to their own kith and kin – the women of the country'. In summer 1958, the SCW held a rally to discuss monogamy.[10] In an address to 150 women leaders and social workers in October 1958, the Chief Minister and the Labour Minister urged women leaders to 'fight for your rights'.[11] The Labour Party government emphasised gender equality education.[12] The People's Action Party (PAP), under pressure from members of its Women's League – many of whom were young, Chinese educated and markedly socialist in their ideals – took the strongest stand on women's rights.[13] For the May 1959 General Elections, it was the only party to campaign openly on the 'one man one wife' slogan, and its leaders urged women to play a 'greater role in nation-building'. Women came out in full force on voting day.[14] Lena Cheng was among them.

In 1960, after graduating from the University of Malaya (renamed the National University of Singapore in 1980), Cheng took a job with the English-language *Straits Times* newspaper. Working with Gillian Mills, editor of the Woman's Page, she oversaw the establishment of *Her World*, a new women's magazine. The first issue featured seven sections: 'fashion, beauty, fiction, home, letters, good advice, good cause'. Cheng's first article in the inaugural issue of July 1960 covered campus fashion, specifically in the Teachers' Training College and the University of Malaya.[15] In August, she covered the dormitory life of undergraduate women in the largest residential college at the University.[16] Her article for September focused on the women in the National Workers Brigade, which the government formed in February 1960 to provide employment to youths and help build the infrastructure in Singapore.[17] When she visited the camp in Pasir Ris, northeast of Singapore, forty women out of the site's 200 workers were cutting back the under-growth and clearing debris on the Brigade's first project, which was to build a sixty-foot wide canal at Sungei Api Api.[18] A few women remained behind in the camp to cook and clean. In October, Cheng followed a cocktail dress back to the Malayan Weaving Mill in Johore, north of Singapore, where she interviewed women factory workers on their working conditions and experiences.[19] Her articles in the November issue on women participating in voluntary social service and the work of the National Association Women's Institutes Federation of Malaya (WI) documented a historical moment where women were present and active participants in the 'road to independence'.[20] She also visited the headquarters of the WI in the Ibu Pejabat, where women living in the rural kampongs paid a nominal subscription fee to get together to discuss and 'learn how to be better wives, mothers, and citizens'.

Cheng's time with *Her World* was short-lived. In 1961, she returned to her first love: books. 'At least books can't answer back!' she said when asked about her time as a reporter.[21] After her journalistic stint, she worked in various libraries, first in the University of Malaya, where she was elected to the management committee of the Varsity Society in April 1961 and discovered the works of Southeast Asian scholars and authors. In 1959, Kennedy G. Tregonning, Raffles Professor of History and head of the university's history department, began developing its library into the 'most comprehensive on Malayan history in the world' and a centre for the study of Southeast Asian history.[22] Tregonning joined the university as a senior lecturer in 1953 after delivering a world history course with an emphasis on Asia and then later Malaya, which he felt had been 'treated as a colony'.[23] Tregonning convened the first international conference on Southeast Asian history and established the *Journal of Southeast Asian History* in 1960 (renamed *Journal of Southeast Asian Studies* in 1969).[24] His teaching and scholarship on Southeast Asia influenced Cheng's own commitment to the region and its cultural offerings.

Cheng married William Siew Wai Lim (known to most as Willy) in 1962 and took a leave of absence from the University library nine months later to pursue a Diploma in Librarianship at University College London, which she completed in 1964. Upon her return, she joined the Hong Kong-published *Asia Magazine* as chief librarian, and later worked for the *Singapore Herald*.[25] Willy co-founded the multidisciplinary Singapore Planning and Urban Research group (SPUR) that year. SPUR published two volumes containing essays by its members and affiliates. In 1969, with two children aged two and four, Lena worked as a part-time library consultant for professional firms, including her husband's Design Partnership Architects (renamed DP Architects in 1975).[26] Founded in 1967, the same year the Urban Renewal Authority (URA) launched its first Sale of Sites programme for private development, Design Partnership's first large project commissions were two modern shopping malls, the Golden Mile Complex and the People's Park Complex. Lena developed a cataloguing system for Design Partnership's books, magazines, reports, and documents.[27] Lena and Willy's family and professional lives intertwined until his passing in 2023.[28]

## GEOPOLITICS OF MODERN ARCHITECTURE

On the economic and cultural front, the first decade of independence, achieved in 1965, witnessed the consolidation of Singapore's place in Southeast Asia through research and knowledge exchange, public campaigns, and commerce, this last as manifested in a plethora of tourist shops, shopping centres and hotels. Design Partnership Architects received commissions to design four shopping centres in four districts across the island. In March 1971, in a lecture at the Rotary Club entitled 'What Sort of Singapore Do We Want to Give Our Children?', Willy called for planning criteria that advocated for the benefit of all citizens.[29] In the same year Lena joined the non-governmental organisation Asian Mass Communication Research and Information Centre (AMIC) as programme specialist. Founded that February by the Government of Singapore and the Friedrich Ebert Foundation, which was associated with the German Social Democratic political party, AMIC published books, reports, and academic journals focused on the development of media and communication theories, strategies, and from Asian-Pacific perspectives on practices to enable 'the flow of information about Asian research among Asians'. She set up their documentation library for 'what they call fugitive or grey material', in other words, articles and seminar papers.[30]

In January 1972, the seven-storey Tanglin Shopping Centre, designed by Design Partnership Architects, opened five hundred meters down the road from AMIC in the commercial district of Orchard Road.[31] From 1970, the Singapore government promulgated shopping as a regional and national pastime as the air-conditioned shopping complex – 'the thing of the future' – anticipated the city-state's changing consumption habits.[32] However, what set Tanglin Shopping Centre apart from the other complexes was the establishment of the private Singapore Medical Centre which accommodated eighteen medical practitioners with up-to-date hospital facilities, spearheaded by Dr Arthur Lim, the president of the Singapore Medical Association and Willy's elder brother.[33] The Medical Centre was part of a wave of medical specialists clustered in the new shopping complexes along

Orchard Road, which peaked in 1979 with the opening of the Mount Elizabeth Hospital and helped establish Singapore's reputation as a regional medical hub. Chee Guan Chye, managing director of Tanglin Shopping Centre and a member of the Pacific Area Travel Association (PATA), expressed that its 150 shops and kiosks carrying goods made in Singapore, Southeast Asia, and beyond would draw tourists to Singapore, making it the 'shopping paradise of Southeast Asia.'[34]

Design Partnership completed three other shopping complexes in the early 1970s. In May 1971, Golden Mile Complex, a monumental mixed-use development comprising a shopping centre, 208 offices, and 84 apartments above, opened on Beach Road.[35] The Lims moved into an apartment in the complex soon after it opened. Next, Singapura Developments commissioned the firm to design a new eight-storey Katong Shopping Centre, another 'under one roof' shopping complex in the affluent residential area on the island's east coast.[36] By the end of 1971, there were already six shopping complexes in operation in Singapore, with four more almost ready to open, three on the drawing board and more in conception. Tanglin Shopping Centre, which opened in 1972, was under construction and Katong Shopping Centre on the drawing board. In Tanglin Shopping Centre's first year, Lufthansa marked its tenth anniversary by moving to the ground and second floors. Genexco International, the exclusive distributor of the top five US manufacturers of home products, opened its first Singapore outlet on the first floor, where the Czech shoe store Bata could also be found.[37] Art connoisseurs Marius and Millie Jalbaud opened an antique shop named 'Connoisseur'. At the same time, first-time entrepreneurs like Marianne Pereira sold Singapore-made items in Imagination, her shop on the second floor.[38] Like Lena, Pereira had a background in journalism. She regularly wrote articles on fashion and beauty as a journalist for the *Straits Times* from 1967 to 1970 and became a public relations officer for a large hotel before setting up Imagination in early 1973.

## UNCOMFORTABLE KNOWLEDGE

Lena attributed her entrepreneurial beginning to her husband. During her years of librarianship, including her last stint at AMIC, she was increasingly uncomfortable with 'the flow of information from west to east in the world of learning'. In September 1972, the Centre held the Asian Conference of Editors of Mass Communication Periodicals in the recently opened Ming

Figure 10.1: Select Books on the second floor of Tanglin Shopping Centre, Singapore, c. 1976. Photograph © Select Books.

Court Hotel, where over twenty editors of specialised periodicals from eleven Asian countries gathered to discuss the need for a regional mass communication journal.[39] She saw the systemic prejudices against Asian scholars and authors, evident in the conference debates where no agreement was reached on government involvement in the regional journal. Eventually Nanyang University (known as Nantah) formally launched its independent Department of Mass Communications after collaboration talks with AMIC fell through in 1976.[40] That year, Lena resigned from her position at AMIC and, in her own words, became 'a librarian without a library'.[41] While she deliberated, she recounted how 'Willie was determined to stop me from dithering so he had Select Books registered as a company'.[42] On 1 October 1976, Lena and two other shareholders opened Singapore's first independent bookshop on the second-floor corner of the seven-storey air-conditioned Tanglin Shopping Centre (Fig. 10.1). Willy was the chairman 'with the business sense', and Lena was the managing director. She invited Nancy Chng, whom she had met at AMIC while she was taking a gap year from college, to build up the bookshop's inventory.[43] Chng spent many evenings with the Lims, and together they lamented the fact that there was no independent bookstore that catered mainly to Southeast

Asian titles. They knew of some small but well-regarded bookstores in the region that carried books not solely published in Europe or North America and were inspired to offer a range of titles to scholars and students of Southeast Asia. When Chng returned to Singapore after graduation, the Lims invited her to be a co-founder and director, and she worked closely with Lena to make their 'dream a reality'.[44]

From the outset, the architectural, the literary, and the regional intersected in the bookshop. Lena, 'who loved working with books', wanted Select Books to be 'a centre for ideas on current world and Asian issues' such as development, social change, population, environment, ecology, urban studies, and delinquency.[45] She intended it to be a safe space for readers, writers, thinkers, critics, artists, architects, and 'dreamers' partaking in Southeast Asia's literary and visual worlds. She was explicit in her emphasis on education and in reaching various sectors. Lena told a journalist from the Malay news daily, *Berita Harian*, that she decided to open the bookshop specialising in books published in the region because there were very few in Singapore. 'Although there are many books on Asia written by authors published outside of the region, there are few published here', she added.[46] She travelled to Hong Kong and ASEAN countries to find books and buy them to fill her bookshop. She prepared a nook for children to read while their mothers looked for their favourite books to instil an interest in reading in the young. When asked how she would cultivate the use of Mandarin, she consistently advocated using a 'positive approach' to 'encourage the use of Mandarin', believing in the perpetuation of cultural values through dialects at home, and suggested that the teaching of Chinese as a second language should begin with offering students engaging textbooks and reading materials to stimulate their imagination.[47]

Select Books pushed the boundaries of social and political discourse. It carried titles that were typically deemed 'off-limits' by mainstream bookshops, and prominently displayed in the window titles by Singapore opposition leaders and outspoken critics such as J.B. Jeyaratnam, Chee Soon Juan, and James Gomez, to ensure readers could access these books.[48] Aside from providing an annotated periodic list of new titles for their customers, another activity which set Select Books apart from other bookstores was the holding of 'Meet the Author' sessions. Usually held on Saturday afternoons, they invited authors – both local and visiting writers – to speak about their work and served tea, coffee, wine, cheese, and canapes (Fig. 10.2). Chng helped arrange several sessions,

Figure 10.2: Readers at a reading corner in Select Books, Singapore, c. 1976. Photograph © Select Books.

including one with Balinese dancers for which she had the store decked out with Indonesian decorations. One memorable occasion involved a near fist-fight between a guest speaker who was the author of a book on the infamous Malaysian communist leader. He got into a heated verbal exchange with the then American ambassador about the existence of weapons of mass destruction. On yet another occasion, Chng arranged for a Singaporean cookbook writer to speak but could not introduce her due to a medical emergency. Her husband, who had no connection with the bookshop 'except as a longtime customer' and was 'clueless in the kitchen' had to step in as her replacement!

## PUTTING SOUTHEAST ASIAN WORKS ON THE GLOBAL BOOKSHELF

Select's publishing arm began when Lena realised there was little interest from Anglo-American publishers in Southeast Asian authors and book projects. Select Publishing's earliest publication was a book edited by Chng, with a foreword by William Lim, chairman of the Southeast Asia Study

Group, and comprised of essays by group members. Alex Josey's scathing review in the *New Nation* reinforced Lena's point on the Eurocentrism of publications. Josey began his review by stating,

> One glaring weakness of this slim volume concerns the identity of the contributors. They are all members of what is called the South-east Asia study Group. But who are they? What are their credentials? It would be nice to know something about them.[49]

For the rest of his article, he focused on the essay by the one 'intellectual of eminence' – Soedjamoko, the former Indonesian ambassador to the United Nations, paying no attention to the rest of the essays. If he had bothered to find out more about the authors, he would have realised that they were active members of the region's intelligentsia, including a Singapore architect-urbanist and founding member of the SPUR, a Thai lawyer-activist, and a Filipino anthropologist who was later a commissioner of a Constitutional Commission. The book marked the shift in Chng's prolific journalistic career, which focused on developments in Singapore and the region. Beginning in 1978, she authored over 500 newspaper articles, reporting on Singapore youths and Southeast Asia's political and cultural happenings, before moving to Jakarta to join a securities firm as a political analyst in 1987.[50] A series of feature articles she wrote on preserving buildings and monuments in April 1979 anticipated rising interest in built heritage in the 1980s.[51]

Lena aggregated the intellectual and creative output of Singapore and Southeast Asian authors. Select began distributing books dismissed by Anglo-American publishers and distributors as too 'local', 'regional', or specific to be relevant for their readers. In the 1980s, it began producing a quarterly annotated book list called *Selections on Southeast Asia*, which it mailed to individuals and institutions in Singapore and abroad. As the Singapore agent for the Library of Congress, Select also recommended to the Washington-based library titles of significance that were published in across the region.[52] Despite the increased economic and political interest, Southeast Asian publications mainly covered economic and political development. In April 1984, Select Books published journalist Gretchen Liu's *Pastel Portraits: Singapore's Architectural Heritage*, the first book on the topic. Encapsulating a decade of interest in pre-war shophouses, it was a crucial document for spurring the conservation of Singapore's built environment. *Pastel Portraits* was the first of many books that Liu, a *Straits Times* journalist since 1979, would write and edit on Singapore's built heritage and identity.[53] In April, a ten-person committee chaired by Willy Lim founded the non-profit, non-governmental organisation Heritage Society, which focused on 'research, education and advocacy on issues relating to Singapore's history, heritage and identity'.[54] Many members of the committee were on a panel comprising three architects, a banker, an environmental planner, and property owner brought together by *Business Times* the previous year to discuss the conservation of Chinatown – the area given the most attention in *Pastel Portraits*.[55]

The Lims fought alongside the literary heritage and built heritage fronts with other advocates for Singapore and Southeast Asia. As a young university graduate, Lena argued at a women's rights forum that equal rights for women meant rights for men as well.[56] As a founding member and the first president of the Association of Women Action and Research (AWARE), founded in 1985, she worked to raise awareness among the privileged and to reach and support women in less privileged socioeconomic situations.[57] Among AWARE's first tasks were the ridding of domestic violence, the call for maternity leave (like national reservist duty), and family planning.[58] Lena urged the Education Ministry to change the policy of offering domestic science as a mandatory subject only for girls, arguing that it should be optional for both girls and boys, as should technical subjects.[59] Willy shared Lena's position on gender equity and supported synergies with her literary commitments. At the opening launch in March 1986, when a journalist asked Willy why he was there, he replied, 'I am Mr Lena Lim'.[60] This was shortly before he co-founded the Singapore Heritage Society of which he was Chairman till 1997. Through the bookstore and Select Publishing, Lena showcased, distributed and published many books on Singapore and Southeast Asian architecture.[61]

## INTERCULTURAL SPACE

The late 1980s witnessed a shift in racial consciousness in Singapore following several policies designed to maintain racial distribution and prevent segregation while preserving distinctiveness, These addressed such topics as representation in governmental posts and demographics in public housing estates.[62] Since 1989, public discussions and debates on Singapore's multi-racial identity have followed the Presidential address on 'what is a Singaporean identity'.[63] Among these was a panel discussion on Singaporean identity chaired by the *Straits Times*, which included Constance Singam, the second president of AWARE, who championed multi-culturalism as a means to identify links and similarities rather than highlighting differences.[64] Her position on racial equity was consistent with AWARE's stance on gender equity and the forum on feminism held the previous year in March 1989, where Lena, the first speaker, asserted that, 'feminism liberates men and women and in the long term benefits society as a whole'.[65]

Lena and Willy championed multiplicity and interculturality. In 1990, Select Books published Willy's *Cities for People: Reflections of a Southeast Asian Architect.*[66] Willy reflected on and critiqued urban life and public spaces through the lens of his experiences fronting research think tanks, running an architectural practice, and participating in advocacy.[67] He reflected on SPUR's 'radical transformations' to modernise the region that would be sensitive to the local way of life, the imagination of a city where 'work, play and living is mixed and concentrated, an efficient rapid transport system and the abundance of clean parks and open spaces would connect everything'. He also drew attention to how developments in post-independence Singapore focused on the physical aspects of the city, with less attention on the cultural, spiritual, and environmental, revisiting DP Architects' shopping complexes as 'city rooms' designed to be in a continuum with the street. That same year, he established and was president of AA Asia with other graduates of his alma mater to create a platform for architectural discourse in Asia. He published five more books with Select: *Asian New Urbanism (1998), Alternatives in Transition: The Postmodern, Glocality and Social Justice* (2001), *Alternative (Post)modernity: An Asian Perspective (2003), Have You Been Shanghaied? Culture and Urbanism in Glocalized Shanghai (2004), and Architecture, Art, Identity in Singapore: Is There Life After Tabula Rasa? (2004).* Besides publishing, Lena was regularly cited in these publications, and her involvement included commenting, proofreading, and editing.[68] All the while she continued to champion women's rights and gender equity issues through public discussions, while pushing for literacy and cultural knowledge of the region.[69]

A key component of AA Asia meetings involved visits and travelling workshops to cities in Asia and companion publications documenting the visits and the conversations they had triggered with architectural and urban practitioners, artists, and officials. Lena travelled with the contingent of architects and architectural enthusiasts and affiliates to cities across East and Southeast Asia, including Bangkok, Jakarta, Jogjakarta, Kuala Lumpur, and Seoul, Beijing, Chongqing, Guangzhou, Hong Kong,

Shanghai, Shenzhen, Taipei, Mumbai, Tokyo, and even down to Melbourne. She assisted in and edited many of Willy's writings about them, as well as on different local Singaporean case studies, including Bukit Brown, The Railway Corridor, Hawker Centers, and Void Decks.[70] Her own contributions to Singapore and Asian book publishing included reviews on Singapore's English Literature such as her review of Koh's *Singapore Literature in English: An Annotated Bibliography* (2008), and extend to commentaries of contemporary issues on gender, history, and society.[71] In 2000, she co-authored an article on 'Women NGOs in Patriarchal Singapore: Interaction between State and Civil Society' in *State-society relations in Singapore*, with her frequent AA Asia travel companion, Koh Tai Ann, Dean of the School of Arts from 1994 to 2000, whom she met through Select Books.[72]

The Lims' literary and architectural practices reimagined place-identity and re-centred creative production. In 2002, on their fortieth-wedding anniversary, Lena prepared to retire as managing director, handing over Select Books to its new owners, and joined Willy on his architectural travels. However, the attention was on him. Select Books published *Nolimits: Articulating William Lim* edited by Robert Powell to celebrate the architect-urbanist's seventieth birthday.[73] Joining many contributors in tribute to his work, Lena contributed an essay titled 'Willy, the unconventional conventional', which began with the heading 'Family Man' and concluded with the final section, 'Quality vs Quantity', where she described Select Books' effort to offer comprehensive and in-depth contents titles about the region. Reflecting on her 'apparent business failure' where quality did not yield quantity (in profit), she concluded: 'I am comforted to know that Willy too has never been willing to compromise quality or professional integrity, in his own architectural practice for monetary returns, social status or influence.'

In 2005, on the fiftieth anniversary of the Afro-Asian Conference in Bandung, the editors of the transborder collective *Inter-Cultural Asia Studies journal* issue on Third Worldism invited Lena to reflect on her work with Select Books in relation to the evolving definition of Asia and knowledge production of those living in the region.[74] Lena began by describing how in 1976 she decided to make a career change from librarianship to bookselling and publishing. She detailed the entire process including her quest against the 'Eurocentric hang-up' and the parochial interest of international publishers. 'What has Select Books achieved in its initial twenty-eight years?' she mused. Not only was it a bookshop but it

Figure 10.3: Lena in her study, 23 May 2004. Photo by the author.

was a cultural space where friends, customers and authors met, and '[its] legacy may have been that we were in some ways opening the eyes of the public as well as institutions, both locally and overseas, that there were architects trained in Asia.' She concluded: 'it is my hope that Select Books managed to open a tiny channel for the works of Southeast Asian authors to emerge from the region and penetrate the west.'[75]

In light of Lena's bookshop, it is fitting to conclude with the editor's note at the beginning of her article:

> Select Books is the only bookstore on earth that specializes in books produced in or about Asia. It is not only a national treasure for Singapore, but also an indispensable institution for the global intellectual community. Thirty years ago, Lim U Wen Lena single-handedly created the Select Books. Her persistent willpower has made the project an Asian pride. In 2004, Lena retired from the enterprise. In producing this special issue on Third Worldism, the Journal invited her to critically reflect on the history of Select Books in the spirit of the Bandung.[76]

As an entrepreneur, cultural figure, literary, and heritage patron, and women's rights advocate, Lena Lim (Fig. 10.3) built forms of solidarity with individuals and groups on the frontlines of postcolonial knowledge production to envision an intercultural Asia. Select Books' reach was also multi-generational. Longtime colleague and friend Chng recalled attending a talk in a very small independent bookstore focusing on Islamic titles owned by 'a younger generation Malay Singaporean'. When he discovered that she was a co-founder of Select Books, he exclaimed: 'I am in the presence of royalty!'[77] Acting on her discomfort with uncomfortable knowledge to create and foster a place for Southeast Asian culture and discourse, Lena and her bookshop testify to the full and imaginative life of a 'liberated woman', with solidarity with not only other women, as postulated by Susan Sontag, but also with others in a rapidly changing region.[78]

## NOTES

1 Yong Shu Chiang, 'A new chapter for the little bookstore that could', *The Straits Times*, 1 September 2004.

2 The decade saw communist bombings, assassination plots and covert information wars, which were underplayed in public discourse.

3 Lena Lim U Wen, interview with Eunice Seng, 23 May 2024.

4 'The New Dynamism of Asia', *Singapore Standard*, 15 April 1955. '"New Dynamism Of Asia" Nehru On Bandung Confab', Indian Daily Mail, 17 April 1955.

5 'Three Malayans Oft To Bandung [...] And Two Are P.A.P. Men', *Singapore Standard*, 16 April 1955.

6 'Conference On S.E. Asia', *Indian Daily Mail*, 25 October 1955, 1.

7 'S-E Asian Varsities Meet and Establish Closer Ties', *Singapore Standard*, 17 January 1956, 8.

8 'New Chinese Literary Guide Boost For Store', *The Straits Times*, 9 January 1957, 8.

9 'Malay language conference', *The Straits Times*, 9 July 1956. The first meeting of Southeast Asian Historians met in Penang in 1957. 'S.E. Asia Historians To Meet In Penang', *Singapore Standard*, 2 May 1957, 7.

10 Taking advantage of the politically conducive climate, the SCW was inaugurated on 4 April 1952, five months after its Secretary-General Shirin Fozda convened a meeting of women to discuss women's rights in Singapore.

11 'Call to Singapore women: Fight for your rights', *The Straits Times*, 20 October 1958, 2.

12 'Equality is Govt. Education Policy', *The Straits Times*, 8 May 1959, 5.

13 Kwa Geok Choon, the wife of PAP Secretary-General Lee Kuan Yew, gave a speech in a Radio Singapore election broadcast on the PAP's policy on women, emphasising the party's support of equal pay among gender. 'Equal pay: PAP will go easy, says Mrs. Lee', *The Straits Times*, 9 May 1959, 7.

14 '"The greater role of women in nation-building" – by women', *The Straits Times*, 30 October 1959, 4.

15 Lena Cheng, 'Campus Clothes: TTC Girls Lead the Varsity in Dress Sense', *Her World* (July 1960): 10.

16 Lena Cheng, 'Eusoff College is Home from Home', *Her World* (August 1960): 62–65.

17 Lena Cheng, 'The True Meaning of Life', *Her World* (September 1960): 14–17.

18 Ibid. 'Anti-flood canal first big job for new work force', *The Straits Times*, 17 March 1960, 4.

19 Lena Cheng, 'Fine Fabrics From A Malayan Mill', *Her World* (October 1960): 26–27.

20 Lena Cheng, 'Why Not Spare A Mahjong Morning and Aid A Good Cause?' *Her World* (November 1960: 7; 'The W.I. does a big job', *Her World* (November 1960): 24–25.

21 She said that she 'ran to the seclusion of bookshelves in the university library'. Anne Millington, 'Bookshop that once had no books', *The Sunday Times*, 4 October 1981, 1.

22 'Big Plan For A Malayan Library', *The Straits Times*, 2 February 1959, 4.

23 Kennedy Gordon Tregonning, interview by Jason Lim, *Development of Education in Singapore*, Oral History Centre, National Archives, 24 July 2003.

24 'In Memoriam: Dr K. G. Tregonning', 157. 'First international meeting of specialists to find new approach to history of Asia', *The Singapore Free Press*, 31 August 1960. 'Problem for historians', *The Straits Times*, 17 January 1961, 7.

25 Issued as a weekly supplement to Asian newspapers, *Asia Magazine* ran for 36 volumes from 1961 to 1998.

26 'Today's supermum battles on', *The Straits Times*, 27 December 1987, 21.

27 Lena Lim U Wen, interview with Eunice Seng, 23 May 2024.

28 Their collaborations are evident in the publications, the bookshop events, the many activities such as symposia, workshops, and AAAsia trips that Lena invariably attended, and their patronage of arts and culture in Singapore. Willy regularly acknowledged Lena for her intellectual and editorial contributions to his writing. See William Lim, *Asian new urbanism and other papers* (Singapore: Select Books, 1998); Lena Lim U Wen, 'Willy: The Unconventionally Conventional', in *Nolimits: Articulating William Lim*, ed. Robert Powell (Singapore: Select Publishing, 2002), 121–31.

29 William S.W. Lim, 'What Sort of Singapore Do We Want to Give Our Children?' *New Nation*, 8 March 1971, 9.

30 Women through the Years: Economic & Family Lives Interview with Lim Lena U Wen, Accession Number 001635, National Archives of Singapore.

31 'Tanglin Centre completed', *The Straits Times*, 20 January 1972, 7.
'Designed to please', *New Nation*, 13 May 1972, 13.

32 'Can Singapore accommodate the coming shop glut?' *New Nation*, 11 September 1971, 12. See also, Judith Yong, 'Hey big spender, happiness is a many splendoured shopping centre', *The Straits Times*, 26 July 1970, 12.

33 'First day hospital will be at Tanglin Shopping Centre', *The Straits Times*, 17 October 1971, 11; 'Three Newcomers', *The Straits Times*, 8 November 1971, 14.

34 'Shopping in a tropical paradise', *Singapore Herald*, 26 January 1971, 14.

35 '$18 million Shopping Complex Along Beach Road', *Eastern Sun*, 21 August 1970; Mok Sin Pin, 'Golden Mile Complex', *The Straits Times*, 12 January 1970, 12.

36 '$15 Mil Shopping Complex For "Affluent" District', *The Straits Times*, 26 February 1971, 7. 'A New Dimension in Shopping: Katong Shopping Centre – The Biggest and Most Modern Shopping Complex in Katong', *The Straits Times*, 6 March 1971, 6.

37 'The big five', *New Nation*, 24 June 1972, 17.

38 'An imaginative display of Singapore-made goods', *New Nation*, 1 February 1973, 12. 'Modern touch for antiques', *New Nation*, 11 March 1972, 9.

39 'Singapore Ideal Information HQ', *Eastern Sun*, 4 February 1971, 3; 'Meeting of Asian journal editors', *The Straits Times*, 29 September 1972, 15.

40 'Nantah, AMIC link-up plan is off', *New Nation*, 23 November 1976, 3.

41 Anne Millington, 'Bookshop that once had no books', *The Straits Times*, 4 October 1981, 1.

42 'Bookshop That Once Had No Books', *The Straits Times*, 4 October 1981, 1.

43 Nancy Chng, email correspondence interview with Eunice Seng, 17 November 2024.

44 Ibid.

45 'Lena furthers romance with books', *New Nation*, 26 September 1976, 4.

46 '*Syarikat menjual buku2 mengenai Asia dibuka esok*' ('*The Company Selling Books on Asia Opens Tomorrow*'), *Berita Harian*, 30 September 1976, 5.

47 'A positive approach', *New Nation*, 7 April 1978.

48 Nancy Chng, email correspondence interview with Eunice Seng, 17 November 2024.

49 Alex Josey, 'Another earnest look at S.E. Asian progress', *New Nation*, 2 October 1977, 23.

50 Chng joined *The Straits Times* (Singapore) in 1979 as a feature writer and became the newspaper's correspondent for Thailand from 1982 to 1986. Her interest in Indonesia began when she joined the informal study group on Southeast Asia whose members included some of Indonesia's most-respected intellectuals: the diplomat Soedjatmoko, journalists Goenawan Mohamad and Mochtar Lubis, and cleric Abdurrahman Wahid, who later became the country's president. Articles she

wrote in 1978 include: Nancy Chng, 'Family planning: Its success linked to nation's development', *The Straits Times*, 10 March 1978, 33; 'All the information you want – at the touch of a button', *The Straits Times*, 20 June 1978, 12; 'Singapore's youths and their problems [...],' *The Straits Times*, 9 August 1978, 9. I am struck by her empathy in this article: 'Who are the Urban Poor?' *The Straits Times*, 9 December 1978, 3. Her reflective review of Bruce Stokes' *Worker Participation* is a far cry from Josey's ill-informed dismissive one of her book. Nancy Chng, 'Worker's role in management decisions', *The Straits Times*, 23 December 1978, 1.

51 'About the old giving way to the new [...]', *The Straits Times*, 12 April 1979, 10; 'The old must give way to new but not completely [...]' *The Straits Times*, 12 April 1979, 1; 'Age no excuse for pulling down our heritage', *The Straits Times*, 21 April 1979, 17; 'New things to do with old buildings', *The Straits Times*, 21 April 1979, 1.

52 According to Chng, this task was laborious but was meaningful work for the staff.

53 These include 'One Hundred Years of the National Museum', and two volumes she edited for the National Museum centenary celebrations in 1987: *Nineteen Century Prints of Singapore* and *Treasures of the National Museum*. Irene Hoe, 'Scenes you will never see again', *The Straits Times*, 26 September 1987, 2.

54 'Society to preserve Singapore's heritage launched', *The Business Times*, 28 April 1987, 16.

55 'A blueprint for heritage', *The Business Times*, 18 April 1986, 4.

56 Valerie Lee. 'Shoulder to Shoulder against sexual inequality', *The Straits Times*, 12 January 1960, 4.

57 'Aware's elected officers', *The Straits Times*, 7 December 1986, 17. Cf. 'Lena Lim, President AWARE', *Berita Harian*, 8 December 1986, 3.

58 'Women's group to study home violence', *The Straits Times*, 10 March 1986, 8.

59 'Bigger families: Call to give men perks too', *The Straits Times*, 9 March 1987, 12.

60 Lee Siew Hua, 'New women's "think group" set up to fight discrimination', *The Straits Times*, 2 March 1986, 10.

61 These included six books written by William Lim between 1990–2004, and five books written by writer-academic Robert Powell over a ten-year span between 1995 and 2005. Select Books distributed Robert Powell and Luca Invernizzi's *Living legacy: Singapore's architectural heritage renewed* in 1994; then published Powell's *The Asian House: Contemporary Houses of Southeast Asia*, 1995; *The Tropical Asian House*, 1996, 2005; *The New Singapore House*, 2001; *The New Thai House*, 2002; and *The New Asian House*, 2005. An ambitious project was *Asian Architects Vol. 1 and 2* (2000), edited by Tan Kok Meng, which was intended to be a six-volume project.

62 'Melting pot not for S'pore', *The Straits Times*, 18 January 1989, 16; 'Ensuring survival of the Chinese language in a multi-racial context', *The Straits Times*, 8 July 1988, 26.

63 'Confronting our own ethnicity', *The Straits Times*, 19 January 1990, 2; 'Singapore's big wish', *The Straits Times*, 27 January 1990, 16.

64 'Ethnic roots and identity', *The Straits Times*, 7 April 1990, 2.

65 'Feminists say no to anti-men', *The New Paper*, 6 March 1989, 9.

66 Publishers focusing on the region and Asia have increased to at least seven: Cannon International, EPB Publishers, Europhone Language Institute, Heinemann Publishers Asia, Institute of Southeast Asian Studies, Pan Pacific Publications, and Select Books. The Institute of Southeast Asian Studies (ISEAS) published SPUR member and Willy's ex-DP partner Tay Kheng Soon's *Mega-Cities in the Tropics.*

67 'Cities are for people', *The Business Times*, 23 June 1993, 26.

68 Lim, *Asian new urbanism and other papers*, 2; *Alternatives in transition – The Postmodern, Glocality and Social Justice* (Singapore: Select Books, 2001), XVI; *Alternative (post)modernity: An Asian Perspective* (Singapore: Select Publishing, 2003), 174.

69 In conjunction with International Women's Day in 1994, AWARE held a roundtable discussion on 'Visions of Singapore Women in the Next Lap'. 'Singapore women in The Next Lap', *The Straits Times*, 8 March 1994, 8. 'A poly course for booksellers?' *The Straits Times*, 20 March 1994, 23.

70 William Lim, *Public Space in Urban Asia* (New Jersey: World Scientific Publishing, 2013).

71 Lena U Wen Lim, *Book Review: Singapore English Literature. BiblioAsia* 5, no. 2 (2008), https://biblioasia.nlb.gov.sg/files/pdf/vol-5/issue-2/v5-issue2_EnglishLiterature.pdf

72 Gillian Koh and Ooi Giok Lin, eds., *State-Society Relations in Singapore* (Oxford: Oxford University Press, 2001), xx.
73 Robert Powell, ed., *Nolimits: Articulating William Lim* (Singapore: Select Publishing, 2002).
74 Hee-Yeon Cho & Kuan-Hsing Chen, 'Editorial introduction: Bandung/Third Worldism', *Inter-Asia Cultural Studies*. 6, no. 4 (2006): 473-475, https://doi.org/10.1080/14649370500316711.
75 Lena U Wen Lim, 'Select Books – the struggle of an independent bookshop', *Inter-Asia Cultural Studies* 6, no. 4 (2005): 590, https://doi.org/10.1080/14649370500316901.
76 Ibid., 581.
77 Email correspondence with Nancy Chng, 17 November 2024.
78 Susan Sontag, *On Women*, ed. David Rieff (New York: Picador, 2023), 86–88.

# PART 4

# SOCIAL ENTREPRENEUR-SHIP

# Chapter 11
# The Invisible Hand
## Female Bureaucrats and the Architecture of Foreign Aid in Post-Independence Kenya

*Maryia Rusak*

On a not-so-bright day in May 2023, having braved the perpetually heavy traffic and the busy crowds of Nairobi's Moi Avenue, I settled into a two-week routine at the Kenyan National Archives. Following a series of back-and-forth negotiations with archival custodians and a deep search in the archival storage, I was kindly provided with long-displaced and dusty folios of the Kenyan Ministries of Work, Health and Economic Development and Cooperation from the 1960s and 1970s. Patiently delivering new volumes, the archivists still did not seem convinced I could discover anything of historical value there. In my research, I was primarily interested in the traces of Nordic architectural and infrastructural projects constructed in post-independence Kenya through networks and institutions of foreign aid, hoping to find the usual sources – drawings, project documents, and reports. Instead, I found myself amidst a chest of treasures: heaps of the seemingly faceless files revealed a vibrant historical snapshot of several Kenyan governmental agencies coloured by enthralling internal politics, staff shortages, international hires, global political alliances, endless negotiations of projects and responsibilities and – most importantly – an array of individual professionals engaged with various interdisciplinary ventures.

A recent project and publication of the Canadian Centre for Architecture, *Fugitive Archives: A Sourcebook for Centring African in Histories of Architecture*, questioned the role of the archives in writing architectural histories of the Global South. In an accompanying editorial, the curators explored the notion of archival 're-centring' and suggested that such a revision would require expanding the set of primary sources and including new media and documents which might not have seemed worth preserving. In a follow-up conversation on the ephemerality of archives, the researchers argued in favour of the sources that 'speak of

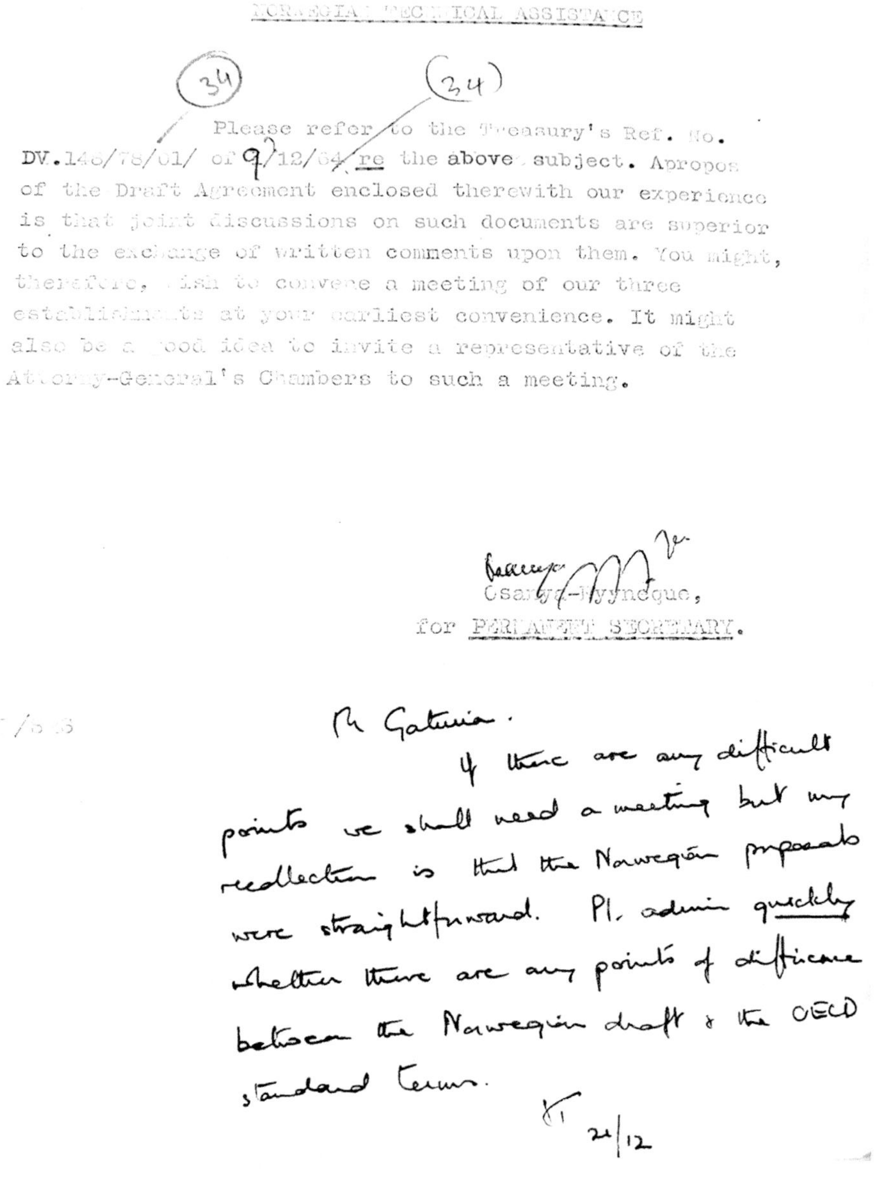

NORWEGIAN TECHNICAL ASSISTANCE

(34) (34)

Please refer to the Treasury's Ref. No. DV.148/78/01/ of 9/12/64 re the above subject. Apropos of the Draft Agreement enclosed therewith our experience is that joint discussions on such documents are superior to the exchange of written comments upon them. You might, therefore, wish to convene a meeting of our three establishments at your earliest convenience. It might also be a good idea to invite a representative of the Attorney-General's Chambers to such a meeting.

Osanya-Nyyneque,
for PERMANENT SECRETARY.

Mr Gatuiria.
If there are any difficult points we shall need a meeting but my recollection is that the Norwegian proposals were straightforward. Pl. advise quickly whether there are any points of difference between the Norwegian draft & the OECD standard terms.
JT 21/12

Figure 11.1. An archival document which jump-started the research: a note on the margins from Joan Tyrrell to her colleagues at the Kenyan Treasury, relaying information about the proposal for the Norwegian Technical Assistance. 21 December 1964. Files of the Ministry of Health, Kenyan National Archives.

the process, the atmosphere, and the context within which material was created'.[1] These 'ephemeral' artefacts prioritise the processes over the final product and highlight the agency of actors overlooked and obscured in more 'official' narratives. In my search, it was precisely the multitude of bureaucratic documents, and not architectural archives, which served as such 'ephemeral' artefacts, accumulating a unique historical record of the many people, processes and negotiations long before any construction project was set in place.

Few records are as ephemeral as handwriting on the margins, a small note on a typed letter, or an abbreviated signature re-appearing across official pages. While browsing through the many folios related to Nordic aid projects in Kenya, I encountered a small, handwritten signature of 'JT', which appeared as a sign-off on an increasing number of documents (Fig. 11.1). From single files scattered across different Ministries, an entire volume from 1967 was signed and archived by the mysterious 'JT'.[2] JT seemed busy at work, negotiating a wide range of agreements from educational qualifications of overseas architects and the bureaucratic intricacies of international compensation to aspects of new regional planning, administration of cooperative construction companies and concrete details of new university buildings. As I read through more files, I grew increasingly curious about who this person was. For a researcher who spent some time in bureaucratic archives, they are far from faceless entities. Tracing back-and-forth correspondence files, one gets to know the many individual characters involved and gets drawn into the many plot twists and turns of political negotiations often worthy of a soap opera. Who was this mysterious JT? Soon, I discovered that 'JT' stood for 'Miss Joan Tyrrell', a woman who adopted the abbreviation for time-saving purposes for the myriad documents and draft letters she had to sign. Appointed as an under-secretary to the Treasury on March 15, 1964, less than half a year after the end of the seven decades of British rule, Joan Tyrrell occupied a curious (and largely invisible) position in Kenyan bureaucracy.[3] More important for my research, she was the key person liaising between the Nordic officials and the political decision-makers of the Kenyan state, turning the many projects of the Nordic physical planning infrastructure into reality.

## THE INVISIBLE HAND

As I read further, I learned more about the invisible hand of Joan Tyrrell, which stirred Kenya's developmental projects of the 1960s. She occupied a crucial position in the Kenyan Treasury, overseeing the government's capital development budget and negotiations with international aid donors.[4] In the post-independence Kenyan government, an entire Technical Assistance Department of the Treasury was set up to channel foreign aid from the many international donors eager to establish a soft geopolitical presence in a newly independent region. Connecting the interests of the many stakeholders was a tricky position. As the Treasury's General Secretary noted in his letter to Tyrrell, the danger for the Technical Assistance Department was to become a 'glorified mailbox', and the main task of the Treasury officials was to distinguish between the '*bona* and *mala fide* requests'.[5] In the 'decade of development', development was good business for local political actors and international donors, while mismanaged technical assistance often incurred substantial financial burdens in the long term. This meant that Treasury officials had to critically evaluate and assess the viability of the many often unrealistic projects. As was later remembered by the Treasury's employee, 'the main role of the Treasury official was to say no'.[6] To do so, Treasury decision-makers had to develop a broad knowledge of the planning needs of the respective departments and pursue a *realpolitik* approach.

Developmental aid projects in post-independence Kenya were administered through close cooperation between the Ministry of Economic Planning and Development and the Ministry of Finance, the Treasury. The former primarily dealt with aspects of Technical Assistance, while the latter allocated development funds. In practice, as Vince Cable, a Treasury employee in the 1960s, remembered, this meant inevitable tensions: the Treasury controlled the 'sinews of financial power' but 'had a narrow, bean-counting approach to economics', while the Planning Ministry 'occupied the political and intellectual high ground but had no direct control of how money was actually spent'.[7] As the Treasury's under-secretary, Tyrrell played a crucial role in the financial decisions behind development projects and negotiated stakeholders' interests across different state departments and international agencies. Cable, who worked under Tyrrell, remembered she was 'in charge of the government's capital development budget and of negotiations with aid donors. Thanks to her as much as anyone, new roads, water supplies, agricultural credit, tourist lodges, and small-scale industries multiplied rapidly in post-independence Kenya'.[8] The projects she worked on ranged from infrastructural works and concrete buildings to establishing new educational institutions and programmes to educate new Kenyan planning professionals.

However, while Tyrrell's role could be traced in professional documentation and occasional mentions in memoirs, little information could be recovered on her educational background or even details of her early professional career. Before joining the Kenyan Treasury, Tyrrell worked in the colonial administration in Nigeria. When I first encountered Tyrrell's name in the archives, I was immediately invested in tracing the story since it was still uncommon for a woman to occupy such a high position within a state apparatus. She was, in fact, the only woman of such calibre whose name remained in the archives. Indeed, Tyrrell belonged to a different class of actors, often overlooked in architectural history – politicians, bureaucrats, economists, engineers, technocratic decision-makers – who contribute to the many decisions behind any construction or planning project. My research was structurally limited by my initial interest in architectural and planning projects carried out under the auspices of Nordic developmental aid. Following the traces of Tyrrell's invisible hand in archives in Nairobi and Oslo, I could piece together her role in implementing regional planning and construction projects in 1960s Kenya. However, this might be just a fraction of a much larger story, as she worked with other administrative and economic projects carried out by the Treasury. Nevertheless, the many bureaucratic documents signed by or addressed to Joan Tyrrell that I could access reveal a woman with a range of personal and political ties, substantial knowledge of different planning concepts and whose advice was solicited by many professional planners.

## SETTING UP DEVELOPMENT

Tyrrell was engaged with Norwegian development projects from the beginning of her appointment in Kenya, which also corresponded with the start of the official Norwegian cooperation with Kenya. In July 1964, Nairobi hosted an international OECD conference on Technical Cooperation, during which new contacts were established between the interested donor countries and state officials within the Kenyan government.[9] The follow-up correspondence between Tyrrell and J.M. Keriri, a representative of the Kenya President's office, reveals that Tyrrell was a part of the initial contact with the representatives of the Norwegian Agency for International Development (NORAD).[10] Personally familiar with the NORAD representative, Mr Eskild Jensen, Tyrrell sat at the juncture between Kenyan interests and the financial offers of the Norwegian donors – and this juncture was critical for turning an array of ideas into concrete projects and buildings.

The framework of the Norwegian aid was based on the premise of 'empowerment', where original funding requests had to come from the recipient country. In practice, this meant that the funding requests still had to fit into the priority frameworks established by the Nordic countries and had to provide an actionable plan. Through networks of foreign aid, Nordic politicians were working to solidify their geopolitical power in the region based on the image of 'humane internationalism'. With the assumption that the Nordic welfare model could be reproduced in other contexts, Nordic assistance prioritised 'social' programs related to health, population and education.[11] In addition, projects related to cooperatives, agriculture, fishing, and forestry were emphasised since Nordic countries could provide the necessary expertise. The archival evidence suggests a complex negotiation between the Norwegian and Kenyan interests: Norwegian donors preferred specific projects, while Kenyan officials were interested in maximising the potential financial gains. Nordic donors preferred a certain course of action, but the formal request had to come from the Kenyan side. To mediate this complex dynamic, enter Joan Tyrrell: a woman who, first, had the weight and the authority within the Kenyan state apparatus and, second, due to her British background, could foster close ties with the Nordic representatives.

Tyrrell then played a crucial role in mediating between Nordic and Kenyan interests. From the original meeting in July, the Norwegian Ambassador in Nairobi, Inge Rindal, Tyrrell informed the Kenyan side that they were prepared to offer a service of up to ten experts in civil engineering, architecture, hydraulics, surveys, and veterinary services.[12] However, a formal request had to be filed by the Kenyan government, and, as Tyrrell mentioned in her letter, the 'Norwegians wanted some guidelines in inducement for expatriates as they are now recruiting "operational experts"'.[13] Tyrrell then worked on revising a draft Technical Agreement and insisted on its urgent processing so that it could be concluded before the arrival of the Norwegian mission to Kenya in January 1965.[14] Eventually, ten operational experts were to join different fields of the Kenya Civil Service. Tyrrell then served as a point of contact, liaising with different Ministries regarding the pressing manpower needs.

One of the severely understaffed agencies was the Ministry of Works. W.J.S. Symes, the Ministry's Engineer-in-chief, pleaded with Tyrrell for more staff, underlining that the Ministry was 'desperately short of architects, and this shortage is likely to be a long-term one'. At the risk of 'appearing greedy', the Ministry wanted to ask for at least four architects to be seconded to the Kenya government, with two-year contracts.[15] Indeed, following Kenyan independence, there were only six architects at the Ministry of Works, and it was thought that foreign assistance was necessary to fill in 'the many vacancies in the professional cadres'.[16] As Symes underlined in another letter to Tyrrell, an architect with 'experience of low-cost housing or of schooling or hospitals' would be very much needed.[17] If the Norwegians were to furnish an engineer, an engineer with experience in the design of the roads would be particularly useful. The letter pleaded: 'If you can inform the Norwegians that we have got a very real need for an Architect and an engineer, you will be doing us a service'.[18]

Concurrently with the process of expert allocation, Tyrrell was responsible for formalising the terms of service of Norwegian experts. Through close correspondence with 'dear' Norwegian Ambassador Rindal in December 1964, she suggested that Norwegian contracts would be modelled after the British payment schemes and forwarded documents describing the British terms.[19] With her background in British colonial administration, Tyrrell indirectly framed Norwegian technical agreements following the familiar British framework, testifying to the complex, behind-the-scenes hybridisation of developmental models via individual connections. Subsequently, dozens of Norwegian engineers and architects were hired for the different departments of the Ministry of Works and Development, while the details of terms of service proposed by Tyrrell shaped the lives of many Norwegian experts and their family members who moved to Kenya.[20]

Among the first wave of invited Norwegian experts were E. Irgens, a civil engineer from Arendal who took a position in road administration, architect Karl Nøstvik from the Directorate of Public Construction and Property in Oslo, and architect Finn Bø, the head of a private firm in Hamar for the Ministry of Works.[21] The two architects would embark on a stellar career in Kenya, delivering commissions of a scale unimaginable at home. A municipal architect with virtually no practice, Nøstvik would become a Kenyan star architect, completing the landmark Kenyatta Conference Centre in 1973 and setting up a successful office after his career was kickstarted at the Ministry of Works. Bø would go on to complete a

## HOSTEL FOR NURSERY STUDENTS

**Åsmund Dahl**

Åsmund Dahl har bygget meget for sykehusavdelingen i M. O. W. (Ministry of Works), men det aller meste er i samarbeid med andre, og tildels fullført av andre. Ett hus var spesielt, hybelhuset for sykepleierelever ved *Mathare Mental Hospital*, nord øst for bysentret i Nairobi (tvers over elven for det overutnyttede, men høyst levende slumområdet Mathare Valley). Huset er en stor kvadratisk blokk med en svær brønn av et atrium midt i. Foreløpig er atriet ikke tilplantet, når blomstrende trær vokser opp mot himmelen blir det et deilig rom, nå er det nakent.

Alle de 96 hyblene har ellers balkong til alle fire verdenshjørner. De som bor der føler seg som en privilegert klasse som setter pris på sin bolig.

Første etasje har fellesrom med kjøkken, kontorer og noen undervisningsrom.

Sykehuset, der resten av undervisningen foregår, ligger rett over gaten.

### Norske, arkitekter på NORAD-oppdrag i Kenya

| *Navn:* | *Arbeidssted:* | *Kontrakts-periode:* |
|---|---|---|
| Bø, Finn Egil | M. O. W., Buildings Branch | 09/65–04/69 |
| Dahl, Aasmund | M. O. W., Buildings Branch | 11/67–11/69 |
| Drage, Håkon Per | M. O. W., Buildings Branch | 05/70–06/75 |
| Grimsgaard, Einar Krog | M. O. W., Buildings Branch | 10/69–10/71 |
| Holm, Olav | M. O. W., Buildings Branch | 04/68–05/70 |
| Hyll, Gunnar | Engineering Dep. Architectural Section, Nairobi City Council | 05/72–05/75 |
| Høivik, Ivar Andreas | Eastern Province Planning Team, Embu | 02/69–02/71 |
| Kove, Kjell | M. O. W., Buildings Branch | 11/71–11/75 |
| Mund, Jørg | M. O. W., Buildings Branch | 04/68–04/73 |
| Nøstvik, Karl Henrik | M. O. W., Buildings Branch | 09/65–09/71 |
| Åmli, Leif Arvid | M. O. W., Buildings Branch | 03/70–03/75 |

*Vi har ikke fått med arbeider av alle de norske arkitektene, og bare litt av det de har gjort som er med. Hovedparten av arbeidet gjøres i samarbeide med mange andre, av mange nasjonaliteter på mange kontorer.*

Figure 11.2: An example of some of the construction projects built in Kenya in the late 1960s, designed by Norwegian architects employed at the Ministry of Works, Buildings Branch. The list of Norwegian architects working in Kenya is on the right. A page from the 1974 issue of the Norwegian architectural magazine *Byggekunst* 56, no. 3 (1974), dedicated to Norwegian construction projects in Kenya.

large NORAD-funded project of the Thika School for Community Nursing and designed a series of standardised hospital buildings for rural Kenya.[22] Indirectly, Tyrrell played a key role in bringing these projects into reality (Fig. 11.2). Mediating between the interests of Kenyan ministries and

Norwegian donors, she pursued a *realpolitik* approach. Official Technical Cooperation agreements finalised by Tyrrell paved the way for new concrete planning and development projects.[23]

## REGIONAL PLANNING

One of the first large projects financed by NORAD was the regional development plan of the Taita and Busia districts, located in the Coast Province. In 1965, the Kenyan government assembled a working party to investigate the development problems and prospects of Taita and Busia, but due to the lack of funds, recommended actions were not carried out.[24] The project envisioned land consolidation and modernisation of agriculture. In addition, the concentration of farmers in selected regions led to overpopulation. As farmers were persuaded to move into lower areas, they had to be provided with new agricultural methods and farming systems. Thus, new residential Farmer Training Centres in Taita and Busia were to offer short courses for farmers and their wives.[25] In addition, the regional plan envisioned new roads connecting the district centres to the railway lines, water and forest development projects, and strengthening cooperative societies.

Tyrrell was at the centre of project negotiations for Norwegian funding. Preparing a draft application, planner Ole David Koht Norbye from the Ministry of Economic Planning and Development consulted 'Dear Miss Tyrrell' on various aspects of the project. Attaching his project description, he suggested she would 'undoubtedly have a number of changes to suggest, particularly on points which are squarely your field of responsibility'.[26] In the closing parts of the letter, he maintained: 'I would like to discuss land consolidation in the Taita Hills with you.'[27] While it is impossible to trace Tyrrell's opinions on the land consolidation, from another letter sent by the Treasury, we learn that there was a certain sense of urgency in implementing the planned developments of Taita District, where several aspects, including road construction, had to be tackled simultaneously.[28]

The project envisioned the construction of new Farmer Training Centres, as they were believed to represent 'excellent methods of implementing the agricultural revolution that ultimately must change the outlook and methods of about one million small-holders in Kenya'.[29] Several applications were filed with NORAD detailing the construction costs for three centres in Busia, Taita and Barino. A new thirty-bed Centre was proposed for Taita

District and a sixty-bed Centre for Busia District, and the projects included the construction of several teaching buildings, office and administrative blocs, housing for students and staff, a store, dining halls, and a common room, with an overall cost of 42,000 pounds.[30] Eventually, the Training Centres were constructed with Norwegian financial support, and while it is impossible to establish the role Tyrrell played in this project, scant archival evidence suggests that she was consulted on several crucial decisions. A successful project implementation was assured by the financial application undoubtedly filed with her invisible hand.

This regional development project revealed more systematic issues of understaffed Kenyan planning ministries and the lack of professional spatial planners. Up until then, Kenyan planning was largely academic, formulated on the national level and with little communication between the provinces and the central government.[31] Following on earlier conversations, Norway suggested supporting a team of planners in the Eastern Province and hiring two or three technical professionals for a period of five years. Consulted by Norbye, Tyrrell once again contributed advice on different planning stages, helped secure Nordic financing and facilitated hiring 'a Norwegian consultant firm with substantial experience in the field of regional planning' to ensure its completion.[32] Eventually, a Norwegian consultancy firm of Andersson and Skjånes from the Institute for Planning and Development undertook a large-scale survey of the Eastern Province and set up a project group of five Norwegian planners to work on different aspects of the province's economic and spatial development.[33] The group dealt with questions of rural housing and designed measures around self-help housing, among others.[34] These interventions resulted in a pilot project in Mbeere province, which included cooperative and educational institutions, Farmer Training Centres and housing.[35] With first-hand experience of planning shortages, Tyrrell played a crucial role in the project's realisation, advising on its early stages.

In her largely invisible position, Tyrrell contributed to the early-stage project negotiations and helped secure Norwegian funding. The project description written by the treasury, which promoted ideas of agricultural 'modernisation' and 'revolution', betrays her as an undoubtedly modernising agent. Through personal connections with Norwegian representatives, she encouraged the hiring of a Norwegian technical consultancy, facilitating the importation of a Nordic techno-scientific paradigm based on 'modern' techniques of surveying, land management and computer processing. Embedded deep within the state decision-making system, Tyrrell's involvement exemplified the process of 'modernisation by invitation', in which political elites in countries receiving aid ascribed to and internalised Western ideas of progress and modernity.[36]

## INSTITUTIONAL PLANNING

Tyrrell's impact did not end with singular developmental projects but also encompassed large-scale structural interventions that impacted the Kenyan planning profession. In 1964, the United Nations planners Lawrence N. Bloomberg and Charles Abrams produced a report investigating the main challenges of the Kenyan construction industry and put forward several proposals.[37] Among them was the establishment of a new educational institution that would address building problems specific to Kenya and the East African region. The Housing Research and Development Unit was conceived as a joint venture of the new Central Housing Board of Kenya and the University College in Nairobi. It was to serve as a pilot programme before establishing new departments of Physical Planning Studies and Environment Design Studies at the Faculty of Architecture, Design, and Development.[38] Over an initial three-year programme, the unit was to build up a body of knowledge 'with an emphasis on urgent problems of housing in urban and rural areas in East Africa'. It was expected to serve the Government of Kenya in 'exploring the social and economic problems of housing and community planning'. It was to produce prototype designs, test building systems and, in collaboration with the Central Housing Board, construct experimental housing projects and community facilities.[39]

However, as with all projects, its realisation was contingent on successful fundraising. Once again, Tyrrell was involved, investigating various financial opportunities. Building on the original report produced by UN planners, it was thought that the Unit could be financed through the UN special fund. Tyrrell worked closely with the British professor, David Oakley, in adapting the proposal to the strategic objectives of the UN office.[40] In May 1966, in discussion with Tyrrell, Oakley prepared two white papers expanding on the Unit's educational program and related them to the work undertaken by the UN.[41] Tyrrell then mobilised her internal contacts with the UN representatives to proceed with the application, writing to 'Dear Miss Davis', an assistant Resident Representative of the UN Development Program in Nairobi.[42] From the correspondence, Tyrrell's enthusiasm for the project shines through. She seemed knowledgeable about current Kenyan planning problems and earlier evaluations produced by the UN's Ernest Weissmann to S.M. Orlic, Chief of Section for Africa. Entrusted by the Treasury to negotiate the project with international aid organisations, Tyrrell wrote: 'I am now in a position to provide you with the Government's answers to the questions in the memorandum [regarding the Housing Research Unit].'[43]

And while there was 'certain scepticism' in Ministerial circles regarding the operations of the Unit, based on her previous experience with Kenyan planning, Tyrrell was convinced that new professionals were 'needed very badly throughout Kenya to execute the housing program and other building work envisaged in the Development Plan'.[44] The correspondence around the Unit's establishment reveals that she had intimate knowledge of the educational tracks of different professionals – architects, engineers and geographers, and was well-versed in practical details of how different degrees and qualifications could be integrated. She advocated a close connection between teaching and research and believed that planning education had to be tied to knowledge of specific East African conditions.[45] In another letter, she maintained: 'The theory is that the teaching of architecture in East Africa must be based on research of local conditions, materials and needs. Otherwise, the teaching will not be related to local needs. We also expect the unit to produce results of use to our housing programme.'[46] She seemed set on the course of the programme: 'There is little doubt in our minds about the professional and technical requirements of our programme, but we would welcome advice on organisation and method.'[47] Seemingly convinced by Tyrrell's arguments, the UN had reviewed the project proposal and suggested that an evaluation mission composed of Weissmann and Kenneth Watts would come to Kenya to examine the proposal on site.[48]

Tyrrell then played an essential role in developing the unit's overall educational strategy and positioning it within the broader developmental discourse. Her enthusiastic support brought concrete results: while the UN processed the project's application, the Ministry of Development was persuaded to allocate £10,000 to match the same contribution from the Treasury to support the interim functions of the Unit.[49] By 1967, the Housing Research and Development Unit (HRDU) at the University College of Nairobi was fully operational. It became a unique international research institution, which engaged with questions of development from a first-hand perspective and attracted a pool of researchers from the

Global South. Its research focused specifically on local conditions and produced a wealth of unique reports on building research in Kenya, many of which were incorporated into reports and developmental strategies of the regional office of the United Nations and laid the ground for future Habitat programs.[50] It also served as a training ground and a point of contact between the researchers from both northern and southern hemispheres. Tyrrell's ardent support was instrumental in making the lofty project visions a reality as she mobilised her international donor contacts and secured initial project funding through internal contacts within the Ministries.

## BUILDINGS FOR DEVELOPMENT

Beyond institutional building, Tyrrell was also involved in concrete construction projects. For example, she played a mediating role in the building committee for Thika School for Nurses Training. As a representative of the Treasury, she sat in the preliminary Committee meetings, which brought together representatives of the donor agencies and the WHO, medical and nursing professionals, and the Ministry of Health and Economic Planning and Development.[51] Project correspondence shows that Tyrrell was working on drafting an application for Norwegian assistance and closely worked with the Norwegian ambassador, Inge Rindal.[52] The proposed Norwegian School for Community Nurses was a pilot scheme to provide basic three-year training for community nurses in clinical practice, midwifery and health visiting. The new training Centre was to be built near a hospital and consist of school buildings, boarding schools housing for the staff and buildings for the health centre. The nurses were to play an essential part in implementing the Ministry's policy of curative and preventive care.[53] In the discussions leading to the project, the project required at least £50,000 of financial support, but, as Tyrrell indicated in correspondence, it would be hard to finalise the details 'until the Norwegians have decided whether they will construct the buildings for us or give us the money to do the job'.[54] Eventually, Norwegian architect Finn Bø – hired earlier for the Ministry of Works via Tyrrell – completed the project in the late 1960s (Fig. 11.3). With an overall cost of 5 million Norwegian kroner, it was a significant project expected to serve as a blueprint for similar centres across the country.[55]

Similarly, Tyrrell was a part of the building committee for new facilities at the University College of Nairobi. The University needed new buildings

## SCHOOL OF COMMUNITY NURSING

## THIKA

**Finn Bø**

Da arkitekt mnal **Finn Bø,** som en av de første NORAD-folk, kom til Kenya for å planlegge helsestasjoner og små sykehus, fikk han oppdraget å tegne en skole for helsepersonell i Thika, 45 km nord for Nairobi. Der lå et gammelt distriktsykehus bygget på britisk vis av huggen stein.

Bergartene i Kenya er i stor utstrekning en nokså løs vulkansk stein som lett kan hogges til gode murformater, et arbeid som krever lite maskinelt utstyr, men en god del tålmodighet. Det siste finnes mye av i Kenya, arbeidet med denne steinhoggingen er ganske populært, og det ferdige resultatet i form av vegger er solid og godt.

Finn Bø brukte denne byggemåten til sitt skolebygg, og han la tak over med Eternit fra den østafrikanske fabrikken i Uganda.

Vinduer og vindusdører av jern, et par formater, enkelt vedlikehold.

Ellers er dørene av tre, snekret på lokale verksteder, og de overdekkede svalganger som forbinder alle hus konstruert av tømmer, men på stolper av jernrør, for å forhindre termitt-angrep.

På afrikansk vis ligger bygningene i en etasje utover en stor tomt, og det er plantet trær og blomstrende busker overalt.

*Fra inngangsplassen inn mot fellesbygget og til internatet.*

*Plan av Administration & Tuition 1:500. Møbler stort sett tegnet til huset og produsert i Kenya.*

Figure 11.3: School of Community Nursing, designed by Finn Bø in Thika, Kenya, with financing from NORAD and managerial support of Joan Tyrrell. A page from the 1974 issue of the Norwegian architectural magazine *Byggekunst* 56, no. 3 (1974), dedicated to Norwegian construction projects in Kenya.

for education and student housing, and the earliest proposals for Norwegian aid included bids for new facilities.[56] While the original proposal listed a range of buildings – from a second science and art building to alterations and extensions to the Library – one of the first projects constructed with Norwegian assistance was the Nutritional Laboratory at the Department of Animal Production at the Faculty of Veterinary Science.[57] Once again, Tyrrell appears in the documentation, signing off on the letter to NORAD as the 'College Planning Officer' as she worked to resolve the issues of paying the project architect.[58] Tyrrell actively participated in the architectural and financial discussions between resident and project architects and negotiated Norwegian payments. In adapting the pronoun 'we', she acted on behalf of the University College and revealed – once again – her continued close relationship with Norwegians. In one of the letters, she noted, 'it seems to us that this sum may not be adequate and that we may have to ask NORAD to switch a small sum from building costs to fees'. From other project documentation, it becomes clear that Tyrrell was a part of the University administration, which dealt with all new construction plans. For example, she also participated in discussing the plans for a new Physical Science building, which was funded by the Norwegian donors and completed by a Norwegian engineering consultancy firm, Norconsult, in 1973.[59]

## THE HISTORICAL LENS

From the limited evidence in bureaucratic archives related to the Nordic aid projects, it is possible to trace Tyrrell's impact as she worked to realise a range of administrative, planning and construction projects. Her story offers a unique insight into the daily realities of post-independence Kenyan bureaucracy and suggests a more nuanced understanding of the relationship between the donor and recipient countries than the usually implied top-down hierarchies within the developmental framework. Indeed, as many scholars like Joe Nasr and Mercedes Volait have argued, decolonisation processes can hardly be characterised by an abrupt end to the export or import of developmental models and perspectives.[60] Local elites in newly independent states often ascribed to the same ideas of socio-economic progress and modernisation, which differed little from the previous paradigm. The many bureaucratic files of the Kenyan Ministries show that the Kenyan decolonisation processes were neither linear nor abrupt. Elaborate negotiations between Departments and risky bids for more financing reveal a new level of agency within the 'recipient' country and a more nuanced power matrix. In rebuilding the nation and its statehood, Kenyan politicians reached out for technical and financial support to various international donors, casting their net far and wide in ambitious and challenging proposals. While the Nordic aid emphasised the recipient's agency, the projects were often first discussed informally, put on the table by the Nordic representatives, and then retroactively matched with local interests.

Tyrrell's place in post-independence Kenyan bureaucracy was particularly interesting. Working as the Treasury's under-secretary, she occupied a key position within the internal structure of the Kenyan government. She served as the main point of contact between the interests of different Ministries and the many often-competing political interests and agendas within the state system. At the same time, she also served as a liaison between Kenyan and Nordic interests, mediating a complex political dynamic through personal contacts with Nordic donors and representatives of global organisations like the United Nations and the WHO. These contacts were often mobilised less formally before the final agreements were concluded. Her position as a former British colonial staff member, negotiating on behalf of Kenyan interests with international aid donors, was undoubtedly mediated both by her gender and race. As a bureaucrat descending from the former colonial power, she certainly occupied an ambiguous power position.

Being a white woman in the Kenyan government in the 1960s could not have been easy. Tyrrell's former subordinate, Vince Cable, later described her as a 'formidable woman [...] with a fearsome reputation for rigorous standards, workaholism, and not suffering fools gladly'.[61] Cable expanded on their relationship: 'After initially regarding me as a particularly hopeless case, useful only for feeding parking meters and carrying files, she discovered, during a long absence, that I could cope, and we developed some rapport.'[62] In a more contemporary note Cable argued that 'she was highly competent and effective but somewhat irascible though basically very nice'.[63] Other colleagues remembered Tyrrell's 'strong, robust character' and 'formidable work ethics'.[64] Indeed, there were two facets to her power as a woman. On the one hand, she developed a personal rapport with a wide range of stakeholders, facilitating agreements and streamlining procedures with her invisible 'female' hand. On the other hand, despite being a woman, she had to develop a robust, strict character to maintain power within an entirely male-dominated Kenyan bureaucracy and a changing sentiment towards British officials.

The case of Joan Tyrrell also provides a historical lens, tracing the evolving place of expatriate experts in post-independence Kenya. According to the memoirs of Vince Cable about his time at the Kenyan Treasury, towards the end of the 1960s, 'the administrative centre of gravity shifted decisively from white to black [...] The era of white expatriate civil servants in the Treasury was over'.[65] The new Kenyan elites 'regarded white faces a symbol of the past from which they were trying to escape', and Tyrrell was asked 'to retire early', a decision reinforced by what Cable described as a 'habit of bawling out dimmer colleagues, with a splendid indifference to colour or rank'.[66] Without direct evidence, it is hard to ascertain, but it is likely that through her earlier involvement with the Faculty of Architecture at the University College of Nairobi after Treasury, Tyrrell transitioned to a new position as the College Planning Officer. She dealt with the financial decisions behind the construction of university buildings, effectively mobilising her networks within both the state and the Nordic donors.

While not an architect and without any formal education in planning or design, Tyrrell contributed to bringing buildings and regional plans to fruition. Without intending to promote a specifically modernist architecture, she was, based on her position, a modernising agent, and her rationale most likely aligned with the modernist form language – that of efficiency, rationality and economy of means. Responsible for incoming financing, she was directly involved in negotiating early technical frameworks, constructing individual buildings, and setting up large-scale regional planning projects and new educational institutions. Through her experience with the bottlenecks of regional planning, she obtained a first-hand understanding of the importance of planning education and advocated for establishing the Housing Research and Development Unit, which developed into an internationally important educational institution. Over time, Tyrrell developed personal contact with professional planners based in Kenya – Norbye or Oakley, and international UN experts such as Weissmann or Abrams. During her earlier stint at the British colonial administration in Nigeria, Tyrrell may have come in contact with Jane Drew and Maxwell Fry, who worked there before Nigerian independence.[67] There is undoubtedly more to be discovered about her career and contacts in both Nigeria and Kenya.

## SEARCHING FOR TYRRELL

Searching for Tyrrell was not an easy task. When I first encountered her name in the Ministerial files, I expected to find a story of a woman living in the former colonial country following a husband stationed in some political office. However, as I reached out to over fifty people and institutions in Kenya and abroad, I learned that her case was different: that of a woman of an uncompromising character who built a robust career but whose story could be pieced together only as told by men. For example, Tyrrell makes several appearances in Cable's memoirs. However, it was almost impossible to trace her whereabouts precisely. After the Kenyan Treasury, Tyrrell served as Financial Secretary to the British Virgin Islands, joining the Overseas Development Institute (ODI) first as a secretary in 1973 and then as an administrative director in 1974.[68] Between 1974 and 1985, she played an important role in keeping in check the tight ODI budget in the post-Thatcher years and overseeing the ODI fellowship placements.[69]

However, when I reached out to the ODI's press office, none of my numerous requests submitted to publication managers, secretaries, or archival custodians were returned. Despite my arguments about the unique importance of the project, highlighting the role of female political actors and Tyrrell's role as the administrative director of ODI for more than ten years, the think-tank did not even seem to have her picture on file – or was unwilling to cooperate. After multiple attempts, Karen Triggs, a former Chief Press Officer who has since left ODI, was kind enough to follow up on the request and reach out to Tyrrell's former colleague for short testimonies. However, many seemed convinced that her work could not have possibly *anything* to do with 'much architecture'.[70] Another of ODI's sources maintained that 'while JT's name might appear as the Finance Office on aid-assisted building projects, the real story of urban design choices would be better explored [elsewhere]'. Instead, they pointed me to other men, 'people such as Percy Johnson-Marshall'.[71] Indeed, what role could a woman who did not even have 'an economics degree' could have played in architecture or urban design?[72]

In the following decades, Tyrrell's name appears in prefaces to several books including *State and Market* by Barbara Harriss-White, *The Marketing of Leisure* by Edwin Ornstein and Austin Nunn, and *Multilateral Mediation* by Swiss diplomat Victor Umbricht. Eventually, my search for Tyrrell, which started in Nairobi, led me to the most unexpected place: an archive at the ETH Zürich located 250 meters from my office, which contains correspondence related to Umbricht's book on mediation (Fig. 11.4). And while 'Miss Joan Tyrrell of Leatherhead, England' is acknowledged in the book's introduction, the letters show that she not only furnished her expertise on the dissolution of the East African Community but also edited multiple chapter drafts, as well as prepared papers and notes for many of Umbricht's lectures on the subject. So much so that when the book project was completed, as Tyrrell wrote to her newly acquired friend, Umbricht's secretary Dorothea Brun, she would bring 'a large old suitcase' with all the files to Switzerland to 'abandon at the town dump' in Basel.[73]

18 Manor House Court,
West Street,
Epsom,
Surrey KT18 7RN
England.

27 June 1984

Dear Dr Umbricht

I spoke to Peter Adams at Cooper and Lybrand a day or two ago to ask him whether you yet had a starting date for writing up your recent work following the break-up of the East African Community and whether you had chosen whom you wanted as your research assistant for this purpose. Since he could not give me any news on these points Mr Adams suggested that I write to you direct.

Having worked in the Kenya Treasury in the 1960s and having visited Kenya, Uganda and Tanzania at intervals since then in the course of my employment, I am very much attracted by the possibility of assisting in some way in this project, and I hope that you in turn would find me useful and adaptable. I have just retired from the Overseas Development Institute in London after ten years as Administrative Director. I shall not be looking for further permanent employment so could be available at short notice if you so wished and as required during the coming months.

If you would like to know more about my capabilities Sir George Bishop, who is Chairman of the Overseas Development Institute and whom I believe you know, has said that he would be happy to act as referee. Perhaps you would let me know if you are likely to ask him for a reference as I should like to warn him in advance.

I should very much appreciate hearing what the prospects are that you might take me on as your assistant for this project.

Yours sincerely,

Joan Tyrrell

(Miss Joan Tyrrell)

Dr V.H.Umbricht,
Ciba Geigy,
Klybeck Strasse141
Basel 4002.

Figure 11.4: Correspondence between Joan Tyrrell and Victor Umbricht, regarding the research assistance for Umbricht's book on the dissolution of East African Community, 27 June 1984. Archiv für Zeitgeschichte (AfZ), ETH Zurich.

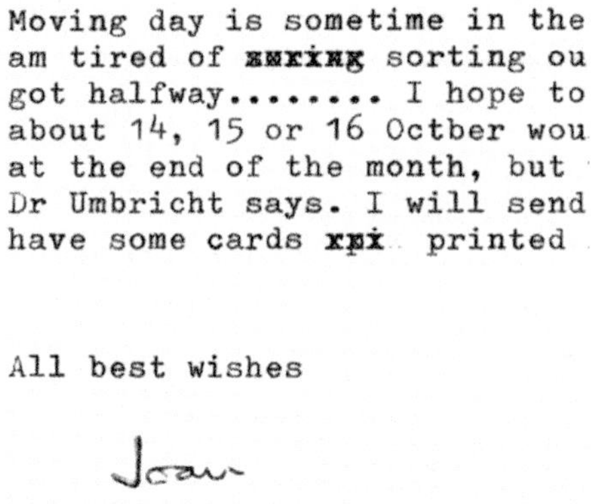
Moving day is sometime in the
am tired of xxxxxx sorting ou
got halfway........ I hope to
about 14, 15 or 16 Octber wou
at the end of the month, but
Dr Umbricht says. I will send
have some cards xxx printed

All best wishes

Joan

Figure 11.5: A signature of Joan Tyrrell on correspondence with Dorothea Brun, 25 September 1985. Archiv für Zeitgeschichte (AfZ), ETH Zurich.

The story of Joan Tyrrell is the story of the thousands of women overlooked in official decision-making roles who have operated – and continue to operate – mostly behind the scenes, on the fringes of history. They negotiate, type in, and reiterate countless documents, which keep bureaucracies running worldwide, but their hands remain invisible. Not only was it impossible to locate more biographical information on Tyrrell, but it was also impossible to track her image. While many documents – virtually any official document that left the Kenyan Treasury – were researched, negotiated, typed, and finalised by her, they were signed by her boss, John Michuki. Michuki, not Tyrrell, was featured in the photographs of official document signing sessions, representing the Treasury. Her image was impossible to track both during her time in the Treasury and her later administrative role at ODI. Even the latest iterations of OpenAI can provide some details about Tyrrell's male colleagues at the Treasury – Libby, Michuki, Keriri – while providing no information on Tyrrell's political role or biographic details. It is important to remember that Tyrrell was no ordinary woman – she worked in high political offices, authored multiple documents and books, and was an administrative director of one of the largest British overseas organisations. Hers is the fate of many women in bureaucracies worldwide who spent countless hours behind desks but whose work remains invisible, uncredited, and unidentified. When I presented this research at the University College Dublin, many women – particularly those working in administrative positions who heard the story – came to talk to me afterwards, emphasising how much they could relate to this story even today.[74]

Philosopher Gayatri Spivak, in her essay 'Can the subaltern speak?' questioned whether the subaltern – women – could find a voice within the existing structures of power.[75] The bureaucratic archives of the Kenyan ministries became the only source where the actual voice of Joan Tyrrell could be found. The many official documents authored and signed off by Tyrrell (Fig. 11.5), with seemingly ephemeral notes on the margins reaching out for her advice, constitute a parallel archive of the woman busy at work, building the many technical frameworks behind the architecture of foreign aid. While Tyrrell was not a powerless woman – that of a British colonial power descent – her story is the story of many women in state bureaucracies around the world. As another of the ODI sources (most likely a woman) pointed out: 'I think there's probably a story to be told about a strong woman working in a difficult environment, which was perhaps not as appreciated as she should have been.'[76] Gender, along with race, played an important modifying role in Tyrrell's career. Ben Kafka, in his book *The Demon of Writing: Powers and Failures of Paperwork,* explored the history of bureaucracy and the role of paperwork, its tools and techniques in producing politics, history and myths.[77] In the case of Tyrrell, her story and her power were recorded and can be told through the bureaucratic documents scattered across archives of different ministries across several continents. These documents testify not only to the complex place of women in power but also to the transformation from colonial to postcolonial political imagery, the role of the state institutions and the reach of former colonial British agents within the state. With this contribution, I hope to encourage other scholars to discover more untold stories in the seemingly faceless documents of bureaucracy.

## NOTES

1 Doreen Adengo, Warebi Gabriel Brisibe and Ramota Obagah-Stephen, Rachel Lee and Monika Motylinska in *Fugitive Archives: A Sourcebook for Centring Africa in Histories of Architecture,* ed. Claire Lubell and Ragico Ruiz (Montréal: CCA/Jap Sam Books, 2023), 157–58.

2 See, for example, volume AMB/17/26, 'Technical Assistance from Norway', 5 January 1967 to 7 June 1967, in Kenyan National Archives, the archive of the Ministry of Economic Planning and Development. All the files in the volume have been indexed and signed in with the initial JT.

3 'Miss Joan Tyrrell', *Kenya Government Gazette,* no. 1, 1 January 1964.

4 Vince Cable, *Free Radical* (London: Atlantic Books, 2009), 87.

5 'Technical Assistance for Fisheries and in General', J. Laulanie, 14 August 1968, AMB/14/59, Kenyan National Archives.

6 Cable, *Free Radical,* 87.

7 Ibid., 81.

8 Ibid., 80.

9 See letter from J. M. Keriri to J. Logie, Forest Department, Ministry of Natural Resources, 24 August 1964, AMB/14/59.

10 Tyrrell to Mr. Keriri, 17 July 1964, 3/A in AMB/14/59.

11 Sunniva Engh, 'The Nordic Model in international development aid: explanation, experience and export', in *The Making and Circulation of Nordic Model, Ideas and Images*, ed. Haldor Byrkjeflot, Lars Mjøset, Mads Mordhorst and Klaus Petersen (London: Routledge, 2021), 125–28.

12 See J.M. Keriri to the Directorate of Personnel, 22 September 1964, AMB/17/19.

13 See a note from JT, 18 December 1964, AMB/14/11.

14 See a note from JT, marked 21 December 21, 1964, on the margins of the letter 'Norwegian Technical Assistance' from the Ministry of External Affairs, 19 December 1964, AMB/14/11.

15 W. J. S. Symes to the Directorate of Personnel, 30 September 1964, A.13.04 AMB/17/19.

16 D.M. Mutiso, head of the Kenyan Ministry of Works, interview in *Byggekunst* 56, no. 3 (1974): 63.

17 'Norwegian Technical Assistance', Engineer-in-Chief W.J. Symes, Ministry of Works, to Joan Tyrrell. 7 December 1964, AMB/17/19.

18 Ibid.

19 Tyrrell to Inge Rindal, 22 December 1964, DV 148/78/01 in AMB/17/19.

20 Norval Hagen, Councillor, NORAD to the ministry of Economic Planning and Development, 22 April 1965, AMB/17/19.

21 NORAD to the Ministry of Economic Planning and Development, 22 April 1965, AMB/17/19.

22 For a detailed description of the projects, see *Byggekunst* 56, no. 3 (1974).

23 'Technical Cooperation with Norway', J. G. Shamalla, 16 March 1965, AMB/17/26.

24 'Development of Taita District', a working document in AMB/17/26.

25 'Proposals for the establishment of a Farmers Training Centre at Wundanyi in the Taita District of Coast Province', a working document in AMB/17/16.

26 O.D.K. Norbye to J. Tyrrell, 8 February 1967, AMB/17/26.

27 Ibid.

28 Letter to the Ambassador of Norway, prepared by the Treasury, 20 February 1967, DV148/78/02 AMB/17/26.

29 O.D.K. Norbye, draft letter to NORAD, 8 February 1967, AMB/17/26.

30 Ibid.

31 Working document of provincial development, AMB/17/26.

32 O.D.K. Norbye, draft letter to NORAD, pending revisions by Tyrrell, 8 February 1967, AMB/17/26.

33 The trip took place between 3-22 March 1967, and the delegation consisted of the financial specialist Bjørn Larsen, architect Tor Skjånes, and economist Arne Finstad from Andersson & Skjånes A/S.

34 'Kenya. Regional utviklingsplan for Eastern Province', E/Ea/Eaa/L0170 in Riksarkivet.

35 For more material on the Mbeere District Development, see NORAD's project 115, E/Ea/Eaa/L0169-L0173, in Riksaerkivet, Oslo, Norway.

36 Luce Beeckmans, 'The Architecture of Nation-building in Africa as a Development Aid Project: Designing the capital cities of Kinshasa (Congo) and Dodoma (Tanzania) in the post-independence years', *Progress in Planning* 122 (2018): 1–28.

37 Lawrence N. Bloomberg and Charles Abrams, *United Nations Mission to Kenya on Housing* (Nairobi: United Nations, Commissioner for Technical Assistance, Dept. of Economic and Social Affairs, 1964).

38 'University of East Africa. Housing Research and Development Unit', working document 1/1, KY/17/8.

39 Ibid.

40 'University College, Nairobi. Housing and Planning Research Unit', Tyrrell to C. Davis, Resident Representative, UN Development Programme, 16 June 1966, KY/17/8. For a brief recap of Oakley's career, see Robert K. Home, 'Knowledge networks and postcolonial careering: David Oakley (1927-2003)', *ABE Journal*, no. 4 (2013), https://doi.org/10.4000/abe.3388.

41 'Note of Meeting in the Ministry of Housing on Thursday, June 2, 1966', file MH/67 in KY/17/8.

42 'University College, Nairobi. Housing and Planning Research Unit', J. Tyrrell to Davis, Resident Representative of the U.N. Development Programme, 16 June 1966, KY/17/8.

43 Ibid.

44 'Housing Research', Ministerial Letter, MH/67 in KY/17/8. 'Housing Research & Development Unit', letter to Mr. Gathiuni, File Hou. 381, 8 February 1967, KY/17/8.

45 'University College, Nairobi. Housing and Planning Research Unit', 16 June 1966, KY/17/8.

46 Letter to Gathiuni, File Hou. 381, 8 February 1967, KY/17/8.

47 'University College, Nairobi. Housing and Planning Research Unit', 16 June 1966, KY/17/8.

48 'University College, Nairobi', K. 5-1-3, Cecile I.G. Davis to J. Tyrrell, 5 December 1966, KY/17/8.

49 'Housing Research Unit—University College', J.M. Tusker to J. Tyrrell, KY/17/8.

50 Currently, a substantial archive of the HRDU is held at the University of Nairobi and offers a wealth of potential material for future research.

51 'Record for the file', 10 August 1965, BY/24/42.

52 Tyrrell to the Permanent Secretary, Ministry of Health and Housing, 21 August 1965, BY/24/42.

53 'Memorandum by the Minster for Health and Housing', Norwegian Aid for Proposed School for Community Nurses, in BY/24/42.

54 'Norwegian Assistance for Community Nurses Training Center', O.S. Knowles to the Ministry of Health and Housing, copy to J. Tyrrell, Ministry of Finance, 20 March 1965, BY/24/42. Tyrrell to the Permanent Secretary, Ministry of Health and Housing, 21 August 1965, BY/24/42.

55 'Kenya—helsesentret i Thika', 20 June 1967, E/Ea/Eaa/L0109.

56 The Treasury, J. M. Michuki to the Ambassador of Norway, 20 February 1967, in AMB/17/26.

57 Helge Bergh, 'Kvartalsrapport i for 1969', E/Ea/Eaa/L0145.

58 'Norad Assistance for Department of Animal Production', 11 July 1969, Joan Tyrrell to S. Hammer, NORAD Resident Representative, E/Ea/Eaa/L0145.

59 O. Lønsjø, 'Uttalelse vedrørende forslag om reising av bygg for de fysiske fag ved University of Nairobi', undated, 1972, E/Ea/Eaa/L0168.

60 Joe Nasr and Mercedes Volait, *Urbanism: Imported or Exported?* (Chichester; Hoboken, NJ: Wiley-Academy, 2003).

61 Cable, *Free Radical*, 80.

62 Ibid.

63 In this line of inquiry, I thank Karen Triggs, former Chief Press Officer of the British Overseas Development Institute (ODI), who, following my request, collected brief testimonies from Tyrrell's former colleagues from her time as an administrative director of ODI between 1974 and 1985. Here, the ODI source was identified by the initials of VC, but it is easy to determine that it refers to Vince Cable, who had worked with Tyrrell in several institutions.

64 ODI Source, identified as PG.

65 Cable, *Free Radical*, 80.

66 Cable, *Free Radical*, 80.

67 On projects of Jane Drew and Maxwell Fry in Nigeria, see Hannah le Roux, 'The networks of tropical architecture', *Journal of Architecture* 8, no. 3 (2003): 337-354, https://doi.org/10.1080/1360236032000134835.

68 See ODI online archives, particularly yearly reports from 1974 to 1985, which mention Tyrrell as administrative director. She is listed as a Secretary in ODI Annual Report from 1973.

69 ODI source, identified as PG.

70 ODI source, identified as AH.

71 ODI source, identified as JH.

72 ODI source, identified as AH. The entire sentence is as follows: 'No, Joan Tyrrell was never an ODI Fellow herself. Wrong generation and arguably without the economics (though Bloomsbury Economics got you far in those days, at least in UK).'

73 Tyrrell to Umbricht on 2 November 1985. In Umbricht, Victor H./9. Mission and Mediation: East African Community/9.6. History of the East African Community Mediation /9.6.3. Correspondence, 1984-1986, Tyrrell, Joan, research assistant, correspondence and notes. Archiv für Zeitgeschichte ETH Zürich, Switzerland.

74 See the conference 'Minding her Business: Women, Architecture, and Design', University College Dublin, 13-15 June 2024. https://expanding-agency.com/conference/.

75 Gayatri Spivak, 'Can the subaltern speak?' *Die Philosophin* 14, no. 27 (1988): 42-58.

76 ODI source, identified as PG.

77 Ben Kafka, *The Demon of Writing: Powers and Failures of Paperwork* (New York: Zone Books, 2012).

# Chapter 12
# Architectural Adjacency
## Sheltered Housing Architectures and the Place-based Practices of Sister Stanislaus Kennedy (RSC) in 1960s–1990s Ireland

*Ellen Rowley and Haylee Derrickson*

## INTRODUCTION: ARCHITECTURAL ADJACENCY AND THICK MAPPING

Our story begins with our amateur recording of a conversation between retired Dublin architect Gerry Cahill and famous local nun-activist, Sister Stanislaus Kennedy in May 2023. We were seated in tension around a table, bright orange walls and incense interrupting, on a warm afternoon in urban Dublin and everyone was shy. If not shy, then diffident and eventually, emotional (Fig. 12.1). This was one of many meetings, of walking and drawing, phone-photographing and note-scribbling in Stanhope Green, a former convent and strange 'other' place, at once protective institution, sheltered housing and meditation drop-in centre which was marked by fecund growth, gravel paths, big skies, big walls.

We were to come back again in February 2024, this time with more rigour and taking more care, to talk, not to the architect but only to the nuns. Sister Stan, as she is known, was joined by Sister Síle Walsh. Our purpose was, is, indeed, to gather the stories around the collaboration of the nun and the architect in 1980s Dublin. We sought to understand how this place, Stanhope Green and its 70 homes at different scales, hewn out of a late Victorian convent and its gardens, arose. This was a pioneering housing model for late-twentieth-century Ireland where mixed dwelling types were managed under a variety of sheltered and supported conditions on an ungendered basis. Effectively, a new residential architecture of care emerged by the time the scheme opened in 1991. And like all grandiose or extraordinary genesis stories, this one left us barely believing, hardly understanding.

Figure 12.1: Collage: Meeting. Source: Ellen Rowley and Haylee Derrickson, 2025.

Why did the Religious Sisters of Charity give Sister Stan their barely-redundant building in an expensive corner of Dublin? How did the economics work midst an extreme local economic recession? Who qualified for a dwelling here? Was the mother superior sympathetic, and what about that bishop? Why, how, when, why? And Stan, without straying from her steady stance, shrugged, sometimes laughingly herself in disbelief as she recalled, 'We just asked'; 'They just gave'; 'We didn't know what we were doing but we were sure it was the right thing.'[1]

It became clear that this activist-nun found sites, persuaded politicians, worked with designers, instructed contractors and, in short, made housing. She was architect-entrepreneur, activist-fundraiser, developer and care worker in one. Her homeless agency, Focus Ireland, which she established as Focus Point in 1984, and quickly shaped to create the Approved Housing Body (AHB) Focus Housing Association, has today, forty years later, 1,200 homes which it lets to thousands of people.[2] Moreover, the successful making of Stanhope Green, as a pioneering (for Ireland) housing model in the late 1980s and early 1990s, spawned a short-lived but impactful movement whence orders of nuns gifted their near-vacant convents to similar housing bodies. Pointedly, this distinct interchange and transformation of convent buildings which brought about hundreds of multivarious homes has not hitherto been measured or discussed in Irish socio-architectural-religious histories.[3]

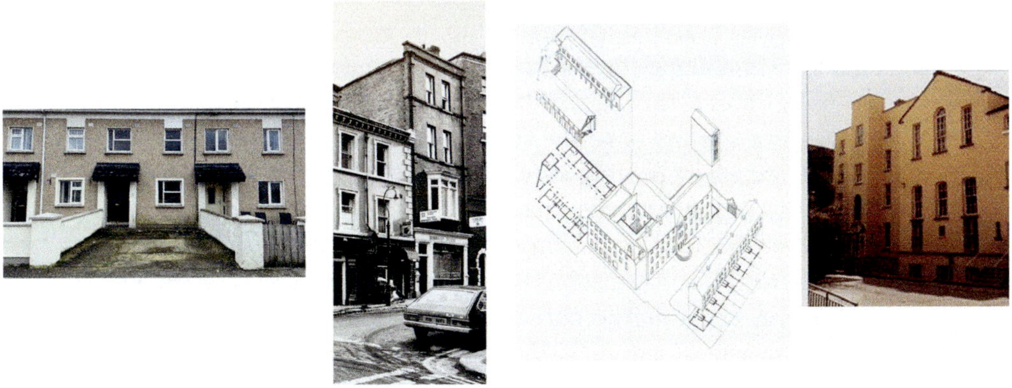

Figure 12.2: Collage: Place-Based Trajectory. Newpark Close – Eustace Street- Stanhope Green – George's Hill, Dublin. Source: Ellen Rowley and Haylee Derrickson, 2025.

It is around such architectural adjacency that we begin to grope and explore. We explore beyond the methods of oral history and site investigation and overlay drawing, conversing, remembering, walking over our readings of Sister Stan's research and publications; namely, *Who Should Care?* (1978/81) and *But Where Can I Go?* (1983/85) which we consume like rare archive material. Seeking to situate the Stanhope Green project, we cast back to our protagonist's formation in the regional county of Kilkenny in south eastern Ireland, during the 1960s and 1970s. Then, physically following our protagonist, we come to the start of Sister Stan's Dublin adventures, namely the Temple Bar experiment and origin of Focus Ireland. In analysing Sister Stan's landmark study into women and homelessness in Ireland's capital city, we employ drawing and collage as methodology. Treating *But Where Can I Go?* as primary source material, we call forth this research-as-territory, thereby contextualising the Temple Bar case study as fundamental to what is being termed Sister's Stan's 'place-based practices of care.'

Carried out in an open-ended and speculative manner, the drawings and collages take the form of parallel mapping exercises; two so-called 'thick maps,'[4] which reflect Sister Stan's distinction between visible and hidden homeless women.[5] From this perspective, the Temple Bar project is uncanny in how it chimes with contemporary architectural theories around reimagining historical Dublin, and in how it readies the way for Stanhope Green. Stanhope Green is in turn presented for its own sake through a 'durational' section – what we call, 'A Day in the Life' section drawing of the site – but also as prescient: prescient in terms of unfolding histories of convent transformations into the twenty-first century, happening before and alongside the disclosure of abuse scandals within the Irish Catholic Church, through the later 1990s and beyond (Fig. 12.2).

As a version of immersive site-recalling, our chapter moves between media and methods, following Sister Stan's own experiences as she intuitively evolved deeply effective space and place-based practices in 1980s and 1990s Ireland. Much is thrown open in relation to recent Irish social and building histories. The case of the religious sister as developer, operating outside of usual market forces and as designer, navigating the 'as found' with architects and builders, begins to name the neoliberal profit-driven city. It calls forth social marginalisation and housing shortage. Ultimately, it points to radical activism from within Irish Catholicism, and it paints a more nuanced portrait of the nun as a later-twentieth-century female actor. Here, Sister Stan becomes a spatial agent.[6]

## GATHERING SISTER STAN: COMBATING POVERTY IN 1960S AND 1970S IRELAND AND THE KILKENNY SOCIAL SERVICES

We first place Sister Stanislaus Kennedy in a poverty stricken housing estate, Newpark Close, then recently completed, outside Kilkenny City in the South-East of Ireland, where she was overseeing a pilot scheme for social services. Newpark Close was an early 1970s development of 120 all-electric two-storey houses, built by the National Building Agency (NBA). The NBA had been charged with housing provision in the heady days of the 1963 Dublin housing protests, erecting Ireland's first tower block housing and largest mechanised housing scheme from 1965, at Ballymun (demolished in 2015).[7]

The cement dust was only settling at Ballymun on the city's edge when the Newpark Close scheme was under development, and both projects, as well as all housing by the NBA at this time, should be understood as technocratic housing-crisis solutions. As Sister Stan wrote of Newpark, in 1978:

> The estate is four years old. This type of house was chosen because it was thought that they were quick to build and would be the answer to the long housing list at the time.[8]

In singling out the material and formal idiosyncrasies of the Newpark Close houses, Sister Stan was setting up the visceral context for her pilot social services scheme. It is interesting to note how place-based and architectural her statistical presentation was already, as she described the 'wooden, cement and aluminium structure(s)' and the composition of blocks 'around a square with the four fronts facing on each other'.[9] The setting for this radical social-services scheme could not be forgotten.

The pilot scheme sought to better understand (and consequently better support) the 'plight of poor families throughout Ireland'.[10] Working with Dr Peter Birch (1911-81), the reforming Bishop of Ossory, Sister Stan was at the helm of the innovative Kilkenny Social Services. Birch joined Ossory, a diocese encompassing 935 square miles of rural and largely agricultural territories in counties Kilkenny, Laois and Offaly, in the early 1960s. He immediately recognised what he termed, 'a cloud of depression' over the area, as reflected in the stagnation of new industry and in the population decline from 202,420 in 1841 to just 60,463 in 1966.[11] In housing terms, the area had a high proportion of old housing stock; 36.5% was over 100 years old.[12]

While much about Bishop Birch's diocese was specific and particular, Kilkenny's (or Ossory's) story of rural depopulation, insanitary housing and insufficient social infrastructure was a well-known Irish tale: a 1950s and 1960s tale playing out to the backdrop of post-war American imperialism and the potential therein, through the Irish diaspora, of Irish tourism. Birch saw his diocese as typical and thus as the ideal testing ground for prospective wider social reform. So, in 1963, with a Charter championing justice, freedom and marginal people 'who lie low', the Kilkenny Social Services was born.[13]

Chief among the range of social mechanisms was the establishment of the national Combat Poverty Agency, under whose aegis the Newpark Close scheme set off. Case and group workers would live within the Newpark community, listening to the new residents, trying to understand them, or as Sister Stan described:

> [...] helping them to reflect on their lives, attitudes and expectations [...] to ensure that any action undertaken comes from the people and is not undertaken simply because the workers think it is desirable.[14]

In this way, the pilot project was founded within a community, whereby the actual experiences of the residents rather than the relativist projections of the care workers were to guide all matters. Newpark Close became the place, partly because of the residents' physical poverty, exacerbated by the architectonics of these so-called revolutionary flat-roofed houses.

There were no chimneys, in other words, no hearths so houses were to be heated by prohibitively expensive storage heaters. There were no picket fences or divisions between houses, that is, no public privacy. There were no green or play areas, or to put it another way, no amenities.

This was crisis-solution housing: quick to construct, difficult to inhabit. The architecture of Ireland's housing crisis – an endemic crisis which has been ongoing since Irish independence from Britain in 1922 – is typically summarised by two programmes. The first is urban slum clearance, such as Dublin's new housing and flat blocks of the 1930s through the 1960s; the second was the replacement of tenant farmer or landless labourer housing with mass concrete rural cottages, again from the 1930s onwards but through semi-state rural agents like the Land Commission or the *Bord na Mona* (the Turf Board).[15] In this fairly dichotomous narrative, the architecture of new modernist homes on the edges of regional towns has been overlooked.[16] Such a place as Newpark Close muddies the waters of settlement identity in mid-to-later twentieth-century Ireland. As a crisis solution employing prefabricated elements and sporting the formal language of second-generation universal modernism, this scheme surely belonged in the city. But here it stood, on the edge of a regional town speaking as blatantly of 1970s rural depression and marginalisation as a Brian Friel play on the stage of Dublin's Abbey Theatre.[17]

Ultimately, the Combat Poverty pilot project stemmed from a deeply humanist motivation, about which Sister Stan mused:

> While we have been working with these families for a number of years, we still feel remote from them – their hopes, their fears, thinking, attitude and aspirations.[18]

Stan's social work practice evolved from her (we paraphrase) tireless seeking to understand the experiences of poverty and oppression, of gross injustices under which, she claimed, marginalised people live. If these messages underpinned the Newpark Close and greater Kilkenny Social Services agenda, the later Temple Bar experiment, the subsequent Stanhope Green project and ultimately, the Focus Point mission, where did they position her vis-à-vis Irish Catholic Social teaching at this juncture?

In her first book, *Who Should Care?* Sister Stan worked to situate Kilkenny Social Services. Her reading of the 1960s focused on change. Citing Joan Baez, Martin Luther King and Pope John Paul II in one paragraph, she asserted that the Pope opened minds that had been closed to 'the great social questions', such as communists being human too, for instance![19] About Ireland she wrote that 'the new Papacy came at a period when [...] fear of state control was beginning to die away [...]'.[20]

Clearly, the Kilkenny Social Services were aligned with the reforming messages of the Second Vatican Council, and unsurprisingly so, when we learn that Bishop Birch had recently returned from the Council in 1963 where he had encountered, as Sister Stan put it, 'the South American bishops'.[21] Were Bishop Birch and then Sister Stan to be conduits of this way of thinking and working? Certainly the Newpark Close scheme, in its determined responsiveness, might be read in the terms of South American Liberation Theology.[22] And, Sister Stan, as recorded in her ongoing published research, came out of Kilkenny hoping to gain a deeper understanding of Christian liberation and justice, through closer readings of Paulo Freire, Gustavo Gutiérrez, Leonardo Boff, and José Comblin.[23]

Into this reforming soup we must mix the research element. Everything was rooted in on-the-ground research. The research findings underpinned the Combat Poverty Agency as it strove, from the outset, to inform and change national social policy.[24] It was timely; coming when Irish people's conviction 'that things could be improved' rather than 'only get worse', was dawning.[25] As Stan observed, 'At the centre of this growing conviction, in the Kilkenny area, was the uncomfortable prophetic activism of Peter Birch.'[26]

But that prophetic activism was not to endure. In 1981, Bishop Birch died. It was premature and the hierarchy of Sister Stan's religious order had a plan for this very vocal, enormously energetic and by then already somewhat maverick nun. Sister Stan was to go: either up to Donegal, the far northwestern and most remote part of Ireland or, into the fires of Dublin, its beleaguered capital city.

## BUT WHERE CAN I GO?: HOMELESS WOMEN IN 1980S DUBLIN AND PLACE-BASED PRACTICES OF CARE

Between 1981 and 1983, Sister Stan moved to Dublin where she began a senior research fellowship at University College Dublin looking into the experience and extent of homelessness among women in Dublin, a population that until this point had scarcely been acknowledged by Irish society, much less studied.[27] As a result – or perhaps more accurately, as a continuation – of this research, she gathered a small group of researchers and young women from the study in a semi-derelict building in Temple

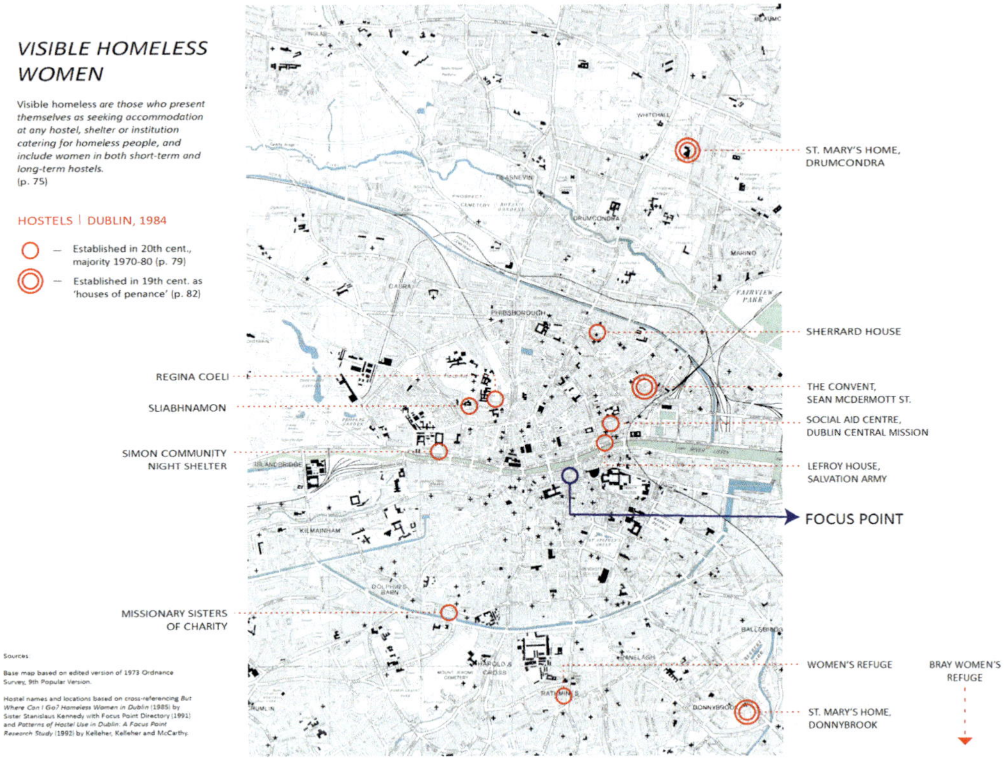


Figure 12.3: Map of Visible Homeless Women. Source: Haylee Derrickson, 2024. Hostel names and locations based on cross-referencing Sister Stanislaus Kennedy, *But Where Can I Go? Homeless Women in Dublin* (1985) with *Focus Point Directory* (1991) and Kelleher, Kelleher and McCarthy, *Patterns of Hostel Use in Dublin: A Focus Point Research Study* (1992); edited version of 1973 Ordnance Survey, 9th Popular Edition used as base map.

Bar for a series of workshops and conversations over the course of a year. This gathering would culminate in the foundation of the homelessness organisation Focus Point (now Focus Ireland).[28]

Adamant about sharing this research, Sister Stan published the book *But Where Can I Go?* Therein, she distinguished between the 'visible homeless', that is those women staying in hostels and shelters, and the 'hidden homeless', a much larger category including women 'squatting, dossing or sleeping rough'. The latter category, the hidden homeless, also comprised women living in convents or other large institutions such as psychiatric hospitals, those in contact with voluntary social services in search of accommodation, women 'doubling up' with friends or family members, and women on the waiting lists of local housing authorities.[29]

In our interpretation of this research, we engage in thick mapping, making two separate but connected drawings. Our first map (Fig. 12.3) traces the geography of visible homelessness, seeking to identify and locate the 14 homeless hostels cited in *But Where Should I Go?* Overlaid onto an edited version of the 1973 Ordnance Survey Map, the hostels circled in red are mapped by cross-referencing the 1991 *Focus Point Directory* and a 1992 Focus Point Research Study, *Patterns of Hostel Use in Dublin*, with the nameless descriptions of hostel attributes in the 1984 study.[30] There is a distinction between large nineteenth-century institutions (established as 'houses of penance'), and the twentieth-century hostels, which were generally smaller.[31] Having opened between 1970 and 1980, the smaller hostels reflected ongoing de-institutionalisation of the mentally ill in Ireland which Stan's research inadvertently captured. Initiated with the re-organisation of the Irish health-care system in 1970, the shift towards community care did not adequately address the needs of people experiencing homelessness, that is those who lost access to the casual wards previously provided in county homes.[32] It is within this context of insufficient state provision and in the existing (spatial) network of homelessness services in Dublin's inner city, that we may locate the Temple Bar experiment, in all its centrality.

While Sister Stan's study estimated that more than 520 'newly homeless' women were accommodated by hostels each year, she approximated the number of 'hidden homeless' women to be much higher, with over 8,000 on the housing waiting list and approximately 680 recorded from other sources.[33] The second drawing (Fig. 12.4), an exercise in narrative mapping and collage, attempts to make visible the conditions of this invisibility. Making speculative map fragments, we trace the stories of three women, as documented in the opening chapter of *But Where Can I Go?* Firstly, the story of a young woman squatting in a doorless, windowless flat in Ballymun provides a glimpse into the lives of the estimated 300 women recorded squatting by Dublin Corporation. Secondly, we mark the repeated references to institutional care which speak of the experiences of women recorded as 'No Fixed Abode' (NFA) at St. Brendan's psychiatric hospital, and thirdly, we note there are the 79 women reported to be living in 24 convents across the city.[34]

While each story illustrates broader trends documented in Sister Stan's study, they also stand individually as a testament to a deeply personal experience. Listening to these experiences and recognising the inherent dignity and agency of the women voicing them, was a fundamental aspect

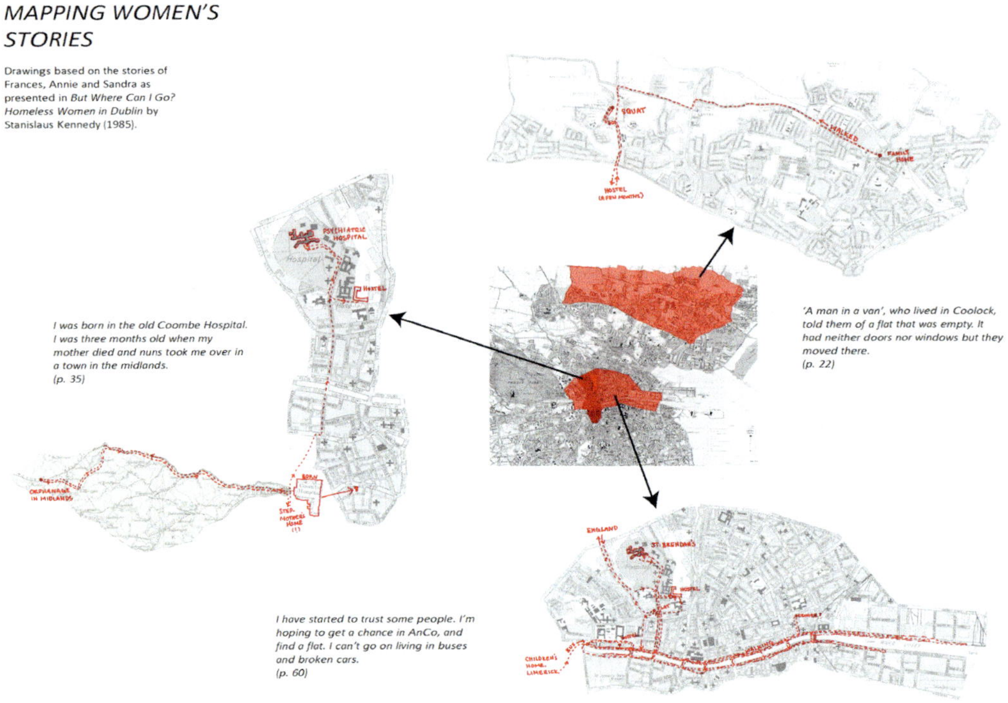


Figure 12.4: Collage: Mapping Women's Stories. Drawings based on the stories of Frances, Annie and Sandra as presented in Kennedy, *But Where Can I Go? Homeless Women in Dublin* (1985). Source: Haylee Derrickson, 2024.

of Sister Stan's practice of care.[35] This direct engagement with people translated to a direct engagement with place, an idea that emerges in the analysis of Sister Stan's research via mapping, and may be further understood through an examination of her actions in Temple Bar over the course of the following year.

'The homeless women we met have great resources', wrote Stan, in the conclusion of her study.[36] And yet, reflecting many years later, she was left feeling that, 'you knew them to a certain extent, but you didn't know enough'.[37] It was this pursuit of deeper understanding, combined with Sister Stan's determination to engage with the capabilities of the women she had met, rather than focusing on their deprivation, that led her to acquire the top floor of a ramshackle Dublin townhouse.

No. 15, Eustace Street was a four-storey nineteenth-century (former merchant) house in Dublin's Temple Bar neighbourhood.[38] At first, Stan leased only the top floor from Córas Iompair Éireann (CIÉ or Irish Rail), the middle floors being occupied by a printing business and the ground floor remaining derelict.[39] The state of the Eustace Street building was typical of the fabric of its neighbourhood. Indeed, it was typical of much of the historic centre of 1980s Dublin. Temple Bar was always noteworthy for its dense urban grain. A rectangular precinct running along the south bank of the River Liffey, it stretched from College Green to Dublin's administrative and ecclesiastic medieval heart. Its centrality led to it being earmarked for demolition by CIÉ for the creation of a new transport hub to be designed by Skidmore Owings Merrill. But while the new station was being planned, the area's use as artists' studios, recording spaces, galleries and thrift shops became embedded in its small streets and former industrial, residential or religious buildings.[40]

Though artists thrived here in the 1970s and 1980s, dereliction dominated and the notion that this underused inner-city urban fabric held value was a radical idea. For Sister Stan, however, a dilapidated Temple Bar townhouse was logical, born of necessity and nurtured by her first-hand experiences of 'making do' in Kilkenny. Her engagement with buildings in terms of their potential utility rather than their obsolescence chimed with the burgeoning building philosophy of many younger Irish architects, particularly that of Gerry Cahill. Cahill's contemporaneous 1979 study of Dublin's medieval Liberties neighbourhood, also undertaken via a UCD fellowship and also culminating in a rich text, *Back to the Street* (1980), lamented the decay of urban fabric and community.[41] He went on to co-organise the Dublin City Quays project, an ideas exhibition and conference held in 1987, which sought to reconsider the river's quayside gap-toothed architecture. This mobilised the architectural community, and arguably culminated in the Temple Bar competition of 1991, which resulted in the area's regeneration.[42]

Pointedly, the dial was moving so that the historic city, with its palette of limestone and granite, copper and slate, was of interest. Perhaps Stan's negotiation with Temple Bar's vernacular architecture signalled the *Zeitgeist*? Or perhaps her chiming with the architectural intelligentsia (the emergent 'Dublin Renaissance' as it became known), was plain old coincidence? Either way, Cahill's and Stan's paths were crossing, physically through a Combat Poverty Agency encounter and culturally through their shared interest in social justice and housing.[43]

This level of engagement certainly informed the strategic acquisition of 15 Eustace Street. Over the course of a year, the top floor of the house took on many functions, primarily that of meeting place for Sister Stan

Figure 12.5: Collage: *But Where Can I Go?* Temple Bar. Source: Ellen Rowley and Haylee Derrickson, 2025.

with fellow nun, Sister Síle, three graduate researchers and eight young women who had been 'intermittently homeless'.[44] In this tiny corner of the city the women held a variety of workshops, cooked meals together, wrote poetry and began a series of conversations that would lead to the eventual formation of the homelessness organisation Focus Point (Fig. 12.5). From playwriting and poetry reading with Eavan Boland and others, generosity was given and received. The eight young women identified several specific needs including a 24-hour emergency phone line, a drop-in information service, outreach services and a low-cost restaurant. Slowly, the group began to acquire the lower floors of 15 Eustace Street in proportion with the scale of their ambitions.[45]

In September of 1985, Focus Point opened the door of its café on the ground floor of the former shopfront, while the middle floors were repurposed as office and meeting spaces for the newly formed organisation's two outreach workers and the approximately 80 volunteers who ran the emergency phone line.[46] In this way, a small, under-utilised building in a corner of the city deemed undesirable became the centre of a new physical and telephonic support network.

## OUTSIDER WITHIN: FEMINIST BIOGRAPHY AND THE PLACE OF THE NUN IN MID-TWENTIETH-CENTURY IRELAND

What is continuously surprising, as we try to map Sister Stan's activism through her architectural agency, was her ability to defy or, more accurately, to test the Irish Catholic hierarchy not only in her own community, The Religious Sisters of Charity, but also nationally, in relation to congregational and diocesan matters. She appeared steadfast in her commitment to a reforming transnational Catholic Church, by evoking the formative influence of Bishop Birch. He provided the example. Writing in *The Furrow* in 1975, Birch stated:

> [...] it is really extraordinary how ready we are, to think that a young, for example, priest or nun, a man or woman of thirty, cannot be depended on to do a little job without referring to superiors for approval at every step. It is the real damning of our training [...] when a person who is probably at the height of his physical and intellectual powers, and maybe his spiritual powers too – is considered precocious or too immature to act independently and well.[47]

Such confident poo-pooing of hierarchical patriarchy, in the face of arguably the most hierarchical Catholic church in the world, reminds us of Bishop Birch's anomalous stance. Just before his death in 1981, he contributed to one of Stan's earliest publications, *One Million Poor*, an academic mapping of poverty in Ireland. His account of community homes is damning; he refers to them as bastions of Pope Paul VI's 'new loneliness', which derive from 'outmoded systems of custodial care where little accommodation has been made to new social thinking'.[48]

This social thinking was influencing the principles of Catholic Social Teaching, as developed in the key 1960s Papal encyclicals, Pope John XXIII's *Mater et Magistra* (1961), and Pope Paul VI's *Pacem in Terris* (1963) and *Populorum Progressio* (1967). Such principles as 'Human Dignity' and 'Solidarity' – that is the interconnectedness of all people and the responsibility of communities to support each other – and of the 'Preferential Option for the Poor and Vulnerable', which required that special attention be given to those who are most in need of attention and support, underpinned the social work that Stan, inspired by Birch, undertook from the 1960s through the 1980s.

Sister Stan's research, social work and ultimately, her private and communal mission were so sure-footed that we can only imagine the strength

Figure 12.6: Collage: Looming Irish Convents. From New Ross to Carndonagh.
Source: Ellen Rowley and Haylee Derrickson, 2025, convent photographs from holdings of the Irish Architectural Archive.

of her vocation. The potency of her actions, as they impacted social policy and produced hundreds of homes, while catalysing the making of thousands more, evidence her conviction of the death of traditional Irish Catholic institutions as places of care. De-institutionalisation would mean a new world order for Catholic (for which read, Christian) practices of care in late-twentieth-century Ireland. Stan's vocation then, was capable of evolving.

As many feminist histories have asserted, mid-century Ireland was dominated by a depressed economy, which in tandem with the Irish Constitution combined to conjure an image of idealised womanhood that positioned women in the home as mother and wife. The most obvious motivation for girls choosing to enter the sisters or become nuns was the alternative this provided to marriage and to an identity as wife and mother.[49] For Sister Stan, joining the sisters provided a freedom and emancipation from marriage.[50] More interestingly, this motivation was superseded by that related to security and ease, what some might indeed consider institutionalisation. For, as Stan's adult life and career developed, and by her own admission in February 2024, she never had to worry or cast a thought as to where her next meal was coming from, or as to where she would sleep that night or that month. As a sister in the

Religious Sisters of Charity, such basic needs were sorted. This echoes an anti-materialism but also nuances Sister Stan's motivation.

Treasa Kennedy joined the order in 1958 and her background, like that of the majority of those Irish women who became nuns at this time, was middle-class and rural. In her case, her homeplace was a mid-sized farm in Lispole in west Kerry which, as a daughter, would not have been hers to inherit or manage, notwithstanding that in the end, none of her siblings took this on, and the farmhouse sits today as a Kennedy family retreat.[51]

Other contexts also matter. During the 1960s, there were 16,000 nuns and 14,000 brothers and clergy in Ireland, making its Catholic Church the most heavily staffed of any in the world.[52] This figure hit peak in 1967, when there were 19,000 nuns. As such, apart from wives and mothers, religious sisters were the most common female presence in Irish society during this time. They were accepted, regularly revered, and often feared. By extension, their institutions and buildings, dotted across Irish towns, cities and villages, were instantly recognisable (Fig. 12.6). In Claire Keegan's novel, *Small Things Like These*, set in a 1980s Irish town, the physical and metaphysical presence(s) of the local convent elide:

> The convent was a powerful-looking place on the hill at the far side of the river with black, wide-open gates and a host of tall shining windows [...] Some said that the training school girls, as they were known, weren't students of anything, but girls of low character who spent their days being reformed [...] Others claimed that it was the nuns themselves who worked their fingers to the bone [...] that they had hearts of gold and problems with their eyes [...] Others swore the place was no better than a mother-and-baby home.[53]

Keegan captures much of the ominous public authority held in the walls of this world within a world, this Catholic citadel looming above and beyond the town still in the 1980s. In Keegan's capable hands, the convent is many things but mostly, it is a profiteering heterotopia.

Returning to motivations and vocations, Yvonne McKenna's oral-history-based research into Irish women who became nuns from about 1930 to around 1960 uncovers how motivations were manifold. They ranged from a search for adventure and heroism, through the experience of becoming a missionary, to a motivation for differentiation and purity, that is for being 'better' than society, and thus from the hope for personal sacrifice to the aspiration for professional advancement.[54] Two motivations, possibly most aligned with our protagonist's story, were the desire for resistance or a form of opposition to contemporary gender terms, as well as the ability and thus the autonomy to choose a particular religious congregation. For Treasa Kennedy, the endemic injustice which she observed in 1950s Dingle town was enough of a motivation to follow in the footsteps of Mary Aikenhead, the founder of the Religious Sisters of Charity.[55] By her own account, the younger Sister Stanislaus Kennedy did not want to become a teacher, nor to be a nurse, but to be active at the forefront of charitable systems within the community. She cited her contempt for Dingle's social inequalities.[56]

In the mid twentieth century, while achieving much as nurse, medic, teacher, missionary, the Irish nun always had limited autonomy, living amidst rules and regulations. Stan understood these rules and structures, yet pushed ahead by working within them. In *But Where Can I Go?* firsthand accounts from women and girls named episodes when nuns managed their care. These episodes were mostly not happy; nuns' perceived or observed behaviour might be outwardly abusive, most often negligent. But Stan did not, could not as a sociologist, and would not as a nun censor these accounts. It is this position of being within, as insider without/outsider within, that confounds and enriches our reading.

## STANHOPE GREEN: NEW HOMES FROM OLD CONVENTS

On the occasion of the publication of *But Where Can I Go?* in 1985, the Irish television broadcaster, RTÉ, broadcast a piece on Sister Stan, which followed her from Temple Bar to her convent at Stanhope Street to the west of Dublin's north inner city.[57] As we watch Sister Stan singing with her fellow sisters in the convent chapel we understand this other-ness, this separation, and we briefly note the communality and ritual underpinning her convent life. This is also a moment in Ireland when both Claire Keegan's semi-fictional regional convent and Stan's non-fictional urban convent were dissipating; they were not quite about to disappear but were, perhaps, finding themselves in the earliest stages of decomposition. The Religious Sisters of Charity could feel their contraction and so commissioned a smaller new building on their existing site. But what of the late-Victorian solid brick building, replete with its Virgin Mary roofline and institutional gloom?

In an anachronistic move, out of time and before its time, Sister Stan asked if she could have the old convent building. Though laden with associations, the convent had potential for reinvention. A standing robust building, albeit damp and with a dysfunctional floor plan, sitting on just-enough ground, provided a good-enough pile of ingredients for Stan's radical cook-up and reformulation.[58] Living in such a communal place meant she had no fear of its architecture.

So it was that at this late-1980s juncture Sister Stan's architectural adjacency was as developer or entrepreneur, one who was collaborative, gathering, persuasive, and caring. First, she got the land; then she gathered the best young idealistic architect, Gerry Cahill. Of course, she had had her client all along, a new type of client, her young women in varying states of homelessness, some with children, most on their own. Next, was her innovative infrastructure, that is, the establishment of the Focus Housing Association (out of Focus Point) onto which Cahill was co-opted so that the typical separation of client, builder, designer, developer was overcome. The architects also contributed to the project's fundraising; the builders also donated some of the materials. Then came government backing, in the form of the 1988 Housing Act. Claiming to tackle homelessness at its heart, it allowed £20,000 per unit created as opposed to £2,000 previously.[59] The Minister of Environment awarded the project £1 million in the 1989 budget.[60]

The making of a community of homes, with priority given to single people, had begun. Both the architect and Sister Stan were united in their mission which was to make as many dwellings as possible by retaining as much of the convent infrastructure as possible. Together they asked, 'what is the smallest unit that won't make you go mad?'[61] As such, there were to be enough homes to meaningfully push at the limits of the building and its land, but not too many to ghettoise the inhabitants. In the main building, the former nuns' cells were to become rooms-as-homes of their own. Each unit contained waste and water infrastructure, ventilation and independent electricity, and behaved as a self-contained kitchen, bedroom, bathroom and sitting room.

What had been a defective floor plan, across the three storeys of the main convent block was transformed through Cahill's design decision to emphasize the building's corridors (see Fig. 12.2). Brightened and widened, they feed the studio flats created out of the former nuns' rooms while containing all the services. Meanwhile, the convent's overwrought floor plan seeks reprieve in new communal areas of courtyard, library and the Fiddler's Green restaurant; such semi-public services and places punctuated Stanhope Green, while attracting non-residents (Fig. 12.7).

Figure 12.7: 'Day in the Life' Section of Stanhope Green. Source: Haylee Derrickson, 2024.

Sheltered and supported, this was to be a new form of housing for Ireland and specifically, the first time that a convent was converted to social housing. While Sister Stan described an ongoing wrangle with political figures to extract enough funding for the project, Cahill outlined the challenges inherent in the institutional architecture. As their memories and reflections, thirty years later, tell it, both were entangled in the pragmatics of the problem and in the prospect of the project. Cahill and his team set about understanding every inch and brick, shrub and stone of the site. Stan pushed. Her agency was two-fold: firstly, in her faith in the adaptive potential of the convent building and secondly, in her dogged rootedness or consciousness of the needs of those experiencing homelessness. Their shared anecdote around procuring extra bricks for free from the contractors – specifically a second leaf of navy brick for the terrace of ten family houses on the site, discussed below – points to their shared determination to realise Stanhope Green without compromising on aesthetic choices and character.

Stan's belief in the convent was developed by Cahill's design interpretation of it as a campus that was at once city and promenade. From this campus-city-promenade premise, two more housing forms were made, to add to the adapted nun's cells in the main and forever gloomy convent building. These were the long-term houses for families: a new diminutive terrace, facing the front of the old building and comprising ten homes of 60 square metres each. Their front doors breach yellow-brick walls,

Figure 12.8: Stanhope Green Cloister, just finished, Gerry Cahill Architects, Dublin, 1991. Source: Bill Hastings for Gerry Cahill Architects.

reminiscent of artisan dwelling terraces in the nearby neighbourhood of Stoneybatter.

The third housing structure, the cloister, is the architectural surprise. It even won the 1991 Irish Concrete Society Award for its deployment of then innovative concrete block system Forticrete (Fig. 12.8). Here a pair of two-storey pitched-roof ranges, with colonnade elevations at ground level, enclose a rectangular courtyard. As a residential setting, it must work harder than most in bringing a mix of long-term homes and shorter-term stepdown dwellings together, into a tight space.

In this way, the architecture is a backdrop, not neutral or passive but never willful or overbearing. The architects chose a roughly textured version of the affordable Forticrete system in order to compliment the convent's rear walls, which were predominately stone. This provides its own structure (Fig. 12.7). Feeling particular to the cloister, it reminds us that we are in another part of the scheme; while unified, each component of Stanhope Green retains its own character. This is the 'city' element of Cahill and his team's design. When it opened in 1991, they had created 96 dwellings: a city, indeed.[62]

## TO END

A lot has transpired since the architects completed the original hard-edged scenography in 1991: today, this place bristles with biodiversity and human activity. It is a secret garden in Dublin's north city (Fig. 12.9).

Out of the Stanhope Green utopia and experiment, emerged an enduring social and financial model – in other words, a new housing type. The project seemed to break a local dam of sorts, unleashing a stream of nuns and mother superiors each with her emptying and decomposing convent building, keen for it to be used and maybe saved.

For instance, the neighbouring Presentation Sisters at George's Hill convent and school, watched the Stanhope Green transformation and by 1992 had invited Sister Stan, representing the Focus Point team, and Cahill to their site to advise them. At George's Hill, the secondary school numbers were dwindling, and the Presentation Sisters saw in their urban buildings the potential to house people. In this, they were investing in

Figure 12.9: Stanhope Green Cloister, Gerry Cahill Architects, Dublin, 2023. Source: Paul Tierney for Dublin City Council, C20th Architecture in Dublin City Project.

their own endurance while alleviating the 1990s housing crisis. Soon afterwards, the Presentation Sisters entrusted George's Hill to Focus Housing Association, where Cahill and project architect Jim Murphy adapted the eighteenth and nineteenth-century blocks while wrapping a new range of two-storey apartments along two of the site's streets (Fig. 12.2). Its 70 apartments opened by 1997. With accommodation for five retired nuns alongside a mixture of family and transitional housing, George's Hill presented yet another model. Then came the Focus Ireland housing apartments at the smaller Religious Sisters of Charity convent at Basin Lane and the nearby Mercy Sisters convent on Cork Street, adapted for housing by Sophia Housing, a related Approved Housing Body.[63] All of these projects emerged outside of Dublin's market forces, through gifts of historic buildings on valuable urban land.

In founding Focus Ireland, Sister Stanislaus Kennedy acted not just as a social innovator but also as a spatial agent, creatively repurposing the architecture of 1980s Dublin in response to the experience of occupying it. Inarguably the resolve to act in this way came from the exigencies of the Kilkenny Social Services project, while the activation of the ramshackle Temple Bar house undoubtedly encouraged her to develop the convent. The brief in all of these contexts – Newpark Close, Eustace Street, Stanhope Green – grew not just as a response to need, but also as a response to place, collectively experienced and imagined. It is in this form of empowered social action, informed by a deep understanding of people and place, that we locate Sister Stan's 'place-based practice of care'.

## NOTES

1 In the conference paper from which this chapter is drawn, we presented a number of mp3 soundbites from a February 2024 conversation which played sporadically. The overlaying of sound bites, our joint oral presentation and the visual material amassed from archive and contemporary sources interpreted the research in performative terms. A multiplicity or cacophony of voices was privileged, which is here translated into collages and drawings as alternative contributory methods to such recent and hyper-local architectural history.

2 Sister Stan, who died in 2025, was Lifetime President and on the board of Focus Ireland. See history of Focus Ireland, in Focus Ireland, *A Place to Call Home. Twenty-Five Years of Focus Ireland* (Dublin: A. & A. Famar, 2011). See most recent annual report at https://www.focusireland.ie/wp-content/uploads/2023/09/Annual-Report-2022.pdf

3 The Evolving Legacies religious architecture project (Ellen Rowley and Philip Crowe, UCD School of Architecture/APEP) maps diocesan churches and convent building transformations. Present studies include Dublin Diocesan and Heritage Council of Ireland (2025–) 'Places of Worship' (led by Shaffreys Architects, Ellen Rowley, Ros Kavanagh and Bushra Mansoor); Bushra Mansoor, 'From Cloister to Community' (M.Arch diss., UCD School of Architecture, 2025), and HeritAct collaboration in Ballina convent, as well as Rún (Open Heart City) by CoLab consortium (UCD, Queens Belfast

and Berlin). Other convent research projects include Rose Luminello, 'Irish Women Religious in the Anglophone World' (Keough-Naughton Institute for Irish Studies, University of Notre Dame); Gillian O'Brien, Danielle O'Donovan and Jessie Castle, 'The Material Culture of Convents, 2020 – ongoing' (John Moores University and Nano Nagle Place, Cork).

4 Mapping as methodology borrows from architecture's method of site analysis as well as methods of narrative mapping in participatory design and interdisciplinary practices of 'thick mapping' as described in Dana Cuff et al., *Urban Humanities: New Practices for Reimagining the City* (Cambridge, MA: MIT Press, 2020), 106-115.

5 The choice to make two separate but connected drawings reflects a key distinction in Sister Stan's study between 'visible homeless', those women staying in hostels and shelters, and the 'hidden homeless', a much larger category including women 'squatting, dossing or sleeping rough', as described later in this chapter; see Stanislaus Kennedy, *But Where Can I Go? Homeless Women in Dublin* (Dublin: Arlen House, 1985), 75-76.

6 The term 'spatial agent' is drawn from Nishat Awan, Tatjana Schneider, and Jeremy Till, *Spatial Agency: Other Ways of Doing Architecture* (Abingdon: Routledge, 2011), 28.

7 There is no history of the NBA researched or compiled to date (2025) though the original and flagship project of the organisation, the Ballymun Estate, has captured the imaginations of geographers, anthropologists, architects, social scientists, and contemporary social historians. Due to the combination of its high-rise mechanised architectonics and later dearth of social infrastructure, the estate has been sung about (U2, 'Running to Stand Still', 1987) and written about such as: John Montague, 'The architecture of Ballymun', in *Memories, milestones and new horizons: Reflections on the regeneration of Ballymun*, ed. Aibhlinn McCrann (Belfast: Blackstaff Press, 2008), 45–76; Sinead Power, 'The Development of the Ballymun Housing Scheme, Dublin 1965–1969', in *Irish Geography* 33 (2000): 199–22; Aisling Prior, ed., *Hotel Ballymun. Seamus Nolan* (Dublin: Breaking Ground, Ballymun Regeneration Ltd., 2008); Ellen Rowley, 'Ballymun, Case Study', in *Art and Architecture of Ireland: Architecture 1600–2000*, ed. Rolf Loeber et al. (New Haven: Yale University Press, 2014), 4:415–16; Robert Somerville-Woodward, *Ballymun, A History. Volumes 1 & 2 c. 1600–1997* (Dublin: Ballymun Regeneration Ltd., 2002). In relation to the 1963 housing protests which were reactions to the collapse of tenement buildings in Dublin city centre in May 1963, see Erika Hannah, *Modern Dublin: Urban Change and the Irish Past, 1957–73* (Oxford: Oxford University Press, 2013).

8 Stanislaus Kennedy, *Who Should Care?* (Dublin: Turoe Press, 1981), Appendix VI, 214.

9 Ibid.

10 Kennedy, *Who Should Care?*, 214-16; and thanks to Donie Butler, Chair of Newpark 60th Anniversary – local history group, 2016.

11 Ibid., Appendix II, 200

12 Ibid. For more on housing in 1960s Ireland, see contemporaneous account by sociologist, Paul Pfreszchner *Dynamics of Irish Housing* (Dublin: Institute of Public Administration, 1965); and histories, Ellen Rowley, *Housing, Architecture and the Edge Condition. Dublin is Building 1935–75* (Routledge, 2018), and Joseph Brady, *Dublin, 1950–1970. Houses, Flats and High Rise* (Portland, OR: Four Courts Press, 2016).

13 Sample points of the Charter include: 'To ensure the dignity of each individual in society and his full development', 'To be accessible and accountable to local people'. See Appendix III, and the Charter of the Communities of L'Arche, in Kennedy, *Who Should Care?*, 203-4.

14 Kennedy, *Who Should Care?*, Appendix VI, 215

15 Irish housing histories such as Rowley, *Housing, Architecture and Edge Condition* and Tom Spalding, *Designed for Life* (Cork: Cork University Press, 2025) focus on urban housing while rural housing has been recorded by Mary McCarthy, 'The provision of rural local-authority housing and domestic space: a comparative North-South study, 1942-60', in *Proceedings of the Royal Irish Academy: Archaeology, Culture, History, Literature*, vol. 111C (2011): 287-309. Exemplary architect-designed schemes are captured in Brian Ward, Gary Boyd, Michael Pike, eds., *Out of the Ordinary* (Abingdon: Routledge, 2019).

16 Other than *Out of the Ordinary* (cited above) or Fergal McCabe, *Ambition and Achievement. The Civic Visions of Frank Gibney* (Dublin: Castles in the Air Publications, 2018), there is a lack of published research on regional modernist housing in Ireland.

17 See for instance Brian Friel, *Philadelphia Here I Come* (1964), Abbey Theatre (Irish National Theatre, Dublin) premiere, October 1972. The internationally acclaimed theatre and literary fiction coming out of 1960s and 1970s Ireland, forcefully and often brutally spoke of rural depression, land grappling and hopelessness.

18 Kennedy, *Who Should Care?*, Appendix VI, 215.

19 Ibid., 15.

20 Ibid., 15.

21 Sister Stanislaus Kennedy and Sister Síle Wall, in conversation with Haylee Derrickson and Ellen Rowley, 27 February 2024.

22 Liberation Theology is a Catholic social justice philosophy which engaged in socio-economic studies to overcome inequalities and perceived social oppression. The term comes in part from the writings of Gustavo Gutiérrez, namely *A Theology of Liberation*, from 1971.

23 The opening paragraph of *But Where Can I Go?* lists these proponents of Liberation Theology. See Kennedy *But Where Can I Go?*, 11.

24 Combat Poverty Agency was set up as a statutory body under the *Combat Poverty Agency Act 1986* (Ireland) ('Act'). According to Eoin Carolan, 'The establishment of the Agency was preceded by the creation of a non-statutory Combat Poverty Organisation ('CPO'), which was asked to review and submit plans for a new specific anti-poverty body to the relevant Minister'. See Carolan, 'Lessons from Anti-Poverty Action in Ireland: Flexibility, Failure and the Pitfalls of a "Fourth Branch" Model', in *Federal Law Review* 51, no. 3 (September 2023): 333-43.

25 This is a paraphrase of Tim Pat Coogan, *Ireland Since the Rising* (London: Pall Mall Press, 1966), cited by Kennedy in *Who Should Care?*, 15.

26 Kennedy, *Who Should Care?*, 15.

27 Kennedy and Wall, in conversation with Derrickson and Rowley, 27 February 2024; Kennedy, *But Where Can I Go?* 13.

28 Ibid., 183.

29 Ibid., 75-76.

30 Presumably, the hostels were described in this way for the sake of anonymity. Sources used for mapping: Focus Point, *Focus Point Directory: Care Accommodation and Housing Support Services in Ireland* (Focus Point Project Limited, 1991); Carmel Kelleher, Patricia Kelleher and Patricia McCarthy, *Patterns of Hostel Use in Dublin: A Focus Point Research Study* (Focus Point Project Limited, 1992).

31 Kennedy, *But Where Can I Go?*, 82.

32 Ibid., 68. For more on post-1960 deinstitutionalisation in Ireland, see Ruth Barrington, *Health, Medicine & Politics in Ireland, 1900–70* (Dublin: Institute of Public Administration, 1987).

33 Kennedy, *But Where Can I Go?*, 169-72.

34 Ibid., 148–49.

35 Sister Stan describes the practice of listening to marginalised voices as an expression of the tenets of Liberation Theology in the Introduction to *But Where Can I Go?*, 11-12. In her concluding remarks, 181-82, she again emphasises the importance of presenting the women's stories in the first chapter of the book, before making any analysis or commentary.

36 Kennedy, *But Where Can I Go?*, 181.

37 Kennedy and Wall, in conversation with Derrickson and Rowley, 27 February 2024.

38 'Focus Ireland, 15 Eustace Street, Dublin 2, DUBLIN', National Built Heritage Service, 19 March 2015, https://www.buildingsofireland.ie/buildings-search/building/50020104/focus-ireland-15-eustace-street-dublin-2-dublin.

39 Kennedy and Wall, in conversation with Derrickson and Rowley, 27 February 2024.

40 For more on Temple Bar's history and its subsequent redevelopment, see the Group 91 essays by Merlo Kelly, 'Irish Film Centre', 'Print Works', and Ellen Rowley, 'Temple Bar Galley + Studios', in *More Than Concrete Blocks, 1973-99*, ed. Ellen Rowley and Carole Pollard (Dublin: UCD Press, 2023), 3:342-402

41 Gerry Cahill was an early proponent of the value of inner-city neighbourhoods in Dublin, a position articulated in his publication *Back to the Street* (Dublin: Housing Research Unit, University College Dublin, 1980). Eimear Arthur and Michael Hayes, eds., *Care and Consideration. On the Work of Gerry Cahill Architects* (Type and Arts Council of Ireland, 2025).

42 A consortium of eight young practices, calling themselves Group 91 won this Temple Bar competition. They had just finished working on 'Making a Modern Street' after contributing to the *Dublin City Quays project*, ed. Gerry Cahill and Loughlin Kealy (Dublin: UCD, 1987). For a comprehensive review of the work of Group 91 in Temple Bar see Patricia Quinn, *Temple Bar: The Power of an Idea* (Dublin: Temple Bar Properties Limited, 1996).

43 Gerry Cahill and Sister Stan first met via the Combat Poverty Agency in the late 1970s. Group conversation, Stanhope Green, May 2023.

44 Kennedy and Wall, in conversation with Derrickson and Rowley, 27 February 2024.

45 Ibid.

46 Focus Point, *Focus Point Directory: Care Accommodation and Housing Support Services in Ireland* (Focus Point Project Limited, 1991).

47 Peter Birch, 'Choosing Helpers', *The Furrow* 26 (1975): 579-586.

48 Peter Birch, 'Poverty and the Church', in *One Million Poor? The Challenge of Irish Inequality*, ed. Stanislaus Kennedy (Dublin: Turoe Press, 1981), 172.

49 Caitriona Clear, *Nuns in Nineteenth-Century Ireland* (Dublin: Gill and Macmillan, 1987). On twentieth-century nuns, see for example, Yvonne McKenna, 'Embodied Ideals and Realities: Irish Nuns and Irish Womanhood, 1930s-1960s', *Éire-Ireland (St. Paul)* 41, no. 1 (2006): 40-63; Deirdre Raftery, 'The "Mission" of Nuns in Female Education in Ireland, c. 1850–1950.' *Paedagogica Historica* 48, no. 2 (2012): 299-313; Deirdre Raftery and Catriona Delaney, 'Teaching Vocation or Religious Vocation: Examining the Changing Identity of Irish Teaching Sisters c. 1940-1970, an Oral History Approach', *Irish educational studies* 43, no. 2 (2024): 329-40.

50 Certainly in February 2024, in response to the question 'why become a nun?', both Sister Stan and Sister Síle heartily agreed that it presented a welcome alternative. Kennedy and Wall, in conversation with Derrickson and Rowley, 27 February 2024.

51 Maurice O'Keefe, 'Sr. Stanislaus Kennedy Interview', in *1922-2022, A Century of Change. Irish Life and Lore* (29 September 2021, Audio, 47:53) https://www.irishlifeandlore.com/product/sr-stanislaus-kennedy/ (accessed May 2023).

52 Tony Fahy, 'The Catholic Church and Social Policy', *The Furrow* 49, no. 4 (April 1998): 203; Daithí Ó Corráin. 'Catholicism in Ireland, 1880-2015: Rise, Ascendancy and Retreat', in *The Cambridge History of Ireland*, ed. Thomas Bartlett (Cambridge: Cambridge University Press, 2018), 726-64.

53 Claire Keegan, *Small Things Like These* (Faber & Faber, 2021), 37-39.

54 Yvonne McKenna, 'Entering Religious Life, Claiming Subjectivity: Irish Nuns, 1930s-1960s', *Women's History Review* 15 (2006): 189-211. McKenna sought to revise the narrative whereby women became nuns as an 'almost passive response to the scarcity of eligible bachelors and their own acceptance of the limited opportunities available', 196

55 Marie O'Leary, 'Mary Aikenhead', entry in *Dictionary of Irish Biography* (Cambridge: Cambridge University Press, ongoing), https://www.dib.ie/biography/aikenhead-mary-a0072.

56 In her conversation with Derrickson and Rowley on 27 February 2024, Sister Stan spoke of witnessing the 'haves' and 'have nots' in 1950s Dingle town, Co. Kerry.

57 'A Day in the Life of Sister Stan, June 5, 1985', RTE archives, https://www.rte.ie/archives/2015/0605/705991-a-day-in-the-life-of-sister-stan/.

58 For an architectural history of this Stanhope Green project within its later twentieth-century context, see Ellen Rowley, 'Stanhope Green', in *More Than Concrete Blocks, 1973-99*, ed. Ellen Rowley and Carole Pollard (Dublin: UCD Press, 2023), 3:334.

59 See Irish Statute Book, https://www.irishstatutebook.ie/eli/1988/act/28.

60 Kennedy and Gerry Cahill, in conversation, Stanhope Green, May 2023.

61 Gerry Cahill in conversation with Ellen Rowley, Stanhope Green, July 2023.

62 In 2011, some changes due to an extensive retrofit in response to housing standards and accessibility regulations, reduced the number of housing units from 96 to 71.

63 The adaptation of the Mercy Sisters Convent for Sophia Housing Association (SHA) was the Association's first housing project. SHA was established after Focus Ireland and was founded with a similar mission by Sister Jean Quinn and Eamonn Martin, see https://www.sophia.ie/about-us#:~:text=Sophia%20was%20founded%20by%20Sr,break%20the%20cycle%20of%20homelessness.

# Chapter 13
# Representing Black Women?
## Black Philanthropy, Architectural Design, and the Cosby Academic Center at Spelman College, 1988–1996

*E. James West*

In November 1988, Black comedian Bill Cosby and his wife Camille Cosby sent shockwaves through American higher education by announcing a donation of $20 million to Spelman, a liberal arts college for Black women located in Atlanta, Georgia. Made more than two decades before his unmasking as a sexual predator, Cosby remained one of America's most popular and beloved entertainers.[1] The enormous success of *The Cosby Show* (1984–1992) had made him one of the highest paid entertainers in the country, and by the late 1980s the comedian, alongside his wife Camille, had begun to funnel this financial windfall back into a range of philanthropic endeavours.[2] As reported in the *New York Times* and other media outlets, the gift was the largest donation ever made to an Historically Black College or University (HBCU) and one of the largest single donations to any college in the nation's recent history. In announcing the gift at a black-tie dinner in Atlanta, Johnnetta Cole, Spelman's newly inaugurated president, admitted that she had 'pinched myself to see if it [was] a dream'.[3]

The bulk of the Cosbys' gift was earmarked for the construction of a landmark new academic centre on the Spelman campus – envisioned as a 'mecca' for Black women's studies – that was to be named in Camille's honour.[4] Given its location and significance, it seemed fitting that both the Cosbys and Spelman's leadership prioritised finding a Black female architect to lead the project. After an eventful search, they settled on Donna deJongh, a co-partner in deJongh Associates, a Black architectural firm based in the US Virgin Islands. Despite a protracted building process, the Centre's completion in 1996 was heralded as an extraordinary achievement that 'sets the standard for what an academic facility should be' (Fig. 13.1).[5] President Cole declared that the building 'truly represents the ideas and values of Spelman College' and was a testament to 'the role

Figure 13.1: Camille Olivia Hanks Cosby Building at Spelman College, deJongh Group, Atlanta, Georgia, c. 1995. Spelman College Photographs Collection, Spelman College Archives.

of African American women' in the making of the modern world. Camille Cosby echoed these sentiments, dedicated the centre to all 'women representing the African diaspora'.[6]

This chapter focuses on the three Black women – philanthropist Camille Cosby, college president Johnnetta Cole, and architect Donna deJongh – at the heart of the building's development. For Camille, the construction of the Cosby Center offered a unique incentive to step beyond the shadow of her superstar husband, with an account in the media considering that she was 'forging a new beginning [...] in the public eye' and taking her place within a longer history of Black female philanthropy.[7] For Cole, the building's construction provided concrete evidence of her visionary leadership as Spelman's first Black female leader and, completed shortly before her departure from the institution, reiterated her standing as Spelman's beloved 'Sister President'.[8] And for deJongh, the project was a unique opportunity to elevate the profile of her practice and to cement her position within a new generation of Black female architects who came of age during the 1980s and early 1990s.[9]

However, while the building was named for Camille Cosby, media coverage of the project tended to centre her husband. Similarly, although Spelman stressed the significance of deJongh, as a Black woman, being the project's lead architect, the difficulties she faced made the project a more protracted and collaborative endeavour than initially envisaged. Furthermore, although the Cosby Center was initially planned as a bold architectural statement befitting its importance as a 'monument' to Black women and as a 'national landmark' for Black colleges, these ambitions were tempered by competing demands to align with the college's 'traditional red brick character'.[10] Addressing these and other tensions, this chapter asks: why was the construction of the Cosby Academic Center such a significant moment for the Spelman community? And how did deJongh Associates – and Donna deJongh in particular – grapple with 'working for two masters' who understood this significance in different, albeit overlapping, ways?

Spelman College was founded as the Atlanta Baptist Female Seminary by Harriet Giles and Sophia Packard, two white teachers from Massachusetts. With support from the Reverend Frank Quarles, the school opened in 1881 in the basement of the Friendship Baptist Church, a Black congregation located in Atlanta's Castleberry Hill district. Giles and Packard's efforts to establish Spelman place them within a larger wave of northern white educators and philanthropists who established new Black schools and colleges across the South in the aftermath of the American Civil War. However, as Evelyn Brooks Higginbotham notes, while the school's founders were white, financial support from Black Atlantans was vital during 'the critical first year of Spelman's existence'. Sustained support for local African American supporters helped to attract more significant funding from northern white Baptist organisations such as the American Baptist Home Mission Society (ABHMS).[11]

The fledgling seminary's most significant early backer was business magnate and philanthropist John D. Rockefeller, who was introduced to Packard and Giles at a church conference in Cleveland, Ohio. Buoyed by Rockefeller's support, Giles and Packard were able to purchase a nine-acre parcel of land close to the church, and the seminary officially moved to this new site in 1883. The following year, in recognition of the Rockefeller family's contribution to the seminary's development, Giles and Packard changed the name of their institution from the Atlanta Baptist Female Seminary to Spelman Seminary, to honour Rockefeller's wife, Laura Spelman Rockefeller and her family. In 1886, the Rockefellers' continued financial support enabled the construction of Rockefeller Hall, the first permanent campus building. Two years later, the seminary was formally chartered, with Packard installed as its first president.

Figure 13.2: Rockefeller Hall at Spelman College, c. 1890, Atlanta, Georgia. Spelman College Photographs Collection, Spelman College Archives.

As Tiffany Momon notes, Rockefeller was actively involved in the design process for Spelman's first major building.[12] In letters to other Spelman benefactors such as Henry Morehouse, the secretary of the ABHMS and namesake of Spelman's 'brother' institution, Morehouse College, Rockefeller detailed his wish that Rockefeller Hall be 'made of brick [and] three stories in height'. Although Rockefeller recommended an 'attractive' exterior, he advised against 'elaborate ornamentation' – perhaps as a reaction to the popularity of Collegiate Gothic, a subgenre of Gothic Revival architecture that became a fixture of many American campuses during the late nineteenth and early twentieth century.[13] The building's round-arched polychrome brick architecture, replete with semicircular dormer windows and a cupola, set the tone for subsequent buildings such as Giles Hall (1893), described by the American Institute of Architects as a 'Victorian' style structure with 'gables and pavilions on each end that echo the larger pedimented central portion' (Fig. 13.2).[14]

For much of the twentieth century, Spelman's institutional and building development was spearheaded by three figures: Lucy Hale Tapley, who served as its president between 1910 and 1927, Florence Matilda Read, who succeeded Tapley and stayed in post until 1953, and Albert Edward Manley, who became Spelman's president after Read's retirement and served until 1976. Under the leadership of Tapley and Manley, Spelman Seminary became Spelman College, and was incorporated into the larger Atlanta University system. The college also erected a number of new buildings, including Bessie Strong Hall, a residential building completed in 1917, and Tapley Hall, the college's new science building, which was completed in the mid-1920s. Perhaps the most significant addition to Spelman's campus during this period was Sisters Chapel (1927), a temple-like structure fronted with white Doric columns. All three sites were designed by Hentz, Reid & Adler, a white-owned architectural firm.[15]

Manley, Spelman's first male and first African American president, significantly increased its enrolment and continued to expand its physical campus. This included the construction of Spelman's first modernist building, the John D. Rockefeller Fine Arts Building, which was completed in 1964.[16] However, Manley's tenure was also marked by tensions between the college's student body and its administration. As Harry Lefever notes, despite Spelman's strong tradition of liberal arts education, in many ways its campus remained 'a parochial and conservative place' into the 1950s. Spelman installed strict social do's and guidelines for 'correct' student behaviour, student rooms were regularly inspected, and if students wished to leave the campus, they needed to provide written permission from parents.[17] At the same time, the desire of many Spelman students to take on a more active role in the coalescing civil rights struggle placed them at odds with its traditionally conservative administration, a fight that reflected broader tensions within the developing Black campus movement.[18]

Tensions spiked again in April 1975, after Manley announced his retirement, effective from June of the following year. The college's faculty and student body were 'ready for a paradigm shift', something that was intimately linked to the appointment of a Black woman as its president.[19] After the Spelman College Board approved the appointment of Dr Donald Stewart, a prominent Black political scientist, enraged students locked the Board members in a conference room.[20] While student protests would ultimately fail to halt Stewart's appointment, they demonstrated the depth of student dissatisfaction, something that Stewart sought to ameliorate through actions such as the election of Black activist and Spelman alumna Marian Wright Edelman to the college's Board of Trustees, and the creation of a Women's Research and Resources Center.[21] However, when Stewart retired in 1986, it was clear that students would accept nothing less than a Black woman to replace him.

In 1987, Spelman's Board of Trustees selected anthropologist Johnnetta Cole as the college's first Black female president. Marian Wright Edelman, who by Stewart's departure had been appointed as the Chair of Spelman's Board of Trustees, declared that Cole's 'commitment to Spelman's history and traditions, academic leadership qualities and vision for the institution' made her the stand-out candidate for the post.[22] For her part, Cole was also quick to emphasize her 'progressive' credentials, perhaps eager to reassure students wary of the school's historically conservative administration.[23] Cole's willingness to accept the post was shaped by her desire to cement Spelman's standing as 'a renowned center for scholarship by and about black women [...] [and] a place where black women leaders of the world are nurtured, trained and developed'.[24]

Cole's appointment was based on her academic credentials. A leading Black anthropologist, Cole had helped to establish one of the nation's first Black Studies programs at Washington State University before developing a distinguished teaching and research career at the University of Massachusetts and Hunter College in New York City.[25] However, her administrative prowess and links to the African American elite were undoubtedly attractive. When Edelman described Cole as 'the right leader at this vital time of challenge', she alluded to the growing need for philanthropic support in the face of financial crises facing many Black colleges.[26] The underfunding and financial precarity of Black colleges was hardly a new phenomenon, but it had been exacerbated by the desegregation of American higher education during the 1960s – something that had provided a boon for Black students eager to attend elite, majority-white institutions, but which had a significant impact on Black college enrolments.[27]

The poster child for Black college malaise was Fisk University in Nashville, Tennessee, which saw its enrolment and endowment shrink by more than two-thirds. Fisk's financial problems became so acute that, by the early 1980s, the college was unable to pay its heating and electricity bills. *Black Enterprise* magazine contended that the challenges facing Fisk were 'merely a microcosm of the problems threatening many of the nation's 105 traditional black colleges', with cutbacks in federal funding, declining enrolments, and ageing infrastructure leaving Black colleges fighting for survival.[28] In an effort to address these issues, Black colleges sought closer ties with the wave of Black celebrities, politicians, and business leaders who had reaped the financial windfall of desegregation. Although Spelman's board did not explicitly articulate it, Cole's links to Black philanthropists and track record of securing financial patronage likely factored into her appointment, with Spelman gambling on her ability to establish connections with the new Black elite.

This included entertainer Bill Cosby, who by the mid-1980s had emerged as one of the nation's leading Black educational philanthropists. Cosby's had started out as a stand-up comedian during the early 1960s, before he gained crossover success as a television star. Cosby decided to step back from his media work in the early 1970s to pursue a doctorate in education, and began to take a more visible public role in supporting Black colleges. From the late 1970s, he was a regular feature of Black college fundraisers organised by entities such as the United Negro College Fund, and, after the extent of Fisk's financial woes became public, Cosby helped to lead a national fundraising campaign.[29] Cosby's efforts were celebrated by *Ebony* and other Black publications as a model of Black celebrity activism.[30] Cosby's interest in Black education was heavily influenced by his wife Camille, whose parents had both attended Black colleges. Although Cosby was the financial breadwinner, Camille took an active role in managing his career and had a major influence of the couple's philanthropic activities.

The Cosbys' ability to support HBCUs was significantly expanded by the commercial success of *The Cosby Show*, which premiered on NBC in 1984. Although Cosby was already an established entertainer, the enormous and immediate popularity of *The Cosby Show*, a primetime sitcom focused on the lives of an upper-middle-class Black family living in New York, catapulted him to a new level of celebrity.[31] The show drew a loyal weekly audience in excess of fifty million people, repeatedly breaking records for ratings and audience share, and helped NBC to become the nation's leading television network. By the end of the decade, Cosby was ranked by *Forbes* as the 'highest paid performer in the business', with annual earnings in excess of $110 million.[32] In 1986, the Cosbys donated $1.3 million to Fisk. The following year, they divided another $1.3 million between another four Black colleges – Central State University in Ohio, Florida Agricultural and Mechanical University, Shaw University in North Carolina, and Howard University in the nation's capital.[33]

Just days before Cole was unveiled as Spelman's next president, *The Cosby Show* 'invaded the campus of Spelman' to shoot its 1987 season finale. Spelman had been chosen to represent Hillman College, a fictitious Black college that featured heavily on the show, and Spelman students and faculty members appeared as extras.[34] The following November, at a dinner marking Cole's inauguration, Spelman's new president shocked onlookers by announcing a $20 million gift from the Cosbys, the largest single contribution to a Black college in American history. The gift would be administered by the Clara Elizabeth Jackson Carter Foundation, headed by David Driskell, a leading Black artist and curator, and featuring board members such as Maxine Waters, a California state representative and future member of Congress.[35] It would help fund the creation of endowed chairs in the fine arts and humanities – the first such positions in the college's history – and would also be used to upgrade existing facilities. The bulk of the gift, however, was earmarked for a new academic centre, named for Camille, which Cole believed would help to establish Spelman as the 'mecca' of Black Women's Studies.[36]

The Cosbys' gift to Spelman, and the Cosbys' support of HBCUs more broadly, represented a 'coming out' of sorts for Camille. The couple had met in the early 1960s, when Camille, then a nineteen-year-old sophomore at the University of Maryland, had accepted a blind date with Cosby, who was seven years her senior, and she would remain largely in her husband's shadow during the first phase of his career. One characteristic profile of the young family described Camille as a 'pretty wife [...] swept along by [her] husband's rise to stardom'.[37] However, Camille took control of managing Cosby's career during the 1970s, and also returned to college, completing a Master's in Education at the University of Massachusetts.[38] Whereas Camille's early public persona had been centred on her role as a doting wife and the mother of Cosby's children, by the 1980s she was increasingly recognised as a full business partner and the vice president of Cosby enterprises.

Six months after the Cosbys' gift to Spelman had been announced, Camille was the college's commencement day speaker. For *Essence* magazine, one of a number of Black publications that ran extensive profiles of Camille in the aftermath of the Cosbys' gift, her decision to accept the speaking engagement was an indication that she was 'emerging and forging a new beginning – one more in the public eye than ever before'.[39] Given the size of their donation to Spelman, Camille's embrace of her role as a 'full partner in all of the Cosby enterprises' and philanthropic endeavours, and the fact that the building was to be named in her honour, it is unsurprising that Camille was keen to take an active role in the project's development.[40] From early on in the process, the Cosbys and their foundation prioritised the hiring of a firm led by a Black female architect or that had a Black female architect as a partner. This was significant, given that the terms of the Cosbys' gift dictated that the project's architect would be one of the Foundation's choosing.[41]

If judged against the balance of history, the search for a Black female architect would not be easy. Over the past few decades, a wealth of new scholarship by figures such as Dreck Spurlock Wilson, Melvin Mitchell, and Victoria Kaplan has authoritatively demonstrated that Black people 'contributed significantly, albeit often anonymously, to the architectural heritage of America' since the nation's founding.[42] From quarrying stone and cutting timber to the assembly of roofs and walls, enslaved people literally built the fledgling Republic, including landmarks such as the White House in Washington, D.C.[43] Following emancipation, pioneers such as Robert Robinson Taylor, who graduated from Massachusetts Institute of Technology in 1892, and Wallace Rayfield, who earned a Bachelor's degree from Columbia University in 1899, designed notable landmarks such as Tuskegee University and the Sixth Avenue Baptist Church in Birmingham, Alabama. However, despite such interventions, the number of professionally accredited Black architects remained vanishingly small into the twentieth century.

This was particularly true for Black women, who accounted for a tiny percentage of this already marginal group. Margaret Hicks and Mary Louisa Page were among the first wave of white women to become practising architects during the 1870s and 1880s. By contrast, it would take another sixty years for Beverly Lorraine Greene, widely recognised as the first accredited Black female architect in the United States, to receive a bachelor's degree in architectural engineering from the University of Illinois. Pioneering Black female architects such as Greene, Georgia Louise Harris Brown, who graduated from the University of Kansas in 1944, and Norma Sklarek, who graduated from Columbia University in 1950, faced the 'double jeopardy' of race and sex discrimination. As in the case of Brown, who emigrated to Brazil in the early 1950s, some were forced abroad to pursue professional advancement. Tellingly, in Dreck Spurlock Wilson's landmark 2004 collection *African American Architects*, which provides a biographical introduction to more than 150 Black architects practising between 1865 and 1945, less than ten of the architects featured are Black women.[44]

However, the educational and professional opportunities afforded to Black women were expanded by the impact of the civil rights and women's rights movements, which contributed to a new wave of Black women becoming accredited architects during the 1960s and 1970s. Norma Sklarek's election as a fellow of the American Institute of Architects in 1980 was hailed as an important breakthrough for Black women into the architectural mainstream. Three years later, Sklarek was the keynote speaker at a landmark conference for minority women in architecture hosted by Howard University in Washington, D.C.[45] In 1984, *Ebony* magazine profiled more than a dozen Black women who 'combine[d] education, licenses and hard work to gain acceptance and build lasting careers' in the architectural profession.[46]

One of the Black women profiled in *Ebony*'s 1984 article was Donna deJongh, a Texas native who had studied at Howard University during the 1960s. Alongside her husband Robert, whom she had met at Howard, she established an architectural practice called deJongh Associates in the US Virgin Islands, an American overseas territory in the Caribbean where Robert had been raised. The firm quickly established a strong reputation and a client base that included local and federal government agencies, banks, resorts, and residential developers. One of the firm's most significant commissions was the Alexander Farrelly justice complex, a multi-building complex designed for the municipal government of the Virgin Islands in St. Thomas which was featured in *Ebony*'s 1984 profile.[47] By the time of Cole's appointment as Spelman's president, deJongh Associates was the largest architectural and engineering firm in the eastern Caribbean. Its reputation received another timely boost shortly after the Cosbys' gift had been made public, when it was recognised as the best young Black architectural firm in the nation by Howard's School of Architecture and Planning.[48]

Donna deJongh recalls that the firm were working on a long-term project for the University of the Virgin Islands when they received news that Spelman and the Cosbys were soliciting qualification statements – an initial statement of information about a firm's experience often requested as a screening mechanism for major construction projects. The College and the Carter Foundation had worked together in a 'pre-design phase' during 1989 and 1990 to establish a range of demands and selection criteria.[49] This included the need for the project's chosen architect to demonstrate existing knowledge of 'the architectural heritage, tradition and symbolism of Spelman College' and a willingness to maintain 'a cohesive campus identity'. For Spelman's leadership, it was essential that any new building was 'compatible' with the 'traditional red brick character of the college's older buildings'. This was managed down to specific recommendations on architectural features, including 'elements of the Neo-Georgian and Romanesque Revival styles of the late 19th century, such as Flemish bond brick detailing, arched openings, hipped roofs, and contrasting granite window sills, caps and cornice'.[50]

Similarly, deJongh notes that the call was 'very insistent' regarding Spelman's desire to have a Black women lead the project, something that significantly limited the number of potential applicants.[51] Even by the end of the 1980s, the number of Black female architects in the United States who owned their own firms, or who were partners for established firms, was extremely low. Among the select few women who were likely targeted as potential collaborators by Spelman and the Cosbys were Roberta Washington, who founded her own practice in 1984, and Hermine Ricketts, who established HER Architects in Florida three years later.[52] Excited by the opportunity, deJongh Associates submitted their qualifications.

In his own recollections of the Spelman search, Melvin Mitchell contends that Camille Cosby had created a shortlist of potential partners by the spring of 1991. Unsurprisingly, 'the most prominent finalist' was Norma Sklarek, who by the early 1990s had cemented her position as the nation's leading Black female architect.[53] Several years earlier, Sklarek had joined forces with Margot Siegel and Katherine Diamond to form Siegel, Sklarek, Diamond – the largest women-owned architecture firm in the nation.[54] Mitchell also alleges that Roberta Washington, a 'solid New York based practitioner' and a former student of Mitchell's at Howard, was a finalist.[55] The deJonghs were another of Camille's shortlisted candidates. The firm was subsequently invited to present to the Spelman Board in Atlanta, where Donna deJongh outlined their initial ideas and, alongside Robert, conducted campus walks to observe and photograph the site. The following week, the couple flew to Manhattan to present their proposals directly to the Cosbys.[56]

Whilst Mitchell contends that Camille Cosby's shortlist was limited to three, deJongh recalls that there were at least five other groups that submitted for the project and that were invited to present to the Cosbys in New York.[57] Unbeknownst to deJongh at the time, the Cosbys had already selected another architect for the project, but they were dropped due to professional differences.[58] Whilst I have been unable to confirm the identity of this architect, anecdotal evidence suggests that it might well have been Sklarek. This would make sense, given her prominence within the field. Irrespective of the politics preceding their own bid, deJongh Associates were awarded the contract. News of their selection was a happy surprise, but brought an array of challenges. DeJongh remembers the contract process being far more involved than any previous project the firm had worked on. Because the Cosbys had 'already been through one set of architects [...] their attorney was insistent that they properly vet [the deJongh's credentials]'.[59]

The deJonghs also had to adjust to expectations and demands that came with working in Georgia (generally) and Atlanta (specifically). Some of these issues were practical, for example, applying for an architectural license to practice in the State. More broadly, the couple navigated the often complex politics of Atlanta's Black community. For more than a century, Atlanta had been celebrated as an 'atypical' southern city – a bastion of racial liberalism and Black opportunity in the Deep South. Violent flashpoints such as the city's 1906 race riots and uprisings of the 1960s complicated but did not derail this notion. As Maurice Hobson notes, Atlanta's importance as a breeding ground for 'black educated and business elite[s]' was consolidated by the passage of the 1965 Civil Rights Act and 1965 Voting Rights Act, which reinforced the city's reputation as a Black 'mecca'.[60] Cole's own characterization of her move to Spelman – 'I didn't come to the South. I came to Atlanta' – speaks to deeply-rooted beliefs in Black Atlantan exceptionalism and the particular qualities of the city's Black business and political elite.[61]

As outsiders to this community, the deJonghs encountered a degree of resistance. Donna recalls the feeling of being sized up by local members of the National Organization of Minority Architects (NOMA), a professional organisation for architects of colour that had been established by a group of Black male architects at the annual meeting of the American Institute of Architects in 1971. In 1991, Atlanta hosted the organisation's annual convention and William Stanley, an Atlanta-based architect, was elected as NOMA's president. It is possible that a degree of professional jealousy influenced the deJonghs reception within NOMA. Donna reflects that, given 'there were other [Black] architects in the Atlanta area [...] why would they [the Cosbys and Spelman] choose us over someone who was there?'[62] However, the award of building contracts to Black-owned companies ensured some degree of local involvement, with two Black Atlantan firms overseeing the majority of the construction. The first, H.J. Russell & Company, was founded in the early 1950s by Tuskegee graduate Herman J. Russell.[63] The second, C.D. Moody Construction, was led by C. David Moody, who had graduated from Howard's architectural programme before pivoting to construction.[64]

By the time that groundbreaking occurred in April 1991, nearly two-and-a-half years had passed since the Cosbys' donation was first announced.[65] Much mainstream media coverage of the event focused on Bill Cosby's involvement, with headlines such as 'Cosby Keeps School Smiling' reflecting a broader trend to frame the Spelman gift as solely Bill's, rather than as a shared decision by Bill and Camille Cosby.[66] In contrast, the *Spelman Messenger* emphasised Camille Cosby's assertion that 'when we break ground today, we honor our African-blooded sisters'. Reiterating why it was so important for her to select a Black woman to lead the project, Camille stressed the importance of positive representation for Spelman's students: 'these children see in their own image that which is going to be extraordinary'.[67] Building on Camille's words, coverage of the ceremony in Spelman publications and Black media outlets leaned heavily on the project's symbolic importance and the significance of deJongh's involvement, noting that she was the first African American *and* the first woman to design a Spelman building in the college's history.[68] In her own remarks, deJongh added to the anticipation, contending that 'we are about to begin an extraordinary building'.[69]

Media coverage of the groundbreaking event also helped to establish a timeline, albeit an inconsistent one, for the building's anticipated completion. The *Atlanta Constitution* relayed deJongh's claims that the building would be finished by the Spring of 1993, and *Jet* magazine also reported that the build was 'expected to be completed in about two years'.[70] The *Spelman Messenger* was more cautious, listing the buildings anticipated completion date as September 1994.[71] However, conflicts over the building's design and function meant that neither deadline would be achieved. In deJongh's retelling, many of the construction issues stemmed from the same foundational tension: deJongh Associates was 'working for two masters' – the Cosby family, via the Carter Foundation, and the Spelman board of trustees and administration – both of whom had different and, at times, conflicting priorities and desires.

From the outset, Camille Cosby expressed strong opinions about the building's design. As her descriptions of the building's function at its groundbreaking and in broader media coverage demonstrate, Cosby envisioned the building as a monument to 'all African-blooded women' and 'our African-blooded sisters'. These rhetorical appeals to diasporic unity paralleled her own interest in African-inspired architectural design. In particular, she was intrigued by the circular concepts present in many forms of indigenous and vernacular African architecture, including rondavels – a traditionally one-room rounded structure with a thatched roof.[72] Camille Cosby invited Donna deJongh and her team to Massachusetts, sharing pictures of buildings she had seen during her travels in Africa, and scheduling a tour of local Shaker buildings that also incorporated circular designs.[73] Her enthusiasm was hardly unique: African inspired circular concepts, both in terms of individual building design and as an organising spatial principle, became a source of fascination for many

Figure 13.3: Plaza of the Charles H. Wright Museum of African American History, Sims-Varner & Associates, Detroit, Michigan, 1997. Photo by Chuck Anderson.

African-American architects during the 1980s and 1990s, as part of ongoing efforts to create a 'distinct' African-American architecture.[74]

Perhaps the most striking articulation of efforts to fuse 'contemporary American' architectural motifs with 'antecedents leading back to Africa' during this period came from the Charles H. Wright Museum for African American History in Detroit.[75] Founded as part of a wave of Black museums during the 1960s, the Wright had already outgrown several previous sites in downtown Detroit by the end of the 1980s.[76] The museum broke ground on a new facility in 1993, which was designed by Sims-Varner & Associates, a Black architectural firm founded in 1968 by Howard Francis Sims and widely regarded as the oldest Black architectural firm in Michigan. Sims-Varner's African-inspired design was organised around an enormous central rotunda, with African flags circled below a 55-foot-tall glass dome (Fig. 13.3).[77]

It was this type of circular concept, albeit on a far less dramatic scale, that Camille Cosby 'wanted to incorporate [into] the characteristics [of] into the building on Spelman'.[78] However, these ambitions represented a significant challenge to the established aesthetics of the campus. Over the previous century, it had largely adhered to the architectural mores of its early brick buildings. Even more recent additions such as the John D. Rockefeller Fine Arts Building, constructed in 1954, replicated 'the tripartite design of the college's 19th-century buildings'.[79] Although Spelman and the Carter Foundation moved away from the dogmatic guidance and requests for specific architectural features such as 'Flemish bond brick detailing' and 'granite window sills, caps and cornice' articulated in pre-design documents, both entities were concerned that a more unconventional design would deviate from the college's established architectural principles.[80]

Alongside pushback from Spelman's administration, the possibility of a more radical architectural design met with resistance from members of the Rockefeller family, who continued to be heavily invested in the college's development. Laurance Rockefeller, the son of John D. Rockefeller, Jr., had been among the guests of honour at the building's groundbreaking ceremonies in April 1991, and the family maintained an active presence on the college's Board of Trustees. In addition to preserving the college's architectural heritage, the Rockefellers were concerned by the building's proposed size. In deJongh's recollection: 'the first schematic was so large [...] that it ran over in front of the [Rockefeller] Fine Arts Building. That was a no-no [...] you could not disrespect the Rockefeller family.' As a result, deJongh Associates had 'to redesign within a specific site limit that would give [...] the Fine Arts Building its due' and ensure that the Cosby Center would be a respectful continuation of, rather than a dramatic departure from, the college's established architectural motifs.[81]

Tensions over the building's design, size, and campus location took time to resolve. DeJongh recalls that 'just getting the schematic design down to the point that it would be acceptable took almost a year', and there were multiple further issues that demanded additional alterations. Despite the heavy emphasis placed on her role as the project's architect, by the Fall of 1992 Spelman and the Carter Foundation appeared to be losing faith in her ability to keep the project on track. In September, Spelman noted that continued difficulties to 'achieve a building size that can be built within the budget and a satisfactory schematic design have caused the Architect to be substantially behind schedule'.[82] Critically, until the building's schematics were approved by both Spelman's board of trustees and the Carter Foundation, Spelman could not receive additional funds from the Cosbys' gift.[83] To ensure the project's progression, deJongh Associates agreed to form a joint venture with Robert L. Brown & Associates, another local Black-owned firm that would consult on design and take charge of the construction phase.[84]

While the decision to establish a joint venture provided deJongh with much-needed additional resources, cost was also becoming an issue. When the Cosbys' gift was announced, few specific details about the scope of the Camille Cosby Academic Center were revealed, aside that its construction had been allocated 60 percent, or $12 million, of the Cosbys' total endowment.[85] However, by the building's groundbreaking in 1991, media outlets were circulating a more specific list of facilities, including an African-American Art Museum, a media centre, a library and archives, and a range of specialised learning spaces.[86] The *Spelman Messenger* added further amenities to this list, including a gift shop, an 'Inter-disciplinary Center' and an auditorium.[87] It quickly became apparent that designing a building to budget, but which included all of these features, was close to impossible. This tension precipitated a conflict between the Cosby family, which was reluctant to budge on the percentage of their endowment earmarked for building expenses, and the Spelman Board of Trustees, which was reluctant to forego facilities that they saw as essential to the college's continued growth, and which had already been broadcast to an expectant study body and wider public.

To address any potential financial shortfalls that would hinder the building's completion, Cole stepped up her fundraising activities. Spelman's faith in her fundraising abilities would be repaid with interest. By the early 1990s, Cole was averaging around two presentations a week in her efforts to solicit contributions from Spelman alumni, wealthy African Americans, and other potential funding sources. Spelman's efforts were bolstered by the publicity generated by the Cosbys' gift, and the continued success of *The Cosby Show* and its subsequent spin-off *A Different World*, with Spelman's campus continuing to stand in for the fictional Hillman College. Eager to capitalise on Spelman's newfound visibility within American popular media and in the minds of prospective supporters, Cole inaugurated the college's 'Initiative for the '90s' – a fundraising drive designed to significantly increase the college's endowment, enhance its academic programme and establish new physical facilities.

As noted by the *Journal of Blacks in Higher Education*, Cole's 'remarkable ability to raise funds' underpinned a sustained and enormously successful funding drive.[88] Around a year after breaking ground on the Camille Cosby Academic Center, Cole announced that Spelman had received a gift of $37 million from the DeWitt Wallace/Spelman College Fund, which established a new benchmark for the largest gift ever made to a Black college.[89] Other significant donations to Spelman's 'Initiative for the '90s' – a

Figure 13.4: Exterior of Camille Cosby Academic Center at Spelman College, deJongh Group, Atlanta, Georgia, c. 1997. Courtesy of deJongh Group Architects.

fundraising drive designed to increase the college's endowment, enhance its academic programme and establish new physical facilities – included a $1 million donation from Black talk show host Oprah Winfrey.[90] Between 1993 and 1996, Spelman was able to secure $114 million in endowment funds, reported to be 'by far the most successful [drive] ever undertaken by a historically black college' and one of the most lucrative campaigns ever mounted by a liberal arts college anywhere in the country.[91]

The financial security provided by Spelman's funding drive, coupled with the additional support provided by Robert L. Brown & Associates, allowed deJongh to push ahead with the completion of the Camille Cosby Academic Center – albeit with some significant concessions. As Figure 13.4 demonstrates, any circular motifs for the building's exterior that were part of early renderings were significantly pared back. Although some accents, such as porthole windows and rounded bays on the first and second floors, remained, the Center's final design can be characterised as a staid postmodern style. The building's exterior rendering complements the palette of the campus's existing red brick architecture, but does not completely mesh with existing structures such as Rockefeller Hall. At the same time, it lacked the architectural panache to be the 'National

Landmark' for Black colleges that Spelman craved. Writing in 2024, this architectural innovation arguably continues to remain absent from the college's campus, although Spelman's new Center for Innovation and the Arts, a Studio-Gang designed site currently in the final stages of construction, may change this narrative.[92]

DeJongh was, however, more successful at incorporating some elements of African-inspired design into the building's layout, most notably through the idea of multiple buildings organised around a central gathering space – a characteristic feature of many African settlements. As she recalls, 'the aspect of being able to stand in a somewhat rounded area and look out to each of the areas of the campus from the classrooms' was an essential part of this concept. The firm's efforts to incorporate the type of diasporic design elements favoured by Camille also shaped the interiors in a more sustained and successful way than the exterior, most notably through its extensive use of mahogany and custom-built furniture pieces that maintained 'the circular motif of African design.'[93]

In keeping with the rationale for the project's significance outlined by Camille Cosby and Johnnetta Cole, the opening of the Cosby Center was celebrated as a moment of Black diasporic unity and an opportunity to celebrate Black female excellence. Spelman students and faculty began using the site in January 1996, and the building's formal opening came the following month. To celebrate the opening of what Cole described as 'the most extraordinary academic center any of us could have imagined', Spelman organised a four-day period of festivities featuring a range of events. Highlights included a public lecture by Darlene Clark Hine, one of the nation's premier Black women historians and a Professor of History at Michigan State University, plus a reception to mark the opening of the college's new Fine Arts Museum, which was housed in the Cosby Center.[94] To celebrate the building's official opening, Varnette P. Honeywood, Spelman's in-house artist, created an original piece titled 'Lifelong Learning', which featured Camille Cosby and Johnnetta Cole alongside two notable Black women from history – the nineteenth-century scholar and educator Anna Julia Cooper, and the eighteenth-century poet Phyllis Wheatley – as well 'composite' figures representing 'a prototype of a 1996 Spelman College student' and 'an African woman.' This emphasis on Black diasporic unity was maintained through an Afrocentric ribbon-cutting ceremony, and performance by Spelman students and African drummers (Fig. 13.5).

Despite deJongh not being included in 'Lifelong Learning', it was clear that the building's opening represented an opportunity to resituate the

Figure 13.5: Cosby Dedication Dancers, 1996. Spelman College Photographs Collection, Spelman College Archives.

building as the work of a Black female architect. Reiterating the significance of the building being designed by a Black woman and built by a cohort of Black firms, Cole argued that Atlanta had a new educational landmark that rivalled the Martin Luther King, Jr. Center. Spelman's president declared that the Center 'truly represents the ideals and values of Spelman College; educational excellence, creativity, generosity and the role of African American women in history, literature, languages, philosophy and religion'.[95] Downplaying the intervention of Robert L. Brown & Associates in the project's latter stages, Camille emphasised deJongh's status as the project's 'master builder' and dedicated its erection to all 'women representing the African diaspora; those who came before us, those who are here now, and those of the future'.

The opening of the Camille Cosby Academic Center was a landmark moment for both Spelman College and the Black college community. As the most significant new addition to Spelman's campus for more than thirty years, and as arguably the most important building erected at Spelman since the completion of Rockefeller Hall more than a century earlier, the Cosby Center provided concrete evidence of Spelman's status as one of the nation's leading liberal arts colleges. Writing in the Cleveland *Call & Post,*

Black journalist Anita Polk contended that 'Spelman College will NEVER EVER be the same'.[96]

Upon its completion, the Cosby Center provided an alternative vision for what the modern Black college could be; one that contrasted with dominant media narratives of a Black college 'crisis'. For many Black colleges, an inability to invest in new buildings or to modernise ageing infrastructure was indicative of broader monetary worries. These financial issues became significantly more acute during the 1980s, on account of stagnating (and in some cases, falling enrolments) and a decline in federal funding. For critics, the decaying campuses of Black colleges were indicative of wider malaise, with 'tall, unkempt grass and old, unrestored buildings that appear just a slight wind's blow away from crumbling to the ground.'[97] When the Cosbys unveiled their gift to Spelman in the late 1980s, they made clear that the money was given 'not just as a gift but as a challenge to other black Americans to support black colleges.'[98] From this perspective, Spelman's gleaming new academic centre was an important public statement on the importance of Black colleges and the need for the Black community and the broader American public to support their organisational and infrastructural development.

The project was also significant for the three Black women at its centre. For Camille Cosby, the Cosbys' unprecedented donation to Spelman, and the construction of the Cosby Center in particular, provided her with a unique opportunity to craft a new public persona. Stepping out from the shadow of her superstar husband, the Cosby Center afforded her 'a new beginning – one more in the public eye than ever before.'[99] Prior to the building's announcement, *Essence* magazine contended that she 'never sought the limelight and rarely [gave] interviews.' By the building's formal opening in 1996, she was a regular on corporate boards, had completed a Doctorate in Education from the University of Massachusetts to go alongside an honorary degree from Spelman, had published her first book, and had co-produced a Broadway play.[100]

For Cole, the completion of the Cosby Center created a tangible marker for the ways that her presidency had transformed Spelman over the previous decade. Several months after the building's opening, she announced that she was resigning from her post, effective of June the following year. Since her appointment, Spelman had more than tripled its endowment, and Cole had personally overseen the most successful fundraising drive at any Black college in the nation's history.[101] Perhaps most significantly, Cole had delivered on her promise to transform Spelman into a 'mecca' for

Black women's studies – a promise embodied in its new academic centre, which housed the college's Women's Research Center.[102]

For deJongh, the project had both short-term and long-term ramifications. The publicity generated by her involvement in the project helped to solidify her position in the vanguard of a new generation of African-American women architects who had 'risen to the top of their field' over the previous fifteen years.[103] In turn, the deJonghs' collaboration with Spelman helped to significantly raise the profile of their firm, although it did attempt to keep its offices 'to a boutique size.'[104] However, Donna deJongh also found her collaboration with the Cosbys and Spelman 'difficult' and, at times, 'overwhelming.' In retrospect, many of the project's challenges stemmed from her need to juggle competing 'masters', and the practical and aesthetic challenges of incorporating Black or African-inspired design elements into more conventional architectural forms. Ultimately, Camille Cosby's desire for the building to 'honor our African-blooded sisters' was accomplished less through its architecture than through the facilities it provided and the symbolic weight attached to it by the Cosbys, the Spelman board, Black media, and the broader African-American community.

## NOTES

1 Mark Whitaker, *Cosby: His Life and Times* (New York: Simon & Schuster, 2014); Nicole Weisensee Egan, *Chasing Cosby: The Downfall of America's Dad* (New York: Seal Press, 2019).

2 'Cosby Heads Forbes List of Highest Paid in Show Biz', *Jet*, 1 October 1990.

3 'A Black College Gets Cosby Gift of $20 Million', *New York Times*, 8 November 1989.

4 Johnnetta B. Cole, 'Another Day Will Find Us Brave', *Sage* 6, no. 1 (1989), 85.

5 'Cosby Building Dedicated at Spelman', *Atlanta Voice*, 2 March 1996.

6 'Spelman's Dedication of Cosby Center', *Atlanta World*, 18 February 1996.

7 'Camille Cosby', *Essence*, December 1989.

8 '"Sister Prez" Takes a Sabbatical', *Ebony*, August 1997.

9 'Black Women Architects: A Blueprint for Success', *Ebony*, June 1984; 'Top Women Architects', *Ebony*, August 1995.

10 Symbolic Statement of Cosby Academic Center, n.d., Box 58, Johnnetta B. Cole Papers (hereafter: JBC Papers), Spelman College Archives.

11 Evelyn Brooks Higginbotham, *Righteous Discontent: The Women's Movement in the Black Baptist Church, 1880–1920* (Cambridge, MA: Harvard University Press, 1994).

12 Tiffany Moman, 'Constructing Traditions: Architecture, Material Culture, and the Higher Education Experience at Spelman College, 1850-1925', (PhD diss., Middle Tennessee State University, 2019), 34–5.

13 Henry L. Morehouse to Sophia B. Packard and Harriet G. Giles, 2 April 1885, Sophia B. Packard Collection, Box 2, Spelman College Archives.

14 Isabelle Gourney, *AIA Guide to the Architecture of Atlanta* (Athens: University of Georgia Press, 1993), 168–69.

15 Jeane Cyriaque, 'Preserving a Sense of Place: The Spelman College Campus Heritage Plan', *Reflections* 6 (2006).

[16] Monique Robinson, 'Restoring Spelman's Rockefeller Fine Arts Building', *National Trust for Historic Preservation*, 14 September 2021.
[17] Harry G. Lefever, *Undaunted by the Fight* (Atlanta: Mercer University Press, 2005), 15.
[18] Ibram X. Kendi, *The Black Campus Movement: Black Students and the Radical Reconstitution of Higher Education, 1965-1972* (New York: Palgrave, 2012).
[19] Richard D. Benson, 'Naming Our Own and Claiming Black Womanhood: The Spelman College Protest of 1976', *Palimpsest* 10, no. 1 (2021): 43–63.
[20] 'Held as Hostages, Trustees Yield to Angry Spelmanites', *Jet*, 13 May 1976.
[21] Beverly Guy-Sheftall, 'Black Women and Higher Education', *Journal of Negro Education* 51, no. 3 (1982): 282.
[22] 'Johnnetta Cole named as the first Black woman leader of Spelman', *Macon Telegraph*, 26 April 1987.
[23] Glenn Collins, 'President Fills Blank Spot in Spelman History', *Fort Worth Star-Telegram*, 2 August 1987.
[24] 'Johnnetta Cole named as the first Black woman leader of Spelman.'
[25] 'College Honors Three', *Spokane Chronicle*, 4 May 1970; Cole, *Anthropology for the Eighties: Introductory Readings* (New York: Free Press, 1982).
[26] 'Johnnetta Cole named as the first Black woman leader of Spelman.'
[27] 'Black College Enrolment Has Doubled since 1970', *New York Times*, 18 May 1981.
[28] Nathan McCall, 'Terms of Endowment', *Black Enterprise*, September 1985.
[29] 'Help for Black Colleges', *Chicago Metro News*, 3 November 1979; 'Lou Rawls Hosts a Telethon for UNCF', *Ebony*, April 1980; 'A Move to Save Fisk', *Black Enterprise*, March 1984.
[30] 'Are Superstars Forgetting Their Roots?' *Ebony*, May 1979.
[31] Linda K. Fuller, *The Cosby Show: Audiences, Impact, and Implications* (London: Bloomsbury Academic, 1992).
[32] 'Cosby Heads Forbes List of Highest Paid in Show Biz', *Jet*, 1 October 1990.
[33] Robert E. Johnson, 'Bill and Camille Cosby: First Family of Philanthropy', *Ebony*, May 1989.
[34] 'Cosby Show Shoots at Spelman College', *Atlanta World*, 16 April 1987.
[35] Antonia M. Grumbach to Johnnetta Cole, 8 November 1988, Box 58, JBC Papers, Spelman College Archives; Congressional Directory, 113th Congress (Washington, D.C.: U.S. Government Printing Office, 2014), 40.
[36] Cole, 'Another Day', 86.
[37] 'Life with Bill Cosby', *Ebony*, September 1966.
[38] Ronald E. Kisner, 'Cosby Makes Millions Teaching Manners and Moral Lessons on TV', *Jet*, 11 May 1978; 'People Are Talking About...', *Jet*, 19 June 1980.
[39] 'Camille Cosby', *Essence*, December 1989.
[40] Johnson, 'Bill and Camille Cosby'.
[41] Antonia M. Grumbach to Johnnetta Cole, 8 November 1988, JBC Papers.
[42] Melvin L. Mitchell, *The Crisis of the African-American Architect: Conflicting Cultures of Architecture and (Black) Power* (New York: Writers Advantage, 2003); Victoria Kaplan, *Structural Inequality: Black Architects in the United States* (New York: Rowman, 2006); Dreck Spurlock Wilson, ed., *African-American Architects: A Biographical Dictionary, 1865-1945* (New York: Routledge, 2004).
[43] Lina Mann, 'Building the White House', *The White House Historical Association*, 3 January 2020.
[44] Wilson, *African American Architects*.
[45] Nancy Anita Williams, 'Howard Conference a Rallying for Black Female Architects', *Washington Post*, 15 December 1983.
[46] 'Black Women Architects: A Blueprint for Success', *Ebony*, June 1984.
[47] 'Black Women Architects'; 'Alexander A. Farrelly Justice Complex', *deJongh Associates*, https://dejonghgroup.com/index.php/project-gallery/alexander-farrelly.
[48] 'DeJongh Associates Honored as Young Firm of the Year', *Los Angeles Sentinel*, 23 February 1989.
[49] Arthur J. Clement to Johnnetta B. Cole, 27 November 1990, Box 58, JBC Papers.
[50] New Academic Complex, 18 February 1988, Box 58, JBC Papers; Architectural Selection Considerations, n.d., Box 58, JBC Papers; Pre-Design Phase Objectives, n.d., Box 58, JBC Papers.
[51] Donna deJongh, interview with E. James West, 21 March 2024.

52 'Top Women Architects'.
53 Mitchell, *The Crisis of the African American Architect*, 86–87.
54 'Women Architects Build Joint Career', *Los Angeles Times*, 27 July 1986.
55 Mitchell, *The Crisis of the African American Architect*, 87.
56 Donna deJongh, interview.
57 Mitchell, *The Crisis of the African American Architect*, 87; Donna deJongh, interview.
58 Donna deJongh, interview.
59 Ibid.
60 Maurice J. Hobson, *The Legend of the Black Mecca: Politics and Class in the Making of Modern Atlanta* (Chapel Hill: University of North Carolina Press, 2017); 'Atlanta: Black Mecca of the South', *Ebony*, August 1971.
61 'Building Sturdy Black Bridges'," *Georgia Trends* 6, no. 2 (1990): 81.
62 Donna deJongh, interview.
63 'History', *H.J. Russell,* https://www.hjrussell.com/history.
64 'Mett C. David Moody, Jr. of C.D. Moody Construction Company', *Voyage ATL*, 18 July 2018. https://voyageatl.com/interview/meet-c-david-moody-jr-c-d-moody-construction-company-inc-lithonia.
65 'The Groundbreaking', *Spelman Messenger,* 107, no. 2 (1991).
66 'Cosby Keeps School Smiling', *Atlanta Constitution*, 12 April 1991
67 'The Groundbreaking'.
68 'Bill and Camille Cosby Attend Groundbreaking', *Jet*, 29 April 1991.
69 'The Groundbreaking'.
70 'Cosby Keeps School Smiling'; 'Bill and Camille Cosby'.
71 'The Groundbreaking'.
72 Ali Sayigh, *Sustainable Vernacular Architecture: How the Past Can Enrich the Future* (Springer, 2011); Gerald Steyn, 'The Indigenous Rondavel: A Case for Conservation', *SAJAH* 21, no. 1 (2006): 21 38
73 Donna deJongh, interview.
74 Mitchell, *The Crisis of the African-American Architect.*
75 Robert Sharoff with William Zbaren, *American City: Detroit Architecture, 1845-2005* (Detroit: Wayne State University Press, 2005), 108.
76 Mabel O. Wilson, *Negro Building: Black Americans in the World of Fairs and Museums* (Berkeley: University of California Press, 2012), 248.
77 'Celebrities Celebrate Museum's Opening in Glittering Style', *Detroit Free Press*, 12 April 1997.
78 Donna deJongh, interview.
79 Robinson, 'Restoring Spelman's Rockefeller Fine Arts Building'.
80 New Academic Complex, JBC Papers
81 Donna deJongh, interview.
82 Spelman College Contract, 28 September 1992, Box 58, JBC Papers.
83 Antonia M. Grumbach to Johnnetta Cole, JBC Papers.
84 Spelman College Contract, JBC Papers.
85 'Cosbys Give Spelman Record $20 Mil.', *Jet*, 21 November 1988.
86 "Bill and Camille Cosby."
87 "The Groundbreaking."
88 'Johnnetta Cole's Resounding Triumph', *Journal of Blacks in Higher Education* 13 (1996): 18.
89 'Spelman Receives $37 Million, Largest Gift to a Black College', *Jet*, 25 May 1992.
90 'Oprah Gives $1 Million to Spelman College's Science Fund', *Jet*, 27 November 1995.
91 'Johnnetta Cole's Resounding Triumph.
92 Spelman College Center for Innovation & the Arts, *Studio Gang*, https://studiogang.com/projects/spelman.
93 Donna deJongh, interview.
94 'Spelman's Dedication of Cosby Center Runs from Feb. 22 to Feb. 28', *Atlanta World*, 18 February 1996; 'Cosby Center Generates Excitement', *Spelman Spotlight*, 15 February 1996.
95 'Spelman's Dedication of Cosby Center Runs from Feb. 22 to Feb. 28.'
96 'Anita Polk', For the Record, *Call & Post*, 14 March 1996.

97 'Terms of Endowment'.

98 Kathleen Teltsch, 'Blacks' Charities Struggle to meet Cosby Challenge', *New York Times*, 15 January 1989.

99 'Camille Cosby'.

100 'Camille Cosby's Broadway Play, "Having Our Say", Wins Critical Acclaim', *Jet*, 1 May 1995.

101 'Dr. Johnnetta B. Cole to Resign as Spelman Prexy', *Jet*, 23 September 1996.

102 Cole, 'Another Day Will Find Us Brave'; 'What's in It?' *Spelman Spotlight*, 15 February 1996.

103 'Black Women Architects'.

104 Donna deJongh, interview.

# Bibliography


Adamson, Glenn. 'Perriand's handmade modernism'. In *Charlotte Perriand: The Modern Life,* edited by J. McGuirk, 156-65. London: Design Museum Publishing, 2021.

Adengo, Doreen, Warebi Gabriel Brisibe, Ramota Obagah-Stephen, Rachel Lee and Monika Motylinska. In *Fugitive Archives: A Sourcebook for Centring Africa in Histories of Architecture*, edited by Claire Lubell and Ragico Ruiz. Montréal: CCA/Jap Sam Books, 2023.

Aggregate Architectural History Collaborative. *Writing Architectural History: Evidence and Narrative in the Twenty-First Century*. Pittsburgh: University of Pittsburgh Press, 2021.

Aggregate Architectural History Collective. *Governing by Design: Architecture, Economics, and Politics in the Twentieth Century*. Pittsburgh: University of Pittsburgh Press, 2012.

Altikes, Pablo. 'Caso No7'. *Arquitectura Moderna*, 24 February 2014. Accessed 28 July 2025. https://www.arqmodern.com/2014/02/24/caso-no7/.

Appleton, Marc, Stephen Gee and Bret Parsons. *Master Architects of Southern California 1920–1940: Paul R. Williams.* Santa Monica, CA: Angel City Press, 2020.

Arnold, Dana. *Reading Architectural History*. London and New York: Routledge, 2002.

Arnold, Dana. *Re-Presenting the Metropolis: Architecture, Urban Experience and Social Life in London 1800-1840*. Aldershot: Ashgate, 2000 and 2nd ed London: Routledge, 2017.

Arnold, Dana, ed. *Women and Architectural History: The Monstrous Regiment Then and Now*. London and New York: Routledge, 2024.

Arthur, Eimear, and Michael Hayes, eds. *Care and Consideration. On the Work of Gerry Cahill Architects* Type and Arts Council of Ireland, 2025.

Attfield, Judy. *Wild Things: The Material Culture of Everyday Life*. New York: Fairchild Books, 2020.

Awan, Nishat, Tatjana Schneider and Jeremy Till. *Spatial Agency: Other Ways of Doing Architecture.* Abingdon: Routledge, 2011.

Banchero, Siña Renzo. 'Las Cajas de Previsión y su papel en la urbanización del barrio alto: El caso de la población El Belloto de Ñuñoa 1950–53'. BA dissertation, Universidad de Chile, 2020.

Bärnreuther, Andrea, ed. *Taking a Stand? Debating the Bauhaus and Modernism*. Berlin: Bauhaus Archiv, 2021.

Barrington, Ruth. *Health, Medicine & Politics in Ireland, 1900–70*. Dublin: Institute of Public Administration, 1987.

Basáez, Patricio, ed. *Ciento cincuenta años de enseñanza de la arquitectura en la Universidad de Chile 1849–1999*. Chile: Universidad de Chile, Facultad de Arquitectura y Urbanismo, 1999.

Baykal, Erol A. F. *The Ottoman Press (1908-1923)*. Leiden: Brill, 2019.

Beddoe, Deirdre. *Back to Home and Duty: Women between the Wars, 1918-1939*. London: Pandora, 1989.

Beech, Nick. 'Social Condensation in the Metropole: Locating the First New Left'. *The Journal of Architecture* 22, no. 3 (2017): 488-511.

Beeckmans, Luce. 'The Architecture of Nation-building in Africa as a Development Aid Project: Designing the capital cities of Kinshasa (Congo) and Dodoma (Tanzania) in the post-independence years'. *Progress in Planning* 122 (2018): 1-28.

Beetham, Margaret. *A Magazine of Her Own? Domesticity and Desire in the Woman's Magazine, 1800–1914*. London: Routledge, 1996.

Benson, Richard D. 'Naming Our Own and Claiming Black Womanhood: The Spelman College Protest of 1976'. *Palimpset* 10, no. 1 (2021): 43-63.

Benton, Tim. 'Pessac and Lège revisited: standards, dimensions and failures'. *Massilia: Anuaire d'etudes corbuseennes*, 64-99. Barcelona: Associació d'Idees, 2004.

Birch, Peter. 'Choosing Helpers'. *The Furrow* 26 (1975): 579-586.

Birch, Peter. 'Poverty and the Church'. In *One Million Poor? The Challenge of Irish Inequality*, edited by Stanislaus Kennedy, 164-74. Dublin: Turoe Press, 1981.

Bloomberg, Lawrence N., and Charles Abrams. *United Nations Mission to Kenya on Housing*. Nairobi: United Nations, Commissioner for Technical Assistance, Dept. of Economic and Social Affairs, 1964.

Bölükbaşı, Rıza Tevfik. *Mufassal Kamûs-i Felsefe*. Istanbul: Matbaa-i Amire, 1914.

*The Book of English Fireplaces*. Feltham: Country Life, 1968.

Bostancı, Kahraman. *Mehmet Vahit Bey ve Güzel Sanatlar Üzerine Bir Terminoloji Risalesi*. Istanbul: Arkeoloji ve Sanat Yayınları, 2003.

'Boston Suburban Architecture'. *Architectural Record* 21, no. 4 (April 1907).

Boyington, Amy. *Hidden Patrons: Women and Architectural Patronage in Georgian Britain*. London: Bloomsbury, 2023.

Brady, Joseph. *Dublin, 1950–1970. Houses, Flats and High Rise*. Dublin: Four Courts Press, 2016.

Brittain, Vera. *Women's Work in Modern England*. London: Noel Douglas, 1928.

Burlando, Daniele. '"Moroccan" Artek – Colonized Textiles within 1930s Modernist Interiors'. *Journal of Design History*, no. 35 (2023). https://doi.org/10.1093/jdh/epac035.

Cable, Vince. *Free Radical*. London: Atlantic Books, 2009.

Cahill, Gerry. *Back to the Street*. Dublin: Housing Research Unit, University College Dublin, 1980.

Çakır, Serpil. *Osmanlı Kadın Hareketi*. Metis Yayınları, 2016.

Carolan, Eoin. 'Lessons from Anti-Poverty Action in Ireland: Flexibility, Failure and the Pitfalls of a "Fourth Branch" Model'. In *Federal Law Review* 51, no. 3 (September 2023): 333-43.

Casey, Christine. *Making Magnificence: Architects, Stuccatori, and the Eighteenth-Century Interior*. New Haven: Yale University Press, 2017.

Castellanos Gómez, Raúl, and Débora Domingo Cañabuig. 'Bloques normales'. *Revista EN BLANCO*, no 6. Vivienda Unifamiliar (2011): 6-11.

Chaloner, Len. 'The New President of the Women's Engineering Society: A Glimpse of Mrs. Willson's Remarkable Career'. *The Woman Engineer* 2, no. 5 (December 1925): 109.

Chamberlain, Rudolph. *There Is No Truce: A Life of Thomas Mott Osborne*. New York: Macmillan Company, 1935.

Cho, Hee-Yeon, and Kuan-Hsing Chen. 'Editorial introduction: Bandung/Third Worldism'. *Inter-Asia Cultural Studies* 6, no. 4 (2006). https://doi.org/10.1080/14649370500316711.

Christensen, Peter H. *Precious Metal: German Steel, Modernity, and Ecology*. State College: Penn State University Press, 2022.

Clay, Catherine, ed. *Women's Periodicals and Print Culture in Britain, 1919–1939: The Interwar Period*. Edinburgh: Edinburgh University Press, 2017.

Clear, Caitriona. *Nuns in Nineteenth-Century Ireland*. Dublin: Gill and Macmillan, 1987.

'Coade Stone in Georgian Gardens'. *Journal of Garden History Society* 16, no. 2 (Autumn 1988): 109-33.

'Coade's Artificial Stone Works'. In *Survey of London: Volume 23, Lambeth: South Bank and Vauxhall*, edited by Howard Roberts and Walter H. Godfrey, 58-61. London: 1951.

Cole, Doris. *From Tipi to Skyscraper: A History of Women in Architecture*. Boston: i Press, 1973.

Cole, Johnnetta B. 'Another Day Will Find Us Brave'. *Sage* 6, no. 1 (1989): 85.

Cole, Johnnetta B. *Anthropology for the Eighties: Introductory Readings*. New York: Free Press, 1982.

Colomina, Beatriz. 'Battle Lines: E.1027'. In *The Sex of Architecture*, edited by Diana Agrest, Patricia Conway and Leslie Kanes Weisman, 167-82. New York: Harry N. Abrams, 1996.

Çon, Esra. *A Decollete Journal for the Ottoman Turkish Women: 'Süs' (16 June 133 [1923]–26 July 1340 [1924])*. PhD diss., Boğaziçi University, 2007.

Conkling, Philip. 'A Practical Visionary, Remembering Emily Muir'. *Maine Magazine* (May 2017). https://www.themainemag.com/a-practical-visionary/.

Coogan, Tim Pat. *Ireland Since the Rising*. London: Pall Mall Press, 1966.

Cook, Max B. 'A Girl with a Very Practical Dream'. *The American Magazine* 92, no. 3 (September 1921): 62.

Corráin, Daithí Ó. 'Catholicism in Ireland, 1880–2015: Rise, Ascendancy and Retreat'. In *The Cambridge History of Ireland*, edited by Thomas Bartlett, 726-64. Cambridge: Cambridge University Press, 2018.

Crawford, Elizabeth. *Enterprising Women: The Garretts and their Circle*. London: Francis Boutle Publishers, 2002.

Cuff, Dana, Anastasia Loukaitou-Sideris, Michael Osman, Todd Presner and Jeffrey Schnapp. *Urban Humanities: New Practices for Reimagining the City*. Cambridge, MA: MIT Press, 2020.

Cyriaque, Jeane. 'Preserving a Sense of Place: The Spelman College Campus Heritage Plan'. *Reflections* 6 (2006): 1-4.

Darling, Elizabeth. 'The Avant-Garde in the Drawing Room: Women, Writing, and Architectural Modernism in Britain'. In *Women, Periodicals, and Print Culture in Britain, 1890s–1920s: The Modernist Period*, edited by Faith Binckes, and Carey Snyder. Edinburgh: University of Edinburgh Press, 2019.

Darling, Elizabeth. 'Robertson [née Lewis], Doris Adeney, Lady Robertson (1899–1981), architect, interior designer, and writer'. *Oxford Dictionary of National Biography*. July 11, 2019. https://www.oxforddnb.com/view/10.1093/odnb/9780198614128.001.0001/odnb-9780198614128-e-369119.

Darling, Elizabeth, and Lynne Walker. *AA Women in Architecture: 1917–2017*. London: AA Publications, 2017.

Davies, Colin. *A New History of Modern Architecture*. London: Lawrence King, 2017.

Day, Kirsten, and Peter Raisbeck. 'The Last Laugh and its Afterlife: Emerging narratives in 1970s Melbourne Architecture'. *Fabrications* 31, no. 3 (2021): 336-56.

De Groote, C. 'Banco del Estado de Chile, local pago de pensionados Santiago'. *Auca: Arquitectura Urbanismo Construcción Arte*, no. 6–7 (1967): 73-74.

Delaney, Paul. *Literature, Money and the Market: From Trollope to Amis*. Basingstoke: Palgrave, 2002.

Dianat, Alborz. 'The Re-Making of Charles Rennie Mackintosh: A Study of the 1933 Memorial Exhibition'. *Architectural History* 62 (2019): 145-69.

Douglas, Ann. *The Feminization of American Culture*. New York: Alfred Knopf, 1977.

Duffy, Pat, ed. *The David-Foulkes Taylor Years: Invitation Exhibition, WAIT 1982*. Perth: WAIT, 1982.

Edwards, Clive. 'Home Is Where the Art Is': Women, Handicrafts and Home Improvements 1750–1900.' *Journal of Design History* 19, no. 1 (2006). https://doi.org/10.1093/jdh/epk002.

Egan, Nicole Weisensee. *Chasing Cosby: The Downfall of America's Dad*. New York: Seal Press, 2019.

'Electrical Enterprise, Ltd'. *The Woman Engineer* 2, no. 12 (September 1927): 248.

Eliash, Humberto, and Manuel Moreno. *Arquitectura y modernidad en Chile 1925–1965: Una realidad múltiple*. Ediciones Universidad Católica de Chile, 1989.

Ellis, Markman. *The Coffee-House: A Cultural History*. London: Weidenfeld & Nicolson, 2004.

Engh, Sunniva. 'The Nordic Model in international development aid: explanation, experience and export'. In *The Making and Circulation of Nordic Model, Ideas and Images*, edited by Haldor Byrkjeflot, Lars Mjøset, Mads Mordhorst and Klaus Petersen, 125-28. London: Routledge, 2021.

Erdoğdu Erkarslan, Özlem. 'Turkish Women Architects in the Late Ottoman and Early Republican Era, 1908–1950'. *Women's History Review* 16, no. 4 (1 September 2007). https://doi.org/10.1080/09612020701445966.

Erişirgil, Mehmet Emin. *Kant ve Felsefesi*. Istanbul: Büyük Millet Meclisi Hükûmeti Maarif Vekâleti, 1923.

'Exhibition House Group'. *Architectural Forum* 65, no. 1 (July 1936).

Fahri, Ziyaeddin. *Bediiyat*. Istanbul: Devlet, 1927.

Fahy, Tony. 'The Catholic Church and Social Policy'. *The Furrow* 49, no. 4 (April 1998): 726-64.

Fausch, Deborah, Paulette Singley, Rodolphe El Khoury and Zvi Efrat, eds. *Architecture: In Fashion*. Princeton: Princeton Architectural Press, 1977.

Focus Point. *Focus Point Directory: Care Accommodation and Housing Support Services in Ireland*. Focus Point Project Limited, 1991.

Ford, James. 'Trends in Housing'. *Social Forces* 11, no. 4 (May 1933): 517-20.

Fortna, Benjamin C. *Learning to Read in the Late Ottoman Empire and the Early Turkish Republic*. London: Palgrave Macmillan UK, 2011.

'Four Small Houses in E. H. and M. K. Hunter, Hemlock Hill, Hanover, N. H.'. *Architectural Record* 114, no. 5 (November 1953): 154-65.

Frederick, Christine. 'How The American Housewife Achieves Leisure Through Electricity'. *Electrical Age for Women* 1, no. 3 (January 1927): 98-100.

Freestone, Ian, M. Bimson, and Michael Tite. 'The Constitution of Coade Stone'. In *Ancient Technology to Modern Science*, edited by W. David Kingery, 293-304. *Ceramics and Civilization*, Vol. 1. Westerville, OH: American Ceramic Society, 1985.

Freestone, Ian. 'Forgotten but Not Lost: The Secret of Coade Stone'. *Proceedings of the Geological Association* 102 (1991): 135-38.

Friedman, Alice T. *Women and the Making of the Modern House.* New York: Harry N. Abrams, 1998.

Fuller, Linda K. *The Cosby Show: Audiences, Impact, and Implications.* London: Bloomsbury Academic, 1992.

'The Furniture History Society. "Mrs Coade's Gothic"'. *Country Life*, (2 June 1977): 514-16.

Gadsden, Nonie. *Arts & Reform: Sara Galner, the Saturday Evening Girls, and the Paul Revere Pottery.* Boston: Museum of Fine Arts, 2006.

García de Cortázar, Gabriela. 'The Kohn Ratinoff House (1962): A Pioneering Dialogue.' *Revista ARQ* 115 (2023): 29-47.

Garrity, Jane. 'Selling Culture to the "Civilised": Bloomsbury, British Vogue, and the Marketing of National Identity.' *Modernism/Modernity* 6, 2 (1999): 29-58.

Gellhorn, Martha. 'So Awful to Be Young, or, Morning to Midnight in Espresso Bars'. *Encounter* 6, no. 5 (1956): 42-43.

Gibson, Susannah. *The Bluestockings: A History of the First Women's Movement.* New York: W. W. Norton, 2024.

Giedion, Sigfried. *Building in France, Building in Iron, Building in Ferroconcrete.* The Getty Center for the History of Art and the Humanities, 1995.

Giles, Judy. *The Parlour and the Suburb: Domestic Identities, Class, Femininity and Modernity.* Oxford: Berg, 2004.

Gökalp, Ziya. *Türkçülüğün Esasları.* Anadolu Üniversitesi Basımevi, 2019.

Gordon, Beverly. 'Woman's Domestic Body: The Conceptual Conflation of Women and Interiors in the Industrial Age'. *Winterthur Portfolio* 31, no. 4 (1996). https://doi.org/10.1086/496697.

Gorman, Carma. '"An Educated Demand": The Implications of "Art in Every Day Life" for American Industrial Design, 1925–1950'. *Design Issues* 16 (2000): 45-66.

Gosseye, Janina. 'A short history of Silence: The Epistemological Politics of Architectural Historiography'. In *Speaking of Buildings: Oral History in Architectural Research,* edited by Naomi Stead, Deborah van der Plaat and Janina Gosseye, 12-27. New York: Princeton Architectural Press, 2019.

Gourney, Isabelle. *AIA Guide to the Architecture of Atlanta.* Athens: University of Georgia Press, 1993.

Gövsa, İbrahim Alâettin. *Bedi-i Terbiye.* Istanbul: Tanin Matbaası, 1925.

Grahn, Maarit. 'The Noormarkku Ironworks: Places of Memory and Capital'. In *Locality, Memory, Reconstruction: The Cultural Challenges and Possibilities of Former Single-Industry Communities,* edited by Simo Häyrynen, Jopi Nyman and Risto Turunen. Cambridge: Cambridge Scholars Publishing, 2012.

Grahn, Maarit. *Perheyhtiö ja paikallisuus – A. Ahlström Osakeyhtiön historian perintö Noormarkussa.* Turku: Painosalama Oy, 2014.

Griffey, Erin. *On Display: Henrietta Maria and the Materials of Magnificence at the Stuart Court.* New Haven and London: Paul Mellon Centre in association with Yale University Press, 2016.

Grimes, Teresa. 'A Woman in a Man's Profession: Edla Muir and the Architectural Community of Los Angeles.' Master's Thesis, University of California Los Angeles, 1992.

Gropius, Walter, and Sarah P. Harkness, eds. *The Architects Collaborative, 1945–1965.* Teufen AR, Switzerland: Arthur Niggli, 1966.

Gropius, Walter. *The New Architecture and the Bauhaus.* Translated by P. Morton Shand. New York: Faber and Faber, 1935.

Gullichsen, Kirsi. 'Noormarkun Käsitöiden huonekalutuotannosta'. In *Noormarkun Käsityöt,* edited by Anni Saisto. Pori: Pori Art Museum, 2021.

Gutman, Marta. *A City for Children: Women, Architecture, and the Charitable Landscapes of Oakland, 1850–1950.* Chicago: University of Chicago Press, 2014.

Guy-Sheftall, Beverly. 'Black Women and Higher Education'. *Journal of Negro Education* 51, no. 3 (1982): 282.

Hackney, Fiona. 'Women are News: British Women's Magazines 1919–1939'. In *Transatlantic Print Culture, 1880–1940: Emerging Media, Emerging Modernism,* edited by Ann Ardis and Patrick Collier, 114-33. Basingstoke: Palgrave Macmillan, 2008.

Hackney, Fiona, and Julia Bigham. 'A Cottage of One's Own: Making Modern Women Through Word and Image in Interwar Women's Homemaking Magazines'. *The Journal of Modern Periodical Studies* 13, no. 1 (2022): 103-41.
Halbwachs, Maurice. *On Collective Memory.* Chicago: University of Chicago Press, 1992.
Hall, Michael. 'Mending Monuments'. *Country Life*, 14 June 1990.
Hannah, Erika. *Modern Dublin: Urban Change and the Irish Past, 1957–73.* Oxford: Oxford University Press, 2013.
Hård af Segerstad, Ulf. *Modern Finnish Design.* Westport, CT: Frederick A. Praeger, 1969.
Harrison, Harry, Stephen Mullin, Barry Reaves and Alan Stevens. *Non-Traditional Houses: Identifying Non-Traditional Houses in the UK 1918-75.* Garston: Building Research Establishment, 2004.
Hayden, Dolores. *The Grand Domestic Revolution: A History of Feminist Designs for American Homes, Neighborhoods, and Cities.* Cambridge, MA: MIT Press, 1982.
Heathcote Tatham, Charles. *Etchings, Representing The Best Examples Of Ancient Ornamental Architecture; Drawn From The Originals In Rome, And Other Parts Of Italy, During The Years 1794, 1795, And 1796.* London: 1799.
Henderson, Susan R. 'A Revolution in the Woman's Sphere: Grete Lihotzky and the Frankfurt Kitchen'. In *Housing and Dwelling: Perspectives on Modern Domestic Architecture*, edited by Barbara Miller Lane, 248-58. Abingdon: Routledge, 2007.
Herrey, Hermann, Constantin Pertzoff and Erna M. J. Herrey. 'An Organic Theory of City Planning'. *Architectural Forum* 80, no. 4 (April 1944): 133-40.
Heynen, Hilde, and Lucía C. Pérez-Moreno. '"Narrating Women Architects" Histories. Paradigms, Dilemmas, and Challenges'. *arq.urb* no. 35 (September-December 2022): 110-22.
Higginbotham, Evelyn Brooks. *Righteous Discontent: The Women's Movement in the Black Baptist Church, 1880–1920.* Cambridge, MA: Harvard University Press, 1994.
'History of Focus Ireland, in Focus Ireland'. *A Place to Call Home. Twenty-Five Years of Focus Ireland.* Dublin: A. & A. Famar, 2011. https://www.focusireland.ie/wp-content/uploads/2023/09/Annual-Report-2022.pdf
Hobson, Maurice J. *The Legend of the Black Mecca: Politics and Class in the Making of Modern Atlanta.* Chapel Hill: University of North Carolina Press, 2017.
Hoffmann, Alfons. *Immanuel Kant. Ein Lebensbild nach Darstellungen der Zeitgenossen Borowski, Jachmann, Wasianski.* Halle: Hugo Peter, 1902.
Holtby, Winifred. *Women.* London: John Lane the Bodley Head Limited, 1934.
Home, Robert K. 'Knowledge networks and postcolonial careering: David Oakley (1927-2003)'. *ABE Journal*, no. 4 (2013). https://doi.org/10.4000/abe.3388.
Hope, Thomas. *Household Furniture and Interior Decoration.* London: Longman, Hurst, Rees, and Orme, 1807.
Hornstein, Jeffrey M. *A Nation of Realtors: A Cultural History of the Twentieth-Century American Middle Class.* Durham, NC: Duke University Press, 2005.
Hough, David. 'Eating Places'. In *The Historical Encyclopedia of Western Australia,* edited by Jenny Gregory and Jan Gothard, 297-99. Crawley: UWA Press, 2009.
Hunter, Margaret King. 'A Design for Living – or Building'. *Wheaton Alumnae Quarterly* 36, no. 3 (July 1957): 14-15.
Hunting, Mary Anne, and Kevin D. Murphy. *Women Architects at Work: Making American Modernism.* Princeton, NJ: Princeton University Press, 2025.
Hurd, M.K. 'Usonian Automatic: Wright's concrete masonry'. In *Concrete Construction* (1988): 1028-1030.
Huyssen, Andreas. *After the Great Divide: Modernism, Mass Culture and Postmodernism.* Bloomington: Indiana University Press, 1986.
Hyman, Isabelle. *Marcel Breuer, Architect: The Career and the Buildings.* New York: Harry N. Abrams, 2001.
Iskin, Ruth I. *Modern Women and Parisian Consumer Culture in Impressionist Painting.* Cambridge: Cambridge University Press, 2014.
James, Kathleen. *Erich Mendelsohn and the Architecture of German Modernism.* Cambridge: Cambridge University Press, 1997.

James-Chakraborty, Kathleen. 'Ausstellungen erleben. Lilly Reichs Produktdisplays 1927–31'. In *Sowohl als auch dazwischen: Erfarhungsräume der Kunst*, edited by Jörn Schafaff and Benjamin Wihstutz, 57-77. Paderborn: Wilhelm Fink, 2015.

'Johnnetta Cole's Resounding Triumph'. *Journal of Blacks in Higher Education* 13 (1996): 18.

Jordy, William. 'The Symbolic Essence of Modern European Architecture of the Twenties and Its Continuing Influence'. *Journal of the Society of Architectural Historians* 22 (1963): 177-87.

Kadıoğlu, Ayşe. 'Writing to Exist: Mes'adet Bedirhan's Pleas for Ottoman Women'. *Women's History Review* 34, no. 1 (2025), 158-77. https://doi.org/10.1080/09612025.2024.2332857.

Kafka, Ben. *The Demon of Writing: Powers and Failures of Paperwork*. New York: Zone Books, 2012.

Kaplan, Victoria. *Structural Inequality: Black Architects in the United States*. New York: Rowman, 2006.

Keegan, Claire. *Small Things Like These*. London: Faber & Faber, 2021.

Kelleher, Carmel, Patricia Kelleher and Patricia McCarthy. *Patterns of Hostel Use in Dublin: A Focus Point Research Study*. Dublin: Focus Point Project Limited, 1992.

Kelly, Alison. 'Coade, Eleanor (1733–1821)'. Revised by Caroline Stanford. *Oxford Dictionary of National Biography*. Oxford: Oxford University Press, 2004.

Kelly, Alison. 'Coade Stone in Georgian Architecture'. *Architectural History* 28 (1985): 71-701.

Kelly, Alison. *Decorative Wedgwood in Architecture and Furniture*. 1965

Kelly, Alison. 'Furnishings from the Coade Factory in Lambeth'. *Furniture History* 10 (1974): 68-70.

Kelly, Alison. *Mrs Coade's Stone*. Upton-upon-Severn: Self Publishing Association, 1990.

Kelly, Alison. *The Story of Wedgwood*. London: Faber and Faber, 1962.

Kelly, Alison. *Wedgwood Ware*. London: Ward Lock, 1970.

Kelly, Ian. *Peter Parkinson: Theatre Architecture*. Perth: York Theatre Festival, 1987.

Kelly, Jessica. 'Anonymity and Hidden Mechanisms in Design and Architecture'. *Architecture and Culture* 6, no. 1 (2018): 5-15.

Kelly, Jessica. *No More Giants: J. M. Richards, Modernism and The Architectural Review*. Manchester: Manchester University Press, 2022.

Kelsall, Frank. 'Liardet versus Adam'. *Architectural History* 27 (1984): 118-26.

Kendi, Ibram X. *The Black Campus Movement: Black Students and the Radical Reconstitution of Higher Education, 1965-1972*. New York: Palgrave, 2012.

Kennedy, Stanislaus. *But Where Can I Go? Homeless Women in Dublin*. Dublin: Arlen House, 1985.

Kennedy, Stanislaus. *Who Should Care?* Dublin: Turoe Press, 1981.

Keylon, Steven. 'The California Landscapes of Katherine Bashford'. *Eden: Journal of the California Garden & Landscape History Society* 16, no. 4 (Fall 2013): 3-13.

Kinnunen, Ulla. *Ben af Schultén and the Artek Tradition*. Finland: Alvar Aalto Foundation, 2008.

Koh, Gillian, and Ooi Giok Lin, eds. *State-Society Relations in Singapore*. Oxford: Oxford University Press, 2001.

Kolson Hurley, Amanda. *Radical Suburbs: Experimental Living on the Fringes of the American City*. Cleveland: Belt Publishing, 2019.

Korvenmaa, Pekka. 'From Policies to Politics: Finnish Design on the Ideological Battlefield in the 1960s and 1970s'. In *Scandinavian Design – Alternative Histories*, edited by Kjetil Fallan. Oxford: Berg, 2012.

le Roux, Hannah. 'The networks of tropical architecture'. *The Journal of Architecture*, 8:3 (2003), 337-354. https://doi.org/10.1080/1360236032000134835.

Lefever, Harry G. *Undaunted by the Fight: Spelman College and the Civil Rights Movement, 1951–1967*. Macon, GA: Mercer University Press, 2005.

León Echaíz, René. *Ñuñohue*. Buenos Aires: Editorial Francisco de Aguirre, 1972.

Leonora Eyles, Margaret. *The Woman in the Little House*. London: G. Richards, 1922.

LeVere, Richard. 'There From the Start'. *Lighting Design + Application*. 35, no. 2 (2005): 59-60.

Lim, Lena U Wen. 'Willy: The Unconventionally Conventional'. In *Nolimits: Articulating William Lim*, edited by Robert Powell. Singapore: Select Publishing, 2002.

Lim, Lena U Wen. 'Select Books – the struggle of an independent bookshop'. *Inter-Asia Cultural Studies* 6, no. 4 (2005). https://doi.org/10.1080/14649370500316901.

Lim, Lena U Wen. *Book Review: Singapore English Literature. BiblioAsia* 5, no. 2, 2008. https://biblioasia.nlb.gov.sg/files/pdf/vol-5/issue-2/v5-issue2_EnglishLiterature.pdf.

Lim, William. *Alternative (post)modernity: An Asian Perspective.* Singapore: Select Publishing, 2003.
Lim, William. *Alternatives in transition – The Postmodern, Glocality and Social Justice.* Singapore: Select Books, 2001.
Lim, William. *Asian new urbanism and other papers.* Singapore: Select Books, 1998.
Lim, William. *Public Space in Urban Asia.* New Jersey: World Scientific Publishing, 2013.
Livingstone, Karen. *Women Pioneers of the Arts and Crafts Movement.* London: Thames & Hudson, 2024.
Lloyd Thomas, Katie. 'This Strange Interloper: Building products and the emergence of the architect-shopper in 1930s Britain'. In *Suffragette City: Women, Politics, and the Built Environment*, edited by Elizabeth Darling and Nathaniel Robert Walker, 110-35. Abingdon: Routledge, 2020.
Lucey, Conor. 'Women and the Construction Industry in Georgian Britain and Ireland'. *Architectural History* 66 (2023): 127-54.
Luckhurst, Nicola. *Bloomsbury in Vogue.* London: Cecil Woolf, 1998.
MacLean, John C. *A Rich Harvest: The History, Buildings, and People of Lincoln, Massachusetts.* Lincoln, MA: Lincoln Historical Society, 1987.
Mahood, Aurelea. 'Fashioning Readers: The Avant Garde and British Vogue, 1920-9'; *Women: A Cultural Review* 13, no. 1 (2002): 120-29.
Major, Judith. *Mariana Griswold van Rensselaer: A Landscape Critic in the Gilded Age.* Charlottesville: University of Virginia Press, 2013.
Mann, Lina. 'Building the White House'. *The White House Historical Association,* January 3, 2020. https://www.whitehousehistory.org/building-the-white-house.
Marchant, Nick. *Kilkenny Design: Twenty-One Years of Design in Ireland.* London: Lund Humphries, 1985.
Matrix. *Making Space: Women and the Man-Made Environment.* London: Pluto, 1984.
Maulén de los Reyes, David. 'Experiencias docentes. Inclusion/ exclusión del espacio urbano y social 1933/1945/1964'. *Revista De Arquitectura* 12, no. 14 (2006): 52-63.
McAllister, Keith A. 'Connections in the Magic Kingdom'. BA Thesis, Amherst College, 1984.
McCabe, Fergal. *Ambition and Achievement: The Civic Visions of Frank Gibney.* Dublin: Castles in the Air Publications, 2018.
McCarthy, Mary. 'The provision of rural local-authority housing and domestic space: a comparative North-South study, 1942-60'. In *Proceedings of the Royal Irish Academy: Archaeology, Culture, History, Literature*, vol. 111C (2011): 287-309.
McKenna, Yvonne. 'Embodied Ideals and Realities: Irish Nuns and Irish Womanhood, 1930s-1960s'. *Éire-Ireland (St. Paul)* 41, no. 1 (2006): 40-63.
McKenna, Yvonne. 'Entering Religious Life, Claiming Subjectivity: Irish Nuns, 1930s-1960s'. *Women's History Review* 15 (2006): 189-211.
'Mett C. David Moody, Jr. of C.D. Moody Construction Company'. *Voyage ATL,* July 18, 2018. https://voyageatl.com/interview/meet-c-david-moody-jr-c-d-moody-construction-company-inc-lithonia.
Mitchell, Melvin L. *The Crisis of the African American Architect: Conflicting Cultures of Architecture and (Black) Power.* New York: Writers Advantage, 2003.
Moe, Kiel. *Unless: The Seagram Building Construction Ecology.* New York/Barcelona: Actar, 2021.
Moman, Tiffany. 'Constructing Traditions: Architecture, Material Culture, and the Higher Education Experience at Spelman College, 1850-1925'. PhD diss., Middle Tennessee State University, 2019.
Montague, John. 'The architecture of Ballymun'. In *Memories, milestones and new horizons: Reflections on the regeneration of Ballymun*, edited by Aibhlinn McCrann. Belfast: Blackstaff Press, 2008.
Morgan, Keith N. 'Six Moon Hill'. In *Buildings of Massachusetts: Metropolitan Boston,* edited by Keith N. Morgan, Richard M. Candee, Naomi Miller, Roger G. Reed, et al., 438-47. Charlottesville: University of Virginia Press, 2009.
'Mrs Coade's Stone'. *Connoisseur* 197 (January 1978): 14-25.
Murray, Andrew. 'Tee Square Journal, Phi, Aspect, and Aedicule: The Publications of the Architectural Students Association of Western Australia'. *Fabrications* 33, no. 1 (2023): 142-70.

Murray, Andrew. 'What To Do with "Thirty Blow-Ins" at a Housewarming Party: Peripheral Figures and Architectural History'. In *Proceedings of the Society of Architectural Historians Australia and New Zealand* 37, *what If? What Next? Speculations of History's Futures,* edited by Kate Hislop and Hanna Lewi, 584-89. Perth: SAHANZ, 2021.

Nasr, Joe, and Mercedes Volait. *Urbanism: Imported or Exported?* Chichester; Hoboken, NJ: Wiley-Academy, 2003.

Noland, John. 'Mariemont, Ohio – A New Town Built to Produce Local Happiness'. In *Better Homes Manual*, edited by Blanch Halpert, 735-37. Chicago: University of Chicago Press, 1931.

Nummelin, Esko, and Emilia Siltavuori. *Maire Gullichsen.* Kukkila: Pori Art Museum, 2000.

O'Keefe, Maurice. 'Sr. Stanislaus Kennedy Interview'. In *1922-2022, A Century of Change. Irish Life and Lore* September 29, 202, Audio, 47:53. https://www.irishlifeandlore.com/product/sr-stanislaus-kennedy/ (accessed May 2023).

O'Leary, Marie. 'Mary Aikenhead'. *Dictionary of Irish Biography.* Cambridge: Cambridge University Press, ongoing. https://www.dib.ie/biography/aikenhead-mary-a0072.

Oikarinen, Sanna. 'Yritystoiminnan keskeiset vaiheet'. In *Noormarkun Käsityöt*, edited by Anni Saisto. Pori: Pori Art Museum, 2021.

Orwig, Timothy T. 'Joseph Everett Chandler, Colonial Revival Architecture, and the Origins of the Historic Preservation Movement in America'. PhD Diss. Boston University, 2010.

Owens, Patricia. *Erased: A History of International Thought Without Men.* Princeton: Princeton University Press, 2025.

Palmer, Montserrat. *La comuna de Providencia y la ciudad jardín: un estudio de los inicios del modelo de crecimiento actual de la ciudad de Santiago.* Santiago: Ograma, 1984.

Palmer, Sue, et al. *Death and Memory. Soane and the Architecture of Legacy.* London: Sir John Soane's Museum, 2015.

Peck, Amelia, and Carol Irish. *Candace Wheeler: The Art and Enterprise of American Design, 1875–1900.* New York: Metropolitan Museum of Art, 2001.

Pender, Anne. 'Modernist Madonnas: Dorothy Todd, Madge Garland and Virginia Woolf'. *Women's History Review* 16, no. 4 (2007): 519-33.

Penick, Monica. *Tastemaker: Elizabeth Gordon, House Beautiful, and the Postwar American Home.* New Haven: Yale University Press, 2017.

Penner, Barbara. 'Farm Kitchens and Home Economy: Demonstrating Care'. *gta papers* 7 (2021). https://doi.org/10.54872/gta-4647-03.

Pepchinski, Mary, and Mariann Simon, eds. *Ideological Equals: Women Architects in Socialist Europe, 1945–1989.* London: Routledge, 2018.

Pettersson, Susanna. 'Artek – a Bridge to the International Art World'. *FNG Research*, no. 3 (2017). https://research.fng.fi/wp-content/uploads/2017/05/fngr_2017-3_pettersson_susanna_article1_2.pdf.

Pfeiffer, Bruce Brooks. 'Frank Lloyd Wright and the 'textile block' construction system'. *Domus* 737 (1992): 110-16.

Pfreszchner, Paul. *Dynamics of Irish Housing.* Dublin: Institute of Public Administration, 1965.

Phillips, Marion, and A.D. Sanderson Furniss. *The Working Woman's House.* Swarthmore: Swarthmore Press, 1919.

Phillips, Marion. 'The Working Woman's House'. *The Labour Woman* 6, no. 23 (March 1918): 7-8.

Power, Sinead. 'The Development of the Ballymun Housing Scheme, Dublin 1965–1969'. In *Irish Geography* 33 (2000): 199-222.

'The President's New Housing Scheme'. *The Woman Engineer* 2, no. 10, (March 1927): 193.

'Presidential Address by Mrs. L. A. Willson, M.B.E. (Delivered at Leeds University, September 3, 1926)'. *The Woman Engineer* 2, no. 8 (September 1926): 153.

'Presidential Address, Delivered at the Bristol University, September 21, 1928'. *The Woman Engineer* 2, no. 16 (September-October 1928): 311.

Prior, Aisling, ed. *Hotel Ballymun. Seamus Nolan.* Dublin: Breaking Ground, Ballymun Regeneration Ltd., 2008.

Prussin, Labelle. *African Nomadic Architecture: Space, Place, and Gender.* Washington: Smithsonian Institution Press, 1995.

Quataert, Donald. 'Ottoman Women, Households, and Textile Manufacturing, 1800-1914'. In *Women in Middle Eastern History: Shifting Boundaries in Sex and Gender*, edited by Nikki R. Keddie, and Bath Baron. New Haven: Yale University Press, 2008. 161-76.

Quinn, Patricia. *Temple Bar: The Power of an Idea.* Dublin: Temple Bar Properties Limited, 1996.

Raftery, Deirdre. 'The "Mission" of Nuns in Female Education in Ireland, c. 1850–1950'. *Paedagogica Historica* 48, no. 2 (2012): 299-313.

Raftery, Deirdre, and Catriona Delaney. 'Teaching Vocation or Religious Vocation: Examining the Changing Identity of Irish Teaching Sisters c. 1940-1970, an Oral History Approach'. *Irish educational studies* 43, no. 2 (2024): 329-40.

Reed, Christopher. 'A Vogue That Dare Not Speak its Name: Sexual Subculture During the Editorship of Dorothy Todd 1922-26'. *Fashion Theory* 10, no. 1-2 (2006): 39-72.

Reilly, Robin. *Wedgwood Jasper.* London: Thames and Hudson, 1994.

Robinson, Monique. 'Restoring Spelman's Rockefeller Fine Arts Building'. *National Trust for Historic Preservation*, September 14, 2021. https://savingplaces.org/stories/restoring-spelmans-rockefeller-fine-arts-building.

Rowley, Ellen. 'Ballymun, Case Study'. in *Art and Architecture of Ireland: Architecture 1600–2000*, edited by Rolf Loeber, et al. New Haven: Yale University Press, 2014: 415-16.

Rowley, Ellen. *Housing, Architecture and the Edge Condition. Dublin is Building 1935-75.* London: Routledge, 2018.

Rowley, Ellen, and Carole Pollard, eds. *More Than Concrete Blocks, 1973-99.* Dublin: UCD Press, 2023.

Ryan, Deborah S. *Ideal Homes: Uncovering the History and Design of the Interwar House.* Manchester: Manchester University Press, 2020.

Sáez, José Miguel. 'Normativa nacional antisísmica en materia de construcción. Bases y proyecciones'. BA dissertation, Universidad de Chile, 2011.

Saito, Yuriko. *Everyday Aesthetics.* Oxford: Oxford University Press, 2007.

Saniga, Andrew, and Andrew Wilson. 'A League of His Own: Karl Langer's Landscape Australia'. In *Karl Langer: Modern Architect and Migrant in the Australian Tropics*, edited by Deborah van der Plaat and John Macarthur, 232-57. London: Bloomsbury, 2022.

Sarantola-Weiss, Minna. 'Creature Comforts: Soft Sofas and the Demise of Modernist Morality in the 1970s Finland'. In *Scandinavian Design – Alternative Histories*, edited by Kjetil Fallan, 146-47. Oxford: Berg, 2012.

Savola, Kaisu. *Disrespectful thoughts about design: Social, political and environmental values in Finnish design, 1960–80.* Joensuu: Aalto ARTS Books, 2023.

Sayigh, Ali. *Sustainable Vernacular Architecture: How the Past Can Enrich the Future.* New York: Springer, 2011.

Schick, Irvin Cemil. 'Print Capitalism and Women's Sexual Agency in the Late Ottoman Empire'. *Comparative Studies of South Asia, Africa and the Middle East* 31, no. 1 (May 1, 2011). https://doi.org/10.1215/1089201X-2010-067.

Schuldenfrei, Robin. *Luxury and Modernism: Architecture and the Object in Germany, 1900–1933.* Princeton: Princeton University Press, 2018.

Schütte-Lihotzky, Margarete. 'Rationalization in the Household'. trans. Don Reneau, in *The Weimar Republic* Sourcebook, edited by Anton Kaes, Martin Jay and Edward Dimendberg, 462-65. Berkeley: University of California Press, 1994.

Scott, Peggy. *An Electrical Adventure.* London: Jas. Truscott & Sons, Ltd., 1934.

Sharoff, Robert, and William Zbaren. *American City: Detroit Architecture, 1845-2005.* Detroit: Wayne State University Press, 2005.

Simpson, Pamela H. 'Cheap, Quick and Easy: The Early History of Rockfaced Concrete Block Building'. *Perspectives in Vernacular Architecture* 3 (1989): 108-09.

Snow, Jenna, and Andrea Thabet. 'A Women's Project: Mary Louise Schmidt and the 1936 California House and Garden Exhibition'. Los Angeles: Friends of Residential Treasures: Los Angeles, March 2023. https://www.fortla.org/trails-films-research/trails/.

Somerville-Woodward, Robert. *Ballymun, A History. Volumes 1 & 2 c. 1600–1997.* Dublin: Ballymun Regeneration Ltd., 2002.

Sontag, Susan. *On Women*, edited by David Rieff. New York: Picador, 2023.

Spalding, Tom. *Designed for Life*. Cork: Cork University Press, 2025.

Sparke, Penny. 'Elsie de Wolfe and Her Female Clients, 1905–15: Gender, Class and the Professional Interior Decorator'. In *Women's Places: Architecture and Design 1860-1960*, edited by Brenda Martin and Penny Sparke. London: Routledge, 2003.

Sparke, Penny. *As Long as It's Pink: The Sexual Politics of Taste*. Halifax: Press of the Nova Scotia College of Art and Design, 2010.

Sparke, Penny. *Elsie de Wolfe: The Birth of Modern Interior Decoration*. Wellington: Acanthus Press, 2005.

Spivak, Gayatri. 'Can the subaltern speak?' *Die Philosophin* 14, no. 27 (1988): 42-58.

Stanford, Caroline. 'Revisiting the Origins of Coade Stone'. *Georgian Group Journal* 24 (2016): 95-116.

Steyn, Gerald. 'The Indigenous Rondavel: A Case for Conservation'. *SAJAH* 21, no. 1 (2006): 21-38.

Storrow, Helen. 'Better Homes for Negroes in America'. *Opportunity: A Journal of Negro Life* (June 1931): 174-77.

Stratton, Jon. 'Youth Culture'. In *The Historical Encyclopedia of Western Australia,* edited by Jenny Gregory and Jan Gothard. Crawley: UWA Press, 2009.

Stritzler-Levine, Nina, ed. *Artek and the Aaltos*. New York: Bard Graduate Center, 2016.

Stritzler-Levine, Nina. *Svenskt Tenn: Interiors*. London: Phaidon, 2025.

Stroud, Dorothy. *Sir John Soane, Architect*. 2nd ed. New Haven: Yale University Press, 1996.

Summerson, John. 'Sir John Soane and the Furniture of Death'. In *The Unromantic Castle and Other Essays, 135–37*. London: Thames and Hudson, 1990.

Summerson, John. *Georgian London*. New Haven: Paul Mellon Center, 2003.

Summerson, John. *The Life and Work of John Nash, Architect*. Cambridge, MA: MIT Press, 1980.

Swenarton, Mark. *Homes Fit for Heroes: The Politics and Architecture of Early State Housing in Britain*. London: Routledge, 2018.

Talesnik, Daniel. 'Monumentality and Resignification. The UNCTAD III Building in Chile'. In *Latin American Modern Architecture,* edited by Patricio Del Real and Helen Gyger, 132-52. London: Routledge, 2012.

Talesnik, Daniel. 'Tibor Weiner y su rol en la reforma: una re-introducción'. *Revista De Arquitectura* 12 no. 14 (2006): 135-53.

Téllez, Andrés, and Hugo Mondragón. *Arquitectura y construcción Chile 1945–50: una revista de arquitectura moderna*. LOM, 2006.

Thomas, Zoë. *Women art workers and the Arts and Crafts Movement*. Manchester: Manchester University Press, 2022.

'A Thousand Women in Architecture'. *Architectural Record* 103, no. 3 (March 1948): 105-13.

Tolga Cora, Yaşar. 'Female Labor, Merchant Capital, and Resilient Manufacturing: Rethinking Ottoman Armenian Communities through Labor and Business'. *Journal of the Economic and Social History of the Orient* 61, no. 3 (2018). https://doi.org/10.1163/15685209-12341453.

Torre, Susana, ed. *Women in American Architecture: A Historic and Contemporary Perspective*. New York: Whitney Library of Design, 1977.

Tunç, Uğurgül. 'Osmanlı Modernleşmesinde Eğitim, Sanat ve Kadın: İnas Sanayi-i Nefise Mektebi Âlisi Örneği'. MA Thesis., Istanbul Technical University, 2018.

'Ueber Herrn Coade's Lithopodipira oder Kunst Backerstein-Fabrik zu Lambeth in England'. *Journal des Luxus und der Moden* 2 (1787).

Ürekli, Fatma. 'Güzel Sanatlar Eğitiminde Osmanlı Hanımlarına Açılan Bir Pencere: İnas Sanayi-i Nefise Mektebi'. *Tarih ve Toplum* 231, no. 39 March (2003): 50-60.

Veblen, Thorsten. *The Theory of the Leisure Class: An Economic Study of Institutions*. New York: Macmillan, 1899.

Walker, Lynne. 'An Irresistible Movement'. In *AA Women in Architecture, 1917–2017,* edited by Elizabeth Darling and Lynne Walker. London: AA Publications, 2017.

Wallach, Ruth. *Los Angeles Residential Architecture*. Charleston, SC: The History Press, 2015.

Ward, Brian, Gary Boyd, Michael Pike, eds. *Out of the Ordinary*. Abingdon: Routledge, 2019.

Ware, Leonard. *Helen Osborne Storrow, 1864–1944: A Memoir*. Northampton, MA, 1970.

Waterfield, Giles, ed. 'Soane Family Tomb'. In *Soane and Death*. London: Dulwich Picture Gallery, 1996.
Watkin, David. *Thomas Hope and the Neoclassical Ideal*. London: John Murray, 1968.
Whitaker, Mark. *Cosby: His Life and Times*. New York: Simon & Schuster, 2014.
Wigley, Mark. *White Walls, Designer Dresses: The Fashioning of Modern Architecture*. Cambridge, MA: MIT Press, 1996.
Williams Goldhagen, Sarah. 'Something to Talk about: Modernism, Discourse, Style'. *Journal of the Society of Architectural Historians* 64, no. 2 (2005): 144-67.
Willis, Carol. *Form follows Finance: Skyscrapers and Skylines in New York and Chicago*. New York: Princeton Architectural Press, 1995.
Wilson, Dreck Spurlock, ed. *African American Architects: A Biographical Dictionary, 1865-1945*. New York: Routledge, 2004.
Wilson, Mabel O. *Negro Building: Black Americans in the World of Fairs and Museums*. Berkeley: University of California Press, 2012.
Woirhaye, Helena. *Maire Gullichsen – Konstens springflicka*. Helsinki: Konstindustrimuseet, 2002.
'A Woman Builder and Electricity'. *Electrical Age for Women* 1, no. 16 (April 1930): 629.
'A Woman's Housing Scheme'. *The Woman Engineer* 2, no. 4 [Special Number on the First International Conference of Women in Science, Industry, and Commerce] (September 1925): 100.
*Women and Housing: Labour Saving in the Home; Report of a Conference of Women's Organisations Held at the 'Daily Mail' Ideal Home Exhibition, Olympia, London, on February 10th, 1920*. The Garden Cities & Town Planning Association, 1920.
'Women in the Irish Construction Industry: Statistics and Facts'. February 13, 2023. https://www.sig.ie/women-in-the-irish-construction-industry-statistics-and-facts/.
Wood, Alice. 'Housekeeping, Citizenship, and Nationhood in *Good Housekeeping* and *Modern Home*'. In *Women's Periodicals and Print Culture in Britain, 1918–1939: The Interwar Period*, edited by Catherine Clay, Maria DiCenzo, Barbara Green and Fiona Hackney. Edinburgh: Edinburgh University Press, 2018.
Wood, Alice. 'Made to Measure: Virginia Woolf in *Good Housekeeping* Magazine'. *Prose Studies* 32, 1 (2010): 12-24.
Woods, Mary N. *From Craft to Profession: The Practice of Architecture in Nineteenth-Century America*. Berkeley: University of California Press, 1999.
Woolf, Virginia, and Leonard Woolf. 'Are Too Many Books Written and Published?' *PMLA* 121, no. 1 (2006): 235-44.
Woolf, Virginia. 'Professions for Women'. In *The Death of the Moth and Other Essays*, 237-38. New York: Harcourt Brace & Co., 1942.
Woolf, Virginia. *Three Guineas*. New York: Harcourt, Brace and Company, 1938.
Wright, Clare. '"Doing the Beans": Women, Drinking and Community in the Ladies' Lounge'. *Journal of Australian Studies* 27, no. 76 (2003): 5-16.
Wright, Gwendolyn. 'On the Fringe of the Profession: Women in American Architecture'. In *The Architect: Chapters in the History of the Profession*, edited by Spiro Kostof. New York: Oxford University Press, 1977.
Wright, Gwendolyn. *Building the Dream: A Social History of Housing in America*. New York: Pantheon, 1981.
Young, Hilary, ed. *The Genius of Wedgwood*. London: V&A Publications, 1997.
Zerman, Ece. 'Reappropriating the Orientalist Gaze in the Material Culture of Kemalist Turkey: The Formation of an "Aesthetic Nationalism."' In *Kemalism: Transnational Politics in the Post-Ottoman World*, edited by Fabio Giomi, Emmanuel Szurek and Nathalie Clayer, 217-63. London: I.B. Tauris, 2019.
Zipf, Catherine. *Professional Pursuits: Women and the American Arts and Crafts Movement*. Knoxville: University of Tennessee Press, 2007.
Zuckerman, Mary Ellen. *A History of Popular Women's Magazines in the United States, 1792-1995*. Westport: Greenwood Press, 1998.

# About the authors

**Dana Arnold** FSA is Professor of Art and Cultural Heritage at the Sainsbury Institute for the Study of Japanese Arts and Cultures at the University of East Anglia, UK. Her research focuses on feminist and decolonising alternatives to canonical architectural histories and includes *Women and Architectural History* (2024), *Architecture and Ekphrasis* (2020), and *The Spaces of the Hospital* (2014). She is a member of the Arts and Humanities Research Council Advisory Board; Chair of the Programme Board of Research Infrastructure for Conservation and Heritage Science; and Deputy Chair, Research Diversity Advisory Panel for the Research Excellence Framework 2029. Her new book *The Public Consumption of Architecture* will be published by Routledge.

**Alex Banister** is a PhD researcher at London Metropolitan University where her research examines women's writing on architecture and design in interwar Britain. She is a Visiting Researcher on the project 'Making Space: Histories of Architecture and Motherhood' at the University for the Creative Arts, Canterbury, and currently serves as a trustee of the Design History Society.

**Gabriela García de Cortázar Galleguillos** is an architect from Universidad de Chile (2006), MA Architectural History UCL (2010) and PhD Architectural Association School of Architecture (2017). Since 2020 she has been Assistant Professor at the Department of Architecture, Facultad de Arquitectura y Urbanismo, Universidad de Chile, where she directed the Master in Architecture between 2020 and 2024. She recently obtained public funding to lead research on experimental architecture techniques from the 1960s in Chile and abroad.

**Haylee Derrickson** is based in University College Dublin's School of Architecture where they completed a Bachelor of Architectural Science. They are a final year student in the Master of Architecture programme. Their research interests include the design and production of social housing, the adaptive reuse of the built environment, and interdisciplinary practices of spatial justice.

**Alborz Dianat** is an architectural historian at University College Dublin and a postdoctoral researcher on the project, 'Expanding Agency: Women, Race, and the Global Dissemination of Modern Architecture'. Holding a PhD in Architectural History from the University of Edinburgh, Dianat is the author of *Walter Gropius in Britain: Emigration and Collaborations* (Routledge, 2025), and Editor-in-Chief of *Architectural History*, the journal of the Society of Architectural Historians of Great Britain.

**Damla Göre** is an architect and researcher examining the cultural histories of interiors in the Eastern Mediterranean, with a focus on craft and design. She earned her PhD at the Institute for the History and Theory of Architecture (gta) at ETH Zürich in 2025. Her work is positioned at the intersection of material culture, gender studies, and architectural history and has been featured in various journals and edited volumes. Damla is also part of the managerial team of Manazir, a platform connecting art, architecture, and visual culture across the Middle East and North Africa.

**Mary Anne Hunting** is an architectural historian with a PhD from the City University of the New York (CUNY) Graduate Center (2007); an MA in the history of decorative arts from the Copper-Hewitt, Smithsonian Design Museum and Parsons School of Design (1989); and a BA from Vanderbilt University (1980). She is the author of *Edward Durell Stone: Modernism's Populist Architect* (W.W. Norton, 2013) and with Kevin D. Murphy of *Women Architects at Work: Making American Modernism* (Princeton University Press, 2025). She also is a co-contributor to *The Routledge Companion to Women in Architecture* (2021), among other projects.

**Kathleen James-Chakraborty** is Professor of Art History at University College Dublin. She holds a European Research Council Advanced Grant for the project 'Expanding Agency: Women, Race, and the Global Dissemination of Modern Architecture'. Her most recent book, co-authored with Katherine Kuenzli and Bryan Clark Green is *The Belgian Friendship Building: From the New York World's Fair to a Virginia HBCU* (University of Virginia Press, 2025). She was previously the Vincent Scully Visiting Professor of Architectural History at the Yale School of Architecture, and is the recipient of the 2018 Gold Medal in the Humanities from the Royal Irish Academy.

**Kevin D. Murphy** is Andrew W. Mellon Chair in the Humanities and Professor and Chair of the Department of History of Art and Architecture at Vanderbilt University. He is the author, with Mary Anne Hunting, of *Women Architects at Work: Making American Modernism* (Princeton University Press, 2025).

**Andrew Murray** is a Postdoctoral Research Fellow in Architectural History at the Australian Centre for Architectural History, Urban and Cultural Heritage (ACAHUCH) at the University of Melbourne. His research interests include Australian architectural history, and the history of the profession as it developed in the 19th century.

**Alexandra Quantrill** is a historian of architecture and the environment. Her scholarship examines how technology, aesthetics, energy, and political economy converge the making of the built world. Her research on electrification, feminism, modern housing, and infrastructure was awarded fellowships from the American Council of Learned Societies, MacDowell, and the Paul Mellon Centre for Studies in British Art. Her publications in *Architectural Theory Review, Grey Room*, and the *Journal for the Society of Architectural Historians* concerned techniques of environmental management, energy economy, and aesthetics. She holds a PhD in Architecture History and Theory from Columbia University and an MArch from Princeton.

**Sini Rinne-Kanto** is a Paris-based curator and researcher, and is currently pursuing a PhD at Paris 8 University. Her PhD focuses on the history of post-war Finnish design in the context of the Cold War, and her wider research interests include domesticity, collective memories, and the socio-cultural histories of the material world. She has curated several exhibitions in France and internationally that test the boundaries of design and contemporary art, most recently *Surprise Guest* at the Fiskars Village Art & Design Biennale (2024) and *Nordic Noir* at the SIC gallery (Helsinki, 2025).

**Ellen Rowley**, an architectural and cultural historian specialising in Ireland's twentieth-century built environment, is University College Dublin's Lecturer in Modern Irish Architecture. Based in the UCD School of Architecture, Planning and Environmental Policy, Ellen teaches architectural humanities. Her research interests range from obsolescence and everyday architecture, to housing and Catholic patronage, demolition and questions of architectural value. She has published widely and collaborated in various media, such as her monograph *Housing, Architecture and the Edge Condition* (Routledge, 2018); co-editor of the architecture volume of *Art and Architecture of Ireland* (five volume series, Yale University Press, 2014) and *Making Dust* (film, dir. Fiona Hallinan, 2023).

**Maryia Rusak** is an architect and architectural historian, working with transnational architectural histories. She is currently a Junior Research Fellow at the Karlsruhe Institute of Technology (KIT). Her recent postdoctoral project at ETH Zurich explored the Nordic architecture of foreign aid in postcolonial Africa, focusing on the pragmatic and economic rationale behind its production. As a researcher, Maryia is particularly interested in the histories of everyday objects, networks of bureaucratic institutions, obscure intricacies of architectural production and, in general, how buildings are made. Her writings appeared in the *Architectural Theory Review* (2022), *The Journal of Architecture* (2024, 2025), *OASE* (2024), and *Footprint* (2025).

**Eunice Seng** is Head of Department and Associate Professor in the Department of Architecture at The University of Hong Kong. She is the founding principal of the architecture and research practice SKEW Collaborative and a founding member of Docomomo Hong Kong. Her research scholarship focuses on the interaction between historical contingency and the built environments in Asia and Southeast Asia. She explores the interdisciplinary intersections, transnational and transregional connections, and agency in relation to architecture, housing, labour, public space, and women and architectural work in postcolonial Asia. She is the author of *Resistant City: Histories, Maps, and the Architecture of Development* (2020).

**Jenna Snow** has twenty-five years of experience in historic preservation, having worked on at least 150 projects, from National Register nominations to large-scale surveys to adaptive reuse rehabilitations. She holds a Master in Historic Preservation from Columbia University and a BA in Fine Arts from Brandeis. Before moving into consulting, she worked at the Freedom Trail Foundation in Boston and interned at the New York City Department of Design and Construction. In 2004, she took part in a preservation exchange in Transylvania through the International Council on Monuments and Sites, gaining hands-on experience with international conservation efforts.

**Andrea Thabet** is a historian, public speaker, and historic preservation consultant specialising in Los Angeles, urban, and public history. She is currently on the Humanities Faculty at the Colburn School, Conservatory of Music in Los Angeles where she teaches courses on United States history. Dr. Thabet holds an MA and a PhD in US History from the University of California, Santa Barbara. She is an on-camera expert for several programs on the History Channel and has published in both academic and popular journals. She is currently completing a book manuscript on the intersection of cultural institution building and urban renewal in Los Angeles after World War II.

**E. James West** is a Lecturer in Arts and Sciences at University College London. His research interests focus on African American Urban History and Black Print and Visual Culture. He is the author of four books, including the multi-award winning *A House for the Struggle: The Black Press and the Built Environment in Chicago* (Illinois, 2022).

# Index

British Library Cataloguing-in-Publication Data
A catalogue record for this book is available from the British Library

ISBN 978-1-910350-41-6

Distributed outside the United States and Canada by Thames & Hudson Ltd, London

Distributed in the United States and Canada by Harry N. Abrams, Inc., New York

**Royal Academy Publications**
Beatrice Gullström
Alison Hissey
Carola Krueger
Peter Sawbridge
Nick Tite

Design: Myfanwy Vernon-Hunt
Digital imaging consultant and archive coordinator: Roz Woodward
Colour origination: DawkinsColour

Printed in Italy by Graphicom

Illustrations
On the cover: *Axons III*, 2002–04 (detail).
Acrylic collage on canvas, 168 x 340 cm

Page 2: Anne-Katrin Purkiss,
*Anthony Whishaw RA*, 2012.
Silver gelatin print, 27.2 x 23.4 cm

Pages 4–5: *Axons I*, 2002 (detail).
Acrylic on canvas, 168 x 305 cm

Page 154: Edward Woodman,
*Anthony Whishaw in His Acme Studio at Robinson Road (E2)*, 1983. Acme Archive

Page 160: *In Search of Nectar*, 2007–15 (detail).
Acrylic collage on canvas, 172 x 208 cm

**Artist's Acknowledgements**
I would very much like to thank the following for their generous donations in support of the book: Dr Jean Arundale, Sidney and Ruth Lapidus, David and Claire Millar, Dr Tara Naidoo and Colin Whishaw.

I am extremely grateful to all those involved in the production of the book, especially Richard Davey for the effort and research he has put into interpreting my work in his most excellent text, and Myfanwy Vernon-Hunt for her beautiful layout design. I am very grateful to Beatrice Gullström, Alison Hissey, Carola Krueger, Peter Sawbridge and Nick Tite of Royal Academy Publications for their commitment and professionalism. Particular thanks are also due to Roz Woodward for her invaluable work coordinating images, and to my daughter Zoë Whishaw for her help throughout the whole project.

*Anthony Whishaw*

# Contents

# 1
# A Salon hang

Every April since his election to the Royal Academy in 1980 Anthony Whishaw has stood in his studio, surrounded by his paintings, and finalised his selection of the works he will be submitting for the year's Summer Exhibition. April 2015 was no different. In November 2014 Whishaw had already decided on *Come Dance with Me* (2013–15; no. 1), a three-metre-long canvas he had been working on since 2013. Now, with just a month to go before the submission deadline, he had to decide on the others. With every Royal Academician allowed to submit up to six pieces he could have entered another five, but in the end he selected just three more.

The four paintings Whishaw chose challenged the modernist narrative of linear progression, in which artists focus on one defined series of work at a time, and in which one idea flows neatly into the next, always looking forward rather than back. Whishaw doesn't work in this way. The walls of his Kensington studio are covered with paintings that use a variety of visual languages and explore a range of subjects. Paintings of trees and Mediterranean seascapes, abstract colour fields and chiaroscuro still-lifes jostle for attention with no sense of hierarchy or obvious evolution. Whishaw started some of the paintings here thirty years ago, yet he is still adding to and altering them. On their reverse can be seen crossed-out dates that record a lifetime of continued reflection in which nothing is finished until it actually leaves the studio and is no longer in his possession.

The Royal Academy's Summer Exhibition also challenges the modernist narrative by offering a visual miscellany of paintings, prints and photographs that vie for the viewer's attention, with abstract works hung next to more traditional figurative works, still-lifes next to portraits, landscapes next to architectural drawings, just as in Whishaw's studio. In 2015 Whishaw's *Come Dance with Me* was hung high on the south wall of the largest gallery surrounded by the work of his fellow Royal Academicians. This large, abstract painting is a celebration of line and

1
**Come Dance with Me**, 2013–15
Acrylic collage on canvas, 178 x 305 cm

colour, its ribbons of pink, red, turquoise and blue weaving sinuous patterns around the picture surface to suggest a series of joyful, dancing rhythms. Nearby was *St Paul's Multiview II* (2009–10; no. 2), a painting that combines elements of cubism and abstraction, collage, realism and topographical architectural drawing. The composition's fractured space sends the viewer's gaze ricocheting around multiple viewpoints, sometimes sliding off steeply angled geometric planes of colour, sometimes being drawn into distant views of Wren's iconic dome.

Whishaw's two other paintings hung amid the dense grouping of small works in another gallery. Like his depiction of St Paul's, *Flying Above II* (2011–15; no. 4) had an architectural focus. As we look down on the rooftops of a Spanish hilltop *pueblo*, the towers of a church rise out of a blue-and-green mist, with roofs and chimneys tumbling around them in a cubist cascade of multiple viewpoints. Some of these architectural features are painted with a hard-edged clarity while others are left as mere suggestions, half-glimpsed through the fog. *Mirrored Flowers* (1998–2005; no. 5) employs multiple viewpoints too, but that is where the visual similarity ends. Using elements of both abstraction and figuration to create a fantastical Escher-like composition, the work contains conventional landscape elements, with hints of sea and sky, fields and fences, flowers and stars. Yet it is also a fantasy, with two horizon lines, multiple perspectives, and two dark curving lines that evoke the mirror of the title, pulling the viewer, Alice-like, through the surface into a tilting, twisting pictorial space that is at once logical and incoherent.

For those wanting to pigeonhole artists into schools or '-isms', Whishaw's eclecticism can be frustrating. His paintings defy classification. Despite being a

2
**St Paul's Multiview II**, 2009–10
Acrylic collage on canvas, 83 x 220 cm
Private collection

3
**St Paul's Multiview I**, 2009–10
Acrylic collage on board, 38 x 37 cm
Private collection

Royal Academician, and exhibiting widely in group shows with other major British artists, he has never been one to follow trends, or to align himself with a particular stylistic group. He resists art-historical categorisation or contextualisation, pursuing his own unique path and commitment to his materials. One moment he is exploring cubist constructions of space, the next, *trompe-l'œil* playfulness. His use of photocopies and collage, and his application of plastic cups, plastic flies and other objects to his picture surfaces, suggest that he is someone with contemporary concerns and an interest in experimentation. And yet his subjects are often traditional or come from his everyday experience, focusing on architectural details and picturesque scenes reminiscent of the nineteenth or early twentieth centuries. His disregard for stylistic boundaries and subject hierarchies has all the hallmarks of postmodernism, and yet Whishaw's art is without the knowingness and parody of much contemporary work.

The four pieces Whishaw submitted to the Summer Exhibition in 2015 had so little in common in terms of style or content that they could easily have been mistaken for the work of four different artists. But it is this very commitment to diversity rather than uniformity, and a refusal to be defined and restricted by labels, that unites Whishaw's prolific output. Even in his eighties he still wants to explore the boundaries of paint, and to push its ability to inspire, delight, evoke memories, shock and excite, as he has always done – not by focusing in and narrowing down his work into an identifiable visual signature, but by constantly trying new things, hoping to be surprised and intrigued by what might emerge.

4
**Flying Above II**, 2011–15
Acrylic collage on canvas, 91 x 91 cm
Private collection

5
**Mirrored Flowers**, 1998–2005
Acrylic collage on canvas, 122 x 107 cm

# 2
# From Brazil to Spain

In 1939, just months before the outbreak of the Second World War, Anthony Whishaw found himself on a ship crossing the Atlantic. He was nine years old, and travelling with his mother to begin a new life at a preparatory school in England.

Although he had been born in London in 1930, Whishaw had spent the early years of his life in Brazil, where his father was working. But with war looming, his mother wanted to return home to care for her elderly parents who were living at Worthing. Whishaw remembers almost nothing of his childhood in Brazil, and apart from the ritual of 'Crossing the Line', when the ship passed over the Equator, he recalls little of that long sea voyage to England.

When he arrived at Brunswick School, Whishaw had had no previous formal education. He found himself a long way behind other boys in his year, although this didn't worry him. Only weeks after he started, Germany invaded Poland and war was declared. The school, outside Haywards Heath in Sussex, found itself in the path of the German bombing raids and was soon evacuated to Michaelstow, a small village on Bodmin Moor in Cornwall.

Safe in the depths of the countryside, far from London and the front line of the Home Counties, Whishaw found that the war largely passed him by. He remembers swimming in a small pond that seemed huge to a young boy's eyes; racing caterpillars on pieces of slate; and watching with trepidation as a dwarf who lived next door to

6
**Seascape with Boats Diptych**, 2002–07
Acrylic on canvas, 35 x 35 cm
Private collection

the school slaughtered and butchered pigs, and teased the pupils with the sight of his missing thumb tip, which he kept in a matchbox.

At fourteen, Whishaw won a place at Tonbridge School in Kent. After the rural seclusion of Brunswick, Whishaw embraced the new opportunities it offered with enthusiasm. He enjoyed geography and maths, found Latin less interesting, and was a keen sportsman, playing rugby and squash. Painting and drawing, however, became his overriding passion.

Where this interest in art came from, Whishaw doesn't know. Other members of his family were not really interested in art, although he remembers his father drawing geysers that turned into strange monsters. Whishaw recalls making action drawings using an old film spool and rolls of paper while at Brunswick, but it was at Tonbridge, under the guidance of an inspiring art teacher, Hervey Adams, that he really discovered his love of drawing and painting.

During his last two years at the school, Whishaw was one of only three pupils studying art. Painting was something he could do that was distinctive and different, and it provided him with a place of escape in the hurly burly of boarding-school life, where solitude is at a premium. The time he spent drawing in his study, away from the other boys, was precious. He recalls painting imaginary worlds – Stone Age landscapes filled with hunters chasing animals. He also started a drawing correspondence course, each month sending an anonymous critic observational drawings of everyday objects, and eagerly awaiting the response.

At eighteen, with the help of a Judd award from his school, he moved to London and began to study at Chelsea School of Art. After the very traditional environment of Tonbridge, Chelsea came as a culture shock. Suddenly he was part of a large group of people who were all passionate about art and its possibilities. Art was no longer an academic subject, to be practised in the privacy of his study, but a way of experiencing and understanding the world. Everything Whishaw had previously known about painting was challenged. Encouraged by his teachers, Ceri Richards and Prunella Clough, he began to expand his horizons and become more adventurous. They showed him what it was to be an artist: taught him to take risks, to look at things rather than invent them, to feel rather than copy.

Just as important was Whishaw's experience of visiting London's galleries and exhibitions. The art coming from Paris proved a particular revelation. Instead of the 'illustrational' and 'uninspiring' work happening in Britain at the time, he found a vision of what painting could be. Among the work of British artists, only Graham Sutherland's invented, thorny landscapes and Francis Bacon's screaming and distorted figures seemed to be doing anything so authentic and risky.

In the work of artists such as Pablo Picasso and Georges Braque, Whishaw saw a new and dynamic way of treating the human figure and manipulating pictorial space. Here was the emotional directness that he was looking for, the encouragement to experiment and express his feelings. In cubism he found a way to construct space and portray objects so that they appeared at once real and abstract. Picasso's use of tortured bodies and angular, distorted features in *Guernica* and *Weeping Woman* (both 1937) showed Whishaw a way of communicating an emotional reality rather than a mere likeness.

As well as the work of Parisian artists, Whishaw discovered paintings by the Belgian surrealist René Magritte. Although he never adopted an overtly surrealist style in his own works, hints of Magritte can be seen in Whishaw's quirky

7
**Horse Head**, 1956
Oil on canvas, 96 x 83 cm

Fig. 1
Constant Permeke
**The Daily Bread**, 1950
Oil on canvas, 148.5 x 175 cm
Mu.ZEE Oostende

playfulness, visual humour and juxtaposition of unexpected objects to create enigmatic compositions: balls bounce out of the canvas and across the wall, staircases disappear into mid-air, and fake spiders lie in wait for fake flies.

A more obvious influence on Whishaw was another Belgian artist, Constant Permeke. Now largely forgotten in Britain, Permeke is often considered Belgium's leading expressionist painter. He spent most of his life at Ostend, painting everyday objects and ordinary people using a grammar of thick, bold brush strokes, angular forms and a dark palette. Whishaw discovered Permeke's work at an exhibition in London, and was immediately attracted by his ability to transform ordinary situations into serious subject-matter (fig. 1). Whishaw's paintings *Two Men Eating* (1958; no. 9) and *Two Men Drilling* (1958; no. 10) show a clear debt to Permeke, as do other images of seated and sleeping figures he made during the 1950s and early 1960s.

In the summer before his final year at Chelsea, Whishaw and six friends went on holiday to Ibiza, a fortnight that began his lifelong passion for Spain. In the early 1950s Spain was overshadowed by a brutal civil war and ruled by the authoritarian military government of General Franco. Immortalised by Ernest Hemingway, Laurie Lee and George Orwell, life in Spain still felt raw and visceral. It was a place of dust, heat and poverty in which bullfights and religious spectacles were central parts of everyday life.

Having grown up in South America, Whishaw immediately felt at home in Ibiza's Spanish culture. If Paris had shown him how to paint reality, Spain offered him a reality he felt compelled to paint. During this holiday he went to his first bullfight, and discovered for himself the intense ritual that had inspired Hemingway's *Death in the Afternoon* (1932): man and beast engaged in a drama that celebrated both courage and fear, life and death.

8
**Last Supper**, 1959
Oil on board, 122 x 488 cm
Christchurch, Kensington

9
**Two Men Eating**, 1958
Oil on board, 122 x 183 cm
Private collection

10
**Two Men Drilling**, 1958
Oil on board, 180 x 122 cm
The Herbert Museum and Art Gallery, Coventry

Fig. 2
Pablo Picasso
**Guernica**, 1937
Oil on canvas, 350 x 782 cm
Museo Nacional Centro de Arte
Reina Sofia, Madrid

11
**Bullfight with Falling Picador**, 1951–52
Oil on canvas, 122 x 137 cm

On his return to England, Whishaw began work on *Bullfight with Falling Picador* (1951–52; no. 11). The foreground of this large oil painting is dominated by the bull, whose massive, muscled presence is seen from behind. Sticking out of its shoulders is the unseated picador's lance. As the bull lunges forward, the picador's terrified horse rears and we are confronted by its gaping mouth, flared nostrils and flying mane – details that, with the body of the fallen picador, Whishaw had clearly borrowed from Picasso's *Guernica* (1937; fig. 2). To emphasise the primeval energy of this life-and-death struggle, Whishaw looked to the geometric proto-cubism of Paul Cézanne. He deconstructed his subjects' bodies, and turned them into angular, multifaceted forms that appear to have been chiselled out of stone. The figures of the picador, bull and horse are placed against an abstract blue background, which bathes them in a strong light so that their multiple surfaces create a cubist chiaroscuro of intense highlights and deep shadows, all reinforcing the drama and physicality of the scene.

At the end of his four years at Chelsea, Whishaw won a place at the Royal College of Art, where his contemporaries included Bridget Riley and Frank Auerbach. But he found a very different environment there. His tutors, John Minton and Carel Weight, exemplified the style of British painting that Whishaw had rejected when he first moved to London. Instead of encouraging him to take risks, they suggested he needed to go away and learn how to draw. Reacting against this comment, he did just that, working in his studio off campus and going in only for tutorials and life classes.

Spain and Spanish artists became Whishaw's new tutors. He made a number of further visits, including one with his future wife, Jean Gibson, a sculptor and fellow student, whom he had met at the Royal College. They took the ferry to Vigo on the northwest coast, travelled around a number of regions and cities, including Galicia and Seville, and ended up in Madrid, where they visited the Prado. It was there that Whishaw first saw Goya's 'Black Paintings' (fig. 3). These haunting images, dating from 1819 and 1823, were private works never intended for public viewing, in which Goya explored dark and frequently difficult themes, including murder, witchcraft and cannibalism. Designed specifically for his house in Madrid, many of the paintings have a long, narrow format that turns their compositions into a theatrical spectacle. Frequently set in nocturnal semi-obscurity, they are filled with processions of people whose closely

Fig. 3
Francisco de Goya y Lucientes
**The San Isidro Pilgrimage**, 1820–23
Mixed method on mural transferred to canvas, 138.5 x 436 cm
Museo Nacional del Prado, Madrid.
Inv.P00760

12
**Corrida**, 1955–56
Oil on canvas, 100 x 300 cm
Tate London

packed faces offer character studies of ugliness, fear, ecstasy, horror and evil.

Goya's fourteen 'Black Paintings' were a revelation to Whishaw, showing him both the ugliness to be found in beauty and the beauty to be found in ugliness. His work soon began to reflect Goya's. He adopted the Spanish artist's limited, earthy palette and his unflinching portrayal of human emotions and the drama of everyday life. One of the first and most significant of his Goyaesque paintings was *Corrida* (1955–56; no. 12), another bullfighting scene, but this time focused on the crowd of spectators rather than the activity in the arena.

Cubism had taught Whishaw how to deconstruct and reconfigure solid forms, while Permeke had shown him how to give grandeur to the ordinary. From Goya, he learnt how to use the composition and structure of his paintings for dramatic effect, and that crowds could be manipulated to generate emotional intensity. His adoption of the long, narrow landscape format of the 'Black Paintings' gave *Corrida* a claustrophobic atmosphere, squeezing the narrative action into two horizontal bands that, while connected, are also distinct. The bottom third of the painting

13
**Bullfight**, 1956–57
Oil on canvas, 122 x 153 cm
Private collection

14
**Flying Above**, 2010–13
Acrylic collage on canvas, 183 x 168 cm
Private collection

is dominated by a riderless and panicked grey horse, whose elongated body creates a wave of energy and movement across and beyond the wooden panelling surrounding the arena.

Mirroring this undulating wave, the spectators occupy the top two thirds of the canvas. They act as a dramatic chorus, reflecting the whole range of human emotions, from boredom and indifference to fear. Although some are clearly watching the bullfight, the majority are not. They turn and chatter to their neighbours, they look up into the sky, they look down, they yawn, they peer over each other's shoulders, eavesdropping on conversations. The variety of these positions and postures brings both a sense of physical and emotional reality to the visual drama, and a three-dimensional plasticity to the work's composition. The horse's body seems flat and frieze-like in comparison.

Goya often places his subjects on the edge of his compositions rather than at their centres, and this results in a partial view and truncated bodies. The viewer is placed *in media res*, forced to participate in the action rather than to watch from a detached distance. The effect of this is sometimes to make his paintings feel more like impromptu snapshots than complete narratives. In *Corrida* Whishaw uses the partial glimpse to brilliant effect. He paints just the upper body of the riderless grey horse, its extended form caught in a moment of headlong flight. There is fear in its eyes and its ears are pinned back flat to its head, but the source of danger is omitted. By relying on facial expression alone, a technique often used in horror films, Whishaw heightens the painting's emotional intensity, transforming it from an illustration into a visual melodrama. *Corrida*'s narrow CinemaScope format sucks the viewer in, and also occupies the field of peripheral vision so that nothing seems to exist beyond this momentary drama.

The following year Whishaw painted *Bullfight* (1956–57; no. 13). The matador and the bull are placed at the edge of the canvas; squashed into the bottom left-hand corner so that their truncated bodies are fused together into a dance of death from which they cannot escape, their white forms overwhelmed by a sickly yellow background that evokes the blood-soaked sand of the arena. The matador's back is arched over the bull's body, his head lying at an impossible angle on his shoulders, while his facial features are distorted into a swirling vortex of agony around a screaming mouth, which finds an echo in the gaping mouth of the bull. Although the composition of *Bullfight* continues to reflect some of Goya's influence, the change in emotional drama from fear to terror owes more to Francis Bacon and his 'Screaming Popes' than Goya.

When Whishaw left the RCA in 1955 he was awarded a Royal College of Art Travel Scholarship, an Abbey Minor Travelling Scholarship and a scholarship from the Spanish Government. With no restriction on where he could travel, inevitably he went to Spain. He lived there, on and off, for the next two years, spending time in Barcelona, Madrid, Ibiza and Andalusia, particularly visiting the area around Cádiz. He travelled along dusty country roads, coming across small hilltop towns and almost deserted villages, where he sat at bars in squares studying the scenery and buildings and watching the world go by. He immersed himself in Spanish culture, living in an old *bodega* and learning to take a siesta in the heat of the afternoon. He went to bullfights and visited museums, discovering the paintings of Velázquez and Zurbarán as well as more Goyas. He also had his first solo exhibition in Spain, at Madrid's Librería Abril, in 1956.

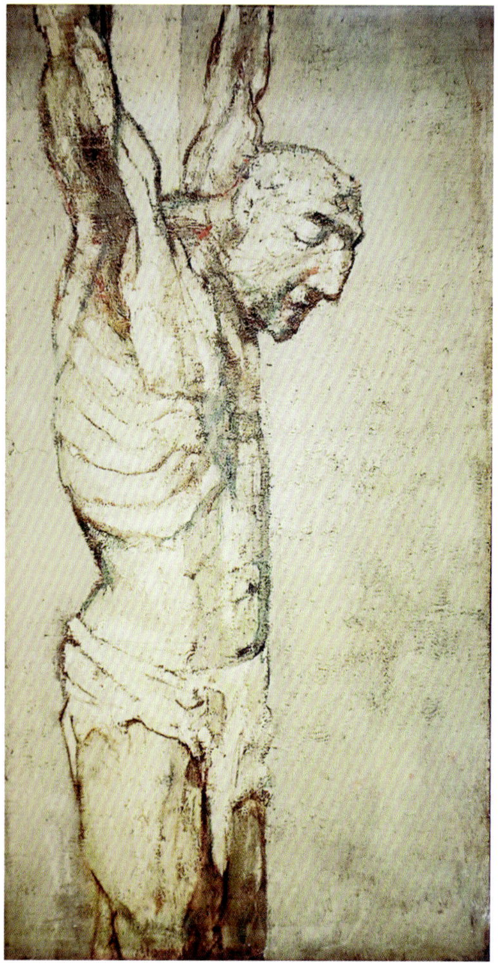

15
**The Crucifixion**, 1956
Oil on board, 344 x 122 cm
Christchurch, Kensington

16
**Still-life with Fish**, 1953
Oil on canvas, 92 x 71 cm

17
**Two Seated Figures**, 1961
Oil on canvas, 167 x 178 cm

18
**Study of an Old Man**, 1955
Oil on canvas, 92 x 67 cm

Like many of the paintings and drawings Whishaw had made since Chelsea, those exhibited at the Librería Abril, and those painted later in England, unashamedly tackled the topic of death and dying. The subjects of his domestic scenes and figure studies were old men and women, his still-lifes were of skulls and dead fish, and he painted bullfights and crucifixions in vivid detail. These dramatic and serious themes expressed in gritty, intense subjects might seem a strange choice for a young man, but they reflect the profound influence Spain had, and continues to have, on his outlook and artistic sensibilities. What Whishaw encountered in Spain, unlike in England, was an attitude to death that didn't hide and sanitise it, but made it a part of everyday life. As his later paintings *Matadero Municipal* and *Matadero Municipal Triptych* (nos 19 and 20) remind us, bars often proudly hang bulls' heads and skulls on their walls, while churches display the bones of saints in open reliquaries and celebrate acts of martyrdom in graphically painted religious statues.

And yet, while the three major bullfighting paintings – *Bullfight with Falling Picador*, *Corrida* and *Bullfight* – clearly reflect Whishaw's concern with the fragile boundary between life and death, they also demonstrate the impact of his distinctively experimental approach, which borrowed widely, and focused as much on the material and expressive possibilities of paint as on the subject-matter.

19
**Matadero Municipal Triptych**, 1983–93
Acrylic collage on canvas, 152 x 416 cm

20
**Matadero Municipal**, 1983–96
Acrylic collage on canvas, 152 x 366 cm

These different visual approaches enabled him to provide a more panoramic study of the rituals and spectacle of the bullring, with cubism allowing Whishaw to depict the bullfight as a moment of intense physicality, Goya turning it into a dramatic spectacle, and Bacon making it a scene of horror and fear.

Whishaw returned to England in 1956. He and Jean were married in 1957 and bought a slightly run-down studio in Kensington that had at one time been the Animal Studio of London, a location for artists to study and draw live animals. This became both their home and workplace. In order to earn a living Whishaw began to teach part-time at Chelsea and a few years later at St Martin's School of Art. But his early, intense experience of Spain, a country he continued to visit annually for many years, never left him. Distant vistas, solitary figures, windows and doorways, colour, light and hilltop towns recur throughout his paintings. It can be found in his references to Spanish paintings, and it is there in the drama, spectacle and emotional intensity of his works; qualities he had first experienced in Spain's *plazas*, fiestas and festivals.

21
**Pradella**, 1991–92
Acrylic collage on canvas,
171 x 183 cm
Ladbrokes

22
**Autumn Burn**, 1981
Acrylic collage on canvas,
122 x 213 cm
Ferens Art Gallery, Hull

# 3
# Moving towards abstraction

Towards the end of the 1960s, approaching his fortieth birthday, Whishaw experienced a crisis of confidence. Looking back, he sees the period from the late 1960s to the mid-1970s as his 'wilderness years', a time of soul-searching and rediscovery during which he was asking himself the same questions he asked of his students: what are you doing and why are you doing it? Not only did he doubt his use of oil paint, but he found himself reassessing his intentions, his influences and his role as an artist.

One of the major factors that contributed to this crisis was the emergence of abstract expressionism. When Whishaw returned from Spain at the end of the 1950s he found the London art world in a state of upheaval and excitement. Wherever he went people seemed to be discussing the work of American artists – Jackson Pollock, Clyfford Still, Willem de Kooning and Mark Rothko. In an austere Britain still recovering from the Second World War these artists offered something radically different. Their large, vibrant canvases appeared confident and modern when compared to those of their British and European counterparts. They looked to a future unencumbered by the past.

Whishaw remembers being profoundly challenged by these works. He had always known where he stood in debates about painting: he was a figurative artist, influenced by Permeke, cubism and Goya, and trained in the discipline of the life class. His subject-matter was drawn from his experience and based in real life, focused on figures and objects whose physicality was emphasised by bold brush strokes and massive, solid forms. He preferred the energy and emotion of expressionism such as Permeke's to the formal purity of abstraction. But the abstraction he now encountered in Pollock's dripped canvases and Rothko's empty colour-fields was very different. Here were abstract paintings full of visual drama and emotional intensity, which teased the viewer and played with reality.

23
**The Twist**, 1960
Ink on paper, 12 x 22.5 cm

24
**Seated Woman**, 1993–94
Mixed media on paper, 31.4 x 43.6 cm
The Royal Collection Trust

Whishaw felt he needed to respond to the questions posed by this disparate group of painters. He did so, first, in a series of ink drawings inspired by the exaggerated movements and unnatural shapes of dancers. One of the earliest was *The Twist* (1960; no. 23), a dynamic black-and-white drawing inspired by the dance craze that accompanied Chubby Checker's 1960 hit of the same name. The angular silhouettes and multiple facial profiles of the drawing's two figures reflected Picasso and the figurative tradition, but the twisting, rotating shapes and energetic lines were something new. Instead of depicting solid figures in a defined space, Whishaw sought the spatial buzz of the abstract expressionists. *The Twist* is dominated by large areas of black ink vying for supremacy with the white of the paper. One moment the black is a solid substance, the next a void. Sometimes the white figures come to the front, standing out as three-dimensional forms; sometimes they fall away, no longer human, but a distant, indefinable space glimpsed through broad fissures in the black. The rapidly drawn lines both carve out the figures' features and dance freely across the areas of white. *The Twist* reveals the future. It is a work rooted in reality, yet fizzing with abstract energy, as Whishaw plays with spatial ambiguities, pulling the viewer into an uncertain space where the distinction between front and back, subject and ground, is no longer obvious. Solidity has been replaced by lightness and energy.

Over the next few years more and more figures joined these dances, until the human form started to dissolve and the dancing figures became dancing shapes. Gradually, the facial and bodily features that are still clearly visible in *The Twist* disappeared, to be replaced by lines and shapes that evoke mere memories of the body in movement: the curve of a back, the shape of an arm, the angle of a leg. Rounded figures became abstract blocks of black and white that dipped, twisted and turned, circled and gyrated across the picture surface. One moment black seemed to take the lead, then white. The individual became lost in a pattern

25
**Dancers**, 1962–63
Watercolour and ink on paper,
29 x 56 cm
Private collection

26
**Dancers**, 1963
Oil on board, 92 x 122 cm
Private collection

of interlocking shapes, a whirling vortex of interwoven movement reminiscent of Pollock's tangled undergrowth of dribbled lines.

Although Whishaw had always been attracted by the human figure as a subject, whether on its own or as part of a wider narrative, he had avoided landscapes, not wanting to engage with the Romanticism of the British landscape tradition. Yet from his first visit to Ibiza in 1951 he had found himself inspired by the Spanish landscape: the high mountains of the sierras, the fertile valleys covered in olive and orange groves, the dusty landscapes of the south, and the compact hilltop towns

27
**Puerto de Santa Maria**, 1963
Oil on canvas, 76 x 120 cm

28
**Arcos de la Frontera**, 1960
Oil on canvas, 155 x 175 cm

and villages glistening white in the sun. He didn't paint these scenes at the time, but they rapidly became a recurring subject when he returned to England.

The same bold brush strokes and fractured, cubist planes that had given monumentality to bullfighters and old men were now used to portray the hilltop towns and seaside villages Whishaw had seen on his travels. Deposited onto the canvas in a thick build-up of paint were his memories of travelling along winding roads on his Lambretta, glimpsing tiled rooftops and tall church towers across dusty hillsides and fields, with the sea occasionally glinting in the distance. But, as with his dancing figures, the figurative substance of these landscapes soon began to disappear into an abstract haze. When he painted *Arcos de la Frontera* (1960; no. 28), an ancient town near Cádiz, Whishaw reduced the individual buildings to a few roofs and walls, represented with the same strokes of burnt umber, sienna, grey and white that he used for the surrounding fields and hills. With the boundary between town and country dissolved, all that remains is a purely abstract pattern of interlocking and intersecting lines, which when studied more closely falls away into light and space. By the time Whishaw painted *Puerto de Santa Maria* (1963; no. 27), another of the seaside villages near Cádiz he had visited regularly, and in which for six months in the early 1960s he had a studio, the buildings had become engulfed by a maelstrom of white, brown and black brush strokes – a wild, choppy sea of paint that has swept away individual structures. Only a jagged skyline, a distant horizon and the title are left as evidence that what we are looking at was once a village within a landscape.

29
**Blue Road Northwards III**, 1967
Oil on board, 51.5 x 60 cm

30
**Blue Road Northwards II**, 1967
Oil on board, 155.5 x 160 cm

31
**Opened Interior**, 1968
Oil on board, 92 x 168 cm

The dark, earthy colours used to capture these Spanish landscapes reflect the relatively limited palette Whishaw had been using since his time at the RCA. They gave his paintings a sense of rootedness and physicality typical of Northern European art. But in the late 1960s this restrained palette underwent a radical transformation. In *Blue Road Northwards* (1967; nos 29 and 30), instead of dark, dramatic hues, we encounter the light and sun of Spain and the manufactured colours of the modern world. And, rather than thick expressionist brush strokes, we find flat, amorphous areas of colour that fizz with visual ambiguity. Dominating these three canvases is the same motif: a dog-leg of intense sky blue that represents a road winding its way through the landscape towards a distant town. It leads the viewer's gaze into a space so insubstantial and full of light that only a few brightly coloured objects within it remain visible: the scalloped edge of a tiled roof, miniature trees, the corner of a building, the terraced contours of hillsides, tiny snatches of the road as it continues through the landscape. Like graffiti, these small figurative details stand out against the pale background of each work, providing a moment of visual interest to arrest the eye and stop the painting sliding away into a purely decorative surface. Whishaw painted the roads blue because that is how he remembered them – as reflections of the sky, dissolving in a heat haze. But this serpentine blue shape also forms a 'zip' down the centre of the painting. It tears a hole in the fabric of reality and divides the composition in two, allowing the division between sky and land to dissolve, and rendering solid ground unstable. There is no front and back, up and down, figurative and abstract. Instead, these three paintings oscillate between different visual realities, one moment forming a nebulous landscape, the next a loose patchwork of colour.

By the time of *Opened Interior* (1968; no. 31), painted the following year, the obviously representational elements of Whishaw's work have disappeared. Their place has been taken by irregularly shaped, flat planes of solid colour, some large, some small, some hard-edged, some more organic in form, all floating in front of a neutral background. As they process across the canvas, these alternating shades of blue, pink and grey create a visual rhythm that pulls in the eye and animates the surface. For, unlike the abstract expressionists, Whishaw couldn't yet let go of the idea of the 'figure' completely. Still wanting his works to be rooted in the world rather than being self-referential and self-indulgent, to be dramatic rather than decorative, in *Opened Interior* he looked to Goya as much as to de Kooning. Like the spectators thronging the stands in *Corrida*, these slabs of colour twist and turn as if in conversation. As they lead the viewer's eye into the painting, they reveal groups of smaller forms huddled in enclosed spaces that are reminiscent of the diners that once filled domestic interiors as in *Two Men Eating*. The figures may have gone, but an abstracted memory of the world and a sense of dramatic narrative remain.

Whishaw's move towards abstraction might appear to be a result of stylistic developments and his response to abstract expressionism. However, what was happening in his life at the time also had an important role to play in these changes. At the beginning of the 1960s he had participated in a number of marches and demonstrations, but soon he stopped, disturbed by the loss of individual identity he had witnessed. It seemed to him that everyone said the same thing, chanted the same slogans and behaved in identical ways, whatever the cause. This experience is reflected in the disintegrating figures of his oil paintings, which were losing their own individuality to become part of an amorphous whole.

# 4
# Acrylic: new medium, new direction

In January and February 1968, 46 of Whishaw's 'semi-abstract' paintings were exhibited in a one-man show at the Cork Street gallery of Roland, Browse & Delbanco, who had represented him since he left the RCA. But this exhibition was to be his last with them. At the end of that year he decided to leave the gallery, wanting the freedom to experiment, push boundaries and explore different techniques and subjects without the pressure to produce work for collectors who he felt just wanted more of the same. Freed from what he saw to be the restriction of a gallery, developing a new, increasingly abstract visual language, and still wrestling with his existential angst, it was at the end of the 1960s that Whishaw made what was to be the most significant change in his practice: he stopped painting in oils.

For the first twenty years of his career Whishaw had painted with them, and he still loves their unique qualities. But by the late 1960s he was becoming increasingly frustrated by their limitations. Oil paint had allowed him to do many things, from creating dramatic chiaroscuro effects to giving his canvases a sense of depth and physical substance. But he wanted to experiment, to play with ideas and to work on many canvasses at a time. Oil paint's drying time was just too slow for him. He could have added fast-drying agents, but these can make the paint brittle and affect its essential properties. Ink drawings helped him to explore his ideas rapidly, but these were only sketches, and he was unable to replicate the effects of the paint itself. So he turned to the relatively new medium of acrylic. This proved to be a moment of liberation. Acrylic is water-soluble, dries quickly and binds to, and with, most things; it was perfectly matched to his eclectic and experimental approach. This was a paint he could play with. He could try things out and test ideas, using it as both tool and subject.

32
**Espot**, 1971
Acrylic on canvas, 130 x 193 cm

Acrylic's flexibility as a medium permits Whishaw to apply it onto the canvas in thick, opaque brush strokes to mimic the physicality of oil. He has mixed it with other materials to build up sculptural surfaces, and at times he has embedded objects into those surfaces. He has painted directly onto canvas and board without previous preparation, and, because acrylic becomes water-resistant when dry, he has drawn onto the painted surface with other materials, including pastel and charcoal, to create dynamic multimedia works.

Whishaw's first acrylic paintings, however, resembled large watercolours, with thin washes of colour painted directly onto 'raw' canvas. Accustomed to working on a prepared surface, which prevents oil paint from rotting the canvas, Whishaw loved the way acrylic pigment could now impregnate the fibres, softening forms and bringing a new, unforeseen spatial dimension to a work. The paint no longer sat in front of the canvas, but pulled the eye through it, occupying a space both within and behind the picture surface.

*Espot* (1971; no. 32) was one of Whishaw's earliest acrylic paintings, a haze of subtly hued shapes blending into one another to form a multi-layered cloudscape of pinks, turquoise, blues, purples, yellows and reds. The composition, which has no obvious subject, took his paintings in a completely new direction. *Espot* is a quiet and subtle work without the overt drama or focus of Whishaw's earlier oil paintings. The interaction of the different layers of colour creates a different form of visual energy, pulsating and subtly shifting like the surface of a Rothko, generating mysterious depths that absorb the gaze. *Espot* could be seen as the culmination

of Whishaw's engagement with abstract expressionism – a self-contained, abstract painting devoid of obvious figurative references. Yet its source is still deeply rooted in his experience of the world: Espot is a valley in the Catalonian Pyrenees that he had visited on one of his trips to Spain, and now his memories of the place resurfaced in the painting's subtle forms, with their suggestion of mountains, clouds and fields, and in its colours, which reflected the shifting patterns of light moving across that mountainous landscape.

Over the next few years the rugged topography of Pyrenean valleys was to inspire many of Whishaw's works. Despite their ethereal appearance, *Blue Valley* (1973/4; no. 33), *Valley* (1975–76; no. 34) and *Valley Green* (1976; no. 35) are grounded in the landscape, their often indistinct shapes hinting at geological formations, the

33
**Blue Valley**, 1973/4
Acrylic on canvas, 183 x 122 cm

34
**Valley**, 1975–56
Acrylic on canvas, 183 x 183 cm
Private collection

35
**Valley Green**, 1976
Acrylic on canvas, 183 x 213 cm
Government Art Collection

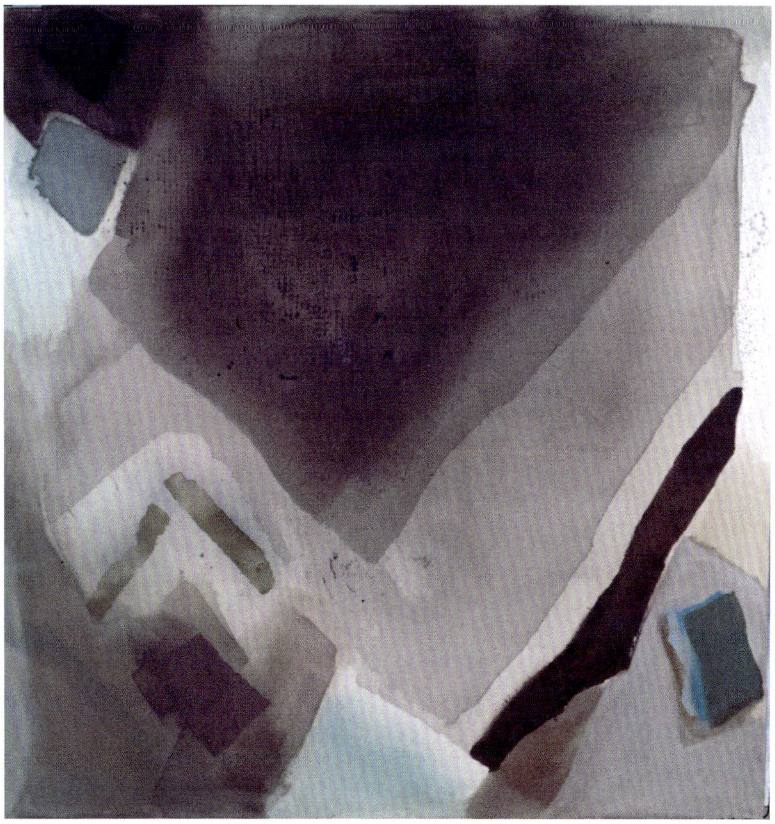

36
**Still Night Sea with Gibraltar in Mind**, 1975–2011
Acrylic on canvas, 229 x 75 cm

weather, fields, valleys and mountains. Yet these are landscapes shrouded in mist, their physical features engulfed in a haze that by turns obscures and reveals them. They tease the eye with glimpses of substance, only for these apparently solid forms to evaporate into clouds of nebulous colour on closer inspection.

*Blue Valley* is a visual crescendo of grey, building in intensity from a spectral light grey through subtle mid-tones to the pulsating deep blue-grey at the centre. The interplay of these muted tones – evoking the misty blues of a mountainous landscape at dusk, or the dark, steel blue of storm clouds standing out against a lowering grey sky – gives the painting its depth and substance. At the centre of *Blue Valley* is a misshapen blue diamond – an area of visual solidity and focus, which appears to hover in front of the picture surface and demand the viewer's attention. But it also establishes a void in the painting's fabric, a portal revealing a space beyond. Like views of distant clouds and mountains, the forms in *Blue Valley* hover between the physical and intangible, between near and far, physical presence and mysterious ambiguity, teasing the eye in the same way as the forms in the *Blue Road* series.

In *Valley* Whishaw uses the playful interaction of complementary colours to suggest optical depth and recession. The pictorial narrative is here provided by a diagonal shaft of sky blue leading up into a cloud of textured purple-pink. Echoing the winding road of earlier oil paintings, this strip of colour leads the viewer's gaze through a 'landscape' of rolling hills, valleys and fields, while forming a deep pool of light in the centre of the canvas.

*Valley Green* was the last and largest of this series of Pyrenean paintings. Combining the crescendo of tonal intensity of *Blue Valley* with the interplay of complementary colours used in *Valley*, *Valley Green* traps the viewer's gaze in interlocking layers of green-black, pale blue-greens, turquoise, yellow-greens and a mist-like off-white. Presented with this beguiling palimpsest of colour, the viewer is pulled in through these successive layers, taken on a journey from light to dark, solid to insubstantial, and back again.

The rectangles, right angles, squares and undefined forms that carry the colours of these first acrylics contribute to the works' spatial narrative. They overlap and intersect each other to suggest layers of visual strata creating a

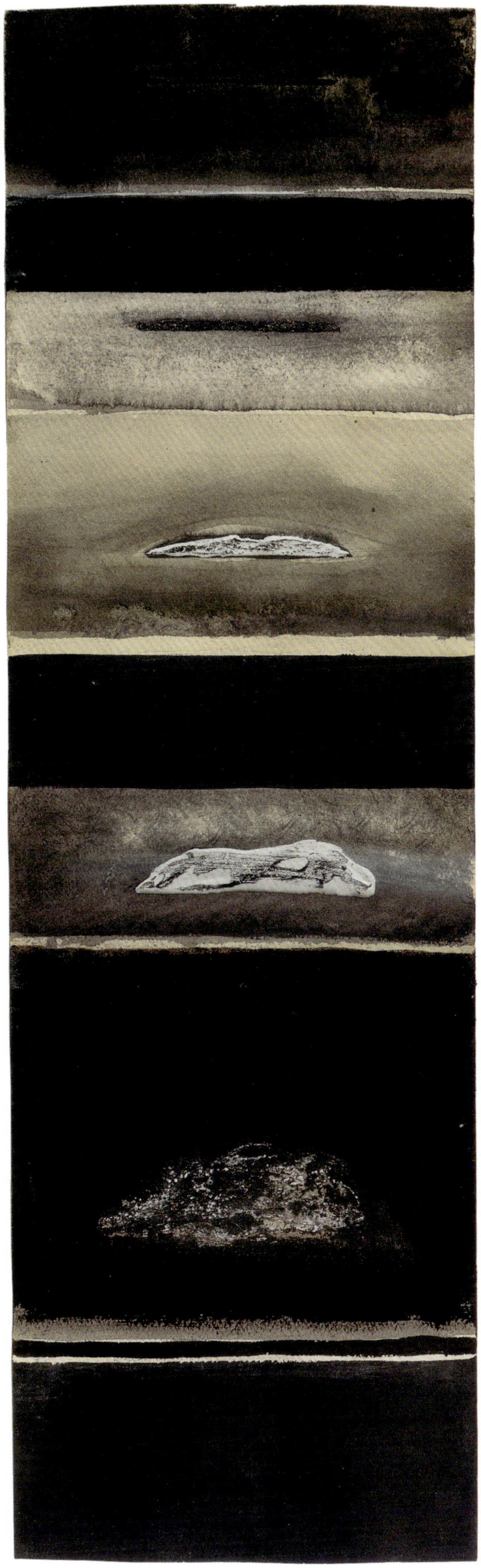

37
**Gibraltar in Mind I**, 1975–76
Mixed media on paper, 71 x 27 cm
(including frame)

38
**Gibraltar in Mind II**, 1978
Mixed media on paper, 71 x 27 cm
(including frame)

39
**Formations I**, 1976–78
Acrylic on canvas, 152 x 51 cm
Private collection

40
**Formations II**, 1976–78
Acrylic on canvas, 152 x 51 cm
Private collection

41
**Formations III**, 1976–78
Acrylic on canvas, 152 x 51 cm
Private collection

42
**Formations IV**, 1976–78
Acrylic on canvas, 152 x 51 cm
Private collection

43
**Formations V**, 1976–78
Acrylic on canvas, 152 x 51 cm
Private collection

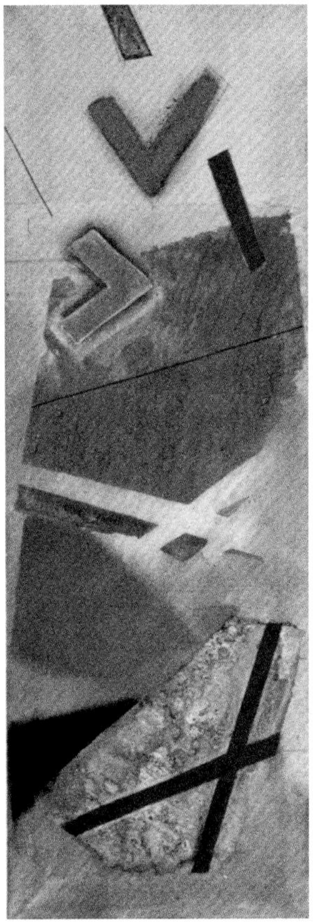

recessional space that constantly pulls the eye in and through the painting. But unlike the three-dimensional forms of *Opened Interior* these colour-shapes appear flat. They offer no three-dimensional or perspectival presence, no sense of solidity, subject, or obvious figurative narrative – only optical recessions of playful colour.

Yet Whishaw has always been a cubist rather than a colourist, more interested in the interaction of forms than in the interplay of colour. However successful his first acrylics might have been as individual works, whatever depth he might have suggested by allowing pigments to soak into the canvas and colours to open up optical spaces, these abstract colour fields ultimately lacked the three-dimensional complexity he sought. They receded from the eye, instead of reaching out and holding the gaze.

In the series of long, narrow *Formations* (1976–78; nos 39–43) that followed these Pyrenean valleys, plasticity returned, however. Geometric shapes cover these canvases, pulling the viewer's gaze into the painting, sending it careening around, across and through the V-shapes, triangles, rectangles and broad, straight lines that lie scattered across each other like a game of 'pick-up sticks' or a geology of shifting tectonic plates. The paintings are full of shadows and highlights, turning flat shapes into three-dimensional forms that thrust themselves into the viewer's space, suggesting objects, figures and solid forms. The picture surface twists and tilts at every turn – a multifaceted, cubist structure that becomes the visual drama and brings the work a sense of narrative and physical presence. We are back among the disintegrating ruins of the Spanish towns Whishaw had painted a decade earlier, picking our way through piles of debris – planks, roofs and wall fragments.

In *Monks Horton* (1976–77; no. 44), *View* (1977), *Garden Early Spring* (1977–78; no. 46) and other landscapes of the late 1970s and early 1980s, Whishaw turned to more local subjects for inspiration: the English countryside in Kent and the North Downs that he visited on family days out with Jean and their daughters Zoë and Phoebe. Pigment-soaked canvases capture the olive and verdant greens of grassy hillsides, the fierce yellow of ripening corn, the warm greys of a winter garden blushed pink with new spring growth, and the rich, ruddy browns and oranges of burnt and burning stubble and ploughed fields. Here is a very English pastoral reverie, based on Whishaw's memories of familiar landscapes.

44
**Monks Horton**, 1976–77
Acrylic on canvas, 178 x 306 cm
The Arts Council

45
**Summer Field**, 1981–82
Acrylic on canvas, 1168 x 457 cm

46
**Garden Early Spring**, 1977–78
Acrylic collage on canvas,
244 x 306 cm

47
**Fire, Wind and Rain**, 1983–84
Acrylic collage on canvas,
168 x 457 cm
Museum of Modern Art, Murcia

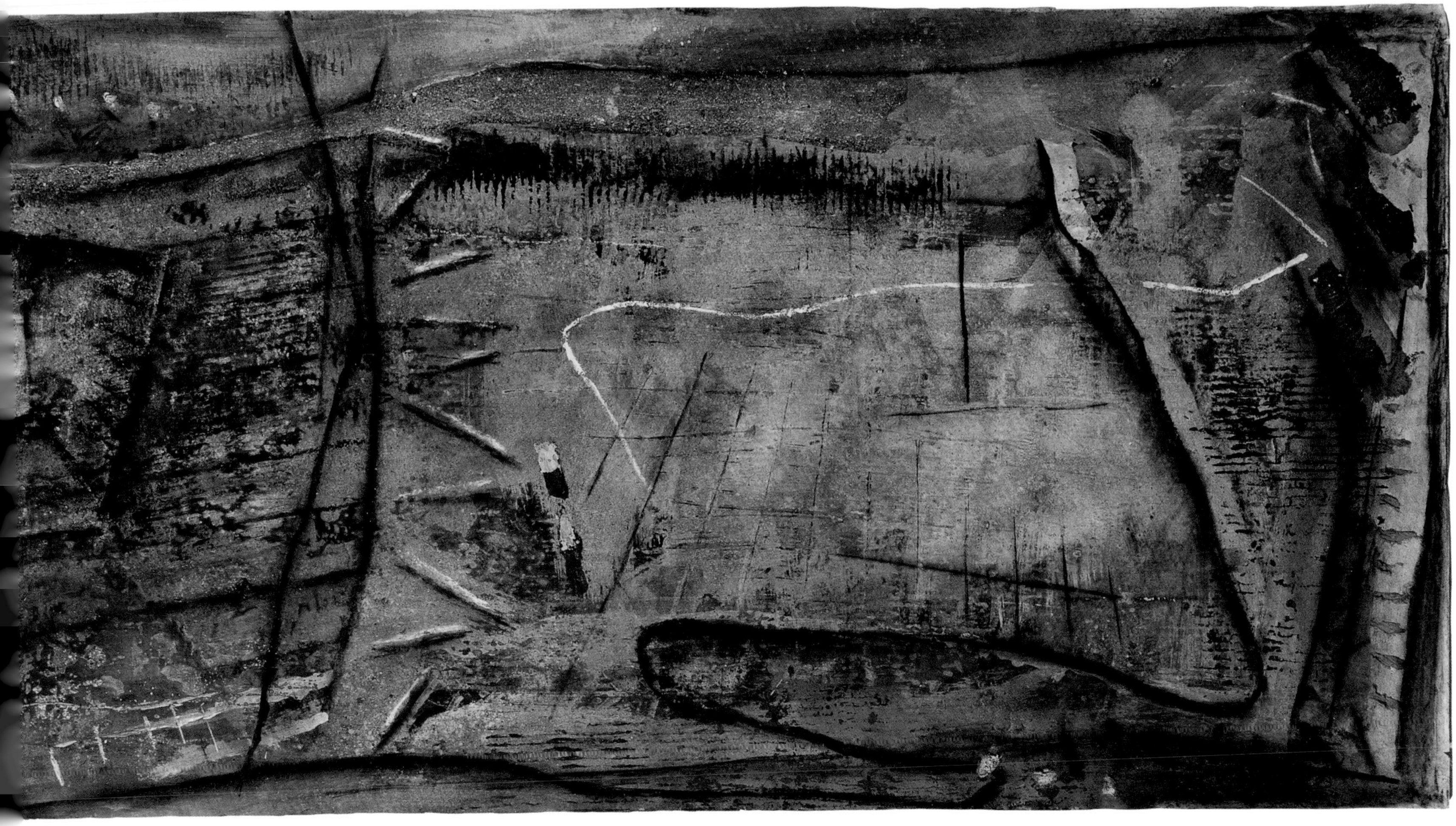

48
**Landscape**, 1983
Mixed media on paper,
80 x 193 cm
Tate, London

But Whishaw wanted his work to capture more than a memory. So he covered these ethereal backgrounds with a calligraphy of lines and shapes that could represent a row of upright fence posts, the curving line of a wall, stalks of waving corn, a stand of trees, the furrowed lines of a ploughed field or a meandering path. These were things he glimpsed out of the corner of his eye as he drove past or walked through the countryside; objects that momentarily brought the landscape into focus like a vivid image emerging from the fog of memory. His cubist sensibility disrupts the rational coherence of perspectival space in favour of the more dynamic and fragmentary space of the glance and sudden view.

However, even these 'solid' forms were not substantial enough for Whishaw. He still wanted to find a way to re-create in acrylic the substance and physical texture of oil paint. The answer, when it came, was simple: he began to draw lines without diluting or mixing the paint, forming a crust of pigment on the picture surface.

As well as creating a dynamic contrast with the thin washes of colour that bled into the canvas, this technique instantly transformed the painting into a tactile, three-dimensional object that reached out into the viewer's space.

When Whishaw painted *Cobbs Hill* (1978; no. 50), a favourite spot for outings, he went further, complementing the thin lines with patches of almost frenzied colour. Filled with swirling dabs of green, ochre and white acrylic, these areas of dramatic visual interest offset the calm offered by the colour wash to break down the painting's spatial coherence. While the thinly applied wash of paint constitutes a portal into infinite space, these areas of impasto detail give us access to the finite space of physical reality, stopping the painting's nebulous background from disappearing into nothingness, and transforming a featureless macrocosm into a microcosm of exquisite detail. In a single glance we see both far-off hillside and a close-up detail so intense that in fact that we can count the individual blades of grass and lumps of soil that cover it.

49
**Garden Diptych**, 1982
Acrylic collage on canvas, 215 x 244 cm

50
**Cobbs Hill**, 1979
Acrylic on canvas, 153 x 153 cm

# 5
# Collage and texture

Acrylic paint brought a new lease of life to Whishaw's art. But the change of medium didn't really alter his essential practice. He still used acrylic in the same way he had previously used oil paint – to 'draw' a design onto a surface. A further development came when he began to collage small scraps of painted paper onto his work. Canvas and board were transformed into sculptural objects, their surfaces covered in pieces of canvas, paper and photocopied drawings that played with reality and asked questions about the nature of painting.

Clearly indebted to the synthetic cubism of Picasso, Braque and Juan Gris, Whishaw's own synthetic compositions finally offered him the complex, constantly shifting surfaces he was looking for. He began to play with different textures, surface layers and material finishes, teasing the eye with unexpected visual experiences that were only revealed when seen close up. Paint could now hide as well as reveal.

In the mid-1980s, paintings such as *Towards Zamora* (1986–88; no. 53), *From Cuenca* (1988–92; no. 54) and *Pueblo II* (1987–2014) saw Whishaw return to the subject of the Spanish *pueblo*. With their long, narrow format, off-set principal subject and restrained palette, they continue to reflect Goya's significant influence. But these are also very much cubist townscapes – a 'Giant's Causeway' of simple geometric forms, erupting like volcanic islands from a sea of opaque colour, their multiple perspectives emphasised by the clusters of parallel black lines, highlights or shadows that Whishaw uses to distinguish each plane.

From a distance, the composition of these works is relatively simple: each town is jumbled, with geometric forms providing a dramatic visual contrast to the flatter, surrounding colour. Like a shaft of light piercing the surrounding gloom, their dynamic patterns send a ripple of optical movement across a formless landscape. But when these works are seen up close, a more complex series of

51
**Downstream, Surface Tensions**,
2001–02
Acrylic on canvas, 210 x 207 cm

52
**Rippled Shallows, Diptych**,
1998–2009
Acrylic collage on canvas,
107 x 214 cm

53
**Towards Zamora**, 1986–88
Acrylic collage on canvas,
122 x 305 cm
Zeneca

54
**From Cuenca**, 1988–92
Acrylic collage on canvas,
122 x 305 cm
Tetrapak UK

55
**Mousehole Harbour**, 1999–2000
Acrylic collage on canvas,
244 x 274 cm

interactions becomes apparent. The opaque sandstorm of ochre paint sweeping across the surface of *From Cuenca*, for example, turns out to be a translucent glaze, while the wisp of white that floats above the right-hand side of the painting is revealed to be part of an extensive structural substrate – a complex, irregular tessellation of triangles, diamonds and parallelograms cut and torn from pieces of paper on which Whishaw has drawn closely clustered, parallel black lines. As these shapes and lines twist and turn, block and connect, they send the eye skittering across the work's surface in pursuit of their chevron pathways. Like the parallel lines Picasso and other cubists used to give direction and angle to otherwise flat planes, Whishaw's black lines help to turn the picture surface into a crumpled, multifaceted playground for the eye. With the translucent ochre paint no longer able to conceal the black and white stripes, and the hand-drawn lines oscillating between positive and negative, solidity and emptiness, the difference between foreground and background becomes increasingly unclear. The painting's stability collapses; instead, our gaze falls through the paint to the stripes, and through the stripes to an indeterminate space beyond.

These optical games give *From Cuenca* the three-dimensional 'buzz' that we have seen before in Whishaw's work. But in this and his other paintings from the early 1980s onwards the impact of the collaged elements is what is new. The structure of these towns is no longer established through the colour and line of paint alone, but also from the pieces of paper that form a distinct physical layer on top of the canvas.

Just as the painting represents the town rising up out of a sea of colour, these layers of paper also rise up off the canvas background, building up islands

56
**Coastal Village**, 2004–05
Acrylic collage on canvas, 24 x 45 cm
Private collection

of dynamic energy that are not only separate from the pigment-soaked canvas beneath but also largely resistant to the layers of paint that flow across their surface. With their imperceptibly raised edges and close-textured surface finish, these collaged elements form their own distinctive layer of visual and physical energy running between the canvas and the top layers of translucent acrylic paint.

If paper had offered Whishaw one way to challenge the coherence of the picture surface, the addition of sacking and canvas gave him another. Beneath dark brown paint, towards the top of the central panel of *Matadero Municipal Triptych* (1983–93; no. 19), Whishaw stuck a long narrow triangle of canvas. It remains hidden until closer inspection reveals its crooked, slightly frayed edges, surrounded by thin, dark shadows. The colour and open texture of the natural canvas remain deliberately visible in places, emphasising both the materiality and tactility of the picture surface. Around this scrap of canvas the painted surface is either opaque with thick pigment, or so drenched with liquid paint that its dense fibres have become infused with colour. In contrast, the strokes of white, red and grey-green paint that skip across the more open weave of the collaged section seem unattached to the surface, floating above it and reaching out into the space between painting and viewer.

Sometimes these canvas patches lie flat, camouflaged on the painting; sometimes, as in *Three Punk Demoiselles d'Angleterre* (1987–2015; no. 57), the collaged canvas is wrinkled and obvious, reiterating the material's skin-like, organic nature. Occasionally Whishaw will stick a piece of canvas onto the painting surface to hide something he isn't happy with, using it as a quick solution – a sticking plaster – rather than having to scrape away layers of paint and start again. More

57
**Three Punk Demoiselles d'Angleterre**,
1987–2015
Acrylic collage on canvas,
206 x 212 cm

often, however, he applies different weaves and textures of canvas to offer himself contrasting surfaces on which to paint, intrigued by the variety of ways paint will soak into, or move across the surface of, different materials.

Around the time that Whishaw was beginning to experiment with the different effects offered by collage, he began to add materials such as Tetrion to his paint. Tetrion, which is a filler, helped turn the paint into a coloured plaster so that it clung like a second skin to the surface of his paintings. Not only did this reduce some of the sheen that can mar the appearance of acrylics when used straight from the tube, it also gave the paintings a physicality that offset their purely visual illusionism. Adding cement, ash, sawdust and soil to paint brought the rough textures and sense of realism Whishaw was looking for, so that in paintings such as *Matadero Municipal Triptych* (1983–93; no. 19), with its depiction of a Spanish municipal abattoir, the gritty physicality of the picture surface reflects the reality of the subject matter – real materials forming a bridge from the picture space into the real world.

Like Whishaw's brush, our gaze also travels at different speeds across the varying terrains of his pictures' surfaces. It lightly skims over the top of corrugated

58
**Into the Garden**, 2003–11
Acrylic collage on canvas,
61 x 127 cm
Private collection

59
**Window View**, 2008–11
Acrylic collage on canvas,
50.5 x 122 cm (including frame)

cardboard or photocopied drawings, but is drawn into the depths of the base canvas. It becomes lost in shadows, among the globules of paint caught in the open weave of rough sacking, and in the lines gouged into Tetrion-bound paint, whose matt colours suck us in like quicksand, while the specks of matter stuck to the surface abrade our retinas with their rough textures. Whishaw has deconstructed the painting, breaking apart the apparent realism of a single perspective space and reassembling it, like a cubist structure, into one of multiple facets. The material surfaces of these works are intended to intrigue us as much as the worlds of reality or abstract imagination they portray.

60
**Interior with King and Queen**, 1985–90
Acrylic collage on canvas, 122 x 305 cm
Royal Academy of Arts, London
(Diploma work)

# 6
# Space

After fracturing his skull at the age of seventeen while playing rugby, Whishaw was unable to play contact sports and turned instead to rifle shooting. More than forty years later, memories of this youthful activity resurfaced in works such as *After Image* (1992–2002; no. 61) and *Taking Aim I* (1990–2015; no. 62). In these idiosyncratic images Whishaw used shooting targets, some still embedded with lead pellets, as both subject and collaged surface.

It would be easy to overlook these paintings as strange diversions in Whishaw's practice. But like so many of the works that he sees as 'mavericks', they provide a vital insight into his concerns and motivations. The collaging together of these two, apparently unrelated activities allowed him to highlight what he saw to be the close links between shooting and drawing. Both activities focus on the making and placing of a mark, in each a line moves through space, and each is completed by the penetration of a surface, either by the lead of a bullet or by paint.

In *Taking Aim I* Whishaw combined gunsights, shooting targets, small, circular impact craters of colour and dark, shadowy bullet holes into a single abstract pattern. Like all Whishaw's works, it exudes optical energy. Black, red and white circles engage in a tussle between foreground and background, while the relationship between the printed circles and the clouds of nebulous colour that surround and hide them creates a shimmering oscillation that radiates out across the surface. But this work is not just about the painted surface and optical space. Looking at it, we find ourselves looking through the gunsights, aiming at the targets. Our gaze follows a line from our eye to the target, then on through a bullet hole to the space behind the painting. As we trace this line we become conscious of the space around the painting as well as the space within it. The coloured dots have become both points of surface interest and a reminder of the unseen space beyond.

61
**After Image**, 1992–2002
Mixed media with shot pellets on wood,
22 x 47 cm

62
**Taking Aim I**, 1990–2015
Mixed media with shot pellets on wood,
28 x 66 cm

1
2
3
4
5
6
7
8
7
6
5
4
3
2
1
STANDARD 25 YARDS, DECIMAL SCORING
NAME
SCORE

63
**Taking Aim II**, 1991–2015
Mixed media with shot pellets on wood,
30 x 60.5 cm

If points of colour pull us through the painting, the mirrors in *Leaded Window, Mirror and Dust Particles* (1999–2004; no. 64) and *Interior with Mirror II* (1991–95; no. 65) push us back out to look at ourselves and what is reflected behind us. And, as we observe the tiny specks of colour that freckle these paintings, we imagine the minute particles of light and dust that fill this space.

But *Interior with Mirror II* doesn't just ask us to look back into the space between ourselves and the painting; it asks us to view this interior from multiple angles and heights, intriguing us with numerous horizon lines and vanishing points. Since vanishing points dictate the position of the viewer in relation to them, we are not just positioned directly in front of this work, but to its left and right, and above and below it. Whishaw asks us to take a 360-degree view of his paintings, which owes much to his fascination with cubism. This reflects his own approach to drawing, which he also passed on to his students during his life drawing classes at both Chelsea and St Martin's. He would teach them to draw an object from four different positions: three from life – moving around the object to see it from

64
**Leaded Window, Mirror and Dust Particles**, 1999–2004
Acrylic collage on canvas, 100.5 x 125 cm

65
**Interior with Mirror II**, 1991–95
Acrylic on canvas, 49 x 122 cm
Private collection

66
**Fly Through**, 1981
Acrylic collage on board, 36 x 36 cm
Private collection

67
**Tree, Window, Sea and Sky**, 1992–93
Acrylic collage on canvas, 43 x 45.5 cm
Private collection

different angles, the fourth from the imagination. As a result, his own paintings can never be seen from one position. They comprise a series of fragments and small parts, each with its own individual identity, with the result that the whole demands circumnavigation. We need to stare at them if we are to discover the hidden, intricate details, but we must also glance at them to catch the momentary blur of colour and pattern that evokes the indistinct landscapes of our dreams and memories.

Whishaw's dynamic spatial approach was already visible in the twisting crowd of *Corrida*, and it continues to inform his multi-horizoned landscapes such as *Tree, Window, Sea and Sky* (1992–93; no. 67), multi-perspective interiors such as *Interior Variations* (1994–2014; no. 71), or works such as *Sudden Flight* (2010–11; no. 69). This latter, an apparently simple image of birds in flight, becomes something more spatially complex when we realise that each bird is flying out of the painting at a different angle, some just to our left, some straight towards us, others off to the right. We no longer experience the work from a disinterested distance, but instead are dragged into it by a shockwave of feathered movement.

Moving away from the centralised, single viewpoint that has dominated Western art since the Renaissance, Whishaw's 360-degree approach celebrates the 'edgelands' of human perception. It offers intriguing details and diverging sight lines, which pull us in rather than leaving us on the periphery as spectators. And once we are drawn in, Whishaw presents us with an experience of space that can leave the viewer feeling dizzy and disoriented, deprived, as in *Vertigo II* (2007–09; no. 70), of

68
**Landscape with Startled Birds**, 1986–99
Mixed media on paper, 132 x 99 cm

69
**Sudden Flight**, 2010–11
Acrylic collage on canvas, 122 x 305 cm

any sense of up or down, front or back. As these familiar architectural structures twist and tilt, reach out and pull away, we enter, as we often do in Whishaw's paintings, an Escher-like world, in which we ascend stairs only to descend into unseen depths. We go inside to emerge outside, and the glance that follows a shaft of light coming from a window straight ahead of us also allows us to look down at a table and into the interior of a vase as if we were standing above it (see *Blue Interior*, 1987–92; no. 113).

Whishaw's architectural interiors throw us off balance because our expectations of reality are called into question. But in his paintings of the sea, water, forests, the stars and electrical impulses racing through the neural pathways of the mind, we become lost because there are no vanishing points, no points of orientation, just a sense of limitless, unbounded space. As a young boy crossing the Atlantic by ship, Whishaw would stand on deck staring out at a vast expanse of water that seemed to extend into infinity. *51° 15′ N 2° 18′ E* (1992–93; no. 74) reflects this childhood experience, the coordinates of the title referring to a location in the North Sea. These numbers and letters reflect humanity's constant attempts to tame the infinite. The painting, however, shows the futility of this, offering the viewer nothing more than an indistinct pattern of black, blue and white. Without a horizon line we have nothing by which to orient our position. Are we looking down or across? Is this a close-up image of gentle ripples disturbing a calm sea, or a distant view of mountainous, storm-tossed waves?

70
**Vertigo II**, 2007–09
Acrylic collage on canvas, 106 x 106 cm

71
**Interior Variations**, 1994–2014
Acrylic collage on canvas, 36 x 129 cm

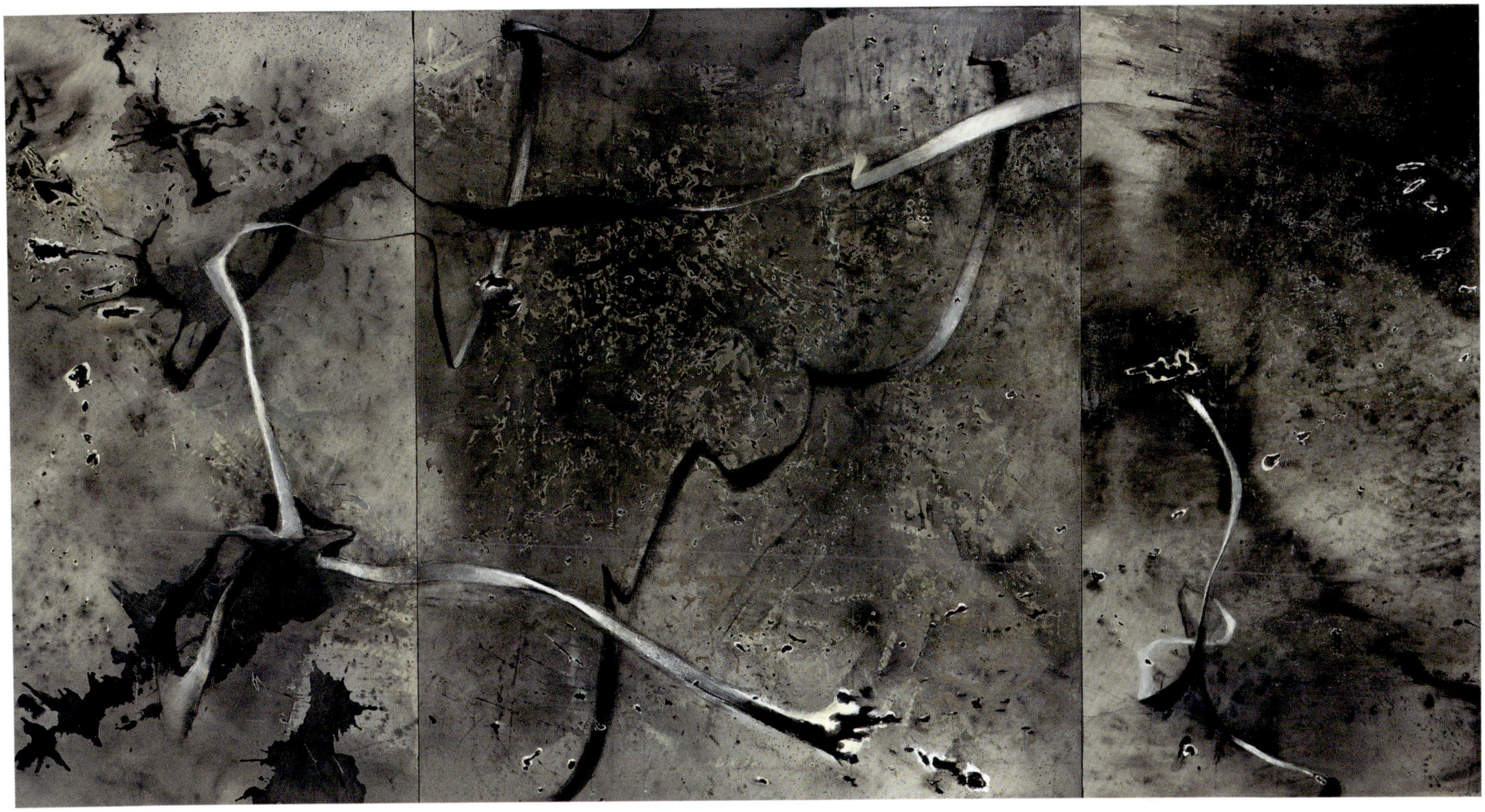

72
**Axons I**, 2002
Acrylic on canvas, 168 x 305 cm

73 (overleaf)
**Axons III**, 2002–04
Acrylic collage on canvas, 168 x 340 cm

74
**51° 15' N 2° 18' E**, 1992–93
Acrylic on canvas, 173 x 427 cm

Whishaw is fascinated by water, particularly the surface patterns that transform it from a glassy mirrored surface into a chaotic pattern of random swirls and interlocking lines, shadows and highlights, areas of movement and stillness. He has returned repeatedly to the simple eddying patterns on the surface of a flowing river, which swirl and straighten, ripple and flatten, reflecting both the depth and nature of the riverbed beneath, just as paint reflects the character of the materials it flows across. Sometimes these rivers are in flood, a tidal surge of turbulence and crosscurrents, carrying flotsam and jetsam in currents that flow and snake in undulating, sinuous ribbons. Others flow gently, meandering diagonally across the surface, a few lines of slightly raised Tetrion creating subtle highlights and shadows

75
**Impact**, 2004–12
Acrylic collage on canvas, 213 x 244

76
**Pond III**, 2001–03
Acrylic collage on canvas
(triptych),
168 x 244 cm

77
**Weir**, 2001–02
Acrylic collage on canvas
(triptych),
168 x 280 cm

78
**Tidal Surge III**, 2010–12
Acrylic collage on canvas, 168 x 457 cm

79
**Downstream Triptych**, 1997–99
Acrylic collage on canvas, 152 x 467 cm

80
**Collapsing Tree**, 2008–10
Acrylic collage on canvas, 213 x 153 cm

that rake the background colour with light. With no horizon or other landscape features to divert our gaze, and the surface of the horizontal world tipped up into a vertical display, Whishaw gives us patterns rather than locations, showing us the organic, natural interconnections of lines that break down the space between land and water, liquid and air. The rich browns, yellows and ochres of *Downstream Triptych* (1997–99; no. 79) suggest a sediment-filled torrent, wave-patterned sand, or wind-bent trees collapsing into a chiaroscuro play of light and dark.

Walking into his studio in Bethnal Green one day, Whishaw became transfixed by the shifting patterns animating a puddle near the entrance. He quickly drew them in ink, creating from memory a bold black-and-white drawing of the positive and negative shapes he had seen. He then photocopied this original, enlarging and reducing it, playing with scale and focusing on particular areas, before cutting and tearing up these sheets into smaller fragments. Whishaw has used this original drawing and its photocopied variants again and again to create intricate collages of seascapes, streams and lily ponds. By painting over areas of a collage, or placing scraps of enlarged drawings next to their reduced counterparts, Whishaw was able to create mesmerising portraits of water surfaces, with pools of deep calm and

emptiness disturbed by wind-rippled areas of energy. Short vertical lines, such as those in *Downstream Thaw* (2007–09; no. 81) and *Downstream Flood II* (2012–14; no. 82), may temporarily provide way-markers and points of orientation to guide our gaze across and through these turbulent waters, but these are quickly lost within the overall play of dark and light.

When Whishaw rotated his photocopied drawing through 90 degrees he found his image instantly transformed. Now standing vertically, the abstract black-and-white pattern became a deeply etched tree trunk fringing a riverbank or pond. But stare closely at the individual marks, and this sense of specific orientation starts to dissolve. Trees blend into water and water into bark, until the distinction between the two becomes harder to read. Is this a tree standing by water, or the reflection

81
**Downstream Thaw**, 2007–09
Acrylic collage on canvas, 113 x 113 cm

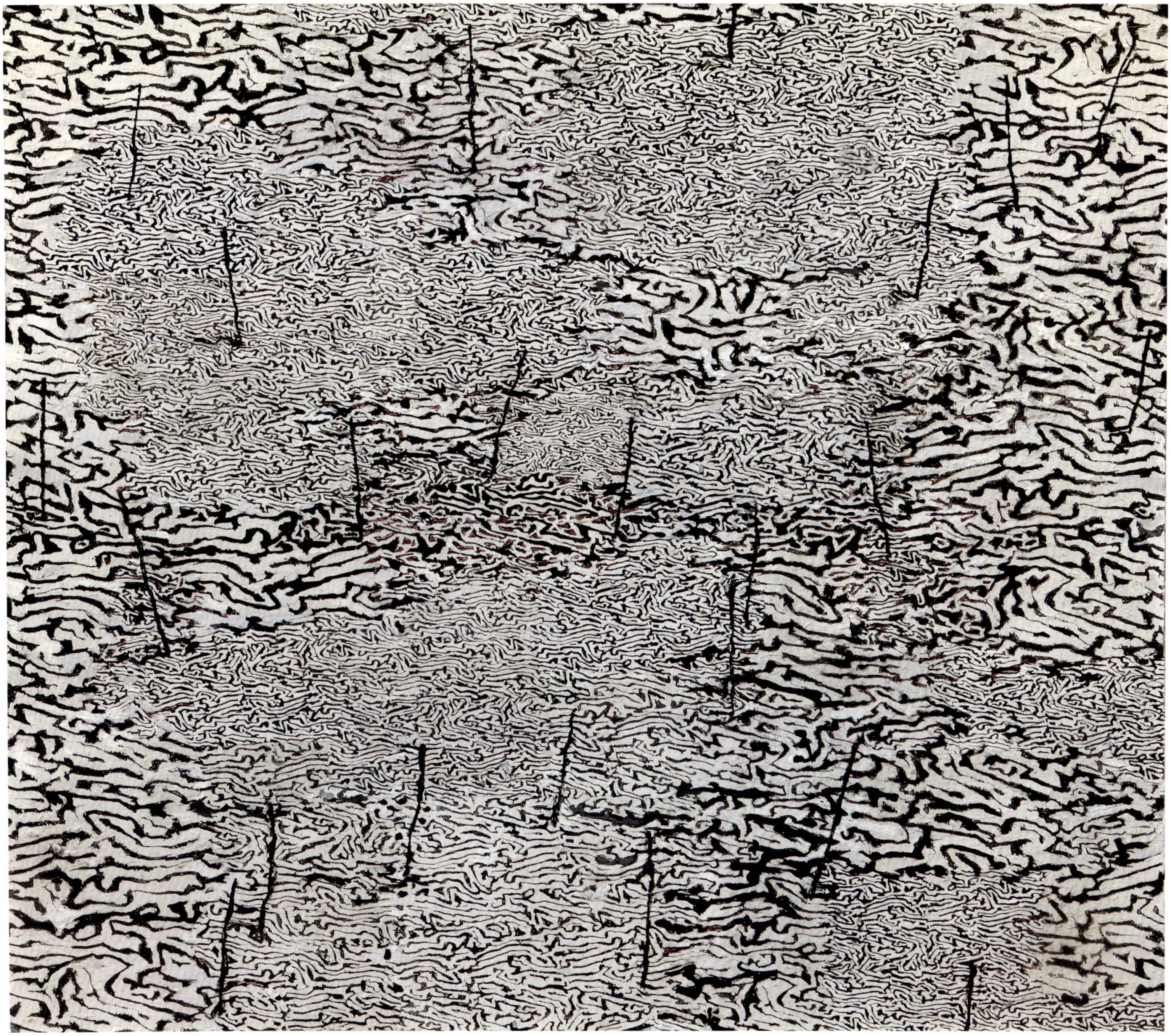

82
**Downstream Flood II**, 2012–14
Acrylic collage on canvas, 123 x 138 cm

83
**Rippled Pond**, 2005–06
Acrylic collage on canvas, 168 x 422 cm
Private collection

84
**Slow Appearance Thameside IV**,
2008–14
Acrylic collage on canvas, 183 x 153 cm
Private collection

85
**Pond VII Triptych**, 2004–05
Acrylic collage on canvas,
212 x 250 cm
Private collection

86
**Rippled Pond with Lilies**, 2005–11
Acrylic collage on board,
76 x 121 cm

87 (previous pages)
**Downstream, Fish Eye, Hook, Tree and Birds**, 2004–07
Acrylic collage on canvas, 183 x 365 cm

88
**Downstream**, 2004
Acrylic collage on canvas, 173 x 457 cm

89
**River Flood**, 2008–10
Acrylic collage on canvas, 122 x 305 cm
Private collection

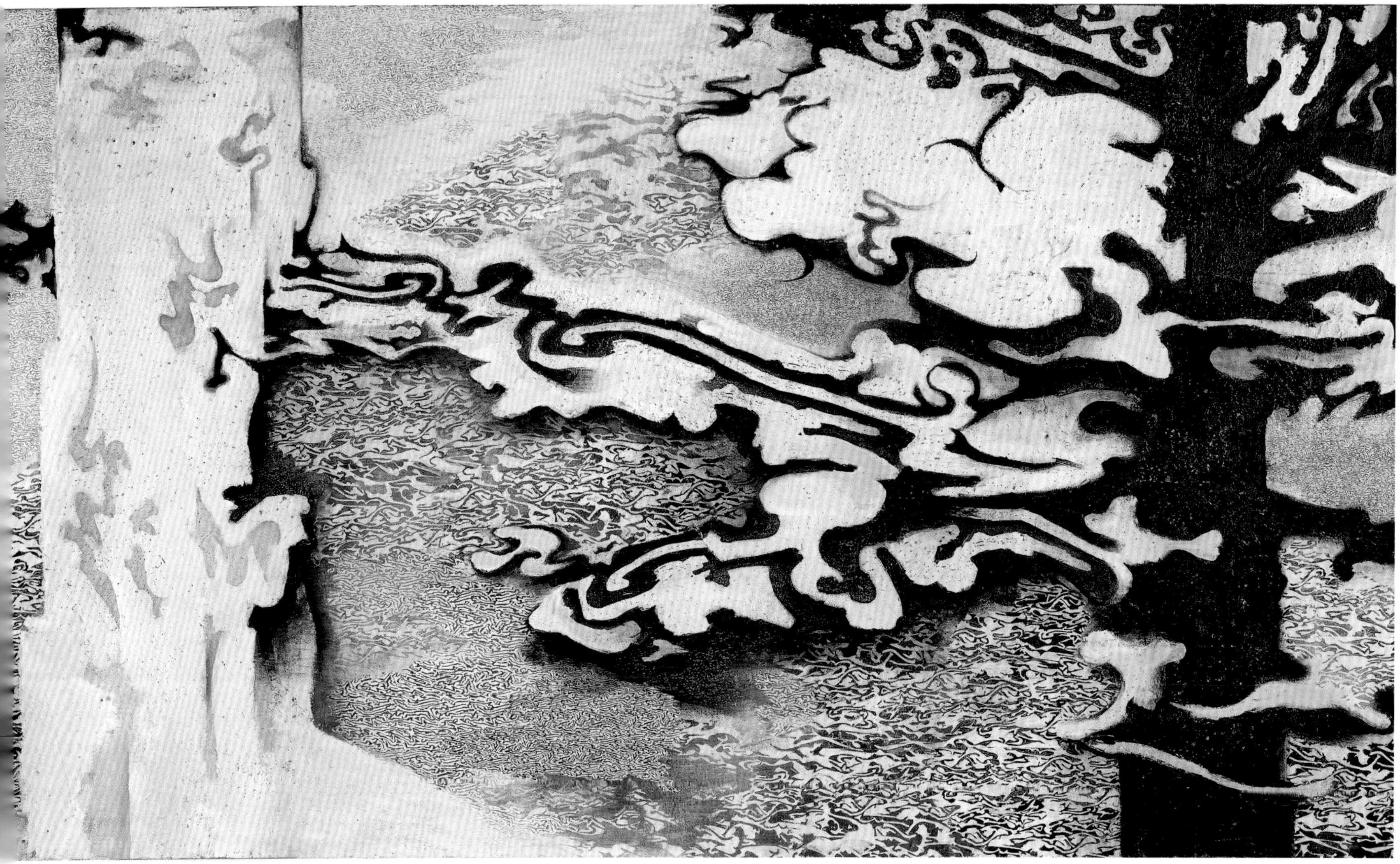

of a tree in water? Even the snaking fishing line with hook that pulls the viewer into *Downstream, Fish Eye, Hook, Tree and Birds* (2004–07; no. 87) gives no specific clues, offering both object and shadow. Whishaw also plays with scale and reality, teasing the borders of microcosm and macrocosm until we are no longer certain of whether we are engaging with the world in intense close up or from a distance: are the trees that dominate the foreground of *Downstream* (2004; no. 88), for instance, massive trunks or tiny saplings?

Whishaw is intrigued by the patterns created by the interplay and overlay of tree branches, twigs and trunks. He often captures their upright vertical thrust, or shows them tumbled sideways, victims of old age or the Great Storm of October 1987, which brought down around 15 million trees in Southern England, and was witnessed at first hand by the artist (see nos 90 and 91). Seen close up, with nothing to give them scale, Whishaw's coppices and woods pull us into spaces of mystery and dark majesty, spattered with flecks and dots of paint that dart and cascade across the composition like blossom and spring leaves, or those flashes of sunlight that dance across them, forming pinpricks of dazzling brightness that both blind us with light and guide us through their dark interiors. As the trunks of whip-thin saplings dissolve in a shower of early spring light or hide in the pink

90
**Knole Park with Deer**, 1987–92
Acrylic collage on canvas, 168 x 458 cm

91
**Knole Park After the Storm,** 1987–2002
Acrylic collage canvas, 122 x 305 cm

92
**December Wind and Rain**, 1994–95
Acrylic on canvas, 168 x 457 cm
Private collection

93
**December Wind**, 1996–2011
Acrylic on canvas, 174 x 305 cm

94
**Coppice III Triptych**, 2000–01
Acrylic collage on canvas,
168 x 401 cm

95
**Aspen Triptych**, 1990–2000
Acrylic on canvas, 168 x 452 cm
Private collection

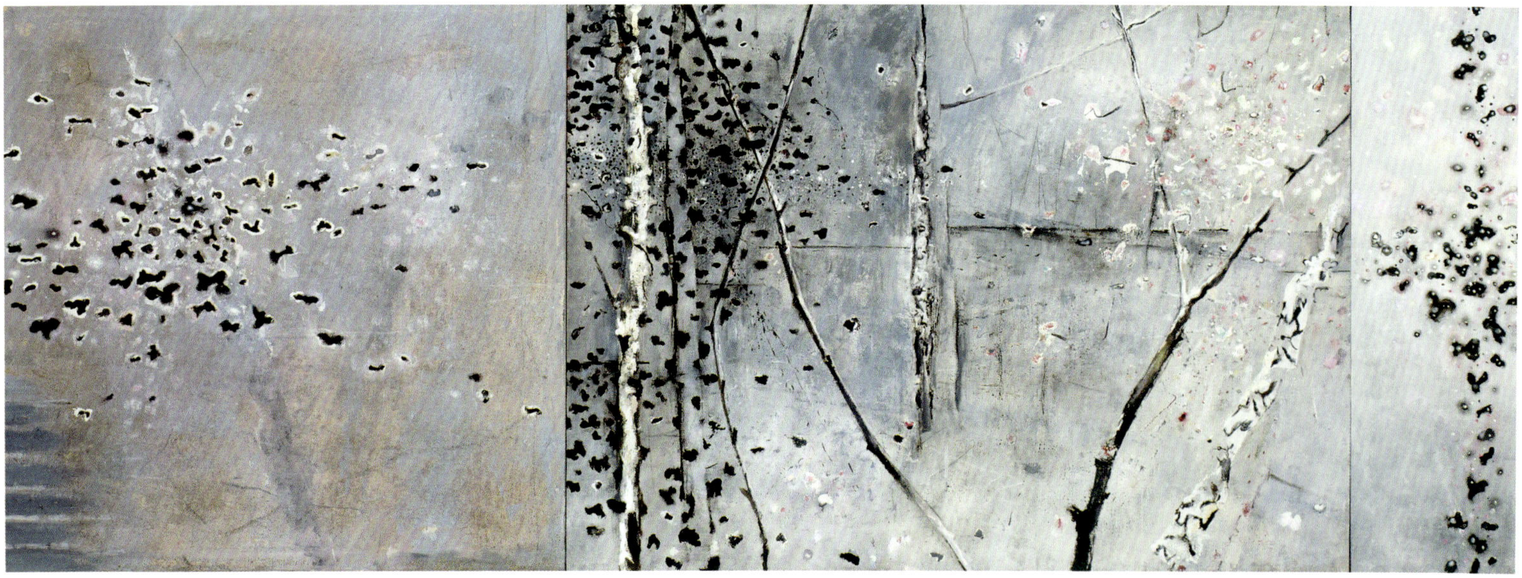

96
**Night Coppice**, 1999
Acrylic on canvas, 173 x 229 cm

97
**Celestial I**, 2007–10
Acrylic on canvas, 168 x 229 cm

half-light of night-time, bare, winter trees, thick and gnarled from age, trap our gaze in the intricate net of their tangled branches. Despite being firmly on land, we feel as though we are in the middle of the sea or among the stars – uncertain of depth and distance, edge and boundary, lost in the sublime immensity of a small patch of ground. This sense of limitless density has intrigued Whishaw ever since he once became lost in Lyminge Forest when walking with his daughters (see *Lyminge Forest*; 1991–92; no. 100). With no external light, or obvious way of finding his bearings, his heightened senses became aware of the more subtle forces of nature that surround us: gentle gusts of wind and delicate shafts of light, those invisible forces that he so often tries to evoke in his work through meandering lines of effervescent dots of colour.

This conflation of space – the persistent intermingling of microcosm and macrocosm – is a recurrent preoccupation. From the small areas of impasto marks in *Cobbs Hill* to the details of bark and tree trunks hovering in the limitless hazy

98
**Winter Landscape,** 1987–93
Acrylic collage on canvas, 168 x 508 cm

99
**Winter Monks Horton**, 1990–92
Acrylic on canvas, 168 x 457 cm

100
**Lyminge Forest**, 1991–92
Acrylic collage on canvas, 242 x 301 cm

101
**Coppice Early Spring Light**, 2000–06
Acrylic collage on canvas, 122 x 305 cm

102
**Forest VI Triptych**, 1982–99
Acrylic on canvas, 168 x 675 cm

103
**Lyminge Forest III Triptych**, 1983–99
Acrylic collage on canvas, 168 x 687 cm
Private collection

colour fields of *In Search of Nectar* (2007–1 5; no. 106) and *Summer Light with Tree and Birds* (2006–14; no. 107), we enter topsy-turvy worlds in which the order of single-point perspective is overturned and we are urged to look at objects individually rather than as integrated elements of the whole.

In *Urban Flood* (2003–12; no. 108) a tree stump stands guard over swirling waters, its dappled bark leaching into the surrounding flood to dazzle the eye with a camouflage that fuses tree and water into a single pattern. Dotted within this fluid design, however, are angular, cubist islands – scraps of paper covered in the parallel lines we associate with Whishaw's urban structures. These abruptly stop the water's sinuous, rhythmic flow, creating a hiatus in the composition's natural momentum and graphically highlighting the difference between nature and the urban environment. Every element of this complex surface plays with scale.

104
**Symphoricarpos**, 1983–99
Acrylic on canvas, 173 x 457 cm

105
**Sunlit Water's Edge**, 2001–10
Acrylic collage on canvas, 100 x 300 cm
Private collection

Minutely detailed drawings blur into a haze of grey, while enlarged fragments introduce tracts of empty, white space and deep black holes. Close up, we become lost in the abstract details of these mesmerising patterns; further away a flooded landscape emerges, an image of cataclysmic deluge that foretells the sunken city paintings that Whishaw made as a visual response to Debussy's piano piece 'La Cathédrale Engloutie' ('The Sunken Cathedral'), and the debris-laden tidal surges that he was to paint after seeing images of the devastating 2004 tsunami and floods in Bangladesh. Stand further away from the work, however, and the stark contrasts in scale resolve themselves and two trees in summer leaf emerge, bathed in strong, shimmering sunlight.

Since his first student paintings of bullfights, Whishaw has regularly explored the relationship between human beings, man-made structures and nature.

106
**In Search of Nectar**, 2007–15
Acrylic collage on canvas,
172 x 208 cm

107
**Summer Light with Tree and Birds**,
2006–14
Acrylic collage on canvas, 213 x 183 cm

108
**Urban Flood**, 2003–04
Acrylic collage on canvas, 122 x 305 cm

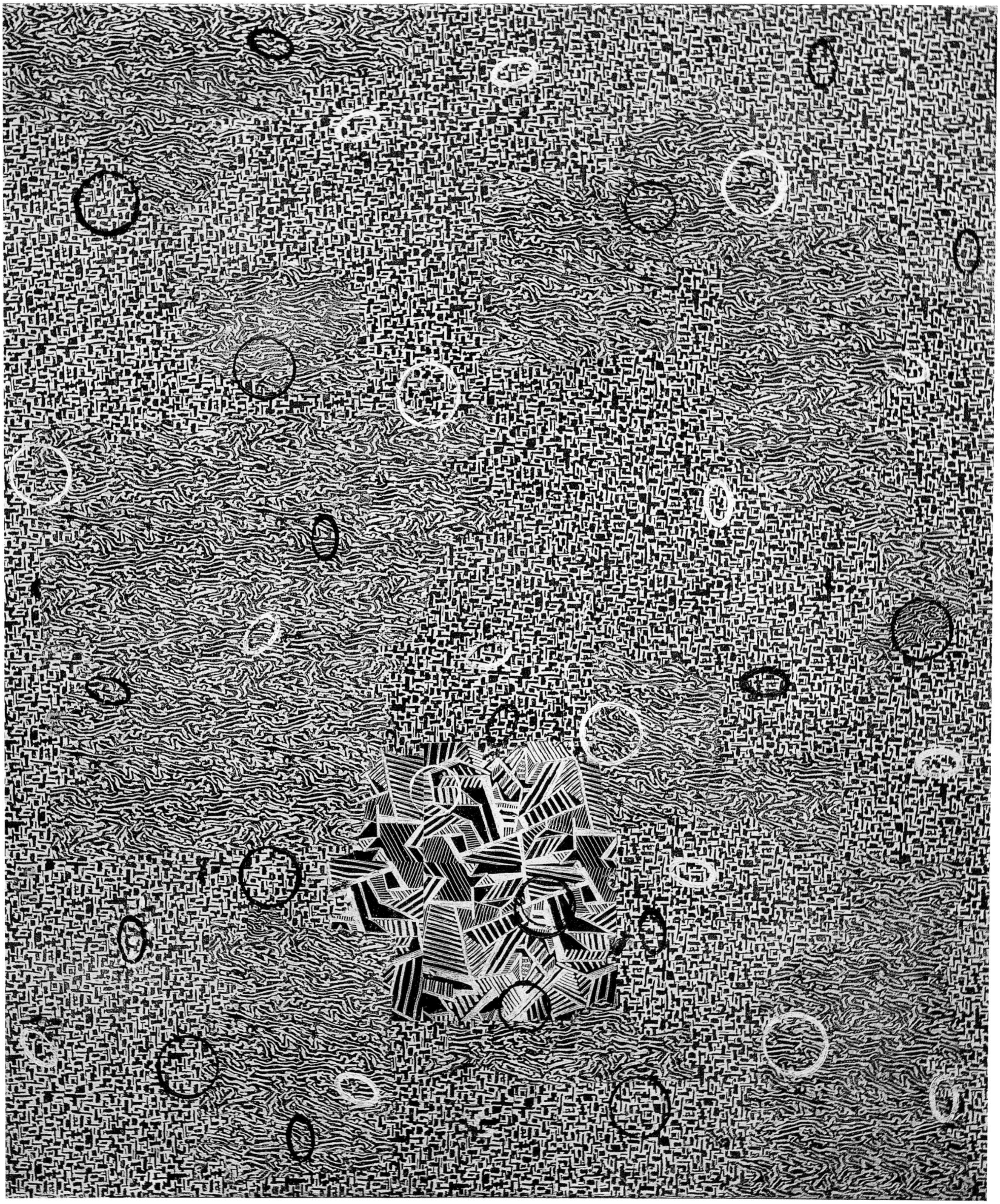

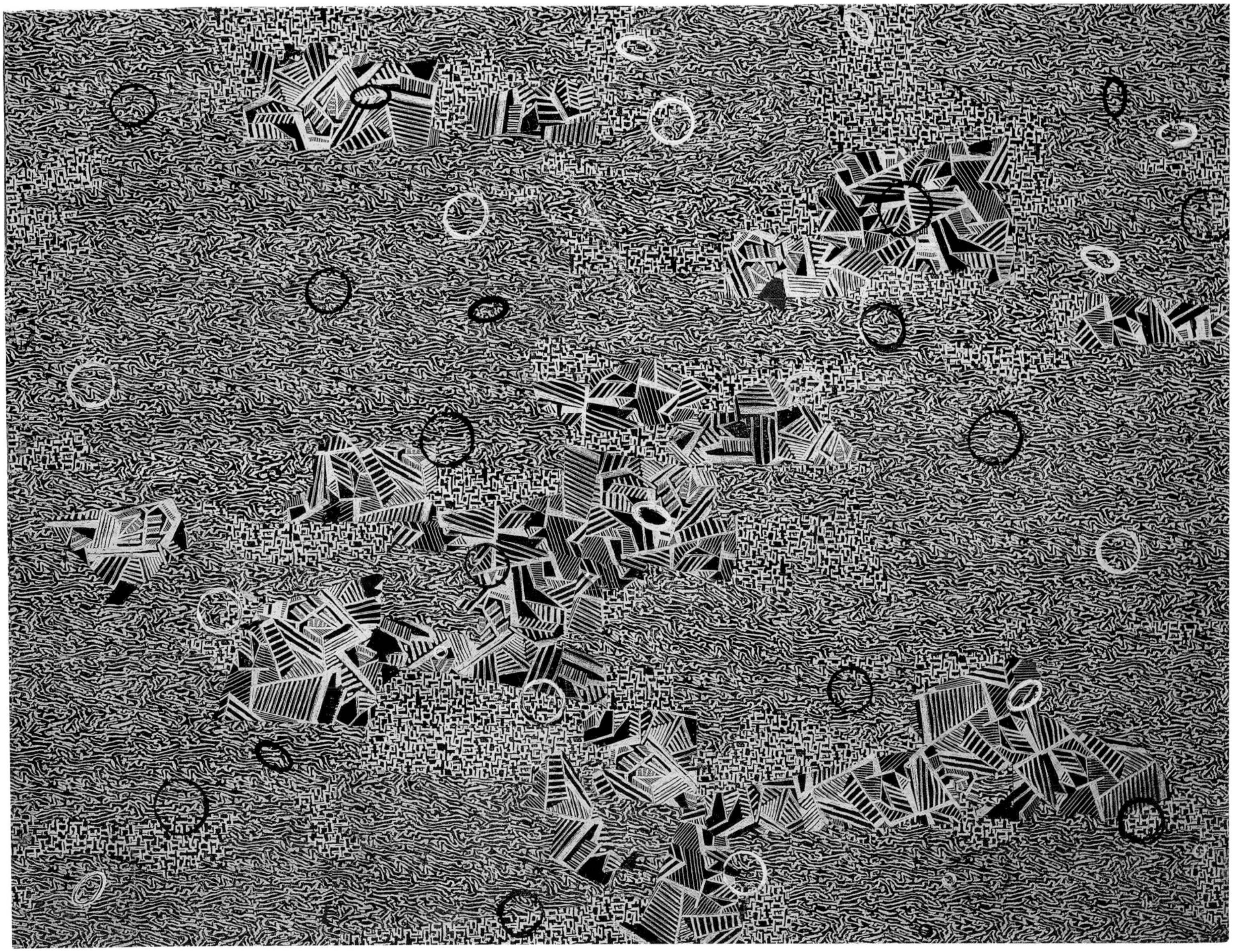

109
**Submerged City II**, 2004
Acrylic collage on canvas,
71 x 91 cm

110
**La Cathédrale Engloutie**, 2004
Acrylic collage on canvas, 73 x 63 cm

Whereas his early works focused on a very particular visceral combat, a series of paintings he began in the early 1990s takes a gentler, more lyrical and surreal approach that breaks down the barrier between interior and exterior, static architecture and living things. Trees now grow inside buildings, the sky and sea become internal walls. With our expectations of reality undermined, we become disoriented. The only reality we can actually focus on is the painting's physical essence, its surface details, paint, materials, pattern and texture.

Whishaw's interiors are filled with hand-drawn parallel lines that contribute to their multifaceted, multi-angled complexity. These stripes lead the eye in one direction before blocking its path and taking it another way. They suggest walls and floors, tables and tilting passageways. They also provide Whishaw with a simplified chiaroscuro shading, as white lines bring intense highlights to areas in deep shadow, their optical vibration silently reverberating on the retina. Like

111
**Tidal Surge I**, 2004–05
Acrylic collage on canvas, 61 x 161 cm

112
**Tidal Surge II**, 2007–08
Acrylic collage on canvas, 168 x 243 cm
Private collection

113
**Blue Interior**, 1987–92
Acrylic collage on canvas,
152 x 152 cm

114
**Bouquet Triptych**, 1988–2010
Acrylic collage on canvas and board,
152 x 226 cm

115
**Red Admiral**, 1982–84
Acrylic collage on canvas,
213 x 231 cm
Private collection

window shutters framing the edge of paintings, they act as repoussoir figures pointing the way, leading us inside or outside, encouraging us to become lost in fragments of constantly unfolding, occasionally confusing space.

The inspiration for Whishaw's pervasive use of hatching comes in part from cubism, but also from the traditional weatherboarding of Kent houses, which he remembers from his time as a pupil at Tonbridge and from many subsequent visits to the county. With *Interior Triptych* (1983–89; no. 116), however, it was not a memory that prompted the painting but the painting that prompted a memory. When he stuck a small patch of painted canvas onto the centre of this image, he was instantly reminded of the open doorway in the background of Velázquez's *Las Meninas* (1656; fig. 4), a painting he had studied in the Prado on many occasions. This small piece of collaged fabric was the key to a whole new body of work, which used elements of Velázquez's great painting to explore the nature of reflected and pictorial space, and reintroduced the human figure after an absence of almost twenty years.

Since earlier works such as *Opened Interior* (1968) and *Yellow Dazzle Woman Interior* (1967), Whishaw had been painting empty 'stage sets' made up of flat and striped planes of colour. Initially working in bright hues, he quickly began to

116
**Interior Triptych**, 1983–89
Acrylic collage on canvas,
152 x 250 cm

117
**Evening Landscape with Trees**, 1990–93
Acrylic collage on canvas, 152 x 254 cm
Private collection

118
**Night Flowers**, 1985–95
Acrylic collage on canvas,
183 x 175 cm

119
**Reflections with Yellow**, 1985–86
Acrylic collage on canvas, 239 x 275 cm

120
**Reflections Interior Triptych**, 1985–87
Acrylic collage on canvas, 152 x 249 cm
Royal Academy of Arts, London

Fig. 4
Diego Velázquez
**Las Meninas**, *c.* 1656
Oil on canvas, 318 x 276 cm
Museo del Prado, Madrid,
inv P01174

use a darker palette of reds, browns and blacks to achieve a chiaroscuro contrast between the large areas of deep shadow and the intense shafts of light flooding in from doorways and windows, or spilling out from light bulbs. As their mysterious, unsettling world was briefly revealed, his paintings took on a deep psychological and emotional intensity.

Whishaw's *Las Meninas* paintings are psychodramas of light and dark that reveal little at a cursory glance. Highlights of bright colour run like ribbons across the surface, their vertical, horizontal and diagonal paths concealing the figures and disrupting the coherence of the setting. Instead of a room we are confronted with a tangled forest of shapes and colour. Whishaw had no desire to re-create the original painting; instead he approached it as he would a life drawing. Rather than adopting a frontal view, he imagined standing within the scene and seeing it from various angles, taking a cubist approach that fractured and then reassembled the original composition, bringing some things into focus and blurring others. The overwhelming size of many of these paintings offers a similar viewing experience, with the frontal, focused gaze disrupted and informed by the peripheral blur of colour that continuously demands our attention.

121
**Reflections I, Grey Interior**, 1984–86
Acrylic collage on canvas, 173 x 477 cm

122
**Margarita, Maria Barbola and Dog Triptych**, 1985–86
Acrylic collage on canvas, 213 x 508 cm

123
**Reflections II**, 1984–86
Acrylic collage on canvas, 173 x 457 cm

Standing in the shadows of these paintings, hidden beneath dazzling highlights, we might find the King and Queen – Philip IV and Mariana, Velázquez, the Infanta Margaret Theresa, her dwarf servant Maria Barbola, or even the Infanta's pet mastiff. The unflinching stare of their returned gaze draws us into these mysterious narratives in a way that the more static visual devices Whishaw normally uses – a fishing line, flock of birds, or shaft of light – never can. At times Whishaw paints these figures with a startling degree of realism; at others, they are reduced to a mass of vigorous Goyaesque brush strokes that only resolve into recognisable form at a distance, their substance reduced into a kaleidoscope of splintered light.

Intrigued by the spatial possibilities offered by the mirror in the background of *Las Meninas*, Whishaw wanted to capture in paint the feeling of being in a hall of mirrors. He became fascinated by the idea of light bouncing backwards and forwards in a constantly reducing ripple of reflections. In *Reflections with Yellow* (1985–86; no. 119) beams of light radiate out across the composition until they come to their natural end, with solid forms dissolving in their path, heightening the sense of mystery and demanding closer scrutiny on the part of the viewer. In paintings such as *Ambiguous Interior* (2009–13; no. 125), *Open Window* (1988–92; no. 128) and *Homage to R. M. Seascape Painting* (1991; no. 129), Whishaw continued to explore ever-decreasing forms, in which frame holds twisting frame, striped plane leads to a smaller striped plane, and interior space leads to ever smaller interior space.

Whishaw also explored the idea of multiplied spaces in the depictions of trees in interior spaces he painted in the early 1990s. In *Tree* (1993; no. 130), *Tree and Clouds* (1993; no. 131) and *Tree in the Quad* (1992–93; no. 127), he leads the eye on an intriguing journey through compositions whose multiple interiors and narratives resemble those of the fifteenth-century Sienese artist Sassetta, who, in his cycle of paintings depicting the Life of St Francis (see fig. 5), breaks down the pictorial space into a series of tantalising glimpses and individual stage sets in which the boundary between heaven and earth has been dissolved. Whishaw's secular

124
**Sundown**, 1996
Acrylic collage on board, 31 x 90 cm
Private collection

125
**Ambiguous Interior**, 2009–13
Acrylic on board (shaped panel),
28.5 x 61 cm

Fig. 5
Sassetta (Stefano di Giovanni),
**The Blessed Raniero of Borgo San Sepolcro Appearing to a Cardinal in a Dream**, 1444
Tempera on panel, 44 x 60 cm
Gemäldegalerie, Staatliche Museen, Berlin

126
**Interior with Figure**, 2004–08
Acrylic collage on board, 34.5 x 67.5 cm

127
**Tree in the Quad**, 1992–93
Mixed media on paper, 69 x 90 cm
Private collection

annunciations break down boundaries, too, bringing the outside inside and the natural world into the manmade.

Not content with the illusion of breaking down boundaries, Whishaw has sought ways to defy conventional straight edges and flat painted surfaces ever since his first collages, striving to push his paintings into the space beyond their frames. Playing with this border between reality and illusion, Whishaw has made a number of abstract, shaped paintings that break out of the straight edge of the frame to deceive the eye with the appearance of three-dimensional solidity (see, for example, *Contradictions*, 2001–02; no. 132), and maverick works such as *Sportif IV* (2002–03; no. 134), in which a series of intersecting circles depict a ball bouncing across the picture space. But suddenly this static representation of a very dynamic subject pushes into new territory: positioned just to the right of the painting in *Sportif I* (2000–01; no. 136) are two more painted circles that continue the ball's inevitable trajectory. The fourth wall has been breached and the painting reaches out into new territory.

But these objects aren't always painted, *trompe-l'œil* visual games. In *Re-appearance II* (1998–99; no. 137) Whishaw attached a short length of rope to the work's surface and then continued it in paint with astonishing illusionistic accuracy,

128
**Open Window**, 1988–92
Acrylic collage on canvas, 31 x 31 cm
Private collection

129
**Homage to R. M. Seascape Painting**, 1991
Acrylic collage on board, 62 x 58 cm
Private collection

130
**Tree**, 1993
Mixed media on paper, 46 x 127 cm
Private collection

131
**Tree and Clouds**, 1993
Mixed media on paper, 46 x 127 cm
Private collection

132
**Contradictions**, 2001–02
Acrylic on canvas (shaped triptych),
40 x 86 cm

133
**White Water Weir**, 1998–2000
Acrylic on canvas (shaped triptych),
73 x 40 cm

using it to trace a serpentine path across the rest of the canvas. The rope also crosses the boundary between the front and back of the painting, often diving through a hole in the surface before reappearing through another elsewhere. In other works, such as *In Search of Nectar* (2007–08) and *Memory Block* (1997–99; no. 135) the mixing of plastic flies and spiders, plastic cups, metal brackets, nails, chains and metal grilles, with their painted counterparts, asks similar questions of identity: is this painting emerging into reality, or is the real world becoming a painting?

Some of the objects and subjects that Whishaw chooses to paint may seem banal: a plastered wall dotted with windows covered in grilles, a Filofax, some rope, bouncing balls, 'windows' being dragged across a computer screen. But like Duchamp's urinal and bicycle wheel, these simple, ordinary objects have been chosen deliberately, not only for the moments of playfulness and humour they offer, but because in their very banality they do not confront viewers with complex narratives, but always bring them straight back to the work's material surface – the space where the real and illusory meet.

134
**Sportif IV**, 2002–03
Acrylic collage on canvas, 68 x 68 cm
Private collection

135
**Memory Block**, 1997–99
Acrylic collage on canvas, 66 x 67 cm

136
**Sportif I**, 2000–01
Acrylic collage on canvas (shaped triptych and separate illusionistic disc), 40 x 96 cm

137
**Re-appearance II**, 1998–99
Acrylic collage on canvas, 41 x 123 cm
Private collection

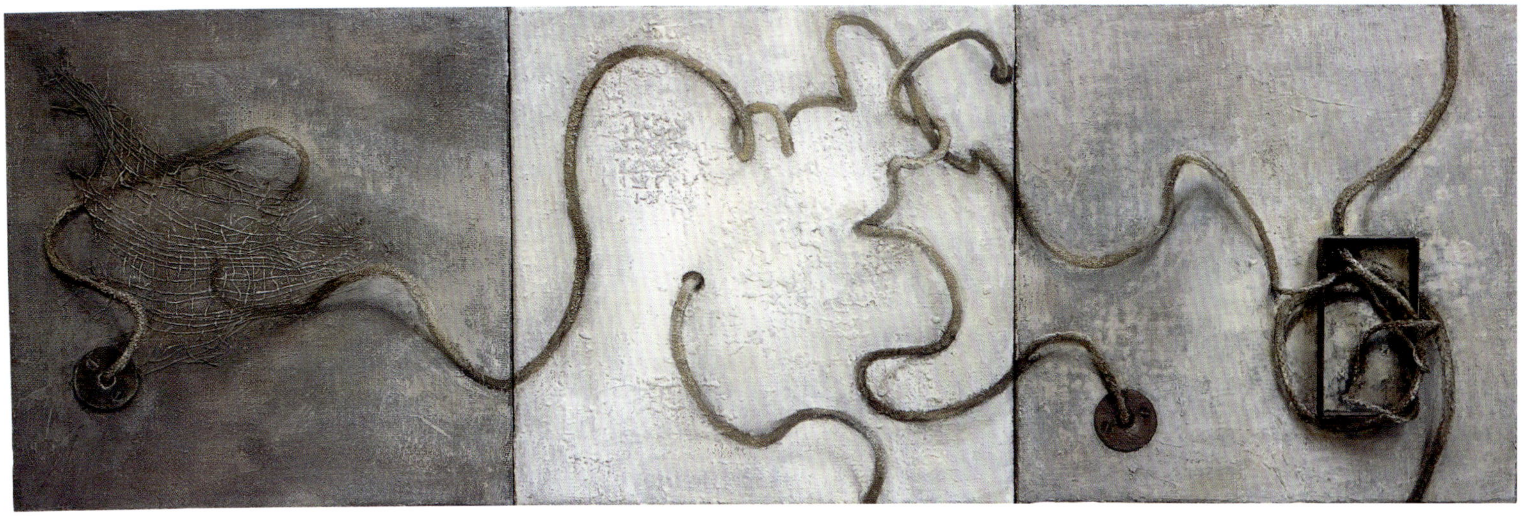

138
**Interior Light**, 1998–99
Acrylic on canvas (shaped triptych), 40 x 85 cm

139
**Filofax Memory Loss**, 1997–2004
Acrylic collage on board, 63 x 61 cm

140
**Dragging**, 2004–07
Acrylic collage on board, 29.5 x 61 cm

141
**Collateral Damage II**, 2004–14
Acrylic collage on canvas, 35 x 41 cm

142
**Collateral Damage I**, 2005–10
Acrylic collage on canvas, 40 x 40 cm

143
**Collateral Damage IV**, 2005–09
Acrylic collage on canvas, 41 x 40 cm
Private collection

144
**Collateral Damage III**, 2004–10
Acrylic collage on canvas, 35 x 41 cm
Private collection

145
**Still Interior**, 2003–12
Acrylic collage on canvas,
110.5 x 110.5 cm
Private collection

146
**The Blind Leading the Blind III – The Trip**, 1987–92
Acrylic collage on canvas, 198 x 168 cm

# 7 Conclusion

In 1988 Whishaw visited a village a few miles north of Madrid. The place – deserted except for an old woman, who sat day in, day out on a chair outside her house, waiting for her son to bring home her shopping – has haunted him ever since. In his poignant series *Reverie* (1988–90; nos 147 and 149) Whishaw painted this woman at twilight among the decaying, crumbling forms of the surrounding buildings, lost in her dreams, hopes and memories as she sat looking down over the village. Sometimes she is confronted by these thoughts, personified in *Reverie III* as multiple figures facing her with her past; sometimes she has been given multiple profiles with which to both look back at the past and imagine alternative futures. This subject became even more poignant for Whishaw when his wife died, after a long illness, in 1991. Suddenly these paintings, which he had started a few years earlier, were transformed into wistful meditations on time compressed and expanded, where the future is unknown and the past is lost into the mists of time. These multiple figures allowed him to express those 'will-o'-the-wisp' fragments of memory that dart in and out of our dreams and waking moments, those snatches of scent, sounds, feelings and images that become fused into an abstracted whole in our mind – a million different moments of an individual's history held in a single moment of time.

During this period Whishaw also revisited other groups of multiple figures he had been working on, including some linked to his large painting *The Blind Leading the Blind*. These became images of the Good Samaritan, or groups of travellers looking towards the River Styx – dark, brooding works pierced by momentary patches of light, which sought to capture the journey of life.

In the late 1990s Whishaw returned again to ideas of memory and its loss in paintings and prints of Filofaxes and skulls, where jumbled letters and evaporating words continue the earlier *Reverie* paintings' reflections on the ephemeral nature of time.

147
**Reverie III Triptych**, 1988–90
Acrylic collage on canvas, 168 x 306 cm

148
**Sentinel**, 1989–92
Acrylic collage on canvas, 242 x 305 cm

149
**Seated Woman Reverie**,
1989–90
Acrylic collage on canvas,
203 x 213 cm

150
**The Blind Leading the Blind II**, 1987–90
Acrylic collage on canvas, 198 x 420 cm

But then we might see the whole of Whishaw's work as a reverie, a dream-like space combining moments of focus with areas that are less defined: a world in which the real and the imaginary blend into multi-layered, multi-perspectival stage sets. His paintings are rarely taken directly from life, instead emerging as snippets and fragments from a sea of memories: a glass, bottle of wine, hammer and nails, and head that evoked memories of Don Pedro, the brother of the owner of a small Spanish *bodega* where Whishaw once stayed (no. 152); distant, tantalising views of landscapes and towns glimpsed from his Lambretta (no. 27); recollections of the Aegean; flashbacks of his car on fire (no. 153).

In our memories and dreams the barriers of time and space are always fluid – past, present and future mingle together. In the same way, dots and ribbons of colour weave their way like brambles across and through Whishaw's works, creating serpentine visual pathways that defy the borders of individual paintings. Whishaw

uses these to link dancers, forests, waves, roads and rolling hillsides into a single whole, making connections that in real life cannot be seen and which, even in his own work, can take decades to emerge. But as he rehangs his studio walls and finds new, temporary partnerships among his paintings, there will often be a moment when he looks at one with fresh eyes, sees an unexpected affinity and finds the solution to an old problem staring him in the face.

Whishaw's paintings can be deceptive in their simplicity and in the ordinariness of their subject-matter. But look beyond the obvious, be drawn through weatherboard stripes into a chiaroscuro, cubist world of intimate and intricate spaces, of richly textured and multi-layered surfaces, and discover worlds of rich invention and tactile complexity that make our eyes dance and our bodies vibrate to their subtle visual energy.

151
**In Search of Memory**, 1997
Digital etching on paper, 14 x 28 cm

152
**Don Pedro**, 1963–2004
Acrylic collage on canvas, 178 x 274 cm

153
**H211 FKE II**, 1997–2005
Acrylic collage on canvas, 91 x 122 cm

DON PEDRO JIMENEZ VARELA

154
**Turbulence II**, 2001–06
Acrylic on canvas, 173 x 414 cm

# Biography

| | |
|---|---|
| 1930 | Anthony Popham Law Whishaw is born on 22 May in St Mary's, Paddington, in London. The family later moves to Brazil, where Whishaw's father works. |
| 1939 | Returns from Brazil with his mother and attends Brunswick School in Sussex. The school is later evacuated to Cornwall during the Second World War. |
| 1944–48 | Attends Tonbridge School in Kent. |
| 1948 | Awarded Judd Scholarship from Tonbridge School. |
| 1948–52 | Studies at Chelsea School of Art, London. |
| 1951 | Makes his first visit to Spain, spending a fortnight in Ibiza. |
| 1952–55 | Studies at the Royal College of Art, London. |
| 1955–56 | Royal College of Art Drawing Prize. |
| 1955–56 | Receives an Abbey Minor Scholarship, an RCA Travelling Scholarship and a Spanish Government Scholarship, which he uses to travel to Spain with Jean Gibson. Here he visits the Prado and sees Goya's 'Black Paintings' for the first time. He lives in Spain for some of the next two years. |
| 1956 | His first solo exhibition is held in Spain, at Madrid's Librería Abril. |
| 1957 | Marries Jean Gibson and buys his studio-house in Kensington. |
| 1960 | Featured in the episode 'Private View' of BBC TV show *Monitor*, following four emerging artists. |
| 1963 | Whishaw's first daughter, Phoebe, is born. |
| 1965 | Whishaw's second daughter, Zoë, is born. |
| 1973 | Perth International Drawing Biennial Prize. |
| 1973 | Bayer International Painting Prize. |
| 1975 | South East Arts Association Painting Prize. |
| 1977 | Greater London Arts Association Grant. |
| 1978 | Arts Council of Great Britain Award. |
| 1979 | Elected to the London Group. His work is included in their exhibitions each year. |
| 1980 | Elected a Royal Academician. He exhibits annually at the Royal Academy of Arts Summer Exhibition. |
| 1981 | Begins working in an Acme studio in Bethnal Green. His routine involves driving to Bethnal Green and working there from 6 am until midday, before returning to Kensington, where he paints in the afternoon. |
| 1981 | Greater London Council Painting Prize. |
| 1982 | John Moores Minor Painting Prize. |
| 1981–82 | Lorne Scholarship. |
| 1986 | Joint winner Hunting Group National Art Competition. |
| 1987–88 | 'Reflections After Las Meninas' at the Royal Academy Diploma Galleries, London, touring to Hatton Gallery, Newcastle; Mead Gallery, Warwick Arts Centre; John Hansard Gallery, Southampton; Space, Exeter. |
| 1989 | Galerie in Faust, Hamburg, and Galerie in Faust, Shanghai, China. |
| 1991 | Whishaw's wife dies after a long illness. |
| 1992 | Elected to the Royal West of England Academy. |
| 1994 | Featured on Channel 4 News, in a feature about his 1989 Galerie in Faust exhibition. |
| 1996 | Korn Ferry Carre Oban International Picture of the Year. |
| 1999 | Featured Artist at Eigse Carlow Arts Festival. |
| 2003 | Elected Honorary RWA. |
| 2006 | Interview with Brian Sewell on 'Divine Art', BBC Radio 4. |
| 2007 | 'Downstream', exhibition at Osborne Samuel, London. |
| 2010 | A series of solo and group exhibitions are held to mark Whishaw's 80th birthday, including at Kings Place Gallery; the Fine Art Society; and Acme Studios, Bethnal Green. |

Edward Woodman, *Anthony Whishaw in his Acme studio at Robinson Road (E2)*, 1983. Acme Archive

# Exhibitions

**Solo and small-group exhibitions**

| | |
|---|---|
| 2016 | 'Woodland Encounters', Art Space Gallery, London |
| 2016 | 'Anthony Whishaw RA: Paintings from the Mid-1960s – 2015', Browse & Darby, London |
| 2011 | 'Eight Large Paintings' (two-person show with Peter Brook), The Gallery in Cork Street, London, and The Richmond Hill Gallery, Richmond |
| 2010 | 'Anthony Whishaw RA at 80', Acme Studios, London |
| 2010 | 'Images on the Edge of Perception', Kings Place Gallery, London |
| 2010 | 'Dancers: Paintings From The Early 1960s', The Fine Art Society, London |
| 2009 | 'New Large Works', Victor Pasmore Gallery, Harrow School |
| 2007 | 'Downstream', Osborne Samuel, London |
| 2007 | 'Arts Unwrapped', Acme Studios, London |
| 2006 | The Dover Arts Club Show, London |
| 2005 | Open Studio, ACME Studios, Bethnal Green, London |
| 2005 | 'Works on Paper', The Walk Gallery, London (with Peter Clossick) |
| 2002 | 'Maverick Images: Shaped, Triptych and Rectangular', Art First, London |
| 2000 | 'Pueblo Landscapes', Royal Academy of Arts, London |
| 2000 | 'Trees', Stephen Lacey Gallery, London |
| 1999 | 'Some Small Works: Maverick Shaped and Chaotic', Art First, London |
| 1997 | 'Images of Ideas, with Memory in Mind', Art First, London |
| 1994–95 | 'On Memory and Reflection', The Barbican Centre, London, touring to Royal Albert Memorial Museum, Exeter; The Maclaurin Art Gallery, Ayr; Huddersfield Art Gallery; R.H.A Gallagher Gallery, Dublin; Hatton Art Gallery, Newcastle; Mappin Art Gallery, Sheffield; Newport and Bolton Museums |
| 1994 | 'Pueblo Landscapes', Art Space Gallery, London |
| 1993 | 'Works on Paper', Art Space Gallery, London |
| 1992 | 'On the Edge of Representation', Art Space Gallery, London |
| 1991 | Blason Gallery, London |
| 1989 | Galerie in Faust, Hamburg, touring to Galerie in Faust, Shanghai, China |
| 1987–8 | 'Reflections After Las Meninas', Royal Academy of Arts, Diploma Gallery, London; Hatton Gallery, Newcastle; Mead Gallery, Warwick Arts Centre; Hansard Gallery, Southampton; Exeter |
| 1986–93 | 'Painting and Works on Paper', Royal West of England Academy, Bristol |
| 1986 | 'Large Landscapes', Royal Academy of Arts, London |
| 1985 | Mappin Art Gallery, Sheffield |
| 1983 | 'Work on Paper', Nicola Jacobs Gallery, London |
| 1982–83 | 'From Landscape', Kettle's Yard, Cambridge, touring to Ferens Art Gallery, Hull, and Bede Gallery, Jarrow |
| 1982 | Open Studio, ACME Studios, Bethnal Green, London |
| 1981 | Nicola Jacobs Gallery, London |
| 1980 | Wapping Open Studios, London |
| 1979 | Newcastle upon Tyne Polytechnic Art Gallery |
| 1979 | New Ashgate Gallery, Farnham (with Martin Froy) |
| 1978 | Oxford Gallery, Oxford |
| 1978 | Acme Gallery, London |
| 1974 | Hoya Gallery, London |
| 1973 | Folkestone Art Centre |
| 1972 | New Art Centre, London |
| 1971 | ICA, London |
| 1960 | Roland Browse and Delbanco, London (also 1961, 1963, 1965 and 1968) |
| 1953 | Ashmolean Museum, Oxford (with Cecil Collins and Willi Soukop) |
| 1956 | Librería Abril, Madrid |

**Annual Group Exhibitions**

| | |
|---|---|
| 1993 – present | Royal West of England Academy Autumn Exhibition |
| 1980 – present | Acme Open Studios |
| 1980 – present | Royal Academy Summer Exhibition |
| 1979 – present | The London Group |

**Recent Group Exhibitions**

| | |
|---|---|
| 2015 | 'Combines', The Cello Factory, London |
| 2015 | 'The Bright Field', The Old Big School Gallery, Tonbridge School, Tonbridge |
| 2015 | 'The Royal Academy at Wolfson College', Cambridge |
| 2014–15 | 'Arboretum', The Royal West of England Academy, Bristol |
| 2014 | 'Four Contemporary Artists', Osborne Samuel, London |
| 2012 | 'RA Now', Royal Academy of Arts, London |
| 2011 | 'The RA's Come to Richmond', The Richmond Hill Gallery, Richmond |
| 2011 | 'Celebrating 25 Years of the Art Space Gallery', Art Space Gallery, London |
| 2011 | 'Revelations', The Richmond Hill Gallery, Richmond |
| 2011 | 'The Invisible Line', 12 Painters from The London Group, London |
| 2010 | 'Images of St Paul's in the 21st Century', St Paul's Cathedral, London |
| 2010 | 'Near and Far', The Royal West of England Academy, Bristol |
| 2010 | 'The RA's Come To Richmond', The Richmond Hill Gallery, Richmond |
| 2010 | 30 years of Eigse Art, Visual Centre for Contemporary Art, Carlow, Ireland |
| 2009 | 'The ING The Discerning Eye Exhibition', The Mall Galleries, London |
| 2009 | Open Exhibition 2009, The London Group, Menier Gallery, London |
| 2008 | Summer Show, The Richmond Hill Gallery, Richmond |
| 2008 | Spring Show, The Richmond Hill Gallery, Richmond |
| 2007–08 | Winter Show, The Richmond Hill Gallery, Richmond |
| 2007 | Bridge Art Fair, The Cynthia Corbett Gallery, London |
| 2006 | Royal Academicians in Dubai |

# Further Reading

Links to all texts and films listed below are available at www.anthonywhishaw.com


Patrick Bourne, *Anthony Whishaw RA: Paintings from the Mid-1960s–2015*, exh. cat., Browse & Darby, London, 2016

David Hare, *Woodland Encounters*, exh. cat., Artspace Gallery, London, 2016

Michael Becket, 'Anthony Whishaw', *Kensington Society Magazine*, 2013

Simon Baker, 'Illusion and Allusion', *RWA Magazine*, Winter 2011

Charles Darwent, 'Anthony Whishaw RA: Images on the Edge of Perception, Kings Place Gallery, London', *Independent*, 28 August 2010

Steve Pill, 'My Studio', *Artists and Illustrators Magazine*, No. 291, September 2010

Stephen Morgan (director), '10-Minute Studio Visit', film, 2007

Brian Sewell, 'Divine Art', radio interview, BBC Radio 4, 27 December 2006

Virginia Boston, 'Portrait of an Artist', *The Artist's and Illustrator's Magazine*, May 2006

Philip Vann, 'Anthony Whishaw', *Face to Face*, Spring 2004

Dr Tharu Naidoo and Keith Patrick, *Anthony Whishaw: Explorations 1963–2003*, exh. cat., ACME Open Studios, London, November 2003

Brian Sewell, 'Report on Anthony Whishaw's Christ Crucified', Christchurch, Kensington, London, March 2003

Laura Gascoigne, 'Visual Games', *The Spectator*, 19 October 2002

Martin Gayford, *Trees*, exh. cat., Stephen Lacey Gallery, London, 2000

Keith Patrick, 'A Keen Sense of Place', *RA Magazine*, Spring 2000

Martin Plimmer, 'A Brush with the Real World', *Evening Standard*, 7 February 2000

Mel Gooding, 'Pieces of Reality', written for Eigse Carlow Arts Festival, Ireland, 1999

Virginia Boston, 'Man of Ideas', *The Artist's and Illustrator's Magazine*, December 1997

Mel Gooding, 'Images of Ideas with Memory in Mind', *Art First*, London, 1997

Virginia Boston, 'Paints and Brushes', *The Artist's and Illustrator's Magazine*, February 1996

'The Winning Picture', *Kensington Post*, 1996

Keith Patrick, 'Anthony Whishaw: Barbican Concourse Gallery', *Art Line International News*, Spring 1994

Norbert Lynton, *Anthony Whishaw: On Memory and Reflection – Paintings Since 1986*, exh. cat., Barbican Centre, London, 1994

Mary Rose Beaumont and Keith Patrick, *Anthony Whishaw: Paintings and Works on Paper 1986–1992*, exh. cat., Royal West of England Academy, Bristol, 1993

Sister Wendy Beckett, *Sister Wendy Beckett on Art and the Sacred*, London, 1992

Anthony Whishaw in conversation with Andrew Lambirth, 'Ambiguous Spaces', *The Artist's and Illustrator's Magazine*, February 1991

Keith Patrick, *Anthony Whishaw: Recent Paintings 1986–1990*, exh. cat., Blason Gallery, London, 1991

Robin Stemp, 'Reflections on the Past: Drawing on Historical Subjects', *The Artist*, March 1988

Michael Phillipson, *Reflections After Las Meninas*, exh. cat., Royal Academy of Arts, London, 1987

Brian Sewell, 'A Passionate Inquisitor', *The Evening Standard*, 8 October 1987

Monica Bohm-Duchen, 'Homage to Las Meninas', *Royal Academy of Arts Magazine*, No. 16, 1987

Simon Vaughan Winter, *From Landscape: Large Paintings Since 1980*, exh. cat., Kettle's Yard, Cambridge, 1982

Hetty Einzig, *Anthony Whishaw*, exh. cat., Nicola Jacobs Gallery, 1981

Terence Maloon, *Recent paintings*, exh. cat., ACME Gallery, London, 1978

Brian Wallworth, 'Profile: Anthony Whishaw', *Arts Review*, 1974

Bruce Laughton, 'Profile: Anthony Whishaw', *Art News and Review*, 20 January 1968

John Schlesinger (director), 'Private View', *Monitor*, BBC TV, 8 May 1960

David Cleghorn Thomson, 'Anthony Whishaw', *The Studio*, November 1956


# Photographic Acknowledgements


Every attempt has been made to trace the photographers and the copyright holders of works reproduced. Specific acknowledgements are as follows:

Photo: Joerg P. Anders © 2016, Photo Scala, Florence/bpk, Bildagentur fuer Kunst, Kultur und Geschichte, Berlin: fig. 5; Douglas Atfield: nos 12, 31, 37, 38, 45, 51, 55, 73, 76, 77, 79, 80, 84, 86–88, 93, 96, 97, 101, 102, 104, 106, 108, 111, 112; John Bodkin/DawkinsColour Ltd: nos 1, 3–5, 78, 89, 106; Photo © Christie's Images/Bridgeman Images: no. 13; © DACS; Photo: AD-Art, Sint-Amandsberg: fig. 2; The Fine Art Society: nos 25, 26; © 2016 Image Copyright Museo Nacional del Prado © Photo MNP / Scala, Florence: figs 3 and 4; © 2016 Photo Art Resource/Scala, Florence/John Bigelow Taylor: fig. 1; Justin Piperger: nos 16, 36, 69, 72, 75; © Anne-Katrin Purkiss/Royal Academy of Arts, London: p. 2; Graham Rees: no. 94; Royal Collection Trust / © Her Majesty Queen Elizabeth II 2016: no. 24; Anthony Whishaw: nos 6, 11, 17, 32, 52, 57, 58, 65, 85, 107, 143–45, 152; Zoe Whishaw: no. 23; Edward Woodman, Courtesy Acme, Acme Archive: p. 154; Roz Woodward: nos 2, 7, 15, 18, 27, 29, 30, 50, 56, 59, 61–64, 70, 71, 81, 82, 109, 110, 125, 126, 132–42, 153

# Index

Page numbers in *italic* refer to the illustrations